Social Trauma - An Interdisciplinary Textbook

AF783557

Andreas Hamburger
Camellia Hancheva • Vamık D. Volkan
Editors

Social Trauma – An Interdisciplinary Textbook

Springer

Editors
Andreas Hamburger
International Psychoanalytic University Berlin
Berlin, Germany

Camellia Hancheva
Department of Psychology
Sofia University "St. Kliment Ohridski"
Sofia, Bulgaria

Vamık D. Volkan
University of Virginia
Charlottesville, VA, USA

ISBN 978-3-030-47819-3 ISBN 978-3-030-47817-9 (eBook)
https://doi.org/10.1007/978-3-030-47817-9

© Springer Nature Switzerland AG 2021
This work is subject to copyright. All rights are reserved by the Publisher, whether the whole or part of the material is concerned, specifically the rights of translation, reprinting, reuse of illustrations, recitation, broadcasting, reproduction on microfilms or in any other physical way, and transmission or information storage and retrieval, electronic adaptation, computer software, or by similar or dissimilar methodology now known or hereafter developed.
The use of general descriptive names, registered names, trademarks, service marks, etc. in this publication does not imply, even in the absence of a specific statement, that such names are exempt from the relevant protective laws and regulations and therefore free for general use.
The publisher, the authors, and the editors are safe to assume that the advice and information in this book are believed to be true and accurate at the date of publication. Neither the publisher nor the authors or the editors give a warranty, expressed or implied, with respect to the material contained herein or for any errors or omissions that may have been made. The publisher remains neutral with regard to jurisdictional claims in published maps and institutional affiliations.

This Springer imprint is published by the registered company Springer Nature Switzerland AG
The registered company address is: Gewerbestrasse 11, 6330 Cham, Switzerland

Introduction

Despite all progress in civilization and technology, collective violence has re-emerged over and again throughout history, afflicting large social groups and leaving traumatic scars not only in the individual survivors' mental life but also in the collective memories of the involved groups. Social trauma influences group identity; it shapes individual and collective coping processes as well as transgenerational transmission. The sequelae of violence targeted against whole groups may embrace psychopathological symptoms in both victims and perpetrators that differ substantially from general traumatic symptoms, but specifically these sociotraumatic experiences afflict also whole social environments. Thus, social traumatizations must be understood and treated in a wider conceptual frame, connecting clinical psychology and psychiatry to all societal aspects. As social trauma is rooted in collective violence, it depends on social mechanisms if and how it leads to long-term clinical symptoms or unconscious transgenerational traces. It may affect whole societies through loss of social and political confidence.

The background of the textbook at hand is a series of teaching and research network, funded by German Academic Exchange Service DAAD, gathering together scholars and students from over 20 nationalities at 7+ universities on the Balkans and Germany. Students shared their research projects and took part in elective (master, postgraduate) Course Social Trauma. For the last 5 years, over 800 students enrolled in the course and many of them are still in the field of social trauma research and/or practice.

The book chapters will explore the intersection of clinical and social aspects of traumatic experiences in postdictatorial and post-war societies, forced migration, and similar circumstances from a variety of perspectives, including conceptual approaches, treatment methods, and research strategies. The book provides necessary knowledge for treatment, which beyond good clinical practice requires interdisciplinary efforts to understand social denial, retraumatization, and transgenerational transmission. Accrued from a 7-year interdisciplinary and international dialogue, the book presents multiple scholarly and practical views from clinical psychology and psychiatry to social and cultural theory, developmental psychology, memory studies, law, research methodology, ethics, and education. It gives a basis for university teaching as well as an overview for all who are involved in the modern issues of victims of social violence.

The book is organized in nine sections:

Part I: Theory of Social Trauma

The opening section of the book brings together chapters that fundamentally outline the concept of social trauma and mark out its interdisciplinary dimension. As Andreas Hamburger explains in his introductory chapter, these are above all Vamık Volkan's concept of "chosen trauma," Jan and Aleida Assman's concept of cultural trauma, the approach to collective trauma advocated by Alexander, Eyermann, Sztompka, and others, and the concept of historical trauma, prominently represented by Jörn Rüsen. In the following chapters, all these approaches are presented by the original authors.

Part II: Clinical Psychology and Psychotherapy of Social Trauma

In comparison to other, more sociologically and historically oriented important textbook in the field, the present volume focusses on connecting the social aspect to the clinical reality of social trauma. As Andreas Hamburger describes in his opening chapter, this does not mean in any way that all individuals affected by or being part of a socially traumatic experience will develop clinical symptoms. But, on the other hand, in psychotherapeutic and practice, we see many patients whose suffering cannot be addressed without taking into account that they are social trauma survivors—even more, in the history of and psychotherapy, they have often been denied recognition as survivors of social trauma. This, however, is a necessary condition to meet their requirements and to provide them with an adequate therapy. The contributions in this section focus on the interdependency of the personal therapeutic relation and the acknowledgment of social conditions. Therapeutic approaches, however, are not only working on the individual level—there is also a social healing dimension that neighbors and expands the traditional clinical approach. In the chapters by M. Gerard Fromm, Gamze Ozcuremez, Diana Ridjic, Thomas Maurer and Willi Butollo, Luise Reddemann and Ljiljana Joksimović, Susanne Metzner, Beatrix Weidinger von der Recke and Konrad Schnabel, a wide range of clinical approaches is discussed, connecting clinical practice and theory with the long-lasting shadows of the past.

Part III: Developmental Psychology of Social Trauma

Developmental issues in social trauma research and practice start with recognition of multiple potential traumatic factors and influences in child development and their long-term consequences in psychological well-being and social functioning of generations of people. Both Streeck-Fischer and Hadžić emphasize the uniqueness of individual experience of social events depending on age-related abilities to integrate emotional experience, and availability of support and help. Environmental conditions influence how the traumatic stress is processed or turned into chronic dysfunction. Recognizing the impact of trauma on personality, cognitive, and emotional functioning of individuals and destruction of sense of social togetherness, Streeck-Fischer warns against the psychiatrization or medicalization of mental disorders, which are more or less socially caused, and points out the importance of moving forward the social trauma perspective. The relational nature of both traumatic and protective factors in development is a shared perspective of all the authors. Holl and Taubner point out the importance of attachment and mentalization in the context of transgenerational transmission of social trauma. They argue that an effective framework for intervention programs to reduce the psychopathological and intergenerational risk of trauma should be based on understanding of mentalization as a protective factor for children at risk. Hancheva describes the impact of social trauma on individual development through the vicissitudes in meaning-making processes, the sense of agency, identity development, and the sense of epistemic trust, which hinder social dialogue and thus the adaptation to ever-changing social and cultural context.

Part IV: Memory Studies

For more than half a century memory research is intricately related to both human sufferings and social processes. Constructions of individual and social life history are a mixture of subjective interpretations of objective facts and events. In their chapter: Neurobiology of Memory in Trauma Survivors, Koso-Drljević and Husremović present results of studies on war veterans, drawing a complicated picture of symptoms, memory and other cognitive dysfunctions and impaired social and personality functioning. Implications of untreated PTSD among traumatized individuals on the creation of collective mainstream beliefs and narratives are discussed. A complicated process of development of autobiographical narrating in regard of traumatic events and/or collective violence is strongly dependent on narrative input of reliable others and social groups to whom person belongs. Habermas and Bartoli point out an optimistic developmental line in the increasing ability of adolescents to contextualize their experience in an autobiographical and social–historical context that makes possible distancing from collective traumatic experiences and at the same time including historical events in their collective identity. The mediating and supporting role of the parents in narrative construction is unquestionable but the existing of subtle, mostly unconscious, processes in transgenerational transmission of trauma is also recognized. Grand and Salberg draw attention to the psychoanalytic perspective on massive trauma, incorporates ethics, history, politics, social justice, and broader acknowledgment of a familial unconscious. In the course of ethical considerations, Hancheva reminds of the need to maintain a difficult balance between relief of suffering and truth recovery when doing research, making therapy or forming an expert position in regard of recovered memories of individual or social trauma.

Part V: Social Psychology of Trauma

Langer and Brehm provide a socio-psychological perspective on social trauma and collective violence. A twofold explanation is developed around group behaviors, in particular social situations, on one side, and historically and socio-culturally anchored prejudices and attitudes, on the other. The authors argue that social trauma in post-conflict societies traced at individual, institutional, and social levels requires both effective practical measures and convincing theoretical developments, taking into account both the perspective of the perpetrator and the victim's narrative. In the same venue, Porobić offers a possible framework for transgenerational recovery, for conflict resolution and reconciliation from war-related social traumas via peace education, enabling educators and students to reflect and self-reflect, to take different perspectives, and to become capable of through experiential learning. An interesting example of psychosocial support model in low-resource settings is provided by Eltayeb. She describes the Ahfad Trauma Centre and its work based on mobilization of the existing cultural norms of trust, social support, reciprocity, and by abiding by strict ethical guidelines. Difficulties in enhancing cultural adaption that encompasses Afro-Arab cultures in addition to gender and political issues are vividly described.

At the organizational level of social functioning, existing of coercive organizational practices is discussed as representative for social trauma and diverse psychological consequences. Hedrih and Husremović make an overview of the most significant existing practices in organization and trace their roots to the collective trauma, prejudices, and stereotypes, preventing recognition of diversity.

The final chapter in this part brings the issue of secondary traumatization that adds another layer to complicated social dynamics of victim-perpetrator groups. Živanović and Vukčević-Marković reveal how social trauma echoes in the helpers being in the position of witnessing indirectly the aftermaths of collusions and traumatic experiences.

Part VI: Legal and Ethical Aspects

Ozcurumez introduces another perspective and language of presenting the social trauma challenge at the level of policy makers, arguing that in the coming years, "trauma sensitive care" and "trauma sensitive policies" shall characterize the discussions on legal and ethical aspects of social trauma globally, nationally, and locally. The multitude of policy actors constituting of policy makers, decision makers, and implementors set the stage of a complicated design of measures to be adopted and implemented. In the next chapter, on Sexual and Gender-Based Violence (SGVB), the author provides a socio-ecological framework for explanation of SGBV in armed conflict and displacement, and links it to social trauma by bringing together structural, individual, family, and community-related processes. As a counterpoint to the sharp-cut policy regulations, an intriguing psychoanalytic approach of Arsenijević brings closer social trauma and environmental violence. The eloquent example of slow environmental violence phenomenon confronts us with another dimensions of suffering, social trauma consequences and subtle, hard to recognize, physical and emotional killing. Another example of consequences of genocide, violence, and complex traumatization is presented by Hirschelmann and Rahman Rasho. They formulate the challenge of devising a framework for elaboration and intervention that incorporates the characteristics of the socio-legal condition and psycho-criminology with the dimensions of the psychological work with the victims.

The difficult field of moral judgment and moral action in regard to social trauma is far from consistent theory, but for the research purposes, Petrović provides practical guidelines and recommendations for prevention of unethical behavior based on ethical standards in trauma research.

Part VII: Specific Methodology and Practice in Social Trauma Research

Social trauma is the subject of multifold and increasing research activities. Students should be aware of the precise conditions and possible pitfalls of such research. Thus, the research section of the textbook presents different approaches of quantitative and qualitative trauma research in the specific field of social trauma. In his introductory chapter, Vladimir Hedrih is using vivid examples and straightforward questions to provoke a critical thinking stance in both interpreters of research results and researchers planning and designing studies on social trauma. The author warns against research causing or justifying social traumatic events by either sided speculations and political agendas or unconscious biases. As a mean for minimizing bias effects, Protić emphasizes the existing standards of good practice in conducting quantitative research and pays special attention to respecting ethical requirements in planning, conducting, and analyzing research in the social trauma field. Another methodological chapter discusses qualitative methods and Stanković proves their potential, especially when dealing with complex and interdisciplinary sociotraumatic phenomena. The importance of giving voice to personal and collective trauma narratives and articulating representations of traumatic experiences is acknowledged. Acknowledgment is a vital part of social trauma recovery and healing process. A powerful example of clash between historical and psychoanalytic reasoning in regard of historical versus reality can be found in Hamburger's chapter on video testimonies of survivors of a traumatic historical event. One of the most difficult lessons, to bear witness and to tolerate uncertainty and ambiguity also in professional position of a researcher or therapist, could be learned through this text.

Part VIII: Social Trauma and Education

Education as one of the main pillars of society represents a complex space of encounter where pupils gain knowledge and skills for future work, but also and even more important, internalize the values and cultural norms important for the society. In the introductory chapter, Husremović and Koso-Drljević discuss through examples of postwar and post-totalitarian states, how nations or interest groups create education outcomes with the goal to install and further sustain collective identities and collective memories to protect large groups, their stereotypes, and internal interests. A vivid example of Serbian experience in education of migrants and vulnerable groups, presented by Kovač-Cerović, supports an interdisciplinary approach and its clear benefits when tackling the social trauma issues. The concluding chapter by Scher and Malmheden is on social trauma education at the university level. It puts into perspective and contextual comparison decades of experience trauma research and education in academic field and the specificity of the international social trauma study course, which provided the breeding ground for the present textbook.

Andreas Hamburger
Camellia Hancheva
Vamık D. Volkan

Contents

Part I
Theory of Social Trauma

Chapter 1
Social Trauma: A Bridging Concept

Andreas Hamburger

1.1 Introduction: Background and Main Theoretical Concepts/Discussions

Social trauma is a clinical as well as a sociopsychological category: (1) as a clinical category it defines a group of posttraumatic disorders caused by organized societal violence or genocide where a social group is the target of planned persecution and therefore not only the individual but also its social environment is afflicted. Therefore, the concept of social trauma also describes (2) the shadowing of the original trauma on long-term social processes, be it on the family, group, or inter-group level.

1.1.1 Clinical Theories of Trauma and Posttraumatic Conditions

Posttraumatic disorders are the only DSM diagnosis defined by an external event. However, the types of traumatizing events are poorly distinguished; especially, post-social-traumatic disorders are not addressed in the diagnostic manuals (see Hamburger, 2020b, this volume). Trauma-related mental illness in general, well known in history, was (re-)acknowledged only lately by rational medicine (Hamburger, 2018c; Kucmin, Kucmin, Nogalski, Sojczuk, & Jojczuk, 2016; Ray, 2008). This picture has changed in the late twentieth century, when the acknowledgment of posttraumatic stress disorder (PTSD), along with its behavioral definition in DSM III, led to a clear-cut diagnosis, but in the same place provoked a steadily widening, even inflationary use of the trauma concept (Kirmayer, Kienzler, Afana, & Pedersen, 2010; Prager, 2011).

A. Hamburger (✉)
International Psychoanalytic University Berlin, Berlin, Germany
e-mail: andreas.hamburger@ipu-berlin.de

© Springer Nature Switzerland AG 2021

A. Hamburger et al. (eds.), *Social Trauma – An Interdisciplinary Textbook*,
https://doi.org/10.1007/978-3-030-47817-9_1

The classical psychoanalytic trauma theory evolved from Freud's early adoption and subsequent rejection of child abuse as the core of hysteria, followed by Ferenczi's concepts of war trauma and child abuse (Hamburger, 2018a), and eventually to a modern psychoanalytic trauma theory that includes the social implications of trauma. There was, however, a remarkable delay in integrating the experience of the Shoah as a massive social trauma into the general psychoanalytic trauma theory (for details, see Hamburger, 2020a, 2020b, this volume; Bohleber, 2007).

Beyond the psychoanalytic discourse, clinical research like Kira's attempts to build a taxonomy of trauma (Kira, 2001) and research on differentiation of traumatic reactions by type of exposure shift the focus of clinical trauma studies from a merely behavioral approach to an increasing awareness of social conditions (discussed in Hamburger, 2020a, this volume).

But still, clinical theories of trauma—besides genocide studies, where the social factor is usually at the center)—often suffer from an individualistic bias, as they rarely take into account that traumatizing events occur in the inter-individual and inter-group space.

1.1.2 Social Theories of Trauma

In social sciences, a vast discussion on social trauma has been evolving since the 1980s—and, not unlike the abovementioned widening of the terminological scope in the clinical trauma concept, has led to a broad and even careless use of the term (Fassin & Rechtmann, 2007/2009). The use of the term trauma in sociology is even more metaphorical than in psychopathology, since social trauma in this perspective is not a reaction to a historical cause at all, but a collective construction. To people, traumatic is what they experience as unsupportable, horrifying, or overwhelming. Trauma as an intuitively understood term is a social fact in itself, and it points to some underlying social experience which can be sociologically reflected. Using trauma in everyday language as a predicate for a societal fact is metaphorical, as it implies a quasi-natural impact that causes a symptom, while in reality social trauma is an ex-post construct (Alexander, Eyerman, Giesen, Smelser, & Sztompka, 2004). Prager (2011) defines social trauma in a theoretical framework that addresses social reality and, at the same time, psychoanalytically reflected individual experience, as "an event or series of events remembered as so dangerous as to be impossible to preserve an equilibrating belief in a world that presumes our presence" (p. 429). He distinguishes three types of social trauma, (1) traumas of lethality, in which the loving self is placed at risk; (2) traumas of violence and bodily harm, where the illusion of safety and security as guaranteed by a social contract based upon equal rights is undermined; and (3) traumas of personal invisibility, when the failure to be recognized as an individual produces anti-social results and, therefore, generates a withdrawal of solidary connections with the larger whole (p. 446).

In the sociological and culturological discussion, different terms and concepts have been proposed, and they will be discussed in the following sections.

1.1.2.1 Cultural Trauma

Alexander et al. (2004) coined the concept of "cultural trauma," underlining that social facts are not causes, but attributions:

> Events are not inherently traumatic. Trauma is a socially mediated attribution. The attribution may be made in real time, as an event unfolds; it may also be made before the event occurs, as an adumbration, or after the event has concluded, as a post-hoc reconstruction. Sometimes, in fact, events that are deeply traumatizing may not actually have occurred at all. (p. 8)

Traumatic events in history are constructed reference points of memory and/or re-projection of societies, serving their group identity.

1.1.2.2 Collective Trauma

Vamık Volkan, in developing the key concept of "chosen trauma" as an identity marker for ethnic, national, or religious group, usually does not draw on the term "social trauma," but uses "collective trauma" instead (Volkan, 1991, 1997; see also Volkan, 2020, this volume). His theoretical approach is based on a psychoanalytic concept of identity and underlines the transgenerational transmission of a shared imagination of the mostly archaic, traumatic event. Thus, the concept of a collectively chosen trauma combines a trauma concept derived from individual psychoanalysis to a sociological approach: the collectively shared imagination of the trauma serves as a symbol that psychologically links large-group members together. Similarly, Hirschberger (2018) describes the collective memory of traumatic events as a:

> dynamic social psychological process that is primarily dedicated to the construction of meaning. The creation and maintenance of meaning comprises a sense of self-continuity, a connection between the self, others and the environment [...], and the feeling that one's existence matters. It is a process of identity construction that comprises the sense of self-esteem, continuity, distinctiveness, belonging, efficacy, and ultimately a sense of meaning. (p. 2)

1.1.2.3 Historical Trauma

The notion of "historical trauma," quite different from the social sciences' term "cultural trauma" or "collective trauma," has been emerging in historiography (Sotero, 2006) since the 1990s. In their seminal books *Unclaimed Experience* and *Representing the Holocaust,* Cathy Caruth (1996) and Dominick LaCapra (1996) opened a debate that challenged historiography over the irrepresentability of the Holocaust (see also LaCapra, 2001, 2004; Rüsen, 2020, this volume). Some historians developed a strong interest in psychoanalytic approaches to individual testimony as a historical source and established empirical cooperations (see Lamparter, Wiegand-Grefe, & Wierling, 2013; Laub, 2005b; Laub & Hamburger, 2017). From the science of history, however, doubts were articulated about the validity and objectivity of testimonies as historical sources (see Laub, 1992a, 1992b, 2005b; Trezise, 2008; and Laub's reply, 2009; for a detailed discussion, see Hamburger, 2020b, this volume).

A second line of historical discourse relates to colonization, consciously alluding to the Holocaust (e.g., Thornton, 1987; see also Brave Heart & DeBruyn, 1998). However, there are huge differences between postcolonial/structural violence against Indigenous people and the Holocaust regarding the spatial, temporal, and qualitative extent of the traumatizing conditions, their social and cultural contexts, and the availability of coping mechanisms. One distinctive element of historical trauma is its persistence over generations.

1.1.2.4 Conceptual Criticism

The use of the trauma concept in sociology, historiography, philosophy, and cultural and literary studies, on the other hand, provoked some fierce criticism. Kansteiner and Weilnböck (2008) objected the concept of cultural trauma as a paradigm error, an understandable but misleading application of a psychopathological concept to society. In a huge, sarcastic essay, Weilnböck (2007) depicted the deep confusion a psychotherapeutically educated reader might experience when reading about the application of the trauma concept in however well-intended philosophical writings (see also Khadem, 2014). Still, the concept of social trauma, if well-defined, is significant, and these critical remarks should remind us to use it properly.

1.2 Learning Outcome Related to Social Trauma

The concept of social trauma describes the psychological and relational consequences of a traumatic experience in the frame of societal occurrences, where a social group is the target of a planned persecution. Genocide and persecution are committed by one group against another and thus affect the holding environment of the victims. It damages the social identity of both the victim and the perpetrator and their societal groups, causing an increased rate of trauma transmission. The concept of social trauma aims at widening the scope of general clinical theories of posttraumatic disorders by including the specificity of the historical circumstances of their traumatic origin, as well as perpetuating conditions, as seen from history, sociology, and political and cultural science. The clinical category of social trauma is related to concepts like massive or extreme trauma, as well as to categories from social sciences like cultural and historical trauma. Consequently, it leads to a relational therapeutic approach, rendering space and giving a voice to the unspeakable through witnessing the "failure to assimilate experience into psychic representation and structure" (Laub & Lee, 2003, p. 433). In its openness to the unspeakable, the notion of social trauma should not be understood as just another entry in the catalogue of diagnostic classifications.

1.3 Preferred Model of Explanation

1.3.1 Clinical Starting Point

The concept of social trauma presented in this chapter started from psychoanalytic research on videotestimonies with Shoah survivors diagnosed with chronic schizophrenia (Hamburger, 2015; see Hamburger, 2020a, 2020b, this volume). Here it became clear that clinical categories are insufficient to understand these patients and their diagnoses, as both their original suffering and subsequent hospitalization are determined by specific social interactions. Thus, the scope of the theory had to be widened beyond the individual patient, considering the interpersonality of both the trauma and the process of witnessing.

1.3.2 Theoretical Implications: Relational Theory

This interpersonal widening of the trauma concept parallels a development in psychoanalytic thought from a biology-based one-body psychology to a relational theory. Following extensions of classical psychoanalysis into ego-psychology, object relations theory, and self-psychology, an interpersonal or relational approach has become prominent in the past few decades (Mitchell, 2009). Both participants, the analyst and the analysand, are subject to unconscious processes; both are striving for an interpretation of this unconscious sense. Such a relational or interpersonal model is much more suitable for the conceptualization of social trauma than the classical theory referring to overwhelming quantities of anxiety (Grand, 2000; Thomas, 2009).

1.3.3 Phenomena Related to Social Trauma

Social trauma is not just a clinical category; however, if survivors display clinical symptoms, they are partly comparable to general posttraumatic reactions. However, there are symptoms like increased guilt feelings, emotional disruption, and adjustment issues that have been described as the "survivor syndrome," like continuous sadness, hopelessness, and social withdrawal (for details, see Hamburger, 2020b, this volume). However, social trauma is in no way defined by a symptom list that allows for a psychiatric diagnosis. Social trauma describes the group-specific reverberation of group persecution; accordingly, its specificity lies in the field of interpersonal communication. Dori Laub, in his paper "Traumatic Shutdown of Narrative and Symbolization" (2005a), described the interactive difficulties that emerge when survivors try to recount their traumatic life story. The co-construction of a coherent autobiographical life history is hampered by splitting off and replacement by screen memories but also by an erasure of emotional resonance and a denial of the trauma, leading to characteristic countertransference reactions on the part of the interviewer/therapist in the form of co-confusion, freezing, and psychosomatic reactions (see Hamburger, 2017a, 2017b).

Beyond the individual, some social phenomena can be regarded as symptoms of social trauma, such as conspiracy of silence, institutional rejection, heroization, avoidance, and blaming (Grand, 2000; Herman, 1992; Rinker & Lawler, 2018). The most specific trait of social trauma, however, that links the individual and transgenerational level to the societal phenomena is the often-reported observation that persecuted families and groups show transgenerational trauma transmission (see Grand & Salberg, 2020). It can be explained by a mentalization model of transgenerational trauma transmission (Hamburger, 2018c).

1.3.4 Mentalization Model of Social Trauma

The crucial difference between social and individual trauma is transgenerational trauma transmission. It has been described and empirically researched mainly among offspring of Shoah survivors (Fromm, 2012; Kogan, 2002, 2012; see Grand & Salberg, 2020, this volume; Fromm, 2020, this volume). Also, survivors of other forms of massive social trauma have been acknowledged and studied (Danieli, 1998; Volkan, Ast, & Greer, 2002). Literature and research on children of individually traumatized persons, however, is scarce (e.g., Kelly, 2018); even the children of war veterans, which might be included in the category of social trauma survivors, are rarely studied (Dekel & Goldblatt, 2008).

The importance of transgenerational transmission for the theory of social trauma is based on the fact that by its being embedded in the social environment it not only impacts the survivors but also their coping through narrativization and recounting of this traumatic impact. While possibly many traumatized parents might hand on some difficult issues to their children, as it has been studied in attachment research (Hesse, Main, Abrams, & Rifkin, 2003; Lyons-Ruth, 2003), in cases where the victim is traumatized as a protagonist of a social group (by a perpetrator, who also acts as a protagonist of a social group, with both groups appertaining to the same overarching society), then the traumatizing event is part and parcel of the social environment and will be recounted (if not by words, then by significant silence) over and over again. It becomes part of history, not only within the family but in the child's overall social environment. Thus, it affects in a much more powerful way the "epistemic trust" (Fonagy & Allison, 2014) or the mental horizon of the child.

The theory of mentalization (Fonagy, 2010; Fonagy, Gergely, Jurist, & Target, 2002) provides an explanatory concept for the interference of emotional development with social circumstances. In its significant relations to caregivers and peers, the infant internalizes the image of himself in the mind of others. This process builds upon a growing ability to read the intentions of others and to emphasize his/her subjective perspective. In order to support this development, caregivers regularly show "marked affects" in playful exchanges with the infant, especially in their mirroring behavior. Thus, the infant learns to connect internal sensations with external affect responses that imitate and underline at the same time the child's own affect displays. Through repeated emphasizing interactions of this kind, the child moves from his/her original *equivalent mode*, where the difference between imagination and reality is not yet established, to the construction of an "inner" and an "outer" world. One major passage toward this difference is pretend play, where children relentlessly make up "as-if" situations. In this genre of universal play, children try to establish an imaginative world, inhabited by persons (including themselves) in possession of a mental life and intentions. This stage that Fonagy et al. (2002) call "pretend mode" is a major prerequisite for mentalization, where the developing individual can distinguish and shift between the perception and imagination of his own feelings to the empathic perception of the feelings and intentions of others. The mentalizing capacity, which is acquired by healthy individuals after about 3 years of life, is, at the same time, a building block for society. Fonagy and Allison (2014) describe "epistemic trust" as the ability to accept new knowledge from another person as trustworthy, developing in secure attachment relations. Reversely, it is also fostered by a stable social environment that offers institutional security and predictability to the caregivers themselves, such as to enable them to help their children to distinguish between anxiety-loaded archaic phantasies and reality in the equivalence mode, to transform them in playful imagination in the pretend mode, and, eventually, to acquire the necessary reflexivity to successfully emphasize mental processes. This social dimension of mentalization is condensed in the proverb "It takes a village to raise a child" (Young-Bruehl, 2012, p. 550); but it makes also clear that, on the other hand, a societal impairment, as it takes place in social trauma, must influence the individual, familial, and societal processes that lead to mentalization and epistemic trust.

> Caregivers under a threat of persecution in reality can hardly provide the secure base the child needs to distinguish between his inner fears, experienced in equivalence mode as outer threats, from reality. And beyond the nuclear family, also the social functions of the wider environment will tendentially be restricted. When a healthy social environment is able to provide a good-enough "eudaimonia" (Young-Bruehl, 2012) through protective social institutions and healing mechanisms like judicial institutions, social security, everyday narratives, urban legends and myths, jokes, and social and cultural events, including the benign subgroup formations celebrated in sports, then all these social processes can be compared to the "pretend play" by which the infant learns to distinguish phantasy and reality and develop pro-social behaviour. If, on the other hand, the social environment itself is under threat of annihilation, many of these pro-social, eudaimonia-producing mechanisms, the digesting capacity of the environment, will fail. (Hamburger, 2018c, pp. 18–19)

Fonagy (1999) describes transgenerational transmission in the case example of the grandchild of a Holocaust survivor as an interplay between attachment and mentalization, meditated by "a vulnerability to dissociative states established in the infant by frightened or frightening caregiving, which, in its turn, is trauma-related" (p. 92). The dissociative core self-originating from this condition "leaves the child susceptible to the internalization of sets of trauma-related ideation from the attachment figure, which remain unintegrated in the self-structure and cannot be reflected on or thought about" (p. 92).

Since "the infant perceives and internalizes the caregiver's representation to form the core of his or her mentalizing or psychological self" (p. 103), it may happen in cases where the caregiver themselves carry an unmourned, unmentalized, or dissociative internal image or a state of persecution that through this gate the caregiver's persecution-imbued images of the child are then internalized and can be handed on through the next generations.

1.4 Practical Implications in the Field of Social Trauma

The theory of social trauma connects clinical psychotraumatology (in a relational psychoanalytic key) to a sociological view. This theoretical connection allows for some changes in practical approaches, be it in psychotherapy or in the understanding of societal phenomena. In the field of mental health, it alerts therapists that the patient is not an insulated individual, but a part of the group, that the traumatic event was shared by this targeted group, and that it took place in the frame of an overarching societal context. Thus, some individual defense mechanisms noticed in the therapeutic work, like repression, denial, and splitting, might well mirror group-dynamic processes. Moreover, the theory of social trauma reminds therapists that such societal defense mechanisms might very well work in the therapist himself. In sociology, on the other hand, the theory of social trauma can make researchers realize (and adequately incorporate in their research designs) that the objects of their studies, societies and groups, are composed of living people who do have an inner world, which, despite (or even because) working partly unconsciously, heavily influences their social behavior and—as symbolic interactionism has emphasized all along—their interpretive participation in societal processes.

1.4.1 Acknowledgment and Witnessing

Working with videotestimonies of Shoah survivors (Hamburger, 2015) is a deep experience of the inescapable entanglement social trauma entails. The testimonial process is an encounter between the survivor and the witness that not only follows the designed path of opening up to the public and transmitting experience but, at the same time, restages the desymbolization and muting resonance of the social environment—the interview dyad itself becomes the site of a narrative annihilation. Only by reflecting this inevitable repetition, not only on the part of the interviewer but also on the part of researchers who work with the testimony, the testimony can be received as a whole. Thus, witnessing is not just listening, but exposing oneself to the blind eye one is so willingly going to turn on the survivor's often fragmented account—the very neglect that makes social trauma so characteristically unspeakable (Laub, 1992a). Psychoanalytic listening acknowledges this entanglement and intentionally exposes itself to uncertainty. This open process may result after some time in a relief for survivors as well as interviewers and staff, as if an unconscious "conspiracy of silence" had been broken (Laub, 2005a; Strous et al., 2005).

1.4.2 Social Healing

The fact that sharing traumatic memories in a holding, witnessing frame can heal individual suffering from posttraumatic disorders has led to the idea that also societies can heal from their traumatic past by establishing reconciliation processes. Starting from the 1980s in South America, truth and reconciliation commissions became famous after the end of the apartheid in South Africa. Today, all over the globe, such processes are at work (Hamber, 2009; Hayner, 2010; Worthington & Aten, 2010). However, it has been remarked that truth and reconciliation commissions are oft assigned a conflicting task, namely to offer an opportunity for a personal voice, while simultaneously aiming at the construction of an accepted national history (Prager, 2008; Thomas, 2009).

Besides government-based practices to provide space for mourning and reconciliation, there are also multiple initiatives of negotiating social trauma; one notable enterprise is the International Dialogue Initiative (IDI), an independent, interdisciplinary building in the psychoanalytic theories and negotiation experiences of Vamık Volkan (see Fromm, 2020, this volume). Volkan and IDI have mediated in many national and ethnic conflicts, trying to understand the conflict in terms of collectively chosen trauma.

Academic cooperation may also contribute to social healing (Delić et al., 2014). The present volume roots in a scientific network that connects universities from countries that were former enemies. It resulted in a nearly decade-long series of cooperative study and teaching on the social scars this enmity had caused and has led to an ever-growing process of exploring conflicts. To give an example: Right at the start of the network, in 2013, Bosnian researchers Amra Delić and Esmina Avdibegović were invited to present their study on war rape during the Yugoslav wars at Belgrade University. It was the first lecture on this topic ever given at the Faculty of Philosophy. The scientific exchange on the former battlefield is an effective way to address social scars and, at the same time, to re-establish mutual epistemic trust; but it is not possible without acknowledging the conscious and unconscious prejudices that even afflict the network process itself (Hamburger, 2018b).

1.4.3 Psychotherapy

As Bohleber (2007) points out, contemporary psychoanalytic treatment technique emphasizes the present transference-countertransference relationship, rather than unearthing buried memories from the past, which had been its major concern in the first place. Trauma, however, is the great exception. "Traumatic memories [...]

constitute a kind of foreign body in the psychic-associative network," requiring "a remembrance and reconstruction of the traumatic events in the analytic treatment" (p. 329; see also Bohleber, 2010).

For social trauma, this twofold approach in psychotherapy is furthermore complicated by the fact of unconscious reenactment. Even if both the therapist and the patient are open to face the traumatic past, social neglect or narrative shutdown will often unconsciously reemerge in the here-and-now—all the more, as the patient and the therapist are part of the same society. Testimony, which Laub emphasizes as an essential element of trauma therapy (see Mucci, 2018, p. 97), takes on a different meaning through the social connections between therapist and patient. In the case of social trauma, the splitting, which in general trauma already begins in the peritraumatic situation and can be gradually dissolved by a holding relationship in therapy, is not an intrapsychic process but a social reality, manifesting itself, for example, in the conspiracy of silence, in denial or trivialization, and in other forms of institutional defense. This split in reality must also be acknowledged and dealt with in the analysis. To treat dissociation processes merely, as in trauma therapy, as intrapsychic, might even retraumatize the socially traumatized patients. Also, silence in therapy can, in the traumatization context that has essentially been perpetuated by silence, bring about this retraumatization or re-staging (see Mucci, 2018, p. 100).

The reflective relationship in transference and countertransference is the essence of psychoanalytic therapy. However, this attitude is particularly challenged in the case of social traumatization by a shared social affiliation to a traumatized society, which leads to a characteristic unfolding of the transference and countertransference different from neurotic or individual-traumatogenic disorders (see also Marcus & Rosenberg, 1988). The individual process of therapy/testimony allows for the interpenetration of external events, personal experience, coping, and resilience. Therefore, in the psychotherapeutic treatment of traumatized patients whose trauma is of a predominantly social nature, an approach is recommendable that reflects on the tendency of social trauma to restage in the here-and-now, with full awareness of the importance of mentalization as the core mechanism of transgenerational transmission. The same mechanism of mentalization, however, can be used to establish a therapeutic contact that focuses on "playful engagement with feelings and beliefs rather than a classical insight-oriented, interpretive approach" (Fonagy, 1999, p. 103).

1.5 Suggested Reading

Hamburger, A. (2018c). New thoughts on genocidal trauma. In A. Hamburger (Ed.), *Trauma, trust, and memory: Social trauma and reconciliation in psychoanalysis, psychotherapy and cultural memory* (pp. 13–22). London: Routledge.

Laub, D., & Hamburger, A. (Eds.) (2017). *Psychoanalysis and holocaust testimony: Unwanted memories of social trauma*. London: Routledge.

References

Alexander, J. C., Eyerman, R., Giesen, B., Smelser, N. J., & Sztompka, P. (2004). *Cultural trauma and collective identity*. Berkeley, CA: University of California Press.

Bohleber, W. (2007). Remembrance, trauma and collective memory. The battle for memory in psychoanalysis. *International Journal of Psychoanalysis, 88*, 329–352.

Bohleber, W. (2010). *Destructiveness, Intersubjectivity, and trauma: The identity crisis of modern psychoanalysis*. London: Karnac.

Brave Heart, M. Y. H., & DeBruyn, L. M. (1998). The American Indian holocaust: Healing historical unresolved grief. *American Indian and Alaska Native Mental Health Research, 8*(2), 56–78.

Caruth, C. (1996). *Unclaimed experience: Trauma, narrative and history*. Baltimore: The Johns Hopkins University Press.

Danieli, Y. (Ed.). (1998). *International handbook of multigenerational legacies of trauma*. Dordrecht: Springer Science & Business Media.

Dekel, R., & Goldblatt, H. (2008). Is there intergenerational transmission of trauma? The case of combat veterans' children. *American Journal of Orthopsychiatry, 78*(3), 281–289.

Delić, A., Hasanović, M., Avdibegović, E., Dimitrijević, A., Hancheva, C., Scher, C., … Hamburger, A. (2014). Academic model of trauma healing in postwar societies. *Acta Med Acad, 43*(1), 76–80.

Fassin, D., & Rechtman, R. (2009). *The empire of trauma: An inquiry into the condition of victimhood*. Princeton: Princeton University Press. (Original work published 2007).

Fonagy, P. (1999). The transgenerational transmission of holocaust trauma: Lessons learned from the analysis of an adolescent with compulsive-obsessive disorder. *Attachment and Human Development, 1*(1), 92–114.

Fonagy, P. (2010). Attachment, trauma, and psychoanalysis: Where psychoanalysis meets neuroscience. In M. Leuzinger-Bohleber, J. Canestri, & M. Target (Eds.), *Early development and its disturbances: Clinical, conceptual and empirical research on ADHD and other psychopathologies and its epistemological reflections* (pp. 53–75). London: Karnac Books.

Fonagy, P., & Allison, E. (2014). The role of mentalizing and epistemic trust in the therapeutic relationship. *Psychotherapy, 53*(3), 372–380.

Fonagy, P., Gergely, G., Jurist, E. L., & Target, M. (2002). *Affect regulation, mentalization, and the development of the self*. New York: Other Press.

Fromm, M. G. (Ed.). (2012). *Lost in transmission: Studies of trauma across generations*. London: Karnac.

Fromm, M. G. (2020). Psychoanalytic approaches to social trauma. In A. Hamburger, C. Hancheva & V. Volkan (Eds.), *Social trauma. An Interdisciplinary Textbook* (pp. 69–76). New York: Springer.

Grand, S. (2000). *The reproduction of evil: A clinical and cultural perspective*. Hillsdale, NJ: Analytic Press.

Grand, S. & Salberg, J. (2020). Trans-Generational Transmission of Trauma. In: A. Hamburger, C. Hancheva & V. Volkan (Eds.), *Social trauma. An Interdisciplinary Textbook* (pp. 209–215). New York: Springer Nature.

Hamber, B. (2009). *Transforming societies after political violence: Truth, reconciliation, and mental health*. Dordrecht: Springer Science & Business Media.

Hamburger, A. (2015). Refracted attunement, affective resonance: Scenic-narrative microanalysis of entangled presence in a holocaust Survivor's testimony. *Contemporary Psychoanalysis, 51*(2), 239–257.

Hamburger, A. (2017a). Genocidal trauma. Individual and social consequences of the assault on the mental and physical life of a group. In D. Laub & A. Hamburger (Eds.), *Psychoanalysis and holocaust testimony: Unwanted memories of social trauma* (pp. 66–91). London: Routledge.

Hamburger, A. (2017b). Scenic narrative microanalysis. Controlled psychoanalytic assessment of session videos or transcripts as a transparent qualitative research instrument. In D. Laub & A. Hamburger (Eds.), *Psychoanalysis and holocaust testimony: Unwanted memories of social trauma* (pp. 166–182). London: Routledge.

Hamburger, A. (2018a). Ferenczi on war neuroses. In A. Dimitrijević, G. Casullo, & J. Frankel (Eds.), *Ferenczi's influence on contemporary psychoanalytic traditions* (pp. 65–71). Milton Park, New York: Routledge.

Hamburger, A. (2018b). After babel—Teaching psychoanalysis on a former battlefield. *International Forum of Psychoanalysis, 27*(1), 1–9.

Hamburger, A. (2018c). New thoughts on genocidal trauma. In A. Hamburger (Ed.), *Trauma, trust, and memory: Social trauma and reconciliation in psychoanalysis, psychotherapy and cultural memory* (pp. 13–22). London: Routledge.

Hamburger, A. (2020a). The complexity of social trauma diagnosis and intervention. In A. Hamburger, C. Hancheva & V. Volkan (Eds.), *Social trauma. An Interdisciplinary Textbook* (pp. 55–68). New York: Springer.

Hamburger, A. (2020b). Videotestimony research. In A. Hamburger, C. Hancheva & V. Volkan (Eds.), *Social trauma. An Interdisciplinary Textbook* (pp. 343–354). New York: Springer.

Hayner, P. (2010). *Unspeakable truths: Transitional justice and the challenge of truth commissions*. London: Routledge.

Herman, J. (1992). *Trauma and recovery: The aftermath of violence—From domestic abuse to political terror*. New York, NY: Basic Books.

Hesse, E., Main, M., Abrams, K., & Rifkin, A. (2003). Unresolved states regarding loss and abuse can have "second generation" effects: Disorganized, role-inversion and frightening ideation in the offspring of traumatized non-maltreating parents. In M. F. Solomon & D. J. Siegel (Eds.), *Healing trauma: Attachment, mind, body and brain* (pp. 57–106). New York: Norton.

Hirschberger, G. (2018). Collective trauma and the social construction of meaning. *Frontiers in Psychology, 9*, 1441. https://doi.org/10.3389/fpsyg.2018.01441

Kansteiner, W., & Weilnböck, H. (2008). Against the concept of cultural trauma. In A. Erll & A. Nünning (Eds.), *Cultural memory studies* (pp. 229–240). Berlin: de Gruyter.

Kelly, K. V. (2018). Heroes at home: The transmission of trauma in firefighters' families. In M. G. Fromm (Ed.), *Lost in transmission* (pp. 203–213). London: Routledge.

Khadem, A. (2014). Cultural trauma as a social construct: 9/11 fiction and the epistemology of communal pain. *Intertexts, 18*(2), 181–197.

Kira, I. A. (2001). Taxonomy of trauma and trauma assessment. *Traumatology, 7*(2), 73–86.

Kirmayer, L. J., Kienzler, H., Afana, A. H., & Pedersen, D. (2010). Trauma and disasters in social and cultural context. In C. Morgan & D. Bhugra (Eds.), *Principles of social psychiatry* (2nd ed., pp. 155–177). Oxford: Wiley-Blackwell.

Kogan, I. (2002). Enactment in the lives and treatment of holocaust survivors' offspring. *Psychoanalytic Quarterly, 71*(2), 251–272.

Kogan, I. (2012). The second generation in the shadow of terror. In M. G. Fromm (Ed.), *Lost in transmission: Studies of trauma across generations* (pp. 5–19). London: Karnac.

Kucmin, T., Kucmin, A., Nogalski, A., Sojczuk, S., & Jojczuk, M. (2016). History of trauma and posttraumatic disorders in literature. *Psychiatria Polska, 50*(1), 269–281.

LaCapra, D. (1996). *Representing the holocaust: History, theory, trauma*. Ithaca: Cornell University Press.

LaCapra, D. (2001). *Writing history, writing trauma*. Baltimore: The Johns Hopkins University Press.

LaCapra, D. (2004). *History in transit: Experience, identity, critical theory*. Ithaca: Cornell University Press.

Lamparter, U., Wiegand-Grefe, S., & Wierling, D. (2013). *Zeitzeugen des Hamburger Feuersturms 1943 und ihre Familien [Eyewitnesses of the 1943 Hamburg firestorms and their families]*. Göttingen: Vandenhoeck & Ruprecht.

Laub, D. (1992a). Bearing witness or the vicissitudes of listening. In S. Felman & D. Laub (Eds.), *Testimony: Crises of witnessing in literature, psychoanalysis and history* (pp. 57–74). New York: Routledge.

Laub, D. (1992b). An event without a witness: Truth, testimony and survival. In S. Felman & D. Laub (Eds.), *Testimony: Crises of witnessing in literature, psychoanalysis, and history* (pp. 75–92). New York: Routledge

Laub, D. & Lee, S. (2003). Thanatos and massive psychic trauma: the impact of the dead instinct on knowing, remembering, and forgetting. *Journal of the American Psychoanalytic Association, 51*(2), 433–463.
Laub, D. (2005a). Traumatic shutdown of narrative and symbolization: A death instinct derivative? *Contemporary Psychoanalysis, 41*(2), 307–326.
Laub, D. (2005b). From speechlessness to narrative: The cases of holocaust historians and of psychiatrically hospitalized survivors. *Literature and Medicine, 24*, 253–265.
Laub, D. (2009). On holocaust testimony and its reception within its own frame, as a process in its own right. *History and Memory, 21*(1), 127–150.
Lyons-Ruth, K. (2003). Dissociation and the parent-infant dialogue: A longitudinal perspective from attachment research. *Journal of the American Psychoanalytic Association, 51*, 883–911.
Marcus, P., & Rosenberg, A. (1988). *Healing their wounds: Psychotherapy with holocaust survivors and their families*. New York: Praeger.
Mitchell, S. (2009), Influence and Autonomy in Psychoanalysis. Hillsdale, NJ: The Analytic Press.
Mucci, C. (2018). *Beyond Individual and Collective Trauma*. New York: Taylor and Francis. [Kindle DX version]. Retrieved from Amazon.com
Prager, J. (2008). Healing from history: Psychoanalytic considerations on traumatic pasts and social repair. *European Journal of Social Theory, 11*(3), 405–420.
Prager, J. (2011). Danger and deformation: A social theory of trauma Part I: Contemporary psychoanalysis, contemporary social theory, and healthy selves. *American Imago, 68*(3), 425–448.
Ray, S. (2008). Evolution of posttraumatic stress disorder and future directions. *Archives of Psychiatric Nursing, 22*(4), 217–225.
Rinker, J., & Lawler, J. (2018). Trauma as a collective disease and root cause of protracted social conflict. *Peace and Conflict: Journal of Peace Psychology, 24*(2), 150.
Rüsen, J. (2020). The wounds of history—About the historical dealing with traumatic experiences. In A. Hamburger, C. Hancheva & V. Volkan (Eds.), *Social trauma. An Interdisciplinary Textbook* (pp. 43–54). New York: Springer.
Sotero, M. (2006). A conceptual model of historical trauma: Implications for public health practice and research. *Journal of Health Disparities Research and Practice, 1*(1), 93–308. Retrieved from http://papers.ssrn.com/abstract=1350062
Strous, R. D., Weiss, M., Felsen, I., Finkel, B., Melamed, Y., Bleich, A., & Laub, D. (2005). Video testimony of long-term hospitalized psychiatrically ill Holocaust survivors. *American Journal of Psychiatry, 162*(12), 2287–2294.
Thomas, N. K. (2009). Obliterating the other: What can be repaired by "truth" and testimony? *International Journal of Applied Psychoanalytic Studies, 6*(4), 321–338.
Thornton, R. (1987). *American Indian holocaust and survival: A population history since 1492*. Norman: University of Oklahoma Press.
Trezise, T. (2008). Between history and psychoanalysis: A case study in the reception of holocaust survivor testimony. *History and Memory, 20*(1), 7–47.
Volkan, V. D. (1991). On "chosen trauma". *Mind and Human Interaction, 4*(1), 3–19.
Volkan, V. D. (1997). *Bloodlines: From ethnic pride to ethnic terrorism*. New York: Farrar, Straus and Giroux.
Volkan, V. D. (2020). Chosen traumas and their impact on current political/societal conflicts. In A. Hamburger, C. Hancheva & V. Volkan (Eds.), *Social trauma. An Interdisciplinary Textbook* (pp. 17–24). New York: Springer.
Volkan, V. D., Ast, G., & Greer, W. F. (2002). *The third Reich in the unconscious: Transgenerational transmission and its consequences*. New York: Brunner-Routledge.
Weilnböck, H. (2007). Das Trauma muss dem Gedächtnis unverfügbar bleiben. Trauma-Ontologie und anderer Miss-/Brauch von Traumakonzepten in geisteswissenschaftlichen Diskursen. *Mittelweg, 2*, 2–64.
Worthington, E. L., & Aten, J. D. (2010). Forgiveness and reconciliation in social reconstruction after trauma. In E. Martz (Ed.), *Trauma rehabilitation after war and conflict* (pp. 55–72). Dordrecht: Springer Science & Business Media.
Young-Bruehl, E. (2012). Civilization and its dream of contentment: Reflections on the unity of humankind. *Psychoanalytic Inquiry, 32*, 543–558.

Chapter 2
Chosen Traumas and Their Impact on Current Political/Societal Conflicts

Vamık D. Volkan

2.1 Introduction: Background and Main Theoretical Concepts/Discussions

2.1.1 Massive Traumas

There are different types of massive traumas. Some are from natural causes, such as tropical storms, floods, volcanic eruptions, or earthquakes. After nature shows its fury, as Robert Jay Lifton and Eric Olson (1976) illustrated years ago, victims ultimately tend to accept the event as fate or as the will of God. A different type of massive trauma can occur due to man-made accidents, like the 1986 Chernobyl accident that spewed tons of radioactive dust into the atmosphere. A huge wildfire, like those that occurred in California in 2019 as well as earlier years, can be started unintentionally by a person or professional mismanagement. After this type of disaster, survivors blame a small number of individuals or professional organizations for their carelessness. If possible, survivors seek compensation or legal settlements for being exposed to accidental man-made traumas. The death of a political leader or another "societal transference figure" by a killer belonging to the same large group or by an accident provokes collective traumatic responses—as did the assassinations of John F. Kennedy and Martin Luther King, Jr., in the United States, Yitzhak Rabin in Israel, Prime Minister Olof Palme in Sweden, National Democratic Party leader Giorgi Chanturia in the Republic of Georgia, and former Prime Minister Rafic Hariri in Lebanon, or the deaths of the American astronauts, especially teacher Christa McAuliffe, in the 1986 space shuttle Challenger explosion. Psychoanalysts have

V. D. Volkan (✉)
Professor Emeritus of Psychiatry, University of Virginia, Charlottesville, VA, USA

President Emeritus International Dialogue Initiative and Past President of Virginia Psychoanalytic Society, International Society of Political Psychology and American College of Psychoanalysts, Charlottesville, VA, USA

© Springer Nature Switzerland AG 2021

A. Hamburger et al. (eds.), *Social Trauma – An Interdisciplinary Textbook*,
https://doi.org/10.1007/978-3-030-47817-9_2

written about societal psychological responses to such events (see, e.g., Erlich, 1998; Moses-Hrushovski, 2000; Volkan, 1997, 2013a, 2013b; Wolfenstein & Kliman, 1965).

Still another type of massive trauma is due to the *deliberate* actions of an enemy large group as in ethnic, national, religious, racial, and political ideological conflicts. Such catastrophes themselves range from chronic mistreatment or oppression of a large group by "Others" within one national boundary to terrorist attack, guerrilla warfare, war, and even genocide and from the traumatized large group actively fighting its powerful enemy in desperation to the traumatized large group being rendered passive and helpless. Such traumas take place because the affected persons and the perpetrators belong to different large groups, and the killing and the destruction is in the name of large-group identity (Volkan, 2006). My own observations on collective traumas have been on this last kind of tragedies. Only this kind of trauma may evolve as a chosen trauma in the future.

As a psychoanalyst I became involved in international relationships following then-Egyptian President's Anwar Sadat's historic visit to Israel in 1977. When Sadat addressed the Knesset, he spoke about a psychological wall between Arabs and Israelis and stated that psychological barriers constituted 70% of all problems existing between the two sides. In response, the American Psychiatric Association's Committee on Psychiatry and Foreign Affairs followed up on Sadat's statements by bringing together influential Israelis, Egyptians, and, later, Palestinians, for a series of unofficial negotiations that took place between 1979 and 1986. My membership in this committee and my chairing it 3 years after becoming a member initiated my decades-long studies of enemy relationships at many locations around the world. In 1988, at the University of Virginia School of Medicine, I opened the Center for the Study of Mind and Human Interaction (CSMHI) with a multidisciplinary faculty and brought together influential "enemy" representatives for years-long unofficial dialogues. I also observed Croats, Bosnians, and Serbians following the collapse of Yugoslavia and witnessed Kuwaitis' response to the Iraqi invasion after the Iraqi forces' withdrawal. Furthermore, I examined societies traumatized by dictators: Romanians and Albanians following the deaths of Nicolae Ceauşescu and Enver Hoxha, respectively (Volkan, 1997, 2004, 2006, 2013a, 2013b).

In this chapter, I will not describe societal traumas I observed at many locations around the world. I will *only* illustrate how the mental image of a past historical event during which ancestors were hurt or at least exposed to a threat against their large-group identity becomes reactivated and how shared feelings and perceptions about it intertwine with perceptions and feelings about the current conflict. A "time collapse" occurs and complicates finding attempts for peaceful co-existence between opposing populations.

2.2 Learning Outcome Related to Social Trauma

Behind political, economic, legal, and historical issues, the central psychological factor in starting or keeping alive a large-group conflict is the protection and maintenance of the large-group identity. CSMHI's helping influential "enemy" representatives to understand and tame "time collapse" opened ways to their having more realistic discussions and finding ways for peaceful co-existence. Now I will briefly focus on what is "large-group identity," as this will help us study "time collapse" better.

2.3 Preferred Model of Explanation

2.3.1 Large-Group Identity

In the psychoanalytic and mental health literature, the term "large group" describes different gatherings of people, from certain therapy groups to rioting masses. I use the term "large group" to refer to tens of thousands or millions of people, most of whom will never know or see each other and who share a feeling of sameness, a large-group identity. Subjective experience of large-group identities is expressed in terms such as "We are Catalan," "We are Lithuanian Jews," "We are Cypriot Turks," "We are Germans," "We are Sunni Muslims," and "We are communists." Elsewhere, I describe in detail how large-group identities develop in childhood (Volkan, 2013a, 2013b, 2018a, 2018b). Existing conditions in the environment direct children to invest in this or that type of large-group belongingness. A child born in Hyderabad, India, for example, would focus on religious/cultural issues as she develops a large-group identity, since adults there define their dominant large-group identity according to religious affiliation—Muslim or Hindu (Kakar, 1996). A child born in Cyprus during the hot Cypriot Turk-Cypriot Greek conflict would absorb a dominant large-group identity defined by ethnic/national sentiments, because what was critical in this part of the world at that time was whether one was Greek or Turkish, and less emphasis was placed on whether one was Greek Orthodox Christian or Sunni Muslim (Volkan, 1979). When one large group is in conflict with another large group due to political, legal, economic, or military issues, the protection and maintenance of large-group identity that develops in childhood becomes a psychological necessity.

In recent years I also described a second type of large-group identity that evolves in adulthood. Employees of a huge international corporation, the tens of thousands or millions of followers of a football team, or the members of an academic organization can be imagined as belonging to this type of large group. However, members of such groups do not drastically modify the large-group identity they developed in childhood. Some religious cults, guerrilla movements, and terrorist organizations, on the other hand, truly represent large groups that evolve during adulthood and lead to their members' losing, or at least drastically modifying, the superego-imposed restrictions that are linked to the large-group identity they acquired as children. These individuals may exaggerate selected aspects of their childhood large-group identities or become believers of ideas that were not available in their childhood environments. Belonging to this second type of large-group identity in adulthood may even allow members to take part in mass suicides, such as what members of

Peoples Temple in 1978 had done. Belonging to a second type of large-group identity also allows horrific sadistic acts to be committed against others, such as ISIS members' cutting their "enemies'" throats without hesitation.

Worldwide, large groups that develop in childhood or adulthood utilize chosen traumas as significant markers of their large-group identity, but in peaceful times they do not pay much attention to it.

2.3.2 *Examples of the Re-inflammation of Ancestors' Historical Images*

Historian Norman Itzkowitz and I studied the Greeks' chosen trauma—the image of the fall of Constantinople (today's Istanbul), the capital of the Byzantine Empire, in 1453—and the Greeks' entitlement ideology which is called *Megali Idea* or the Great Idea (Volkan & Itzkowitz, 1994). Markides (1977), a professor of sociology in the United States, states that Megali Idea is "a dream shared by Greeks that someday the Byzantine Empire would be restored and all the Greek lands would once again be united into a Greater Greece" (p. 10). Markides was born in Cyprus to Greek parents. He also states, "Because the Greeks of Cyprus have considered themselves historically and culturally to be Greeks, the 'Great Idea' has had an intense appeal. Thus, when the church fathers called on the Cypriots [Cypriot Greeks] to fight for union with Greece, it did not require much effort to heat up emotions…. Enosis [uniting Cyprus with Greece] did not originate in the church but in the minds of intellectuals in their attempt to revive Greek-Byzantine civilization" (p. 10). Like Markides, I was born in Cyprus but to Turkish parents and like him migrated to the United States. I did not work or develop projects on the Cypriot Turk-Cypriot Greek conflict on the island—which has been going on, at one level or another, for five decades—by telling myself that to do so would be unacceptable, like a psychoanalyst putting his mother on his couch would be unacceptable. However, I followed many attempts to find a solution for the so-called Cyprus problem very closely and noted how the Greeks' chosen trauma and entitlement ideology has played a significant role in creating obstacles for a solution. Before I go further, I need to say that there are many other realistic and fantasized obstacles to a truly peaceful co-existence on the island.

After the collapse of the Soviet Union, Estonians gained their independence. However, every third person in Estonia at that time was not an Estonian. He or she was a Russian or a "Russian speaker"—a non-Estonian person who had belonged to the former Soviet Union. Overnight the Estonians had become the administrators of their own country, while Russians and Russian speakers—most of them now non-citizens—were left in a state of great confusion. There also was a border dispute between Estonia and Russia. My facilitating team from CSMHI brought together influential Estonians and Russians, such as parliamentarians, for 3-day unofficial diplomatic discussions. We had two meetings in 1994, seven meetings in 1995, and another two meetings in 1996. The Estonians' chosen trauma is unrelated to one specific historical event, but to the fact that they had lived under almost constant dominance (Danish, Polish, Swedes, Germans, Russians) for many centuries. After gaining independence, Estonians were singing and celebrating their newly found freedom. However, my team members and I could see how, psychologically speaking, they had become anxious with their unconscious expectation for disappearing as an independent country once more. During the initial part of the dialogue series, we could see anger on some Estonian team members' faces, but they would not verbalize their negative feelings against their most recent occupiers. Toward the end of the second year of the dialogue series, the Estonian participants started to be more comfortable in referring to their victimization under the Soviet regime, expressing their negative feelings toward Russians to their Russian counterparts.

During one session we were discussing some current issues when an Estonian complained about the Russians' past treatment of his people. A very high-level person from the Russian parliament, who was also a member of the Russian dialogue team, suddenly and very loudly began talking about events that took place from the thirteenth to the fifteenth century: Tatar and Mongol lords occupying many parts of today's Russia, including Moscow. I recall how my facilitating team members and I were surprised. The Russian parliamentarian could not stop talking about what has become known to historians as "the Tatar-Mongol yoke" (see, e.g., Halperin, 2009). The Russian chosen trauma had come alive in the room. The parliamentarian wanted us to realize that the victimized Russians had stood between the Tatar and Mongol perpetrators and the Europeans. If Russia had not existed, the Europeans would have been devastated by the Tatars and Mongols. He was upset that the Europeans did not acknowledge how Russian suffering had saved the Europeans. He described the Russians' entitlement to rule over other large groups, but at the same time being different than the Tatars and Mongols through a behavior that protected the Others under the Russian rule. How dare the Estonians not appreciate living under Russian rule which had brought "good" things to Estonia! I noted that the parliamentarian not only was talking about the Russian chosen trauma but he also was glorifying victimized ancestors who, he believed, had protected the Europeans from a disaster. This brings us to look at the relationship between chosen traumas and chosen glories.

2.4 Practical in The Field of Social Trauma

2.4.1 The Relationship Between Chosen Traumas and Chosen Glories

Like a chosen trauma, a chosen glory refers to the shared image of a historical event that is a significant ethnic, national, religious, or ideological large-group identity marker. This time the image is linked to the ancestors' great accomplishments in dealing with another large group and the ancestors' heroes. I already stated that a chosen trauma is not an image of a rather recent historical event. For example, the Holocaust is not a chosen trauma. Survivors' pictures and some belongings are still at the descendants' homes, and survivors' stories are still "alive." Similarly, a chosen glory also is not an image of a recent event in the large-group history that still actively increases the members' personal narcissism.

While chosen glories increase collective self-esteem, they do not burden the next generations with shared psychological tasks such as being linked to an entitlement ideology and a time collapse. Because of this, chosen traumas, in supporting large-group identity and its cohesiveness, are more complex than chosen glories. In stressful situations, however, a political leader may reactivate a chosen trauma and a hero associated with it. During the first Gulf War Saddam Hussein made many references to Sultan Saladin's victories over the Crusaders as a propaganda tool, even though Saladin was not an Arab but a Kurd, and Saddam Hussein was treating the Iraqi Kurds very badly. Also, sometimes chosen traumas and chosen glories are intertwined, as the Russian parliamentarian during Estonian-Russian dialogue series illustrated.

2.4.2 *Wish to Replace a Chosen Trauma with an Old or New Glory*

New massive tragedies or societal complications can occur when a chosen trauma is inflamed by political leadership with propaganda, sometimes malignant propaganda, that aims not only to humiliate but also to destroy those perceived as the Others, in order to erase the chosen trauma by turning it into a new glory or bringing back an old glory.

Slobodan Milošević and the political circle around him reactivated the image of Serbian chosen trauma—the Battle of Kosovo in 1389—and the entitlement ideology Christoslavism to which it is linked. Prince Lazar was the leader of the Serbians when they fought against the Ottoman Turks in Kosovo and he was killed. Milošević and his advisors arranged a plan to inflame the Serbian chosen trauma. Lazar's 600-year-old remains, which had been kept north of Belgrade, were placed in a coffin and taken, over the course of a year, to almost every Serb village and town where they were received by huge crowds of mourners dressed in black. Again and again during this long journey, Lazar's remains were symbolically buried and reincarnated, until they were buried for good at the original battleground in Kosovo on June 28, 1989. The Serbian people began feeling, without being intellectually aware of it, that the defeat at the Battle of Kosovo had occurred only recently, a development made possible by the fact that the chosen trauma had been kept effectively alive for centuries. Reactivation of the Serbian chosen trauma led to tragic new traumas in this part of the world. Milošević died in 2006 in his prison cell of a heart attack, while being tried for war crimes in The Hague.

I studied this event closely from a psychohistorical angle, including conducting interviews with people who knew Milošević. The chapter space available to me will not allow me to describe further this extremely informative example of the inflammation of a chosen trauma with deadly consequences. I wrote about this event extensively elsewhere (Volkan, 1996, 2013a, 2013b).

Most recently, Finnish historian Jouni Suistola and I (Suistola & Volkan, 2017) examined how the so-called Islamic State of Iraq and the Levant (ISIS) created a new large group in adulthood to "re-establish" the Caliphate with an illusion in order to erase Sunni Arab Muslims' rage and humiliation following the end of Caliphate after the Ottoman Empire collapsed, as described by political scientist Elie Kedourie (1970) and historian Bernard Lewis (1990). The tragedies ISIS has caused still are in our minds.

This introduction to the concept of chosen trauma as well as chosen glory tells us how we need to expand the studies of certain massive societal traumas by noticing the impact of ancestral history and including in-depth psychohistorical observations in order to find ways to tame aggressive actions that seek to protect and maintain large-group identities.

2.5 Suggested Readings and Further Information

Information on the International Dialogue Initiative: https://www.internationaldialogueinitiative.com/

Information on Vamık Volkan's work with traumatized societies: https://www.vamiksroom.org/about-vamiks-room

References

Erlich, H. S. (1998). Adolescents' reactions to Rabin's assassination: A case of patricide? In A. Esman (Ed.), *Adolescent psychiatry: Developmental and clinical studies* (pp. 189–205). London: The Analytic Press.

Halperin, C. J. (2009). *The Tatar yoke: The image of the Mongols in medieval Russia*. Bloomington, IN: Slavica Publishers.

Kakar, S. (1996). *The colors of violence: Cultural identities, religion, and conflict*. Chicago, IL: University of Chicago Press.

Kedourie, E. (1970). *The Chatham house version and other middle eastern studies*. London: Weidenfeld & Nicholson.

Lewis, B. (1990, September). The roots of Muslim rage. *The Atlantic Monthly, 20*, 47–60.

Lifton, R., & Olson, E. (1976). The human meaning of total disaster: The Buffalo Creek experience. *Psychiatry, 39*, 1–18.

Markides, K. C. (1977). *The rise and fall of the Cyprus Republic*. New Haven, CT: Yale University Press.

Moses-Hrushovski, R. (2000). *Grief and grievance: The assassination of Yitzhak Rabin*. London: Minerva Press.

Suistola, J., & Volkan, V. D. (2017). *Religious knives: Historical and psychological dimensions of international terrorism*. Durham, NC: Pitchstone.
Volkan, V. D. (1979). *Cyprus-war and adaptation: A psychoanalytic history of two ethnic groups in conflict*. Charlottesville, VA: University of Virginia Press.
Volkan, V. D. (1996). Bosnia-Herzegovina: Ancient fuel of a modern inferno. *Mind and Human Interaction, 7*, 110–127.
Volkan, V. D. (1997). *Bloodlines: From ethnic pride to ethnic terrorism*. New York: Farrar, Straus and Giroux.
Volkan, V. D. (2004). *Blind trust: Large groups and their leaders in times of crisis and terror*. Charlottesville, VA: Pitchstone.
Volkan, V. D. (2006). *Killing in the name of identity: A study of bloody conflicts*. Charlottesville, VA: Pitchstone Publishing.
Volkan, V. D. (2013a). Large-group-psychology in its own right: Large-group identity and peace-making. *International Journal of Applied Psychoanalytic Studies, 10*, 210–246.
Volkan, V. D. (2013b). *Enemies on the couch: A Psychopolitical journey through war and peace*. Durham, NC: Pitchstone.
Volkan, V. D. (2018a). Refugees as the other. *Group Analysis, 51*, 343–358.
Volkan, V. D. (2018b). *Immigrants and refugees: Trauma, perennial mourning, prejudice, and border psychology*. London: Routledge.
Volkan, V. D., & Itzkowitz, N. (1994). *Turks and Greeks: Neighbours in conflict*. Cambridgeshire, England: Eothen Press.
Wolfenstein, M., & Kliman, G. (1965). *Children and the death of a president: Multi-disciplinary studies*. New York, NY: Doubleday.

Chapter 3
Cultural Memory

Aleida Assmann

3.1 Introduction: Background and Main Theoretical Concepts/Discussions

The rise of an interest in cultural memory went hand in hand with a shift in the structure of Western temporality and political and cultural sensibility. Until the 1980s, the past had been the specialized field of study of historians and attracted little interest as a public topic or endeavor to engage in. Since 2000, memory and the past were suddenly all over the place. These topics entered the public sphere and became potentially everybody's business.

3.1.1 From Afterlife to Aftermath

In the 1980s, new theories of cultural memory emerged. The conceptual beginnings of Jan and Aleida Assmann's approach to cultural memory date back to the late 1970s. At that time, Jurij Lotman and Boris Uspenskij, two semioticians from the University of Tartu, developed a new concept of culture, defining it as the biologically non-inheritable memory of a society (Lotman & Uspenskij, 1970/1977, p. 39). They argued, firstly, that the past is not necessarily past and, secondly, that both the future and the past are constructed in the present: "The culture that is connected to the past through its memory does not only produce its future, but also its past. In this way, it presents a mechanism that runs counter to natural time" (Lotman & Uspenskij, 1970/1977, p. 23).

A. Assmann (✉)
Konstanz University, Konstanz, Germany
e-mail: aleida.assmann@uni-konstanz.de

© Springer Nature Switzerland AG 2021

A. Hamburger et al. (eds.), *Social Trauma – An Interdisciplinary Textbook*,
https://doi.org/10.1007/978-3-030-47817-9_3

Cultural memory is a system of values, artifacts, institutions, and practices that retain the past for the present and the future. It transfers knowledge and supports the emergence and elaboration of distinct identities, because humans define themselves and are defined by their affiliation to one or various cultural groups and traditions.

In equipping humans with a sense of their distinct identity and a necessary supply for the future, cultures create sustainable structures for their "afterlife." In indigenous societies, the practices creating such a temporal continuity focus on *strategies of repetition*: the performance of myths, storytelling, and other practices transmitting multi-media forms of what is now called "intangible cultural heritage," including music, ritual, and dance. Cultures that have developed systems of external storing of information deploy *strategies of duration* and organize diachronic transmission with the help of media such as written texts and images, preserving the thoughts of prominent individuals and historic events, along with buildings, monuments, and other sites of memory.

The birth of the nation in the nineteenth century ushered in a new era of secularization that changed dramatically the structure of cultural memory. Until then, religion and genealogy had occupied the central areas of cultural memory, emphasizing the Biblical canon, prayers and songs, the lives of the saints, and the history of the church on the one hand and the genealogy of dynasties and the aristocracy on the other. The new nation, on the contrary, was to define itself primarily through history and the arts, providing a narrative account of the origin of the nation and celebrating its distinct achievements. The driving force and determining selector in creating this new national memory was pride in the new collective of the nation, publicly perpetuating its collective history and artistic achievements in sacred icons for a perpetual afterlife.

While the nations of the nineteenth and early twentieth century were created in a heroic and self-celebrating mode, the post-colonial nations and later the post-communist nations in the second half of the twentieth century were created in the tragic mode of trauma, victimhood, and suffering. Their national memories were focused on injustice, violence, and suffering as defining features of their national history and identity crystallizing around moments of misrecognition, mutilation, and "historical wounds" (Chakrabarty, 2007). In the structure of national memory, this constituted a decisive change from afterlife to aftermath, from voluntary to involuntary national memory, from active to passive, from heroic to traumatic narratives. In these cases, the (re-)birth of the nation was not triumphant but maimed and scarred; it was tattooed with a wound that was conceived, however, not just as a stigma but as the badge of a distinct and unalienable identity.

In order to analyze this shift from afterlife to aftermath more closely, I want to look at three concepts that were introduced to explain and describe it: "trauma," "impact events," and "historical wounds."

3.1.2 Trauma

A post-colonial discourse developed in the 1950s and 1960s propelling the transformation of the new nation-states from their status as colonies to free states, redefining their new identities. While this early discourse was mainly politically driven, new concepts were absorbed in the 1980s that related to a language of psychic disorders. In this context, the rediscovery of the *trauma* discourse became prominent and had a huge impact on post-colonial identity formation. The introduction of this concept into the Diagnostic and Statistical Manual (American Psychiatric Association, 1980) had indeed unforeseeable consequences. It started with a *medical recognition* of a psychic wound in individuals that does not heal but remains latent over years and decades, requiring belated attention, recognition, and therapy (see Hamburger, 2020, this volume). It was followed by *social and political recognition* of members of groups who had been exposed to injustice and violence in history. This shift from medical to social and political recognition took some time, because it required a new cultural framework in which the former wrongdoers who had inflicted these wounds finally came to acknowledge their responsibility for this history. What evolved in this process among many Western states was a decisive change in their culture of memory, because the avowal of responsibility required that they included this negative history into the framework of their own national narrative. It took its model from the lasting impact and public reception history of the Holocaust starting in the 1980s. In the wake of this recovered memory, new concepts, terms, and values were created that acquired a global resonance. Concepts such as trauma and witnessing now became important key terms to access also other histories of violence (see Assmann, 2010).

3.1.3 Impact Event

Another concept that has been offered to describe the after-effects of trauma is *impact event* which has been introduced by Anne Fuchs in her book on the bombings of Dresden (Fuchs, 2011), drawing on Badiou (2005/2007) and Žižek (2002):

> Impact events can be defined as historical occurrences that are perceived to spectacularly shatter the material and symbolic worlds that we inhabit. Impact also denotes the duration of the after-effects in the material culture and collective consciousness. (...)The emphasis is here on the violent overturning of the social, cultural, and—in the case of extreme trauma—symbolic frames and the destruction of the material world in which we constitute meaning as social beings that inhabit shared social worlds. (Fuchs, 2011, p. 12)

"Impact events" of this sort cause long-term damage because they destroy the bond of a common humanity and thereby also the close social connection between experience, memory, and narrative. It was from the void of this destroyed triad that the concepts of witness and testimony later emerged.

3.1.4 Historical Wounds

The term "historical wounds" was introduced in an influential essay on "History and the Politics of Recognition" by Dipesh Chakrabarty (2007) in which he has emphasized the therapeutic importance of acquiring a language, concepts, and a memory for the traumatized group. He writes: "To be able to speak thus, (…) to speak self-consciously from within a history of having been wounded—is itself a historical phenomenon," which he traces back to the beginnings of post-colonial discourse in the 1950s and 1960s. According to Chakrabarty, historical wounds are built on recognition and are thus "dialogically formed." This important prerequisite, however, did not immediately occur after the Second World War but only a few decades later. It was in the 1990s that acknowledgment was indeed given by "groups seen as givers of the wound in the first place" (78). Chakrabarty emphasizes that the concept is a cultural formation and built on a social consensus; for this reason, "historical wounds"—as he puts it—"live precarious lives." The evidence for them is neither anchored in the historical archives nor firmly rooted in historiography, but in everyday practices of a long unrecorded history of misrecognition and abuse that was perceived as a state of normalcy by the contemporaries of the time. Historical wounds are therefore, to quote Chakrabarty again, "a mix of history and memory" (78) with the memory of the victims supplying what went unrecorded in history and is registered only belatedly. Historical wounds with their claim to protection of minorities and human rights thus depend on a politics of recognition and can easily be dislodged by right wing parties and conservative governments.

Recognizing and acknowledging responsibility for historical wounds by the former colonial states has led to "a politics of regret" which peaked in the 1990s when many heads of state uttered formal public apologies for former injustices, exploitations, and atrocities committed by their governments against defenseless minorities and subalterns. In the United Kingdom, for instance, the result of this shift toward a politics of regret was that a proud memory of empire had all but vanished by 1980 and was increasingly replaced "by a public discussion of empire as a legacy of shame." Taking responsibility for crimes against humanity in the course of their national history has been continuing into the recent past in Australia and is going on in present-day Canada.

In contrast to the post-colonial nations, the post-communist nations that came into being after the demise of the Soviet empire met with a very different experience. While they also based their national narratives on suffering and a history of atrocities and occupation, they did not receive acknowledgment from the giver of their historical wounds. A social consensus, built on a dialogically formed memory, did not evolve in the wake of their self-liberation. The central lieux de mémoire of these nations became sites of suffering; their national museums have telling names such as "The House of Terror" in Budapest, the "Occupation Museum" in Riga, and the "Museum of Genocide" in Vilnius. The lack of recognition and a dialogical consensus concerning this history has had the effect of deepening the scars that were here chosen as the seminal element of the victimized collective self-image. In this case, the divisive character of the wound has been entrenched into the structure of national memory. Within the new framework of the EU, the *aftermath* of traumatic events that had been tabooed and repressed by external oppression for decades and longer was transformed into a public *afterlife* in the stable national framework including annual rites of commemoration and museums with their specific objects, media, and iconic images.

3.2 Learning Outcome Related to Social Trauma

If the Holocaust represents a historic turning point in the extremity of violence involved in mass killing, this change also poses entirely new challenges to individual remembering and collective memory. It is therefore unsurprising that the resonances of this experience have caused the foundations and norms of remembering to shift; at the same time, these so-called anomalies have brought a great deal of academic attention to the process of remembering more generally. As the painful impact of historical and individual traumas exceeds the capacity for being synchronically perceived and processed, the event is blocked, covered up, and accessible only for a belated reception. Individual acts of returning to the trauma and recovering the impact event are embedded within social frames and shaped by them, fostering either recognition or repression, public discussion or ongoing silence. In the "post-traumatic era" in which we currently find ourselves, practices of memory are also linked to theories of memory. We are looking at ourselves, as it were, in the process of remembering. Individual and collective remembering are less and less frequently understood as spontaneous, natural, or sacred acts and more and more frequently recognized as social and cultural constructions that change over time and so have their own history.

In the long shadow of the Holocaust and its belated engagement, an arsenal of concepts and norms has been produced that are now being applied both to contemporary forms of violence such as the sexual abuse of children as well as to other historical forms of violence such as slavery, genocide of indigenous peoples, colonial violence, or the First and Second World War. This conceptual and discursive expansion of research into trauma in no way implies that the Holocaust be relativized or that its singularity be called into question. Rather, it signals a profound moral and cognitive transformation in light of this event, one that permits us to perceive earlier incidences involving the excessive use of violence in new ways and above all to describe and judge such events for which there had previously been no language or public interest.

3.3 Preferred Model of Explanation: Three Frames of Transmission—Identification, Ethics, and Empathy

Little attention has so far been paid to various "frames of transmission" within which individuals perceive their past, depending on the ways in which they are personally anchored and position themselves vis-à-vis a violent history. Dominick

LaCapra (1992) comments on the different subject positions depending on historical affiliations when he emphasized that the same statement can take on different meanings if uttered by people with different connections to the events, and Saul Friedländer added: "If we consider German and Jewish contemporaries of the Nazi period—contemporary adults, adolescents, or children, even the children of these groups—what was traumatic for the one group was obviously not traumatic for the other. (…) The victims of Nazism cope with a fundamentally traumatic situation, whereas many Germans have to cope with a widening stain, with potential shame or guilt" (Friedländer, 1994, p. 257)—and, as I would like to add in updating this statement, the breaking of the silence. I will discuss here three frames of transmission that are all part of our contemporary memory culture but defined by different sites, perspectives, and national contexts: the identification mode relating to the victims, the ethical mode relating to the former perpetrators, and the empathy mode relating to the bystanders.

3.3.1 *The Identification Mode*

From the Jewish point of view, the frame of transmission is that of individual and collective identification. In this frame, the process of transmission is based on genealogical links and guided by the principle of identification with the victims connecting the past of those who died and suffered with the future of succeeding generations. As these victims were not targeted for what they had done but for who they were, the genocidal violence of the Nazis hit all European Jews irrespective of the nations of which they were part, with a special focus on women and children to also destroy also their future. This further explains why individual remembering is closely connected to the collective Jewish history of family, diaspora community, and the nation of Israel.

There rather are different forms in which identification can shape the process of transmission. A prominent example are children of Holocaust survivors who refer to themselves as "2G" (= second generation), defining themselves as a group with seminal common features and a collective identity. These children (over-)identified with their parents by not only sharing their history but also their trauma, appropriating it unconsciously as part of their own self. The distinctive and liberating move of the 2Gs was to transform the unconscious imprint of the trauma that they had come to share viscerally into a conscious *identification* and thus into a central feature of their identity. Identification in the case of the members of 2G meant that the borderline between the identity of the parent and that of the child had become porous and that this was later on acknowledged not only as a handicap but also as an individual asset. We are dealing here not only with the generally acknowledged syndrome of "trans-generational trauma" (see Grand & Salberg, 2020, this volume) but also more specifically with a condition for which Marianne Hirsch (2009, 2012) has supplied the important term "post-memory."

Identification, however, does not only relate to a specific group among the second generation of Holocaust survivors but also applies more generally to Jewish remembering and acts of commemoration across generations. One example is that of taking on the name of a child that died in the Holocaust as a symbolic sibling in the religious ceremony of Bar or Bat Mitzvah. This symbolic gesture confirms not only the personal identification with an individual child victim but also in a more general way the integration of the dead into the living memory of the community. Another collective formative experience is the "march of the living," an educational tour that brings Israeli school-children to Auschwitz where they re-enact and re-experience liturgically the collective trauma of their families and the nation by personally connecting with their historical site of suffering and death. In this case, the flag is used very much like a prayer shawl, providing protection from the trauma that is personally re-enacted at the historical site and, at the same time, symbolizing the community of the living that survived the threat of total extinction. Examples of the identification mode could be multiplied. They are—in different forms and expressions—a defining trait of Israeli and Jewish memory culture.

3.3.2 *The Ethical Mode*

Identification along the lines that I have just indicated is the prerogative of the succeeding generations of Jewish victims and not accessible to other groups. For these, other meaningful links to connect to the traumatic event have been created. There is another frame of transmission of Holocaust memory that I will refer to as the ethical mode. This form of memory was developed by and for those who are genealogically and historically connected to the country of the perpetrators. In Germany, as Raul Hilberg has famously emphasized, the Holocaust was family history. This means that the children of the generation of the Second World War were also intensely linked to the event, but this time through feelings and concepts such as (belated) guilt, shame, responsibility, and regret. While, in the families of survivors, the Holocaust was firmly embedded in the communicative memory of families, anchored in the society and supported by long-entrenched cultural patterns, in German and Austrian families, it was for decades passed over in silence. Recovering this memory for the second generation of Germans involved the very opposite of an act of identification; it required, rather, a conscious facing and working through this history, along with the breaking with oppressive family ties that had reinforced complicity and denial. This is exactly what the ethical mode makes possible: recovering a new and independent stance from both German silence and communicative memory by creating a "negative memory" that is rooted in a new self-critical memory culture.

In Germany, the second generation of the perpetrators wanted to break as thoroughly away from their own parents as the children of the survivors wanted to merge with them. Longing to distance themselves from their own family background, their country, and its history, some of them took a short cut and, bypassing the ethical mode, identified directly with the Jewish victims. Fantasizing a new identity was an act of emotional and moral rebellion verging on conversion, which, however, did not allow for any personal working through or cognitive historical self-orientation. Among Germans, this "emotional fallacy" has become the topic of extensive reflection and criticism (see Jureit and Schneider, 2010). As an opposed strategy, denying any historical link to the perpetrators was common with Germans of the GDR: they focused exclusively on the heroes of resistance, thus imagining themselves exclusively as victims of the Nazi regime without any necessity of taking responsibility for German atrocities. The dimension of perpetration was "externalized" onto the other Germany in order not to taint the heroic national self-image. Their paradigm, again, was that of identification, this time not with Jewish victims, however, which were completely bypassed, but with communist resistance fighters.

As the identification paradigm was ruled out for Germans (except for Neo-Nazis who identify with the perpetrators), they created a new mode: the ethical stance. The succeeding generations of Germans have developed the ethical mode adopting the emotional complex of guilt, shame, responsibility, remorse, and mourning. As the perpetrators themselves tenaciously preferred to forget, to deny, and to justify themselves, the succeeding German generations, who are no longer tainted with guilt, are taking up in a vicarious position a stance that had been totally inaccessible to the perpetrators themselves. This self-critical stance that consists in addressing a guilty past and accepting responsibility for it is at the heart of the new memory culture that has been built into the foundations of the German state. The message of official commemoration includes three dimensions: (1) honoring the victims, (2) preserving the memory of this darkest chapter of German history, and (3) citizenship education: respecting human rights and the principles of democracy.

With the growing temporal distance to the historic events, the strong sense of guilt that had dominated the emotions of the first and the discourse of the second generation has been translated half a century after the end of the war into notions of responsibility and political vigilance. Remembering in the German case connects "anamnestic solidarity" with the victims with a "politics of regret" regarding the historical connection with the perpetrators. It combines historical consciousness (it was in this country where these events happened) with democratic education (this state will actively oppose discrimination and exclusion of minorities). In Germany, the frame of transmission of Holocaust memory is thus considered as an antidote, working in the form of vaccination that helps to make the patient immune to a dangerous disease: never again! This sense of accountability combining the memory of the past with a vigilance toward the future is the core of the ethical paradigm. Remembering in this frame is therefore also a pedagogical tool that is saturated with instructions, admonitions, and warnings.

3.3.3 The Empathy Mode

The third frame of transmission allows to transcend distinctive filiations and affiliations. It creates a stance that provides at the same time more distance than the identification frame and more proximity than the ethical frame. It does not emerge from group relations, starting with the family and extending these ties to the diasporic group or nation, but from a self and its individual stance, thus bracketing the constraints of a collective "we." The empathic mode is not a distinctly separate frame of transmission but one that is also inscribed into the identification mode and the ethical mode. It differs from these frames, however, in offering an individual approach to the atrocities and trauma of the Holocaust that is based on the fundamental difference between self and other.

Empathy is a complex emotion that is based on both cognition and imagination, combining intellect and knowledge with feelings and a concern for others. It has been discovered and redefined by neuroscientists who have taught us in studies emerging since the year 2000 that this pro-social emotion is a general human endowment, developing together with the human brain from early on. The possibility of empathy arises at the age of two and a half years when children are able to acquire a sense of their individual self and its distinctness from another human being. Empathy makes it possible for humans to think in the minds of others and to imagine the suffering of another person. It differs from compassion which is strongly colored by Christian cultural traditions but also from sympathy or identification because it involves a consciousness of the difference between self and other. It is elicited not only in personal interaction but also through the media who have a great potential for staging impressive images of suffering but also for presenting information and knowledge that can serve as a basis or trigger for empathy. Knowledge is of paramount importance to consolidate a mere affective state into a conscious subjective stance. In spite of its promising universal quality, it should not be forgotten that empathy can easily be blocked, be it through a surfeit of images without a clear personal connection, or because of a selective perspective that restricts it exclusively to "thick relations" within one's in-group (Margalit, 2003). The question of similitude between the person who suffers and the person who experiences the emotion was an important criterion for Aristotle's definition of compassion. As Martha Nussbaum has convincingly argued, this emotion was clearly restricted. "All kinds of social barriers—of class, religion, ethnicity, gender, sexual orientation—prove recalcitrant to the imagination, and this recalcitrance impedes emotion" (Nussbaum, 2001, p. 317). Empathy clearly exceeds the culturally defined and highly gendered range of compassion. It builds a bridge between self and other by creating a sensibility for the suffering of others under the premise that the observer could be subject to the same pain. The affirmation of the other can include also distant groups and individuals, provided that they are judged to be "significant others." This means that they must be acknowledged to be "an important part of one's own scheme of goals and projects, important as ends in their own right" (Nussbaum, 2001, p. 320). Only when the other is recognized as part of "my circle of concern" can attention be invested and empathy be released. The political and cultural framework of a memory culture but also media representations channel and stimulate empathy by bringing others into one's circle of concern, turning them into "grievable victims" (Butler, 2009).

3.4 Practical Implications in the Field of Social Trauma

The trans-generational transmission of Holocaust memory is not a purely individual affair, but a process framed by historical affiliations and political cultures. While, in the identification mode, which is exclusively focused on the victims, the roles between the self and other are intentionally blurred in order to generate a sense of belonging and to affirm a collective identity, they are clearly accentuated in the ethical mode that maintains a link to the perpetrators and the responsibility for the historical crimes, thus connecting the commemoration of the Holocaust today with political messages such as "never again," civil education, the protection of minorities, or the prevention of anti-Semitism. The empathy mode once again reconstructs the trauma of the Holocaust from the perspective of the victims. Empathy with the victims is of course also present in the identification mode and in the ethical mode, but the empathy mode is possible without any personal connection to either the victims or the perpetrators. It is the most subjective and generalizable mode that, however, does not give up the basic distinction between self and other. This mode is especially geared to media representations tapping the universal human resource of empathy.

Since the beginning of the new millennium, framing a long-term transmission of Holocaust memory has become a concrete project of politicians, survivors, and professional experts. An official transnational frame of transmission for these different countries has been created by the International Holocaust Remembrance Alliance (IHRA), a network consisting of 31 states and 8 observer countries, most of them from Europe. In this transnational frame, which includes programs for museums, monuments, commemoration dates, scholarship, and education, the empathic mode of Holocaust remembrance has been adopted both as a foundational myth of Europe and as a universally accessible memory. In this process, it has received a normative and inclusive institutional framework and achieved a transnational status with a growing uniformity at the expense of historical specificity. Although Holocaust museums are now being built also in Central and Eastern European countries, this does not necessarily imply that the new transnational memory community initiated from above has penetrated all regions and is all-encompassing in Europe. There are still pockets of silence, denial, or indifference where a self-critical approach to one's own history is still rejected and the national narrative of pride or suffering excludes or covers up the local history of Jewish victims and other minorities.

There are other effects of the official memory frame that could be mentioned. In Germany, for instance, a transnational frame of memory is generally welcomed because it replaces the ethnic and genealogical frames. Seventy and more years after the historical events, the link connecting succeeding generations with the guilt of their (grand)fathers and (grand)mothers is becoming ever more tenuous. While family affiliations were once more activated as the most loaded and direct approach to the Nazi past in the German TV miniseries *Generation War* (2013; in German: "Unsere Mütter, Unsere Väter"), this frame of transmission can no longer serve as a normative model in an ethnically diverse German society. From this point of view, a more transnational framework seems necessary that opens up new points of access and creates a shared space for different perspectives. But there is also a backlash built into the growing uniformity of Holocaust memory: in this narrative the Germans remain tied to the emblematic position of the perpetrators. A German boy with Turkish roots recently discovered this dilemma when he joined a group of adolescents traveling to Auschwitz to learn about the history of his country. At the historic site, he had to experience that simply by speaking the language of the perpetrators he felt automatically stigmatized and was willy-nilly inscribed into this national history.

While guidelines for collective commemorations can and have to be assigned and installed from above, remembering is something that cannot be delegated to politicians or other professional groups. Nor is it something that can be merely continued. As the historical event of the Holocaust is rapidly receding into the past, an urgent question is whether it will become *history* and thus be only the concern of a few historians or whether it will retain the quality of *memory* that has to be transmitted to succeeding generations. Such an affective, living connection to the past will have to be reignited from below by sparking new attention, interest, empathy, and commitment of *individuals*.

3.5 Suggested Readings and Further Information (Best Practices, Web Sites, etc.)

Assmann, A. (2010). The holocaust—A global memory? Extensions and limits of a new memory community. In A. Assmann & S. Conrad (Eds.), *Memory in a global age* (pp. 97–117). Houndmills, Basingstoke: Palgrave Macmillan.

References

American Psychiatric Association. (1980). *Diagnostic and statistical manual* (3rd ed., DSM III).

Assmann, A. (2010). The holocaust — A global memory? Extensions and limits of a new memory community. In A. Assmann & S. Conrad (Eds.), *Memory in a global age* (pp. 97–117). Houndmills, Basingstoke: Palgrave Macmillan.

Badiou, A. (2007). *The century*. Cambridge: Polity. (Original work published 2005)

Butler, J. (2009). *Frames of war: When is life grievable?* Brooklyn, NY: Verso.

Chakrabarty, D. (2007). History and the politics of recognition. In K. Jenkins, S. Morgan, & A. Munslow (Eds.), *Manifestos for history* (pp. 89–99). London: Routledge.

Friedländer, S. (1994). Trauma, memory, and transference. In G. Hartman (Ed.), *Holocaust remembrance. The shapes of memory* (pp. 252–263). Oxford: Blackwell.

Fuchs, A. (2011). *After the Dresden bombing. Pathways of memory 1945 to the present*. Houndmills, Basingstoke: Palgrave Macmillan.

Grand, S., & Salberg, J. (2020). Transgenerational Trauma Transmission. In Hamburger A, Hancheva C, Volkan V (Eds.), Social Trauma. An InterdisciplinaryTextbook (pp. Xx-xx). New York: Springer.

Hamburger, A. (2020). Social trauma—A bridging concept. In A. Hamburger, C. Hancheva & V. Volkan (Eds.), *Social trauma. An Interdisciplinary Textbook* (pp. 3–16). New York: Springer.
Hirsch, M. (2009). The generation of postmemory. *Poetics Today, 29*(1), 103–128.
Hirsch, M. (2012). *The generation of postmemory. Writing and visual culture after the holocaust*. New York: Columbia University Press.
Jureit, U., & Schneider, C. (2010). *Gefühlte Opfer. Illusionen der Vergangenheitsbewältigung*. Stuttgart: Klett.
LaCapra, D. (1992). Representing the holocaust: Reflections on the historians' debate. In S. Friedländer (Ed.), *Probing the limits of representations: National-socialism and the 'final solution'* (pp. 108–127). Cambridge: Harvard University Press.
Lotman, J., & Uspenskij, B. (1977). Die Rolle dualistischer Modelle in der Dynamik der russischen Kultur. *Poetica, 9*, 1–40. (Original work published 1970).
Margalit, A. (2003). *The ethics of memory*. Cambridge, MA: Harvard UP.
Nussbaum, M. (2001). *Upheavals of thought. The intelligence of emotions*. Cambridge: Cambridge University Press.
Žižek, S. (2002). *Welcome to the desert of the real: Five essays on September 11 and related dates*. London: Verso.

Chapter 4
Cultural Trauma

Ron Eyerman

4.1 Introduction

The theory of cultural trauma is the product of a collective intervention by a small group of scholars assembled at the Center for Advanced Study in the Behavioral Sciences (CASBS) at Stanford University (Alexander, Eyerman, Giesen, & Sztompka, 2004; Eyerman, 2019). The results of that year-long project were published as *Cultural Trauma and Collective Identity* (Alexander et al., 2004). The main intention was to provide a constructivist social theory of trauma developed in dialogue with existing psychological and realist uses of the term (Alexander et al., 2004). Further developed as a research framework, the theory of cultural trauma provides a social theory of trauma that is non-pathological and non-essentialist. It highlights how collective suffering is meaningfully manifested through the processes of articulation and representation and the mediating factors of power and access. In developing this framework, a first task was to distinguish *cultural* trauma from the classical psychoanalytic and modern psychological notions that also permeate common usage of the concept (Alexander et al., 2004; Smelser, 2004). In providing a definition, Jeffrey Alexander writes, "cultural trauma occurs when members of a collectivity feel they have been subjected to a horrendous event that leaves indelible marks upon their group's consciousness, marking their memories forever and changing their future identities in fundamental and irrevocable ways" (Alexander et al., 2004, p. 1). By emphasizing "feelings" and "group consciousness," Alexander calls attention to social processes of articulation and representation, as feelings require interpretation and group consciousness collective representation. In the same volume, Neil Smelser (2004, p. 44) made clear the difference between psychological and sociological perspectives on trauma when he defined cultural trauma as "a memory accepted and publicly given credence by a

R. Eyerman (✉)
Center for Cultural Sociology, Yale University, New Haven, CT, USA
e-mail: ronald.eyerman@yale.edu

© Springer Nature Switzerland AG 2021

A. Hamburger et al. (eds.), *Social Trauma – An Interdisciplinary Textbook*,
https://doi.org/10.1007/978-3-030-47817-9_4

relevant membership group and evoking an event or situation which is (a) laden with negative affect, (b) represented as indelible, and (c) regarded as threatening a society's existence or violating one or more of its fundamental cultural presuppositions." Here also attention is turned to representation and, importantly, to memory.

Accompanying this task of differentiation was to distinguish social constructivist and realist notions of trauma. A realist notion (Sztompka, 2004) proposes that a shocking incident can be traumatic in itself, while a constructionist points to the mediating role of interpretation and narrative, claiming, as Smelser (2004, p. 37) does, that traumas are "made not born." A middle position, proposed by Eyerman (2011), argues that a powerful incident that shatters the taken-for-granted foundations of daily life is a necessary but not sufficient factor in setting processes of interpretation and representation in motion. This middle position between realism and constructivism is contained in the idea of the "traumatic potential" contained within the emotionally powerful and unsettling incident that catalyzes a "meaning struggle" to determine what happened and who or what was responsible.

A pathway to the theory of cultural trauma was paved by Kai Erikson (1979), who formulated the idea of collective trauma. In his study of a small American community destroyed by floodwaters, Erikson revealed how symptoms associated with psychological and realist notions of trauma were experienced by those members of the community that were not present to directly experience the disaster that destroyed their town. Their strong identification with people and place was sufficient to evoke an emotional response similar to those who were actually present. This discovery highlighted the importance of collective identification and collective memory with regard to traumatic experience. Contemplating the complex nature of trauma, Erikson later wrote, "trauma has both centripetal and centrifugal tendencies. It draws one away from the center of group space while at the same time drawing one back" (Erikson, 1995, p. 232). An incident of trauma, in other words, can destroy as well as create community. Identification as well as interaction with others is central to a social theory of trauma, where identification links individual suffering to collective suffering, such that the suffering of others can have a cumulative impact on individuals. Such as the suffering of my neighbor intensifies my own suffering. As Eyerman (2019, p. 91) put it, "Individual and collective traumas both issue from shock, and in each instance, the wounds that incur are collective and social as much as they are individual."

Related to collective identification and collective identity is the idea of collective memory. Developed by Maurice Halbwachs (1992), the idea of collective memory makes the case for a social, as opposed to an individual/psychological, theory of memory. Halbwachs reveals how a shared version of past events is crucial in sustaining group cohesion. A collective memory in other words makes collective identity possible. The memory of the flood that destroyed the community in Erikson's study became central to grounding present community life; a reconstructed shared past (factual or mythical) is part of what makes the "we" of any community possible. Eyerman's contribution to *Cultural Trauma and Collective Identity* revealed how the memory of slavery was formative for the idea of the African American, a collective identity that has been passed on over generations as a collective memory grounding collective identification. Arthur Neal's *National Trauma and Collective Memory* (1998), which applies a realist notion of trauma, also brought the idea of trauma and collective memory to the forefront in shaping collective identity, as well as influencing collective response to present events. The focus on the impact of past traumas on national identity would become a focus of cultural trauma research (Eyerman & Sciortino, 2019; Hashimoto, 2015).

As applied in these studies, the theory of cultural trauma has evolved into a research paradigm, being applied in individual case studies and comparative historical analyses. In reviewing the theory's internal development, Giuseppe Sciortino (2018) writes "the core of the CTP [cultural trauma process] is the analysis of the symbolic processes through which suffering—real or perceived—is inscribed with compelling meaning" (p. 9). Several steps conditioned the development from theory to research paradigm. One was the inclusion of performance theory and another the adaptation of Victor Turner's (1974) notion of social drama, both of which lead to describing the "meaning struggle" to interpret what happened and who was responsible following a traumatic experience or incident into a trauma drama, where the construction of trauma narratives and the performance of authorities and "carrier groups" are determinant. Highlighting the role of representation in this process, Alexander and Breese (2013, xxvii) write "Collective traumas are reflections neither of individual sufferings or actual events, but symbolic renderings that reconstruct and imagine them in a relatively independent way." Eyerman's studies of political assassination (Eyerman, 2008, 2011) apply Turner's framework through a performative perspective in explaining the traumatic impact of political assassination. A further step was to apply cultural trauma in a comparative perspective, where various traumatic incidents could be studied from the point of view of where whether or not the trauma drama that followed developed into cultural trauma or not. Here cultural trauma is conceptualized as a tear in the social fabric (an incident with traumatic potential) where the foundations of a collective identity are shattered, triggering a trauma drama, including attempts at social repair. Through this comparative study, several factors were identified as conditioning the emergence of cultural trauma. These were (1) the timing of the incident, (2) the surrounding political context, (3) how authority performed, (4) the content of mass media representations, and (5) the presence, power, and performance of carrier groups. Cultural trauma was analyzed as a contingent process, where the outcome, that is, a cultural trauma, depended on the interplay of these factors.

4.2 Learning Outcome to Social Trauma

Individual trauma always occurs in a social context in which there are varying degrees of access to the means of articulation, representation, and dissemination. As an overwhelming emotional response to an incident whose meaning must be interpreted and communicated, trauma must be narrated in comprehensible form. This requires language and an interpretative framework, as well as process of coming to be and a means of communication to disseminate the trauma. Because the process of understanding occurs in a political as well as a social context, there are power differentials as well as different points of view to account for. The trauma drama processes is a meaning struggle where interpretations compete and where there are varying degrees of access to the means of interpretation, articulation, and communication. This raises important sociological issues concerning who gets to speak and how, that is, through what means and media, as well as how the varying viewpoints are received and themselves interpreted. This is to call attention to the cultural creators, those individuals and carrier groups who construct the trauma narratives and their relative access to the means of representation, as well as their intentions and possible interests. The socio-political context in which trauma occurs is thus an important object of research and investigation. The role and place of mass media for example, including how free and autonomous they are from political and religious influence, is a crucial issue. In contemporary societies, mass media are crucial in the structuring and interpretation of dramatic incidents and thus in the trauma process. This is an important lesson gleaned from a social theory of trauma. It also raises the issue trauma for whom and whose trauma. In Erikson's study of the traumatic impact of a flooded village, the boundary limits of the "community" are relatively clear. However, in Eyerman's (2015) study of Hurricane Katrina, the collectivity impacted was not as clear. Was this a "trauma" only for those directly impacted, or for a larger group overrepresented in that catastrophe, such as African Americans, or even wider for the American nation itself? Such questions can only be raised and studied through a social theory of trauma within a wide historical scope.

4.3 Preferred Model of Explanation

The preferred model of explanation is retrospective historical analysis. Cultural traumas are analyzed after the fact, through a retrospective accounting of a trauma drama. This can be done in the form of a single case study or a comparative analysis of several cases. There are several possible levels at which to carry out such studies, local, regional, and national for example. One could study the traumatic impact of a political assassination, natural disaster, or mass shooting, for example, at the local level, such as a neighborhood or a city, the regional level, or the national level. While the historical comparative approach is the most popular in applying the framework of cultural trauma, other studies have used discourse analysis and other qualitative methodologies. These include Onwuachi-Willig's (2016) analysis of the "trauma of the routine" with reference to African Americans and the violence used against them, Schmidt's (2013) study of the American organization Mothers Against Drunk Driving (MADD), and Zhukova's (2016) study of the ground reaction to the Chernobyl nuclear disaster. A particular innovation with regard to the theory of cultural trauma made by Schmidt is the idea that trauma can be "perpetual" as well as mediated through organizations that act as carrier groups with a remedial function.

Both the "trauma" and the organizations can be studied through qualitative analysis, rather than retrospective historical methods.

4.4 Practical Implications for the Field of Social Trauma

The theory and framework of cultural trauma provides the field of social trauma and its concern for damages to the social body and the targeting of social groups with an extensively applied and rich research paradigm. Cultural trauma offers a comparative framework with which to analyze collective suffering through a cultural sociological lens. This highlights the meaning-making processes in the face of great sufferings and the role of carrier groups and organizations, such as mass media, in the process of making sense of suffering. Incorporated into this process are attempts at social repair, which include the attempt to re-narrate the foundations of collective identity that have been damaged or even shattered. Repairing a damaged social body often includes naming and punishing those who caused the damage, which opens the field of social trauma to studying the legal, political, and cultural processes involved in this.

4.5 Suggested Readings and Further Information

Alexander, J., Eyerman, R., Giesen, B., & Sztompka, P. (Eds.). (2004). *Cultural trauma and collective identity.* Berkeley: University of California Press.

Eyerman, R. (2019). *Memory, trauma, and identity.* New York: Palgrave Macmillan.

References

Alexander, J., Eyerman, R., Giesen, B., & Sztompka, P. (Eds.). (2004). *Cultural trauma and collective identity*. Berkeley: University of California Press.

Alexander, J., & Breese E. (2013). "Introdution: On Social Suffering and its Cultural Construction" in Eyerman et al (2011).

Erikson, K. (1979). *Everything in its path*. New York: Simon and Schuster.

Erikson, K. (1995). Notes on trauma and community. In C. Caruth (Ed.), *Trauma explorations in memory* (pp. 183–199). Baltimore: Johns Hopkins University Press.

Eyerman, R. (2008). *The assassination of Theo van Gogh*. Durham: Duke University Press.

Eyerman, R. (2011). *The cultural sociology of political assassination*. New York: Palgrave Macmillan.

Eyerman, R. (2015). *Is this America?* Austin: University of Texas Press.

Eyerman, R. (2019). *Memory, trauma, and identity*. New York: Palgrave Macmillan.

Eyerman, R., Alexander, J., & Breese, E. (Eds.). (2011). *Narrating trauma*. Boulder: Paradigm Publishers.

Eyerman, R., & Sciortino, G. (Eds.). (2019). *The cultural trauma of decolonization*. New York: Palgrave Macmillan.
Halbwachs, M. (1992). *On collective memory*. Chicago: University of Chicago Press.
Hashimoto, A. (2015). *The long defeat: Cultural trauma, memory, and identity in Japan*. Oxford: Oxford University Press.
Neal, A. (1998). *National trauma and collective memory: Major events in the american century* armonk: M.E. Sharpe.
Onwuachi-Willig, A. (2016). The trauma of the routine: Lessons on cultural trauma from the Emmett till verdict. *Sociological Theory, 34*(4), 335–357.
Schmidt, I. (2013). Perpetual trauma and its organizations: Mothers against drunk driving and drunk driving revisited. *Memory Studies, 7*(2), 239–253.
Sciortino, G. (2018). Cultural traumas. In J. Hall, L. Grindstaff, & M. C. Lo (Eds.), *Routledge handbook of cultural sociology* (2nd ed., pp. 135–143). London: Routledge.
Smelser, N. (2004). "Psychological Trauma and Cultural Trauma" in Alexander et al (Eds.), 2004.
Sztompka, P. (2004). "The Trauma of Social Change: A Case of Postcommunist Societies" in Alexander et al (Eds.), 2004.
Turner, V. (1974). *Dramas, fields, and metaphors: Symbolic action in human society*. Ithaca: Cornell University Press.
Zhukova, E. (2016). From ontological security to cultural trauma: The case of Chernobyl in Belarus and Ukraine. *Acta Sociologica, 59*(4), 332–346.

Chapter 5
The Wounds of History: About the Historical Dealing with Traumatic Experiences

Jörn Rüsen

5.1 Introduction: Crises Make History

Cultural orientation frameworks of human life practice enable human beings to develop their goals and ideas in the course of their life and to pursue these by acting, omitting, and suffering—of course always endangered or disturbed by the experience that things that are important for this action occur in such a way that they cannot be sufficiently understood with the instrumental rationality of human action.

The meaning of a historical event follows a different logic than the logic of instrumental rationality, which is about the appropriateness of means for given purposes. It is the logic of telling a story that makes the contingent events appear sensible and meaningful. Historical narratives bring the temporal change of human life situations into an order in which the contingency of "critical" events is dissolved into a sensible and meaningful concept of the temporal change that the human world as a whole goes through.

The following text presents a strongly modified version of an older reflection on the German approach to the Holocaust (Rüsen, 2001). Translated from German by Dr. Boris Drenkov.

J. Rüsen (✉)
Institute for Advanced Study in the Humanities, Essen, Germany

Witten/Herdecke University, Witten, Germany

© Springer Nature Switzerland AG 2021
A. Hamburger et al. (eds.), *Social Trauma – An Interdisciplinary Textbook*,
https://doi.org/10.1007/978-3-030-47817-9_5

5.1.1 Trauma

Trauma is a crisis that destroys the reference frame of the historical formation of meaning and prevents its renewal into another, which could fulfil the same function as the destroyed one. Trauma can be described as a "catastrophic" crisis and distinguished from other types of crisis by this term.

One can distinguish three types of crises that constitute different ways of historical meaning formation: normal, critical, and catastrophic.

A *normal crisis* can be overcome with culturally given possibilities of historical consciousness. The challenging contingency experience is integrated into a narrative within which it makes sense, so that human action comes to an end with it, in that the already given cultural potential of meaning formation through time experience only needs to be exhausted.

A *critical crisis* can only be solved if new elements are brought into play that substantially exceed the given interpretation potentials of historical culture. In this case, new patterns of interpretation for understanding the past are formed; historical thought develops new paradigms.

A *catastrophic crisis* destroys the possibility of historical consciousness to cope with contingency. In this case, the fundamental principles of meaning formation itself, which stand for the plausibility of the historical narrative, are challenged. They must be crossed into a cultural no-man's-land, or simply abandoned. When a catastrophic crisis occurs, the language of historical meaning falls silent. It takes time (sometimes over generations) to find a language that can express this crisis. This does not mean that there are no attempts to make sense of this crisis and to break its spell over memory. The catastrophic nature of the crisis can be seen in the failure of such attempts.

The Holocaust represents the most radical experience of such a catastrophic crisis in history, at least for the Jews and, in different ways, for the Germans. For each of the two peoples concerned, genocide is unique in its genocidal nature and its radical negation and destruction of the fundamental values of modern culture that they share. When Dan Diner (1990) characterized the Holocaust as a "breach of civilization," he said that, through its mere happening, the phenomenon of the Holocaust had destroyed the cultural possibilities of integrating it into a historical order of time, within which it can be understood in such a way that the life of the present can also be lived in view of this experience. The Holocaust problematizes and even averts any unbroken connection of meaning with the time before and after it.

Nevertheless, events of this kind must be regarded as historical and given a place in the historiographical interpretations of modern history. If we were to place such events beyond history and give them a "mythical" meaning, they would lose their character as actual events of experience. At the same time, historical thinking would be limited in its access to the experience of the past. But that fundamentally contradicts the logic of historical thought. For a myth does not have the same reference to experience that is regarded as a necessary condition of its trustworthiness for historical thought. Therefore, the Holocaust and other traumatic events are "borderline events." They cannot be held at all in the object area of historical thinking. They have always crossed it and reach into the center of the mental procedures of historical thought itself (Rüsen, 2005).

All three types of contingency as crisis experience lead to history, but to very different forms of historical interpretation. In the first case, the narrative order integrates the challenging contingency experience by "lifting" it in the Hegelian sense of the word (negating and preserving at the same time). In the second case, in the "critical" crisis, such integration can only be achieved by changing the narrative order itself. In the case of trauma, the challenging experience is also "historicized," but the historical pattern of interpretation relativizes its claims to a coherent narrative order, or senselessness itself is placed at the center of that order. The traumatic crisis leaves traces of the incomprehensible in the traits of history.

History is always generated by an idea of temporal change that integrates the experience of the past, the present practice of life, and the expectation of the future into the unity of time as a sensible and meaningful order of human life. The traumatic crisis has left its mark on the historical features of the temporal order—disturbances and ruptures. It marks the limits of meaning in the treatment of the experience of time. It provides the coherence between experience and interpretation of time with the signature of ambivalence and ambiguity.

5.1.2 Historical Awareness

Historical awareness synthesizes experiences of the past and expectations of the future. In this synthesis, the past is present as a spiritually moving force charged with all the powers with which the human spirit purposefully (in fear and hope) directs itself toward the future. The awareness of history increases the temporal extension of memory into an intergenerational continuity. The idea of this duration, which corresponds to the need to transcend birth and death, drives cultural practices in which a society reflects and confirms its togetherness and its distinction from others.

With regard to the three types of crisis, the respective conception of continuity differs quite considerably. In the case of a "normal" crisis, it binds past, present, and future into an already-known, solid, and unbroken unity of the respective self. In the case of a "critical" crisis, there is no healing of the temporal order already in place. It must be "invented" by new ways of working through what has happened. This "invention" is not a creation out of nothing, but it restructures the elements of historical narrative into a new concept of temporal order or introduces new elements into this concept. In the case of a "catastrophic" or "traumatic" crisis, the core of the fundamental concept of time, the meaningful unity of past, present, and future, is destroyed.

5.2 Learning Outcome Related to Social Trauma

The knowledge of the fundamentals of historical consciousness as a social processing of experience as well as of the strategies of historicizing crises makes it possible to understand that catastrophic crises (social traumas) cannot be healed by applying new patterns of interpretation of history, but that they fundamentally question the possibility of establishing an image of history. *Historical science is also a cultural practice of de-traumatization, but it remains the necessary function of a fact-based, enlightening critique of the Historization of trauma.*

5.3 Preferred Model of Explanation: Historization of Trauma

Traumatic experience is an experience that cannot be integrated into the context of interpretation, which orientates human action in terms of culture. Axiomatically, it does not make any sense. On the contrary, it destroys the effective concepts of meaning as life-practical orientation systems. Therefore, a traumatic experience means a struggle for interpretation through which it can be overcome. It must be interpreted in such a way that it makes sense, i.e., that it fits into the effective contexts of understanding and interpretation of the practical orientation of life. Such a sense consists first of all in omitting or suppressing all that in the traumatic experience which endangers the effectiveness and security of these patterns of interpretation. The formation of vital meaning through traumata means an alienation, even falsification of experience with the intention of coming to terms with it.

Everyone knows this destruction and alienation. They always occur when you try to talk about an experience that is or was unique and has deeply shaken you. This applies not only to negative experiences with traumatic quality but also to positive ones (e.g., overwhelming experiences of happiness). Those who make such experiences are pushed beyond the boundaries of everyday life and thus beyond the world interpretations and self-understandings that are decisive for this everyday life. Nevertheless, without words, things cannot be kept within the horizon of perception and memory, which have such a shattering quality that they catapult out into the uninterpreted and unintelligible. For only in these horizons of interpreted perception and memorable experience can one come to terms with them.

Even in the dark prison of repression, such experiences tend to express themselves: If those concerned cannot talk about them, they will compulsively compensate for the lack of language and its possible interpretation by a behavior that manifests itself as a lack and break in living. They must "talk" about them in this "language" of coercive acts without words, because they are connected to them and must mentally deal with this connection and come to terms with it.

Historization is a common cultural strategy to cope with the disturbing consequences of traumatic experiences. The moment one begins to tell a story about what happened, the first step is taken to integrate the destructive events into the world and self-understanding. At the end of this path, the historical narrative gives trauma a place in a temporal chain of events. In this chain it makes sense and has lost the power to destroy sense and meaning.

5.4 Practical Implications in the Field of Social Trauma

This *de-traumatization through historization* can be carried out through different strategies of locating traumatic events in a historical context:

- *Anonymization* is widespread. It simply prevents the destruction of symbolic concepts. Instead of murder and crime, of suffering and guilt, one speaks of a "dark" period, of "fate," of a "burglary of demonic forces" into the more or less ordered world.
- Through *categorization,* a trauma is equated with understandable events and developments. It loses its destructive uniqueness for those who are destined by it (mostly, but not exclusively, the victims) by being called abstract terms. Such terms integrate traumas into sensible and meaningful temporal developments. "Tragedy" is a prominent example for this strategy type.
- In *normalization,* the destructive quality of traumatic events is dissolved. In this case, what has happened appears as something that happens over and over again at all times. It is then explained by referring to human nature, which, despite all temporal differences, is ultimately the same. As such a normalizing category, "evil" in humans or in human nature is very often used.
- *Moralization* civilizes the destructive power of historical trauma. The traumatic event takes on the character of a case that stands for a general rule of human behavior: namely that one should not do such a thing. The trauma then takes on the meaning of a message that touches hearts because of its horror. The best example of this is the film *Schindler's List* by Steven Spielberg (1994). Many Holocaust museums in the United States follow the same strategy for formation of meaning. At the end of the tour through the horrors that the Jews had to suffer, the visitors are dismissed with a clear moral message.
- *Teleologization* reconciles the traumatic past with present (or at least later) life forms. A widespread teleologization consists in using the stressful past to historically legitimize an order of life that claims to protect itself from a return of the terrible. This historical perspective appears as a lesson learned from historical experience. A well-known example is the Historical Museum in Israel's Yad Vashem Memorial. The visitors literally follow the course of time by going into the depths of the horror of the concentration camps and gas chambers; then, their path leads them up to the founding of the State of Israel.

- Through *historical-theoretical reflection,* the painful reality of traumatic events can dissolve into the thin air of abstraction. The challenging rupture of time caused by traumatic events raises critical questions about what history in general is, what principles of meaning apply, and what the modes of representation of this past look like. Answering such questions means overcoming the break in the concept of historical change. The traumatically dammed up flow of time (cf. Diner, 1990) in the chain of events flows again and blends into the orientation patterns of contemporary life—when such historical-theoretical questions are answered.

All these historiographical strategies are usually accompanied by mental procedures that are well-known from psychoanalysis. They are concerned with ignoring or at least making more bearable the disturbing features of historical experience. The most effective procedure, of course, is displacement. But it is too easy just to look at whether and to what extent a historical narrative uses repression mechanisms and to ask what it does not tell. It is more fruitful to ask how a narrative brings the past to the fore in order to silence its frightening traits at the same time. Psychoanalysis can teach historians that there are a large number of ways in which the meaninglessness or disturbing nature of past experiences can be transformed into a historical sense by subsequently bringing it to light in a relieving way. Those who know, for example, that they were involved in the crimes of the past and are responsible for them relieve themselves of this past by extraterritorializing it from the realm of their own history and shifting it to the realm of stories that are authoritative for the "others." This extraterritorialization can be achieved by exchanging the roles of perpetrators and victims or by shifting perpetratorship and responsibility to others. Such a "shift" can also take place by drawing a picture of the past in which one's face has disappeared in the representation of the facts, although these facts objectively belong to the events that constitute one's own history.

One can observe all these strategies if one asks about the traces that past traumas have left in historiography and other forms of historical culture that serve the practical orientation of life in the present. The traces are covered by memory and history, as it were, and sometimes it is very difficult to discern the disturbing reality beneath the smooth surface of collective memory and historical interpretation.

The diagnosis of these strategies of historical meaning formation inevitably leads to the question of how the work of historians should relate to them. Is it possible to avoid the alienating and distorting transformation of meaningful traumas into meaningful history? The disturbing answer to this question is No. Of course, this does not mean that careful historical research cannot overcome the abridgments of repressive falsifications and painful connections (including burdensome responsibility). In this respect, historiography has the necessary function of an enlightening critique to bring the facts to light. However, by interpreting these facts (and they, of course, must interpret them), historians cannot use them other than in narrative patterns of interpretation that give historical meaning to the traumatic facts. In this respect, for *purely logical reasons, history is a cultural practice of de-traumatization.* It changes trauma into history. But does this mean that the trauma inevitably disappears in the history of its representation?

The abundance of traumatic experiences in the course of the twentieth century has brought about a change in the historical relationship to trauma. A blurred overshaping of their hurting spines is (no longer) possible, at least as long as the victims, the survivors, the descendants as much as the perpetrators, their descendants, and all those involved in the crimes against humanity are objectively conditioned by this hurtful reversal of human norms and subjectively confronted with the task of looking them in the face.

The problems of such a view into the face of absolute horror have been discussed in detail with regard to the Holocaust but also in dealing with other traumatic experiences (cf. Friedländer, 1992, 1998, 2007b; Frei & Kansteiner, 2013). In this discussion, there is an attempt to maintain the peculiarity of this traumatic event by keeping it in the living memory separate from the strategies of historical meaning developed up to then. This separation was called "mythical" and "historical" by the conceptual pair of opposites. Only a "mythical" relationship to the Holocaust represents the form in which its traumatic character can be protected from dissolution through historization (cf. Broszat & Friedländer, 1988; Rüsen, 1997). But if one de-historicizes the Holocaust in this way, then one robs it of its explosive power in the negation of the usual procedures of historization. If one assigns this trauma an asylum alongside the normality of the usual historical world view, then one cuts it off from the established practices of historical culture. This separation then allows history to be written in the usual way, as if nothing had happened. (This is the danger of establishing "Holocaust Studies" as a separate field of academic research.)

But how can this de-traumatization be prevented then? I would like to propose a strategy of *secondary traumatization.* By this I mean that the way of doing history has to be changed. I am thinking of a new kind of historical narrative, in which the traumatic events narrated leave their traces in the pattern of interpretation of the narrative itself, which determines the interpretation work of historians. The narrative has its unity to give up its smooth ceiling over the chain of events. It must express its "disturbance" within the methodological procedures of interpretation and in the narrative procedures of historical representation (convincingly in Friedländer 1997/2007a).

At the level of fundamental principles of the formation of historical meaning through the interpretation of events, *senselessness itself* must *become a constitutive element of the historical sense itself.*

That means in detail:

- *An anonymization of* horror can be avoided by clearly saying what happened in the shocking nudity of crude factuality.
- Instead of *subsuming* the disturbing events under meaningful categories, these events must be integrated into interpretive frames of reference that problematize the traditional categories of the historical sense itself.
- Instead of a *normalizing* story that dissolves disturbing elements of experience, history has to maintain the memory of the "normality of exception." History has to remember the horror under the thin cover of everyday life, to systematically take into account the banality of evil, etc.

- Instead of *moralizing, the* historical interpretation has to bring to light the inner fragility of morality itself.
- Instead of smoothing time breaks through *teleology,* history has to show how the flow of time accumulates in the relationship between the past of traumatic events and the present of their memory. Discontinuity, the breaking of connections, or brokenness has become a form of historical meaning itself in the ensemble of symbolic ideas about the passage of time.
- And, finally, *historical-theoretical reflection* must take up the disturbing elements of historical experience in their traumatic dimension and incorporate them into the abstraction of concepts and ideas.

The cries of the victims, the laughter of the perpetrators, and the eloquent silence of the spectators die away when the course of time takes on its normal historical form in which it orients people in this progression of time. Secondary traumatization is an opportunity to give this dehumanization back its voices. By remembering the horrors of the past in this way, historical thought gains a chance to prevent their continuation.

5.5 Further Reading

Rüsen, J. (2014). Sinn und Widersinn der Geschichte—Einige Überlegungen zur Kontur der Geschichtsphilosophie. In R. Langthaler & Hofer, M. (Eds.), *Geschichtsphilosophie. Stellenwert und Aufgaben in der Gegenwart. Wiener Jahrbuch für Philosophie* (Vol. 46, pp. 9–26).

Rüsen, J. (2019). Historisierung des Holocaust. Sinnprobleme einer historischen Erfahrung. In E. Kobylinska-Dehe & M. L. Hermanns, Ludger M. (Eds.), *Im Schatten von Krieg und Holocaust. Psychoanalyse in Polen im polnisch-deutsch-jüdischen Kontext* (pp. 25–34). Gießen: Psychosozial Verlag.

References

Broszat, M., & Friedländer, S. (1988). A controversy about the historization of national socialism. *New German Critique, 44*, 85–126.

Diner, D. (1990). Between aporia and apology: On the limits of historicizing national socialism. In P. Baldwin (Ed.), *Reworking the past: Hitler, the Holocaust and the historians' debate* (pp. 135–145). Boston: Beacon Press.

Frei, N., & Kansteiner, W. (Eds.). (2013). *Den Holocaust erzählen. Historiographie zwischen wissenschaftlicher Empirie und narrativer Kreativität.* Göttingen: Wallstein.

Friedländer, S. (Ed.). (1992). *Probing the limits of representation. Nazism and the 'final solution'.* Cambridge: Harvard University Press.

Friedländer, S. (1998). Writing the history of the Shoa: Some major dilemmas. In H. W. Blanke, F. Jaeger, & T. Sandkühle (Eds.), *Dimensionen der Historik. Geschichtstheorie,*

Wissenschaftsgeschichte und Geschichtskultur heute. Jörn Rüsen zum 60. Geburtstag (pp. 407–414). Köln: Böhlau.

Friedländer, S. (2007a). *Nazi Germany and the Jews* (2 vols). New York: Harper Collins. (Original work published 1997)

Friedländer, S. (2007b). *Den Holocaust beschreiben. Auf dem Weg zu einer integrierten Geschichte*. Göttingen: Wallstein.

Rüsen, J. (1997). The Logic of Historization—Metahistorical reflections on the debate between Friedländer and Broszat. *History and Memory, 9*(1–2), 113–144.

Rüsen, J. (2001). Krise, trauma, identität. In J. Rüsen (Ed.), *Zerbrechende Zeit. Über den Sinn der Geschichte* (pp. 145–179). Böhlau: Köln.

Rüsen, J. (2005). Historizing nazi-time. Metahistorical reflections on the debate between Friedländer and Broszat. In J. Rüsen (Ed.), *History. Narration—Interpretation—Orientation* (pp. 163–188). New York, Oxford: Berghahn Books.

Part II
Clinical Aspects of Social Trauma

Chapter 6
The Complexity of Social Trauma Diagnosis and Intervention

Andreas Hamburger

Social trauma is a bridging concept that connects a social and clinical perspective (see Hamburger, 2020, this volume). The chapter explores the use of the concept in the clinical context and describes the vicissitudes of the acknowledgment of post-genocidal traumatic pathology in diagnostic classifications. Moreover, it specifies the basic conditions of healing in cases of posttraumatic disorders in a shared societal frame.

6.1 Introduction

Posttraumatic disorders are the only DSM diagnosis defined by an external event, only that this external event is vaguely defined. Moreover, the type of trauma does not specify the diagnosis, which according to DSM-5 is based on the reported symptoms.

6.1.1 The Concept of Trauma in Psychiatry and Psychotherapy

The category of trauma-related mental illness had a long and variable way of inclusion into the classification systems for mental disorders. Known to clinicians and poets, described in the founding myths, heroic epics, literature, and art throughout history (Kucmin, Kucmin, Nogalski, Sojczuk, & Jojczuk, 2016), the damage that terror and fear inflict on mental health lost relevance when rational medicine took over. The nineteenth-century medical literature mentioned that traumatic

A. Hamburger (✉)
International Psychoanalytic University Berlin, Berlin, Germany
e-mail: andreas.hamburger@ipu-berlin.de

© Springer Nature Switzerland AG 2021
A. Hamburger et al. (eds.), *Social Trauma – An Interdisciplinary Textbook*,
https://doi.org/10.1007/978-3-030-47817-9_6

experiences caused psychological symptoms (mainly in the context of large-scale technology beyond control, like railway accidents; Fischer-Homberger, 1999). When in World War I soldiers and civilians faced the machinery of mass destruction, combat trauma became an issue for military psychiatrists. However, well into the twentieth century, the psychopathological symptoms like dissociations, mutism, and anxiety that were caused by those stressful experiences were ascribed to the mechanical concussion of the "shellshock" rather than to the mental and bodily experience of atrocity (Ferenczi's papers on war neurosis were a rare exception; see Hamburger, 2018a). Only in the aftermath of World War II was the category of traumatic "gross stress reaction" acknowledged and included in the newly issued DSM-I (APA, 1952), only to disappear in DSM-II (APA, 1968) and reappear in DSM-III (APA, 1980) under the category of PTSD (see Hamburger, 2018b; Scott, 1990). However, DSM-III brought with it a merely symptom-oriented description, disregarding the context of the traumatizing event. Thus, all kinds of adverse experiences were likewise accepted as an undefined "exposure." While DSM-III-R (APA, 1987) defined traumatic situations as events "outside the range of usual human experience," recent studies show that trauma exposure appears as a normality. Huge epidemiological studies (Kessler et al., 2017) report high numbers for trauma exposure (70.4% of the respondents had experienced at least one type of a traumatic event in their lifetime). This inflationary use of the trauma concept, however, has been criticized as indistinct (Prager, 2011), culture insensitive (Moghimi, 2012), and excluding the subjective processes that lead from an external event to a mental disorder (Lellau, 2005). Moreover, a trauma concept, based on individual adversities, excludes the social meaning and societal context of the event (see Kirmayer, Kienzler, Afana, & Pedersen, 2010).

DSM-5 (APA, 2013) redefined PTSD by relocating it into the new diagnostic class of "Trauma- and Stressor-Related Disorders," together with Adjustment Disorders. Then it clarified the diagnostic criteria for PTSD, one of whom being exposure to trauma (Criterion A), which was for the first time precisely described, including psychological harm beyond mere physical threat. Four types of exposure are differentiated: direct exposure, witnessing trauma, learning that a relative or close friend was exposed to a trauma, and indirect exposure to aversive details of the trauma, usually in the course of professional duties. For the most important types of direct or witnessed trauma, DSM-5 gives the following list of anchor examples:

> exposure to war as a combatant or civilian, threatened or actual physical assault (e.g., physical attack, robbery, mugging, childhood physical abuse), threatened or actual sexual violence (e.g., forced sexual penetration, alcohol/drug-facilitated sexual penetration, abusive sexual contact, noncontact sexual abuse, sexual trafficking), being kidnapped, being taken hostage, terrorist attack, torture, incarceration as a prisoner of war, natural or human-made disasters, and severe motor vehicle accidents. For children, sexually violent events may include developmentally inappropriate sexual experiences without physical violence or injury. […] Medical incidents that qualify as traumatic events involve sudden, catastrophic events (e.g., waking during surgery, anaphylactic shock). Witnessed events include, but are not limited to, observing threatened or serious injury, unnatural death, physical or sexual abuse of another person due to violent assault, domestic violence, accident, war or disaster, or a medical catastrophe in one's child (e.g., a life-threatening hemorrhage). Indirect

> exposure through learning about an event is limited to experiences affecting close relatives or friends and experiences that are violent or accidental (e.g., death due to natural causes does not qualify). Such events include violent personal assault, suicide, serious accident, and serious injury. The disorder may be especially severe or long- lasting when the stressor is interpersonal and intentional (e.g., torture, sexual violation). (pp. 274–275)

This comprehensive list of possible trauma exposures, however, is of limited clinical use, since it only defines the necessary starting point for diagnosing PTSD, without any contribution to diagnostic content, which is—according to the philosophy of DSM since DSM-III—strictly based on symptom descriptions. Thus, Criterion B describes intrusions, flashbacks, dissociation,, avoidance and arousal; criterion C stated that these symptoms should not exceed the duration of one month; criteria E and F refer to serious impairments and the exclusion of differential diagnoses.

The comprehensive description of different types of trauma exposure currently bears nearly no implications for psychiatric nosology; especially, post-social-traumatic disorders are not addressed in their specificity in the diagnostic manuals (Ehrenreich, 2003; Hamburger, 2017a; 2017b; Kira, 2001; Kira, Templin, Lewandowski, & Shuwiekh, 2018; Stein, Wilmot, & Solomon, 2016); however, DSM-5 mentions a "variation in the type of traumatic exposure (e.g., genocide)" as a "culture-related diagnostic issue" (APA 2013).

6.1.2 Psychoanalytic Trauma Theory

A genuinely psychological trauma theory evolved in Freud and Breuer's early psychoanalytic theory under the influence of Charcot (Herman, 1992)—and, in parallel, in Janet's conceptualization of dissociation (Van der Hart & Horst, 1989). It overcame the former assumption that the symptoms were caused by a physical concussion that had injured the brain and conceptualized psychological trauma as an overflow of unsupportable (mental) experience that caused a "splitting of consciousness" (Breuer & Freud, 1893, p. 12). However, this theory, despite being based on mental processing, suffered since the very beginning from a lack of conceptual clarity regarding the nature of the relation between the external event and its mental processing (Bohleber, 2000; Hillebrandt, 2004; Sandler et al., 1987, S. 28 f). When Freud famously renounced on the "reality" of the childhood trauma in 1897, he certainly did not deny the fact of abuse, but introduced intrapsychic mechanisms explaining the traumatogenic process (for a discussion of the debate on the "seduction theory," see Good, 2005).

However, Freud's concentration on infantile phantasy and inner conflict (Freud, 1905) made trauma nearly disappear from the psychoanalytic discourse and, as a consequence, blinded psychoanalysis for a long time for the importance social interaction. Only when confronted with the shellshock victims of World War I did trauma become again important (Ferenczi, Abraham, Simmel, & Jones, 1921;

Freud, 1955). New and pioneering concepts of sexual trauma reappeared only later through the writings of Sandor Ferenczi (1933/1949) that, however, found a delayed reception in the psychoanalytic discourse.

6.1.3 History of the Social Trauma Concept

A theory of social trauma was widely absent from psychoanalytic theory, despite the experience of the Nazi terror, where many psychoanalysts had been personally threatened. Very few papers addressed it, with the notable exception of Burlingham and Freud (1942) and Bettelheim (1943). Bettelheim's report from his years in Dachau and Buchenwald are among the most insightful first-hand analyses of the concentration camps. It was published in a renowned journal and an abridged version even made it into the 1947 edition of the four-volume *Encyclopaedia Britannica* history of the years 1936–1946, vol. 2, under the entry "Concentration Camps, German" (Bettelheim, 1947). However, it has been criticized as subjectively biased (see Fleck & Müller, 1997; Robinson, 1970). It was not before the 1960s that psychoanalysis put emphasis on social trauma (Barocas, 1975; Chodoff, 1963; de Wind, 1968; Eissler, 1967; Eitinger, 1961; Klein, Zellermayer, & Shanan, 1963; Krystal, 1968; Niederland, 1968; Tuteur, 1966; Wangh, 1964). Since then, the psychoanalytic concept of social trauma has been elaborated through the seminal work of many clinicians (Grand, 2000; Herman, 1992; Kogan, 2018; Krystal, 1968; Krystal & Niederland, 1971; Mitscherlich & Mitscherlich, 1967; van der Kolk, McFarlane, & Weisaeth, 1996) in an ongoing discourse with the humanities.

One starting point of the social trauma discourse within psychoanalysis is Bruno Bettelheim's autobiographical report on detainees in concentration camps. Bettelheim's (1943) report is written in third person and is presented as an interview study, aiming at a description of stages of the camp experience.

Bettelheim's assumptions that prisoners underwent a process of regression to a childlike sense of self and, eventually, even identified with the values of the Gestapo (p. 447 f.) have been heavily criticized; they mirror the basic psychoanalytic trauma definition as a situation where the psyche is overwhelmed.

This view, however, misses the social embeddedness of survivors, including resilience factors possibly due to a defensive abstinence from reflecting its own traumatic history (Bohleber, 2000; Prince, 2009). Traditional psychoanalytic models tend to interpret the traumatic experience in terms of the maternal dyad and the Oedipal triangle, while undervaluing the role of extrafamilial and societal factors for mental development (see Grand & Salberg's transgenerational model, 2020, this volume). Also, such a subjective perspective on trauma renders different types of traumatizing events undiscernible, while a more socio-psychological approach could definitively tell a private hardship from genocide. The difference is that systematic transgression and undermining of morally and culturally accepted values do not only overwhelm the coping capacity of the victim but also the symbolizing capacity of its social environment.

6.1.4 How to Define a Traumatizing Event?

Terr's (1991) influential concept of childhood trauma types was an important step toward inclusion of the exposure type to subsequent pathology.

Terr distinguished two types of traumatic events. Type 1, "single blow trauma," can be recalled in detail and leads to symptoms like cognitive reappraisals ("omens") and misperceptions, while Type 2, "variable, multiple, or long-standing traumas," stirs up emotions like absence of feeling, rage, or unremitting sadness and leads to symptoms like denial, psychic numbing, and sudden or inhibited rage. Furthermore, she defined a Type 1/Type 2 crossover for children, who suffered from one-blow-trauma with lasting consequences; here she observed perpetual mourning and depression to the extent of a personality change.

A more detailed taxonomy was designed by Kira (2001) who distinguished five types of affected individual functioning (attachment trauma, autonomy or identity trauma, interdependence trauma, achievement or self-actualization trauma, and survival trauma). The second classification distinguishes "real" from "factitious" trauma. Real traumatic events take place between two or more persons; they may be simple (Type I), complex/extended (Type II), or complex/extended including a "factitious" component (Type III). Factitious trauma is transmitted in multiple steps or cross-generationally, either through family or collective history or through structural violence. Such a taxonomy is helpful, but still not sufficient to understand the specificity of social trauma.

Other researchers, most notably van der Kolk et al. (1996) and Herman (1992), tried to define a separate diagnostic category for types of trauma that are not or not sufficiently covered by the PTSD category. They did not succeed to establish a new category in DSM-5, where a unified category of PTSD was upheld and compensated by introducing a wider range of traumatic stressors. However, in the forthcoming ICD-11, a new category of "complex PTSD" will be introduced, which allows for an appropriate diagnosing of long-term childhood abuse and social trauma with their specific pathology consequences like emotional dysregulation, negative self-concepts, and difficulties in social relationships (see Streeck-Fischer, 2020, this volume).

6.2 Learning Outcome Related to Social Trauma

Social trauma, besides being a description of a societal phenomenon, can be understood as a specific diagnostic category. A PTSD diagnosis cannot sufficiently describe social traumatization (Becker, 1995; Hernández, 2002). The theory of social trauma embraces a narrower and, at the same time, a wider concept; it is more specific regarding the type of trauma and less concentrating on psychopathology.

The psychoanalytic concept of social trauma roots in survivor testimonies and considers the notion of social trauma as reflected in sociology, history, art, and culture.

6.3 Preferred Model of Explanation: The Concept of Social Trauma

The concept of social trauma is not defined by a symptom list that allows for a psychiatric diagnosis. Social trauma is a concept for the individual experience of being socially persecuted and appertaining to a persecuted social group; moreover, it describes the group-specific reverberation of the persecution.

6.3.1 Psychological Reactions and Clinical Descriptions

Such a social trauma can lead to severe psychological symptoms in the aftermath, but this is by no means necessarily so. There are impressive reports of persons who have survived severe atrocities with a healthy personality (e.g., Ornstein, 2003), and we do not exactly know the conditions that might have enabled them to maintain their mental health (Ferren, 1999; Lomranz, 1995; Rousseau, Drapeau, & Rahimi, 2003). But, on the other hand, many symptoms have been reported in the clinical literature on survivors of social trauma (see the literature review in Barel, Van IJzendoorn, Sagi-Schwartz, & Bakermans-Kranenburg, 2010).

In the late 1960s, the symptoms of concentration camp survivors, like chronic sense of anxiety and depression, feelings of guilt, emotional disruption, cognitive disturbances (especially regarding memory and concentration), and personality problems, were subsumed under the term "survivor syndrome" (Niederland, 1968) or the "concentration camp syndrome" (Eitinger, 1964; Krystal, 1968; see Krell, 1979). Most components of the survivor syndrome were subsequently confirmed (Barel et al., 2010). In later studies, multiple long-term effects of the concentration camp detainment were stated: increased frequency of PTSD and other psychiatric symptoms; lower physical, psychological, and social quality of life; sleep disturbances, nightmares, nervousness, intrusive thoughts, headaches, and exhaustion; and increased emotional distress (e.g., frequent anxiety, irrational fears, uncontrolled anger).

6.3.1.1 Memory

From the clinical and testimony experience, Dori Laub has developed the concept of the Holocaust survivors' fragmented memory as a result of the breakdown of the internal "Thou":

> The traumatic event became an 'absent' experience because at the core of the executioner-victim interaction all human relatedness is undone. The internal other, the 'Thou' to whom one can address one's plea, tell one's story, no longer exists. Therefore the 'story' is never known, told, or remembered. (Laub, 2005a, p. 257; see also Laub & Auerhahn, 1993, Blum, 2007; Laub & Hamburger, 2017).

Memory, however, is not just a private storage; it is constructed by intra- and interpersonal narration (Hamburger, 1998); therefore, societal denial of social trauma and institutional rejection of acknowledgment have an effect on personal memory like a blinded mirror. In this context, also a tendency of modern psychoanalysis to focus on the here-and-now-experience in the consulting room shall go together with unceasing attempts of voicing and reconstructing the past which can be seen as critical in the case of posttraumatic disorders in general and, specifically, social trauma (Bohleber, 2000, 2017).

6.3.1.2 Relatedness and Failed Empathy

The symptom of a fragmented memory, in Laub's (1992) understanding, is intertwined with a rupture in the inner representation of interpersonal relatedness. This basic distrust in a holding environment may be reflected in actual interpersonal relations, mentioned by Hillel Klein as early as 1968, who emphasizes the relational aspects of the survivor syndrome: "Survivors are threatened by the possibility of an intimate relationship" (Klein, 1968, p. 248; see also Laub & Auerhahn, 1989).

For Laub (2016), the failure of empathy in the traumatic situation leads to an internalization of the unresponsive other. Analogously, Ilany Kogan, in her meanwhile classical case analysis *Escape from Selfhood* (2018), traces the boundary confusions that occurred in the course of the treatment back to the patient's unresolved striving for fusion in his early relation with his mother. Both his parents were orphaned Holocaust survivors, and the patient had never left his role of the symbiotic warrant of survival.

6.3.1.3 Fragmented Narratives

In testimonial or therapeutic interactions, where survivors who are usually reticent about their traumatic experiences are encouraged to share their life stories, Laub (2005a) observed a "traumatic shutdown of narrative and symbolization" that characterizes the interactive field when survivors try to recount their traumatic life story. The co-construction of a coherent autobiographical life history is hampered by splitting off and replacement by screen memories but also by an erasure of emotional resonance and a denial of the trauma, leading to characteristic countertransference reactions on the part of the interviewer/therapist in the form of co-confusion, freezing, and psychosomatic reactions (see Grünberg, 2013; Grünberg & Markert, 2012; Hamburger, 2017a, 2017b). In the interpersonal dimension, the trauma can damage the relatedness of the survivor to his social group and to the cultural environment (Rosenbaum & Varvin, 2007). Clinically, this loss of trust in the social environment may contribute to the described adjustment issues in the survivor syndrome, like continuous sadness, hopelessness, and social withdrawal.

6.3.2 *Between the Individual and the Society: Transgenerational Trauma Transmission*

The most specific trait of social trauma is the often-reported observation that persecuted families and groups show transgenerational trauma transmission (see Grand & Salberg, 2020, this volume).

Since first reports in 1967 (Rakoff, Sigal, & Epstein, 1966), a huge body of clinical and empirical research literature has evolved (see literature reviews by Kellermann, 2001; Braga, Mello, & Fiks, 2012), indicating that children of trauma survivors may develop emotional, cognitive, and behavioral problems including posttraumatic symptoms, depression, anxiety, hyperactivity, and conduct disorders. However, meta-analyses (Sagi-Schwartz, van IJzendoorn, & Bakermans-Kranenburg, 2008; Van IJzendoorn, Bakermans-Kranenburg, & Sagi-Schwartz, 2003) showed that in some studies no increase of psychopathology in Holocaust survivor offspring was found. Moreover, Gomolin (2019) argued that, given the weak evidence, intergenerational trauma transmission itself is a countertransference-based construct of involved researchers (criticized by Gerson, 2019).

Still, qualitative research and multiple clinical experience indicate that epidemiological findings, which are usually based on standardized questionnaires, possibly fail the subtler ways how the traumatic experience influences the mental life of persons closely related to a persecuted group (Braga et al., 2012; Scharf, 2007).

Kaplan (2008) distinguishes in her psychoanalytic field study with Rwandan children *generational linking* from *trauma linking* in genocide survivors. The latter is similar to intrusions, flashbacks, and irritability in PTSD and leads to an immersion in the traumatic memory, while *generational linking* allows subjects to shift their attention toward significant people and objects in the past as well as in the present. Laub's (2005b) model of the loss of communication with the internalized other can be understood as a transgenerational mechanism, too.

6.3.3 *Social Symptoms*

Despite the present chapter's focus on the clinical notion of social trauma, the social aspect of this concept must not be discarded. Societies may—although in a metaphorical sense—display symptoms, too. Thus, social phenomena like conspiracy of silence, institutional rejection, heroization, avoidance, hate speech, and victim-blaming may be regarded as social pathologies. As an example, the ambivalent reception of Shoah survivors in postwar Israel might be mentioned, or the contempt and hostility Soviet slave laborers faced after their return from Germany.

6.4 Practical Implications for the Field of Social Trauma

For psychotherapy with patients who were traumatized in the context of social violence or appertain to an involved social group, it is indispensable to actively address this context; it may even retraumatize them to ignore it and treat patients as if their suffering were an individual experience. Mental health practitioners working with socially traumatized patients or groups must be aware that denial is one of the most powerful mechanisms of perpetuation. Moreover, they must be aware that denial or evasive addressing of the trauma may easily take place in the therapeutic situation itself, despite the therapist's best intentions, since it is part and parcel of social trauma to be woven into the fabric of the societal unconscious also therapists are part of. In a relational psychoanalytic perspective, the analytic alliance must be designed and upheld in a way to be able to contain even strong reenactments, including the unconscious entanglement and resistance of the analyst, and to provide a mentalizing space to transform them into symbolic language.

Moreover, societal acknowledgment beyond therapy plays a decisive role. It would again perpetuate the traumatic process and pathologize the survivors, if care for the victims of social violence would be assigned to the mental health system alone. Social violence can be overcome only by social acknowledgment. Therefore, commemoration and historical acknowledgment are necessary for cultural healing (see Assmann, 2020, this volume; Rüsen, 2020, this volume).

6.5 Suggested Reading

Hamburger, A. (Ed.) (2018). *Trauma, trust, and memory: Social trauma and reconciliation in psychoanalysis, psychotherapy and cultural memory.* London: Routledge.

Hamburger, A. (2020). The complexity of social trauma diagnosis and intervention. In A. Hamburger, C. Hancheva & V. Volkan (Eds.), *Social trauma. An Interdisciplinary Textbook* (pp. 55–68). New York: Springer.

Laub, D., & Hamburger, A. (Eds.) (2017). *Psychoanalysis and holocaust testimony: Unwanted memories of social trauma.* London: Routledge.

References

APA [American Psychiatric Association]. (1952). *Diagnostic and statistical manual of mental disorders I.* Washington, DC: American Psychiatric Association.

APA [American Psychiatric Association]. (1968). *Diagnostic and statistical manual of mental disorders II.* Washington, DC: American Psychiatric Association.

APA [American Psychiatric Association]. (1980). *Diagnostic and statistical manual of mental disorders III.* Washington, DC: American Psychiatric Association.

APA [American Psychiatric Association]. (1987). *Diagnostic and statistical manual of mental disorders III R (text revision).* Washington, DC: American Psychiatric Association.

APA [American Psychiatric Association]. (2013). *Diagnostic and statistical manual of mental disorders* (5th ed.). Arlington, VA: American Psychiatric Press.

Assmann, A. (2020). Cultural memory. In A. Hamburger, C. Hancheva & V. Volkan (Eds.), *Social trauma. An Interdisciplinary Textbook* (pp. 25–36). New York: Springer.

Barel, E., Van IJzendoorn, M. H., Sagi-Schwartz, A., & Bakermans-Kranenburg, M. J. (2010). Surviving the holocaust: A meta-analysis of the long-term sequelae of genocide. *Psychological Bulletin, 136*, 677–698.

Barocas, H. A. (1975). Children of purgatory: Reflections on the concentration camp survival syndrome. *International Journal of Social Psychiatry, 21*(2), 87–92.

Becker, D. (1995). The deficiency of the concept of posttraumatic stress disorder when dealing with victims of human rights violations. In R. J. Kleber, C. R. Figley, & B. P. R. Berthold (Eds.), *Beyond trauma: Cultural and societal dynamics* (pp. 99–131). New York: Plenum Press.

Bettelheim, B. (1943). Individual of and mass behavior in extreme situations. *Journal of Abnormal Social Psychology, 38*, 417–452.

Bettelheim, B. (1947). Concentration camps, German. In W. Yust (Ed.), *10 eventful years: Volume two (2, II): Concentration camps to ley* (pp. 1–16). Chicago, iL: Encyclopedia Britannica.

Blum, H. P. (2007). Holocaust trauma reconstructed: Individual, familial, and social trauma. *Psychoanalytic Psychology, 24*(1), 63.

Bohleber, W. (2000). The development of trauma theory in psychoanalysis. In S. Varvin & T. Stainer Popovic (Eds.), *Upheaval: Psychoanalytic perspectives on trauma* (pp. 207–234). Belgrade: International Aid Network.

Bohleber, W. (2017). Treatment, trauma, and catastrophic reality: A double understanding of the "too much" experience and its implications for treatment. In D. Laub & A. Hamburger (Eds.), *Psychoanalysis and holocaust testimony: Unwanted memories of social trauma* (pp. 19–31). London: Routledge.

Braga, L. L., Mello, M. F., & Fiks, J. P. (2012). Transgenerational transmission of trauma and resilience: A qualitative study with Brazilian offspring of holocaust survivors. *BMC Psychiatry, 12*(1), 134.

Breuer, J., & Freud, S. (1893). On the psychical mechanism of hysterical phenomena. *The standard edition of the complete psychological works of Sigmund Freud, Volume II (1893–1895): Studies on Hysteria* (pp. 1–17).

Burlingham, D., & Freud, A. (1942). *Young children in war time, in a residential war nursery.* London: Allen and Unwin.

Chodoff, P. (1963). Late effects of the concentration camp syndrome. *Archives of General Psychiatry, 8*(4), 323–333.

De Wind, E. (1968). The confrontation with death. *The International Journal of Psychoanalysis, 49*, 302–305.

Ehrenreich, J. H. (2003). Understanding PTSD: forgetting "trauma". *Analyses of Social Issues and Public Policy, 3*(1), 15–28.

Eissler, K. R. (1967). Perverted psychiatry? *American Journal of Psychiatry, 123*, 1352–1358.

Eitinger, L. (1961). Pathology of the concentration camp syndrome: Preliminary report. *Archives of General Psychiatry, 5*(4), 371–379.

Eitinger, L. (1964). *Concentration camp survivors in Norway and Israel.* London, England: Allen & Unwin.

Ferenczi, S. (1949 [1933]). Confusion of the tongues between the adults and the child—(The language of tenderness and of passion). *The International Journal of Psychoanalysis, 30*, 225–230.

Ferenczi, S., Abraham, K., Simmel, E., & Jones, E. (1921). *Psycho-analysis and the war neuroses. With an introduction by Prof. Sigmund Freud.* London: The International Psycho-Analytical Press.

Ferren, P. M. (1999). Comparing perceived self-efficacy among adolescent Bosnian and Croatian refugees with and without posttraumatic stress disorder. *Journal of Traumatic Stress, 12*, 405–420.

Fischer-Homberger, E. (1999). Zur Medizingeschichte des traumas [toward a medical history of trauma]. *Gesnerus, 56*, 260–294.
Fleck, C., & Müller, A. (1997). Bruno Bettelheim and the concentration camps. *Journal of the History of the Behavioral Sciences, 33*(1), 1–37. https://nbn-resolving.org/urn:nbn:de:0168-ssoar-235016
Freud, S. (1905). Fragment of an analysis of a case of hysteria. *The standard edition of the complete psychological works of Sigmund Freud, Volume VII (1901–1905): A case of hysteria, three essays on sexuality and other works* (pp. 1–122). London: The Hogarth Press.
Freud, S. (1955). Memorandum on the electrical treatment of war neurotics. *The standard edition of the complete psychological works of Sigmund Freud, Volume XVII (1917–1919): An infantile neurosis and other works, Bd. 17* (pp. 211–215). London: The Hogarth Press.
Gerson, S. (2019). The enduring psychological legacies of genocidal trauma: Commentary on 'The intergenerational transmission of holocaust trauma: A psychoanalytic theory revisited'. *Psychoanal Quart, 88*(3), 501–511.
Gomolin, R. P. (2019). The intergenerational transmission of holocaust trauma: A psychoanalytic theory revisited. *The Psychoanalytic Quarterly, 88*(3), 461–500.
Good, M. I. (Ed.). (2005). *The seduction theory in its second century: Trauma, fantasy, and reality today*. Madison, CT: International Universities Press.
Grand, S. (2000). *The reproduction of evil: A clinical and cultural perspective*. Hillsdale, NJ: Analytic Press.
Grand, S., & Salberg, J. (2020). Trans-Generational trauma transmission. In A. Hamburger, C. Hancheva & V. Volkan (Eds.), *Social trauma. An Interdisciplinary Textbook* (pp. 209–218). New York: Springer.
Grünberg, K. (2013). Scenic memory of the Shoah: "The adventuresome life of Alfred Silbermann". *The American Journal of Psychoanalysis, 73*, 30–42.
Grünberg, K., & Markert, F. (2012). A psychoanalytic grave walk—Scenic memory of the Shoah. On the transgenerational transmission of extreme trauma in Germany. *The American Journal of Psychoanalysis, 72*(3), 207–222.
Hamburger, A. (1998). Narrativ und Gedächtnis [narrative and memory]. In M. Koukkou, M. Leuzinger-Bohleber, & W. Mertens (Eds.), *Erinnerung von Wirklichkeiten. Psychoanalyse und Neurowissenschaften im Dialog. Bd. 1: Bestandsaufnahme [memory of realities. Psychoanalysis and neuroscience in dialogue. Vol. 1: Current Aproaches]* (pp. 223–286). Stuttgart: Verlag Internationale Psychoanalyse.
Hamburger, A. (2017a). Genocidal trauma. Individual and social consequences of the assault on the mental and physical life of a group. In D. Laub & A. Hamburger (Eds.), *Psychoanalysis and holocaust testimony: Unwanted memories of social trauma* (pp. 66–91). London: Routledge.
Hamburger, A. (2017b). Scenic narrative microanalysis. Controlled psychoanalytic assessment of session videos or transcripts as a transparent qualitative research instrument. In D. Laub & A. Hamburger (Eds.), *Psychoanalysis and holocaust testimony: Unwanted memories of social trauma* (pp. 166–182). London: Routledge.
Hamburger, A. (2018a). Ferenczi on war neuroses. In A. Dimitrijevic, G. Casullo, & J. Frankel (Eds.), *Ferenczi's influence on contemporary psychoanalytic traditions* (pp. 65–71). Milton Park, NY: Routledge.
Hamburger, A. (2018b). New thoughts on genocidal trauma. In A. Hamburger (Ed.), *Trauma, trust, and memory: Social trauma and reconciliation in psychoanalysis, psychotherapy and cultural memory* (pp. 13–22). London, NY: Routledge.
Hamburger, A. (2020). Social trauma as a Bridging Concept. In A. Hamburger, C. Hancheva & V. Volkan (Eds.), *Social trauma. An Interdisciplinary Textbook* (pp. 3–16). New York: Springer.
Herman, J. L. (1992). *Trauma and recovery: The aftermath of violence—From domestic abuse to political terror*. New York, NY: Basic Books.
Hernández, P. (2002). Trauma in war and political persecution: Expanding the concept. *American Journal of Orthopsychiatry, 72*(1), 16–25.
Hillebrandt, R. (2004). *Das Trauma in der Psychoanalyse. Eine psychologische und politische Kritik an der psychoanalytischen Traumatheorie [Trauma in psychoanalysis. A psychological and political critique of the psychoanalytic theory of trauma]*. Gießen: Psychosozial.

Kaplan, S. (2008). *Children in genocide: Extreme traumatization and affect regulation*. London: International Psychoanalysis Library and Karnac Books.

Kellermann, N. P. (2001). Transmission of holocaust trauma-an integrative view. *Psychiatry: Interpersonal and Biological Processes, 64*(3), 256–267.

Kessler, R. C., Aguilar-Gaxiola, S., Alonso, J., Benjet, C., Bromet, E. J., Cardoso, G., … Koenen, K. C. (2017). Trauma and PTSD in the WHO world mental health surveys. *European Journal of Psychotraumatology, 8*(5), 1353383. https://doi.org/10.1080/20008198.2017.1353383

Kira, I. A. (2001). Taxonomy of trauma and trauma assessment. *Traumatology, 7*(2), 73–86.

Kira, I. A., Templin, T., Lewandowski, L., & Shuwiekh, H. (2018). A conceptual model and measurement of identity-based, existential annihilation anxieties (EAA). *Psychology, 9*(6), 1306.

Kirmayer, L. J., Kienzler, H., Afana, A. H., & Pedersen, D. (2010). Trauma and disasters in social and cultural context. In C. Morgan, D. Bhugra, & D. (Eds.), *Principles of social psychiatry2* (pp. 155–177). Oxford: Wiley-Blackwell.

Klein, H. (1968). Problems in the psychotherapeutic treatment of Israeli survivors of the holocaust. In H. Krystal (Ed.), *Massive psychic trauma* (pp. 233–248). NY: International University Press.

Klein, H., Zellermayer, J., & Shanan, J. (1963). Former concentration camp inmates on a psychiatric ward: Observations. *Archives of General Psychiatry, 8*(4), 334–342.

Kogan, I. (2018 [2007]). *Escape from selfhood: Breaking boundaries and craving for oneness*. London: Routledge.

Krell, R. (1979). *Medical and psychological effects of concentration camps on holocaust survivors*. New York: Routledge.

Krystal, H. (Ed.). (1968). *Massive psychic trauma*. New York: International Universities Press.

Krystal, H., & Niederland, W. G. (Eds.). (1971). *Psychic traumatization. Aftereffects in individuals and communities*. Boston: Little Brown.

Kucmin, T., Kucmin, A., Nogalski, A., Sojczuk, S., & Jojczuk, M. (2016). History of trauma and posttraumatic disorders in literature. *Psychiatria Polska, 50*(1), 269–281.

Laub, D. (1992). Bearing witness or the vicissitudes of listening. In S. Felman & D. Laub (Eds.), *Testimony: Crises of witnessing in literature, psychoanalysis and history* (pp. 57–74). New York: Routledge.

Laub, D. (2005a). Traumatic shutdown of narrative and symbolization: A death instinct derivative? *Contemporary Psychoanalysis, 41*(2), 307–326.

Laub, D. (2005b). From speechlessness to narrative: The cases of holocaust historians and of psychiatrically hospitalized survivors. *Literature and Medicine, 24*, 253–265.

Laub, D. (2016). Re-establishing the internal "thou" in testimony of trauma. In S. Knopp, S. Schulze, & A. Eusterschulte (Eds.), *Videographierte Zeugenschaft: Geisteswissenschaften im Dialog mit dem Zeugen [Videographed testimony: Humanities in dialogue with the witness]*. Velbrück Wissenschaft: Weilerswist.

Laub, D., & Auerhahn, N. C. (1989). Failed empathy: A central theme in the survivor's holocaust experience. *Psychoanalytic Psychology, 6*, 377–400.

Laub, D., & Auerhahn, N. C. (1993). Knowing and not knowing massive psychic trauma: Forms of traumatic memory. *The International Journal of Psychoanalysis, 74*, 287–302.

Laub, D., & Hamburger, A. (Eds.) (2017). *Psychoanalysis and holocaust testimony: Unwanted memories of social trauma*. London: Routledge.

Lellau, D. P. J. (2005, June). Zum problem des Traumabegriffes in der psychoanalyse [problems of the concept of trauma in psychoanalysis]. *Forum der Psychoanalyse, 21*(2), 143–155.

Lomranz, J. (1995). Endurance and living: Long-term effects of the holocaust. In S. E. Hobfoll & M. W. de Vries (Eds.), *Extreme stress and communities: Impact and intervention* (pp. 325–352). Dordrecht, the Netherlands: Kluwer.

Mitscherlich, A., & Mitscherlich, M. (1967). *The inability to mourn. Principles of collective behavior*. New York: Grove Press.

Moghimi, Y. (2012). Anthropological discourses on the globalization of posttraumatic stress disorder (PTSD) in post-conflict societies. *Journal of Psychiatric Practice®, 18*(1), 29–37.

Niederland, W. G. (1968). The problem of the survivor: The psychiatric evaluations of emotional problems in survivors of Nazi persecution. In H. Krystal (Ed.), *Massive psychic trauma* (pp. 8–22). New York, NY: International University Press.
Ornstein, A. (2003). Survival and recovery: Psychoanalytic reflections. *Progress in Self Psychology, 19*, 85–105.
Prager, E., & Solomon, Z. (1995). Perceptions of world benevolence, meaningfulness and self-worth among elderly Israeli holocaust survivors and non-survivors. *Anxiety, Stress, and Coping, 8*, 265–277. https://doi.org/10.1080/10615809508249378
Prince, R. (2009). The self in pain: The paradox of memory. The paradox of testimony. *American Journal of Psychoanalysis, 69*, 279–290.
Rakoff, V., Sigal, J. J., & Epstein, N. B. (1966). Children and families of concentration camp survivors. *Canada's Mental Health, 14*, 24–26.
Robinson, J. (1970). *Psychoanalysis in a vacuum. Bruno Bettelheim and the holocaust*. New York: Yad Vashem-Yivo Documentary Projects.
Rosenbaum, B., & Varvin, S. (2007). The influence of extreme traumatization on body, mind and social relations. *The International Journal of Psychoanalysis, 88*(6), 1527–1542.
Rousseau, C., Drapeau, A., & Rahimi, S. (2003). The complexity of trauma response: A 4-year follow-up of adolescent Cambodian refugees. *Child Abuse and Neglect, 27*, 1277–1290. https://doi.org/10.1016/j.chiabu.2003.07.001
Rüsen, J. (2020). The wounds of history—About the historical dealing with traumatic experiences. In A. Hamburger, C. Hancheva & V. Volkan (Eds.), *Social trauma. An Interdisciplinary Textbook* (pp. 43–54). New York: Springer.
Sagi-Schwartz, A., van IJzendoorn, M. H., & Bakermans-Kranenburg, M. J. (2008). Does intergenerational transmission of trauma skip a generation? No meta-analytic evidence for tertiary traumatization with third generation of holocaust survivors. *Attachment and Human Development, 10*(2), 105–121. https://doi.org/10.1080/14616730802113661
Sandler, J., Dreher, A. U., Drews, S., Fischer, R., Klüwer, R., Muck, M., Vogel, H. & Will, C. (1987). *Psychisches Trauma. Ein psychoanalytisches Konzept im Theorie-Praxis-Zusammenhang [Psychological trauma. A psychoanalytical concept connecting theory and practice]*. Frankfurt/M.: Sigmund-Freud-Institut.
Scharf, M. (2007). Long-term effects of trauma: Psychosocial functioning of the second and third generation of holocaust survivors. *Development and Psychopathology, 19*, 603–622.
Scott, W. J. (1990). PTSD in DSM-III: A case in the politics of diagnosis and disease. *Social Problems, 37*, 294–310.
Stein, J. Y., Wilmot, D. V., & Solomon, Z. (2016). Does one size fit all? Nosological, clinical, and scientific implications of variations in PTSD criterion A. *Journal of Anxiety Disorders, 43*, 106–117.
Streeck-Fischer, A. (2020). Complex and sequential traumatic stress disorders. In A. Hamburger, C. Hancheva & V. Volkan (Eds.), *Social trauma. An Interdisciplinary Textbook* (pp. 155–162). New York: Springer.
Terr, L. (1991). Childhood traumas: An outline and overview. *American Journal of Psychiatry, 27*, 96–104.
Tuteur, W. (1966). One hundred concentration camp survivors: Twenty years later. *Israel Annals of Psychiatry, 4*, 78–90.
Van der Hart, O., & Horst, R. (1989). The dissociation theory of Pierre Janet. *Journal of Traumatic Stress, 2*(4), 397–412.
van der Kolk, B. A., McFarlane, A. C., & Weisaeth, L. (Eds.). (1996). *Traumatic stress: The effects of overwhelming experience on mind, body, and society*. New York, NY: Guilford.
Van IJzendoorn, M. H., Bakermans-Kranenburg, M. J., & Sagi-Schwartz, A. (2003). Are children of holocaust survivors less well-adapted? No meta-analytic evidence for secondary traumatization. *Journal of Traumatic Stress, 16*, 459–469.
Wangh, W. (1964). National socialism and the genocide of the Jews. *International Journal of Psychoanalysis, 45*, 386–395.

Chapter 7
Psychoanalytic Approaches to Social Trauma

M. Gerard Fromm

7.1 Introduction

In her groundbreaking paper, "Ghosts in the Nursery" (1975), Selma Fraiberg describes vividly a mother who could not hear her baby's cries because, as it turned out, her parents could not hear her childhood cries either, for reasons related to their traumatic history. In the 1970s, the problems of children of Holocaust survivors were also coming to light. Fraiberg's paper and the study of second-generation Holocaust survivors opened a new field of investigation—the transmission of trauma across generations—which has enriched clinical psychoanalysis (Faimberg, 2005; Fromm, 2012; Kogan, 1995; Koh, 2019; Volkan, 2014, 2015) and contributed to the understanding and treatment of traumatic experience. Transmission is one effect of social trauma and the lens through which I will explore its effects on both parties.

The psychoanalytic study of trauma began in 1895, when Freud thought he had discovered the cause of neurotic symptoms in actual child abuse and its repressed memory (Freud, 1895). He shifted this "seduction theory" in subsequent years to the child's developing mind: its immature but powerfully conflicting wishes, fantasies, and emotions (Freud, 1905). But the reality of what actually happened returned to him as he encountered casualties from WWI. Social trauma re-entered and fundamentally broadened his theory (Freud, 1920, 1923).

Others like Ferenczi (1949) and Winnicott (1954) elaborated on developmental trauma in childhood, the former in terms of a parent's chronic empathic failure and the latter highlighting how this failure of attunement leads to annihilation anxiety in the child and a "freezing of the failure situation" (p. 281), in the hope that a human environment might facilitate a resumption of development. Social trauma also

M. G. Fromm (✉)
Erikson Institute of the Austen Riggs Center, Stockbridge, MA, USA

International Dialogue Initiative, Lenox, MA, USA
e-mail: Gerard.Fromm@austenriggs.net

© Springer Nature Switzerland AG 2021

A. Hamburger et al. (eds.), *Social Trauma – An Interdisciplinary Textbook*,
https://doi.org/10.1007/978-3-030-47817-9_7

entered psychoanalytic theory in a way that supported this last line of thought; Anna Freud and Dorothy Burlingham (1943) found that mothers in the London bomb shelters who were able to provide empathic coverage and hope to their children protected them from psychological trauma, despite their dire circumstances. To some degree, trauma is a consequence of aloneness.

7.2 Learning Outcome

Trauma studies have burgeoned in recent years and moved clinical understanding beyond a narrow focus on post-traumatic stress disorder to a broader appreciation of states of extreme arousal, both sudden and sustained, in which adaptive coping mechanisms shut down in favor of massive dissociation (Brenner, 2001; Caruth, 2014; Coates, Rosenthal, & Schecter, 2003; Herman, 1992; Krystal, 1968; Laub, 2018; Niederland, 1968; van der Kolk, McFarlane, & Weisaeth, 1996). In his Introduction to this volume, Andreas Hamburger (2020) follows Freud's trajectory by bridging the gap between trauma in a child's development and the larger context of social trauma.

> One consequence of social trauma is that unbearable, unthinkable experience falls out of social discourse, but often onto and into the next generation, as an impenetrable symptom, an acute affective sensitivity, an encapsulated madness, and sometimes an unconscious mission: for example, to avenge a parent's humiliation or repair a devastating loss. (Fromm, 2012)

7.3 Preferred Model of Explanation: Case Examples

In this chapter, using case examples, I describe a number of features of this clinical work: the intertwining of parental trauma with a child's development; time collapse and speechlessness at the heart of trauma; transmission through actions, images, objects, and names; the special role and authority dilemma a child finds him/herself in; resistances encountered in the context of trauma transmission, including the fear of breakthrough; the process of witnessing within the transference; and the movement from collapsed to generative intermediate space. The chapter concludes by applying this learning to societal conflict.

In the fall of 1940, a 10-year-old British boy and his mother fled their home in London, just in time to escape its being destroyed by German bombing. Later in life, he built a career in the automobile industry, and later still, his daughter attempted suicide in one of his company's cars. When she recovered and after her therapist's vacation, she reported a dream: "There were some ruined buildings. They were partially destroyed by fire. One was a pet shop. There were some guinea pigs in a cage, doing something sexual." The next day, she remembered that the buildings had not been destroyed by fire, but by rain. Her therapist, without knowing the story of her father's childhood, said spontaneously: "There is a kind of rain that brings fire." The patient said "Bombing" and suddenly remembered for the first time a scene from her childhood when she was 10.

Night after night, her father had watched newsreel of the London blitz, as if he was searching for something. His anxious daughter sat next to him and repeatedly asked why he was doing this. He didn't respond. This nightly ritual took place just after the father's mother had died, a woman with whom he was quite close but who seemed to will herself into debilitation and death after her son left home. Her husband had abandoned mother and son before the bombing. The patient was named for this grandmother.

After his mother's death and the phase of searching for his boyhood home, the patient's father entered a long depression that his adoring daughter's liveliness attempted, unsuccessfully, to cure. As she grew into adolescence, this former "pet" of her father felt that she had lost his presence and love completely. She became extremely vulnerable to rejection in love relationships and increasingly convinced that no one could stand the violence, borne of hurt and humiliation, inside her. Following in her namesake's footsteps, she drifted toward suicide in response to the loss of a man she loved.

7.4 Discussion and Implications for the Field of Social Trauma

Life stories are always complex and psychopathology is always multi-determined, especially at what Davoine and Gaudilliere (2004) call the intersection of the Big History and the Little History. This case illustrates how social trauma to one generation—the destruction of a home in war, with its accompanying terror of death and in the context of parental abandonment—falls upon the next generation.

One aspect of that transmission is silence about something urgent and enormously confusing. This patient experienced a fundamental speechlessness from her father, related to his own childhood social trauma. He never spoke about his wartime experience, and his daughter's repeated questions were not answered. But she sensed something, something about the past in the present. Volkan describes this as a "time collapse" (2015, p. 13); Davoine and Gaudilliere describe "time falling into immediacy" (2004, p. 181).

Her father's unspoken, presumably unspeakable experiences were given symbolic form, however. His daughter was passively bombarded with disturbing wartime images and given her grandmother's name. Might these actions on her father's part have been a request that she somehow carry the social trauma for him or with him? Was it meant to liberate her, so that she could discover what the experiences that had all along been affecting her father's behavior meant? Was he simply reliving the past with his daughter or encoding it for the purpose of future discovery, differentiation, and mourning?

A parent's traumatic experiences tend to be interwoven into the fabric of family life and into a child's development, through what Erikson called "minute displays of emotion, minute socioeconomic and cultural panics," and "the subtler methods that…transmit to the human child the outlines of what really counts" (1959, pp. 27–28). But certain children—perhaps because of gender, birth order, physical resemblance, or some other intimate characteristic linking parent and child (note that this patient was 10 at the time of the newsreels, the same age her father was when his home was destroyed)—find themselves in a role that implicates them in a parent's trauma. They feel charged with an energy and a duty and may come to identify with the traumatized parent, living out a special compact in which the parent's needs and the child's desires intertwine in confusing ways. There was certainly an Oedipal dimension to this daughter's relationship with her father and a real danger that her failure to fulfill an impossible mission would lead to suicidal despair.

A person's bringing this kind of experience to psychotherapy represents their seeking a relational venue for an understanding of what they have unconsciously been carrying for a traumatized parent. Meaning opened up through the dream image of buildings ruined by a fire–rain, which led to the recovery of a memory about the patient's and her father's history. Dreaming this dream could be seen as the patient's effort to formulate and take authority for what those wartime images had meant in her family's life. To some degree, the experience of the next generation is "authored" by what had been unspeakable in their parents' histories. This patient may well have been unconsciously "authorized" by her father to bring that trauma into the future. Such transgenerational experience "must come into being as emotional understanding if the (person) is ultimately to take authority for his or her own life as distinct from that of the traumatized parent" (Fromm, 2012, p. 113).

Personal and societal repair is sometimes led by the second and third generations, who face risky decisions. A few years ago, a folksinger named Clare Burson released an album called *Silver and Ash* (2010), which told the story of her grandmother, who had escaped Leipzig in 1938, just before Kristallnacht, and who lost her parents in the Holocaust. Clare wanted to learn whatever she could about these terrible experiences, despite being warned that her grandmother could not speak of it. Later, Clare said that her grandmother had spent "so much time trying not to remember that she successfully blocked the memories" (Jacobs, 2010).

During her college years, Clare decided to study in Germany. Her grandmother was shocked: "Why in the world…?" "She thought I was crazy," Clare said (Jacobs, 2010). They then had a "frank conversation," in which Clare, for the first time, used "incredibly charged words," like "Nazi" (Lunden, 2010). At the end of their talk, her grandmother asked Clare a stunning question: Why she hadn't invited her to go too. Clare said, "I never dreamed you would want to go." Her grandmother's responded: "I will, for you." Clare writes: "The following spring, the memories began to flow… We walked through the market square. She pointed out where her boyfriend Berny had a jewelry shop… the building of her father's business… the building she grew up in" (Jacobs, 2010). "It used to be so green," her grandmother said (Lunden, 2010).

Clare Burson's *Silver and Ash* helped to heal a "rupture…where there was no continuity between my past and my future… It's our duty to hear the stories and incorporate them into our own lives… I'm a grandchild of someone who fled Nazi Germany. I've lived my life feeling the effect of that. And I know I'm not alone" (Jacobs, 2010).

Healing as this inter-generational work can be, the next generation's decision to lead it is felt, sometimes unconsciously, to be enormously risky. These critical moments remind us that the word "decide" has the same root as the words "suicide" and "homicide." Decisions separate; they, in a sense, kill the alternatives. For the London patient, one of those alternatives had been to attempt to cure her father through her love and companionship. Her inevitable failure brought her near death and eventually into treatment and to the different, but also dangerous, path of trying to understand what she was enacting.

A major source of resistance for such patients is the profound fear, even conviction, that, by separating themselves from their unconscious mission—and speaking it to another person is a form of separating from what has been unspeakable—they will destroy the person they love and need. They also are terrified of re-traumatizing their parents: of causing them to re-live unbearable pain and thereby losing them again. Winnicott, addressing his version of time collapse, wrote that the "Fear of Breakdown" (1974) some patients dread has to do with past trauma that is always on a future horizon. To put the trauma into the past, "the patient needs to 'remember'...but it is not possible to remember something that has not yet happened, and this thing of the past has not happened yet because the patient (whose ego was incapacitated by massive dissociation) was not there for it to happen to" (p. 105, my parenthetical addition). The traumatized person's fear of breakdown becomes the next generation's fear of breaking through (Fromm, 2016) to their parents' unbearable history.

This patient played out the transmission of her father's trauma in the transference to her therapist, by allowing herself to react to his vacation with the feelings and images of abandonment formulated in her dream. The psychoanalyst Dori Laub (2018), himself a Holocaust survivor, writes that the treatment of trauma, whether in the first or subsequent generations, involves the communication of "testimony" to a witness "(willing) to be totally present to the survivor, and (to) receive as well as experience what he/she wants to transmit" (p. 102).

The transmission of trauma from one generation to the next could be seen as an ambivalent effort at testimony, potentially dangerous but also essential to the development of the child who has found herself in the role of witness to a parent's social trauma. Psychoanalytically oriented treatment offers that person a new witness, to whom testimony can be brought in its various unconscious forms so that it can be contained, interpreted, and brought into the historical context. The potential space (Winnicott, 1971) that had collapsed between child and parent, because containment of the unbearable was impossible and no Third (Muller, 1996) existed, may become a generative space between patient and therapist, generative of the imagination and strength to make sense of what she has been carrying. When the family's issues are interwoven with social trauma, as Clare Burson so beautifully shows us, the task of the child-now-adult shifts from enacting an unconscious mission to bearing witness, so that the family's deeply personal, indeed tragic, stories are no longer dissociated from the human narrative. This can be a healing process not only for the next generation but for the parent who suffered so profoundly from social trauma.

7.5 Implications for Work with Social Trauma

In practical terms, therapists should consider the nature of the trauma their patients have experienced or might be carrying from preceding generations. This would mean being interested in the life stories, including of parents and grandparents, learning about their social-historical context, developing an "ear" for signifiers of condensed meaning, being curious about names, noticing silent parts of the story, and trusting that one's associations may have potential meaning in the patient's history.

A psychoanalytic lens on trauma is also critical for work at the societal level. Some time ago, a senior diplomat working with the Israel-Palestine negotiating team was asked what happened when people on either side talked about their fears. The diplomat was surprised. "We don't speak of fear," he said, adding, on reflection, that perhaps they should, but that the negotiating group did not know how to. A thousand miles away, a group of Northern Ireland leaders were meeting to discuss a flare-up of violence in Belfast. When the subject of shame came up, one member became enraged. "How dare you speak about shame? There is so much shame here that, if we let ourselves feel it, we would all commit suicide."

Societal conflict is the result of social trauma and leads to social trauma. It's a vicious circle reflecting deeply disturbed relationships between communities of people (Alderdice, 2010). Central to this disturbance are intense feelings, like fear and shame, fantasies about one's own group and the other, and a set of historical events that have shaped large group identity (Volkan, 2013) for both. Because disturbed relationships are its field of study, psychoanalysis can contribute to an understanding of social trauma by generating hypotheses about these disturbances and shaping interventions (Covington, 2016; Friedman, 2019; Rifkind, 2019; Scholz, 2005). In 2007, the International Dialogue Initiative was created by Professor Vamik Volkan for this purpose.

7.6 Suggested Readings and Further Information on Work with Social Trauma

Fromm, M. G. (2012). *Lost in transmission: Studies of trauma across generations*. London: Karnac.

Volkan, V. (2013). *Enemies on the couch: A psychopolitical journey through war and peace*. Durham, NC: Pitchstone Publishing.

Volkan, V. (2014). *Animal killer*. London: Karnac.

Volkan, V. (2015). *A nazi legacy.* London: Karnac.
www.internationaldialogueinitiative.com
www.hmc.ox.ac.uk/centre-for-resolution-of-intractable-conflict/
www.oxfordprocess.com/

References

Alderdice, J. (2010). Off the couch and round the conference table. In A. Lemma & M. Patrick (Eds.), *Off the couch: Contemporary psychoanalytic applications* (pp. 1–15). London: Routledge.

Brenner, I. (2001). *Dissociation of trauma: Theory, phenomenology, and technique*. Madison, CT: International Universities Press.

Burson, C. (2010). *Silver and ash* [CD, Album]. Nashville, TN: Rounder Records.

Caruth, C. (Ed.). (2014). *Listening to trauma: Conversations with leaders in the theory and treatment of catastrophic experience*. Baltimore: Johns Hopkins University Press.

Coates, S., Rosenthal, J., & Schecter, D. (Eds.). (2003). *September 11: Trauma and human bonds*. Hillsdale, NJ: The Analytic Press.

Covington, C. (2016). *Everyday evils*. London: Routledge.

Davoine, F., & Gaudilliere, J.-M. (2004). *History beyond trauma*. New York: Other Press.

Erikson, E. (1959). Identity and the life cycle: Selected papers. *Psychological Issues, 1*, 1–171.

Faimberg, H. (2005). *The telescoping of generations*. New York: Routledge.

Ferenczi, S. (1949). Confusion of tongues between the adults and the child. *International Journal of Psycho-Analysis, 30*, 225–230.

Fraiberg, S., Adelson, E., & Shapiro, V. (1975). Ghosts in the nursery. *Journal of the American Academy of Child Psychiatry, 14*, 387–421.

Freud, A., & Burlingham, D. (1943). *Children in war*. New York: Medical War Books.

Freud, S. (1895). *Studies in hysteria. S. E. 2*. London: Hogarth.

Freud, S. (1905). *Three essays on the theory of sexuality. S. E. 7*. London: Hogarth.

Freud, S. (1920). *Beyond the pleasure principle. S. E. 18*. London: Hogarth.

Freud, S. (1923). *The Ego and the Id. S. E. 19*. London: Hogarth.

Friedman, R. (2019). *Beyond the soldier's matrix*. London: Routledge.

Fromm, M. G. (2012). *Lost in transmission: Studies of trauma across generations*. London: Karnac.

Fromm, M. G. (2016). Fear of breakthrough. *Modern Psychoanalysis, 41*(1), 11–25.

Hamburger, A. (2020). The complexity of social trauma diagnosis and intervention. In A. Hamburger, C. Hancheva & V. Volkan (Eds.), *Social trauma. An Interdisciplinary Textbook* (pp. 55–68). New York: Springer.

Herman, J. (1992). *Trauma and recovery: The aftermath of violence—From domestic abuse to political terror*. New York: Basic Books.

Jacobs, J. (2010, September 16). Silver and ash: Escape from Germany inspires Granddaughter's folk album [Interview with Clare Burson]. *The [Pittsburgh] Jewish Chronicle, 53*(20), 14. Retrieved from https://jewishchronicle.timesofisrael.com/silver-and-ash/

Kogan, I. (1995). *The cry of mute children: A psychoanalytic perspective of the second generation of the holocaust*. London: Free Association Books.

Koh, E. (2019). Cultural work in addressing conflicts and violence in traumatized communities. *New England Journal of Public Policy, 31*(1), Art. 3.

Krystal, H. (Ed.). (1968). *Massive psychic trauma*. New York: International Universities Press.

Laub, D. (2018). Testimony as part of the therapeutic process in psychoanalysis. In E. J. Schreiber (Ed.), *Healing trauma: The power of listening* (pp. 97–108). New York: International Psychoanalytic Books.

Lunden, J. (2010). *Clare Burson: Songs of a haunted past*. NPR Interview with Clare Burson, October 15, 2010. Retrieved from https://www.npr.org/templates/story/story.php?storyId=130568495&t=1579373424256

Muller, J. (1996). *Beyond the psychoanalytic dyad: Developmental semiotics in Freud, Peirce, and Lacan*. New York: Routledge.

Niederland, W. G. (1968). Clinical observations on the "survivor syndrome". *International Journal of Psycho-Analysis, 49*, 313–315.

Rifkind, G. (2019). Preparing the psychological space for peacemaking. *New England Journal of Public Policy, 31*(1), Art. 7.

Scholz, R. (2005). Culture, trauma and identity. *Dynamic Psychiatry, 38*, 377–385.

van der Kolk, B., McFarlane, A., & Weisaeth, L. (1996). *Traumatic stress: The effects of overwhelming experience on mind, body and society*. New York: Guilford Press.

Volkan, V. (2013). *Enemies on the couch: A Psychopolitical journey through war and peace*. Durham, NC: Pitchstone Publishing.

Volkan, V. (2014). *Animal Killer*. London: Karnac.

Volkan, V. (2015). *A Nazi Legacy*. London: Karnac.

Winnicott, D. W. (1958). Metapsychological and clinical aspects of regression within the psycho-analytical set-up. In D. W. Winnicott (Ed.), *Through paediatrics to psycho-analysis* (pp. 278–294). New York: Basic Books. (Original work published 1954).

Winnicott, D. W. (1971). *Playing and reality*. New York: Basic Books.

Winnicott, D. W. (1974). Fear of breakdown. *International Review of Psycho-Analysis, 1*, 103–107.

Chapter 8
Psychiatric Approaches to Social Trauma: From Normal Response to Psychopathology and Psychobiological Conceptions

Gamze Özçürümez Bilgili

8.1 Introduction

Awareness of the role of psychological trauma as a contributory factor in psychiatric disturbances has off and on been a subject of serious study since the second half of the nineteenth century. But it especially became an object of investigation in the twentieth century, when people were exposed to and suffered from social trauma, such as multiple catastrophes and extreme experiences (world wars, genocides, forced migration, political oppression, etc.). The concept of social trauma offers a broad acknowledgment of how the external world can dramatically impinge on a given population's ability to develop freely, promoting instead traumatic deformation (Volkan, 2020, this volume). As van der Kolk, McFarlane, and Weisaeth (2007, p. 25) emphasize, one core function of human societies is to provide their members with traditions, institutions, and value systems that can protect them against becoming overwhelmed by stressful experiences. Therefore, whenever society and its institutions fail to act as a container for individuals and groups, this generates a trauma, social trauma. In the past four decades, there has been considerable increase in research on the mental health effects of social trauma. But it is imperative to keep in mind that numerous other concerns have been identified among survivors as more urgent than the symptoms of trauma. Such concerns include family conflict, sadness and isolation resulting from the loss of social networks (Langer, 2020, this volume), spouse abuse (Özçürümez, 2020, this volume), distress related to the experience of poverty and the inability to provide for one's family (Eltayeb, 2020, this volume), sadness due to separation from loved ones, grief associated with the death or disappearance of family members, and distress regarding the lack of opportunity to

G. Özçürümez Bilgili (✉)
Faculty of Medicine, Department of Psychiatry, Baskent University, Ankara, Turkey

International Psychoanalytic University, Berlin, Germany

© Springer Nature Switzerland AG 2021

A. Hamburger et al. (eds.), *Social Trauma – An Interdisciplinary Textbook*,
https://doi.org/10.1007/978-3-030-47817-9_8

engage in culturally important rituals of bereavement (Miller, Worthington, Muzurovic, Tipping, & Goldman, 2002).

8.2 Learning Outcome Related to Social Trauma

As a psychiatrist, I would like to acknowledge the fact that the psychiatric profession has had a troubled relationship with the idea that the reality in the external world can profoundly and permanently alter people's psychology and biology: "Psychiatry has periodically suffered from marked amnesias, in which well-established knowledge was abruptly forgotten and the psychological impact of overwhelming experiences was ascribed to constitutional or intrapsychic factors alone" (van der Kolk et al., 2007, p. xii). Consequently, from the earliest involvement of psychiatry with traumatized patients, there have been vehement arguments: Is the etiology of these patients' complaints biological or psychological? Is trauma the event itself or its subjective interpretation? Does the trauma itself cause the disorder, or do preexisting vulnerabilities? I prefer not to dwell in such arguments but instead focus first on a normal response to trauma and then to the possible psychiatric outcomes of social trauma and its psychobiological background.

8.2.1 Description of a Normal Response to Trauma

Ever since people's responses to overwhelming experiences were first systematically explored by psychiatry, it has been noted that the psychological effects of trauma are expressed as changes in the biological stress response (van der Kolk, 2014, pp. 74–76). The resultant emotional, cognitive, physical, and behavioral reactions are summarized in Table 8.1:

Forster (1992) described these reactions in three phases: response, adaptation, and recovery. The initial phase of outcry and alarm usually lasts only minutes. A normal reaction shown by perhaps a quarter of victims is to show little response. However, the majority do what needs to be done while they, nevertheless, experience some degree of intermittent anxiety, fear, anger, and withdrawal. These reactions need not be indicative of illness or abnormality. Moving on to the next phase may be delayed if there is a need to concentrate on survival or repair above all else, especially in the case of social trauma. The adaptation phase is typified by alternating states of denial and intrusion. It seems likely that the denial and avoidance symptoms which predominate later are a response to, or a means of coping with, these intrusive symptoms. There may be a decrease in emotional contact, avoidance of others, and a reluctance to talk about what has happened. In this latter part of the normal adaptation phase, there is an increase in vague or ill-defined physical symptoms, with headaches, fatigue, muscle aches, and gastrointestinal upsets. The course of the normal response is predictable only in the broadest terms. It is affected in

Table 8.1 Trauma reactions

Emotional	Cognitive	Physical	Behavioral
• Shock • Fear • Sadness • Anger • Helplessness • Guilt • Shame • Hopelessness • Anxiety • Regret • Doubt • Insecurity • Inadequacy • Loneliness • Numbness • Emptiness	• Denial • Attention/concentration difficulties • Vivid and disturbing dreams • Vivid and disturbing images • Reliving • Dissociation • Depersonalization • Distorted beliefs/thoughts	• Headaches • Chest pain • Nausea • Overreaction to sudden stimuli • Changes in appetite • Fatigue • Difficulty breathing • Changes in sleep • Trembling • Hyperventilation	• Sudden and extreme reactions • Withdrawal • Avoidance • Indifference • Increased risk-taking • Alcohol-substance abuse • Automated movement • Too much or no crying/laughing

populations and individuals by the nature of the trauma, its duration, and its meaning and by the individual's personality, experience, support, and personal role in the society and the family. It may differ in duration, intensity, and specific symptom constellation. Normal symptomatology may continue, though decreasing, for several months after the event, without being followed by chronic symptomatology or significant dysfunction.

8.2.2 Psychopathologies

Although the majority of individuals cope well in the face of a disaster, a substantial proportion experience some psychological impairment, and a smaller proportion will go on to develop mental disorders (Goldmann & Galea, 2014). But it is not easy to classify social trauma from a clinical point of view (Hamburger, 2020, this volume). Those who do develop a significant mental disorder, which follows a social traumatic event and which is postulated to have been caused or precipitated by it, suffer from trauma- and stressor-related disorders such as acute stress disorder (ASD) and posttraumatic stress disorder (PTSD); anxiety disorders such as generalized anxiety disorder (GAD) and panic disorder (PD); affective disorders, most prevalently major depressive disorder (MDD) and prolonged grief disorder (PGD); substance use disorders (SUD); and somatic symptoms.

In the fifth edition of the American Psychiatric Association's (APA) *Diagnostic and Statistical Manual* (DSM-5), PTSD is a mental illness that can follow exposure to a traumatic event and is characterized by reexperiencing of the event through nightmares and/or flashbacks, avoidance of stimuli reminiscent of the event, and numbing of emotional responses, as well as symptoms of hyperarousal (2013). In incidents like terrorist attacks, a number of factors were related to the development of PTSD, including female gender, being single, having a low educational status, being present at the time of the attack, witnessing the blast, being injured, not fully recovering from the injury, grieving due to the death of close friend or family, experiencing economic difficulties after the attack, and being unemployed due to the injury (Glad, Jensen, Hafstad, & Dyb, 2016). Beyond all these factors, Eşsizoglu, Altınöz, Sonkurt, Kaya, and Köşger (2017) reported a striking finding: the negative impact of perceived societal attitudes toward victims following a terrorist attack was associated with the greater possibility of PTSD. Their finding coincides with the notion that societies and institutions can protect individuals against becoming overwhelmed by such stressful experiences.

Depression is, after PTSD, the second most commonly studied mental health condition in social trauma research; however, owing to its large burden in the general population, it may be the most prevalent posttraumatic illness. Studies report a range of MDD prevalence estimates after social trauma because prevalence estimates depend on factors such as MDD prevalence in the study population prior to the trauma, symptom measurement, sampling design, degree of disaster exposure, and post-disaster social support (Goldmann & Galea, 2014).

Studies have reported elevated prevalence of GAD among those affected by a disaster, although it is less commonly studied than PTSD and MDD (Goldmann & Galea, 2014). Death anxiety, PD, and phobias have also been reported among disaster victims, although few studies have focused on these conditions.

Substance use disorders are characterized by problematic alcohol or drug use that results in difficulty fulfilling obligations in work, home life, or school, legal issues, difficulties in social relationships, involvement in dangerous situations, increased tolerance, symptoms of withdrawal, and unsuccessful efforts to quit (APA, 2013). They have been less frequently studied after disasters than has PTSD or MDD. Some studies observed increases in the use of alcohol, drugs, and cigarettes after a disaster, and some evidence shows that disaster victims use substances, particularly alcohol, as a coping strategy. A recent review of the literature argues that the prevalence of substance use disorders does not increase substantially after a disaster and that problematic use is found primarily among those with prior substance use problems or those who developed other psychopathologies in response to the disaster (Goldmann & Galea, 2014).

Somatic symptoms also manifest in the aftermath of disasters. When people are chronically stressed, a constant muscle tension ultimately leads to spasms, back pain, migraine headaches, fibromyalgia, and other forms of chronic pain. The prevalence of these symptoms varies through studies, from 3% to 78% in one review. Although physical symptoms generally subside over time, some persist for years following the disaster (Goldmann & Galea, 2014).

8.3 Preferred Model of Explanation: Psychobiology

When Charcot first described traumatic memories over a century ago, he called them "parasites of the mind": "an idea, a coherent group of associated ideas settle themselves in the mind in the fashions of parasites, remaining isolated from the rest of the mind..." (Charcot, 1885, cited in Ellenberger, 1970, p. 149). In line with Charcot's definition, Janet (1889) postulated that intense emotional reactions make events traumatic by interfering with the integration of the experience into existing memory schemes (Koso-Drljević & Husremović, 2020, this volume; Hancheva, 2020, this volume). Janet coined the term "dissociation" to describe the splitting off and isolation of memory imprints that he saw in his patients. Intense emotions, Janet thought, cause memories of particular events to be dissociated from consciousness and to be stored, instead, as visceral sensations (anxiety and panic), or as visual images (nightmares and flashbacks). He noted that victims had trouble learning from experience: unable to put the trauma behind them, their energies were absorbed by keeping their emotions under control at the expense of paying attention to current exigencies. They became fixated upon the past, in some cases by being obsessed with the trauma, but more often by behaving and feeling like they were traumatized over and over again without being able to locate the origins of these feelings (van der Kolk & van der Hart, 1989).

Freud (1920/1955a) also considered the tendency to stay fixated on the trauma: "after severe ... accidents involving a risk to life, ...dreams ... have the characteristic of repeatedly bringing the patient back into the situation of his accident, a situation from which he wakes up in another fright. ...The patient is ... fixated to his trauma" (pp. 6–7). He initially defined trauma in economic terms, as being bombarded by stimuli, following the collapse of the "protective shield," a hypothetical structure which foreshadowed the role played by the ego in the structural model (Freud, 1920/a). Later, in *Inhibitions, Symptoms and Anxiety* (Freud, 1926/b), Freud connected the psycho-economic view of trauma with his theory of anxiety. The excessive quantity of excitation in the traumatic situation gives rise to a massive anxiety. Here, the trauma is always an *infantile* traumatic situation, which not only involves the subject and a breaking through of his barrier against stimuli but also a life situation, "helplessness" because the physical unpleasure (wetness, hunger, sleepiness) becomes psychic distress the moment the (m)other fails to turn up (Freud, 1926/b):

> Anxiety is not newly created in repression; it is reproduced as an affective state in accordance with an already existing mnemic image. If we go further and enquire into the origin of that anxiety—and of affects in general—we shall be leaving the realm of pure psychology and entering the borderland of physiology. Affective states have become incorporated in the mind as precipitates of primaeval traumatic experiences, and when a similar situation occurs they are revived like mnemic symbols... (p. 93)

Freud's definition of this automatic or traumatic anxiety (Freud, 1926/b, pp. 136–148) is of a chiefly somatic nature and brings Damasio's somatic marker hypothesis (SMH) to mind. According to Damasio (1994), somatic markers are emotional reactions with a strong somatic component that support decision making, including rational decision making. These reactions are based upon the individual's previous experiences with similar situations. Clarifying the relationship between SMH and trauma, Damasio et al. (2000) reported that reliving a strong negative emotion causes significant changes in the brain areas that receive nerve signals from the muscles, gut, and skin and are crucial for regulating basic bodily functions:

> All emotions engaged structures related to the representation and/or regulation of organism state, for example, the insular cortex, secondary somatosensory cortex, cingulate cortex, and nuclei in brainstem tegmentum and hypothalamus. These regions share a major feature in that they are all direct and indirect recipients of signals from the internal milieu, viscera and musculoskeletal frame. (p. 1051)

Their neuroimaging findings showed that "recalling an emotional event from the past causes us to actually reexperience the visceral sensations felt during the original event" (van der Kolk, 2014, p. 95). The author, who coined the illustrious phrase "the body keeps the score," interprets these results as the "elementary self system in the brain stem and limbic system being massively activated when people are faced with the threat of annihilation, which results in an overwhelming sense of fear and terror accompanied by intense physiological arousal" (ib.). The memory of trauma is encoded in the viscera, in heartbreaking and gut-wrenching emotions, and in autoimmune disorders and skeletal/muscular problems. Hence, mind and body are constantly aroused, as if they are in imminent danger. This in turn can trigger desperate attempts to shut those feelings down by freezing and dissociation.

In line with the above explanations, when Kardiner (1941) first defined what is now called PTSD, he called it a physioneurosis in which patients developed "an enduring vigilance for and sensitivity to environmental threat" (pp. 193–198). Even though the trauma is a thing of the past, the emotional brain keeps generating sensations that make the sufferer feel scared and helpless because trauma disrupts and reorganizes homeostatic controls (Hopper, Spinazzola, Simpson, & van der Kolk, 2006).

8.4 Practical Implications in the Field of Social Trauma

Clinical encounters with people who are affected by social trauma have their own special characteristics, sensitivities, and difficulties. While clinical theories are constructed in order to understand the individual's psyche, there might be several difficulties for the clinicians when contemplating expressions and practices for "pluralities" who were exposed to socially traumatic situations and also when detecting direct and indirect interactions in an individual context at the communal level. Frequently, the effects and scope of a social trauma can exceed the limits of an absolute psychopathological and descriptive evaluation, and clinical approaches that are stuck at this level can create the feelings of being misunderstood, not being able to be held and contained properly in the social trauma victims.

Instead of thinking of social trauma as based on a psychopathological view and language that is related only to the traumatic event, it would be meaningful to create a psychiatric encounter space that conceptualizes the traumatic event as an *effect, being affected*, and a *multidimensional psycho/social meeting*, which is customized for individuals, and offers interpretations and associations regarding the referral.

Also, it should not be forgotten that the social trauma conditions, which are influenced by the external reality that is both dominant and distractive, are not only affecting the patients but they are laying siege to the clinical space. It is imperative to remember that clinicians frequently share and become a part (even a victim) of these traumatic conditions and impacts. Without a doubt, this situation and the unconscious fantasies and defenses it creates might prevent an in-depth clinical work or even a proper encounter to be designed. In order to construct a *good enough* space, analyzing the direct and indirect effects that contaminate the clinical sphere and the clinician through the *socialization* processes of the social trauma should be a priority.

8.5 Suggested Readings and Further Information

Ursano, R. J., McCaughey, B. G., Fullerton, C. S., &Raphael, B. (1995). *Individual and community responses to trauma and disaster: The structure of human chaos*. Cambridge: Cambridge University Press.

Ursano, R. J., & Norwood, A. E. (2008). *Trauma and disaster responses and management*. Arlington, VA: American Psychiatric Publishing.

Acknowledgments I would like to thank to Dr. İlker Özyıldırım (Istanbul Psychoanalytical Association), psychiatrist and psychoanalyst, for his extraordinary effort in implementing psychoanalytical treatment for survivors of social violence. His work which reminds of Nâzım Hikmet Ran's verse is not only inspirational but also encouraging:

To live! Like a tree, alone and free
Like a forest in brotherhood

References

American Psychiatric Association. (2013). *Diagnostic and statistical manual of mental disorders* (5th ed.). Arlington, VA: Author.

Damasio, A. R. (1994). *Descartes' error: Emotion, reason, and the human brain*. New York: Grosset/Putnam.

Damasio, A. R., Grabowski, T. J., Bechara, A., Damasio, H., Ponto, L. B., Parvizi, J., & Hichwa, R. D. (2000). Subcortical and cortical brain activity during the feeling of self-generated emotions. *Nature Neuroscience, 3*(10), 1049–1056.

Ellenberger, H. (1970). *The discovery of the unconscious: The history and evolution of dynamic psychiatry*. New York: Basic Books.

Eltayeb, S. (2020). Understanding social trauma in low-resource settings. In A. Hamburger, C. Hancheva & V. Volkan (Eds.), *Social trauma. An Interdisciplinary Textbook* (pp. 243–252). New York: Springer.

Eşsizoglu, A., Altınöz, A. E., Sonkurt, H. O., Kaya, M. C., & Köşger, F. (2017). The risk factors of possible PTSD in individuals exposed to a suicide attack in Turkey. *Psychiatry Research, 253*, 274–280.

Forster, P. (1992). Nature and treatment of acute stress reactions. In L. Austin (Ed.), *Responding to disaster: A guide for mental health professionals* (pp. 25–52). Washington, DC: American Psychiatric Press.

Freud, S. (1955a). Beyond the pleasure principle. In J. Strachey & A. Freud (Eds.), *The standard edition of the complete psychological works of Sigmund Freud.* Volume XVIII (1920–1922). London: Hogarth Press. (Original work published 1920).

Freud, S. (1955b). Inhibitions, symptoms and anxiety. In J. Strachey & A. Freud (Eds.), *The standard edition of the complete psychological works of Sigmund Freud, Volume XX (1925–1926)* (pp. 87–175). London: Hogarth Press. (Original work published 1926).

Glad, K. A., Jensen, T. K., Hafstad, G. S., & Dyb, G. (2016). Post-traumatic stress disorder and exposure to trauma reminders after a terrorist attack. *Journal of Trauma & Dissociation, 17*(4), 435–447.

Goldmann, E., & Galea, S. (2014). Mental health consequences of disasters. *Annual Review of Public Health, 35*, 169–183.

Hamburger, A. (2020). The complexity of social trauma diagnosis and intervention. In A. Hamburger, C. Hancheva & V. Volka (Eds.), *Social trauma. An Interdisciplinary Textbook* (pp. 55–68). New York: Springer.

Hancheva, C. (2020). Social trauma and memory construction. In A. Hamburger, C. Hancheva & V. Volkan (Eds.), *Social trauma. An Interdisciplinary Textbook (pp. 191–200)* (pp. 191–200). New York: Springer.

Hopper, J. W., Spinazzola, J., Simpson, W. B., & van der Kolk, B. A. (2006). Preliminary evidence of parasympathetic influence on basal heart rate in posttraumatic stress disorder. *Journal of Psychosomatic Research, 60*(1), 83–90.

Janet, P. (1889). *L'Automatisme psychologique*. Paris: Félix Alcan.

Kardiner, A. (1941). *The traumatic neuroses of war*. New York: Hoeber.

Koso-Drljević, M., & Husremović, D. (2020). Neurobiology of memory in trauma survivors. In A. Hamburger, C. Hancheva & V. Volkan (Eds.), *Social trauma. An Interdisciplinary Textbook* (pp. 183–190). New York: Springer.

Langer, P. (2020). Social Trauma: A Socio-Psychological Perspective. In A. Hamburger, C. Hancheva & V. Volka (Eds.), *Social trauma. An Interdisciplinary Textbook* (pp. 219–234). New York: Springer.

Miller, K. E., Worthington, G. J., Muzurovic, J., Tipping, S., & Goldman, A. (2002). Bosnian refugees and stressors of exile: A narrative study. *American Journal of Orthopsychiatry, 72*, 341–354.

Özçürümez, S. (2020). Sexual and Gender-Based Violence and Social Trauma. In A. Hamburger, C. Hancheva & V. Volkan (Eds.), *Social trauma. An Interdisciplinary Textbook* (pp. 279-286). New York: Springer.

van der Kolk, B. A. (2014). *The body keeps the score: Brain, mind, and body in the healing of trauma*. New York: Viking Penguin.

van der Kolk, B. A., McFarlane, A., & Weisaeth, L. (2007). *Traumatic stress: The effects of overwhelming experience on mind, body, and society*. New York: The Guilford Press.

van der Kolk, B. A., & van der Hart, O. (1989). Pierre Janet and the breakdown of adaptation in psychological trauma. *The American Journal of Psychiatry, 146*, 1530–1540.

Volkan, V. D. (2020). Chosen traumas and their impact on current political/societal conflicts. In A. Hamburger, C. Hancheva & V. Volkan (Eds.), *Social trauma. An Interdisciplinary Textbook* (pp. 17–24). New York: Springer.

Chapter 9
Cognitive Behavioral Therapy Approaches to Social Trauma

Diana Ridjic

9.1 Introduction: Background and Main Theoretical Concepts/Discussions

The term social trauma refers to an individual's reactions to a traumatic event that affect society. This expression suggests that the tragedy remained in the group's memory. Memory of social trauma is remembered by members of the group who did not witness these traumatic events. Sociologist Kai Erikson describes social trauma and their impact on the self:

> …by collective trauma, I mean a blow to the basic tissues of social life that damages the bonds attaching people together and impairs the prevailing sense of communality. The collective trauma works its way slowly and even insidiously into the awareness of those who suffer from it, so it…[is] a gradual realization that the community no longer exists as an effective source of support and that an important part of the self has disappeared… (Erikson, 1976, pp. 153–154)

Social trauma transforms the way survivors experience the world and understand the relationship between their group and other groups (Alexander, Eyerman, Giesen, Smelser, & Sztompka, 2004; Vollhardt, 2012). Social trauma also destabilizes a fundamental sense of security with long-term effects among second generations of survivors. At the individual level, individuals manifest significantly higher rates of psychological distress (Yehuda, Halligan, & Bierer, 2002), and, at the social level, the second and third generation survivors display heightened individual and collective fear, feelings of vulnerability, injured national pride, humiliation (Lifton, 2005), a crisis of identity, and a predisposition to react with heightened vigilance to new

D. Ridjic (✉)
Department of Occupational Health of Police Officers, Counselling Centre—Domino, Sarajevo, Bosnia and Herzegovina

© Springer Nature Switzerland AG 2021

A. Hamburger et al. (eds.), *Social Trauma – An Interdisciplinary Textbook*,
https://doi.org/10.1007/978-3-030-47817-9_9

threats, so that the pain of the past generations is conflated with threats facing the current generation (Canetti et al., 2017). Trauma can disrupt people's global sense of meaning by exposing them to darker sides of human nature. Establishing a meaning, therefore, is particularly important when groups encounter traumatic life experiences (Park, 2013).

Cognitive Behavioral Therapy (CBT) and different modalities of intervention within CBT (i.e., Trauma-Focused Cognitive Behavioral Therapy (TF-CBT), Trauma-Grief Component Therapy (TGCT), Cognitive Behavioral Intervention for Trauma in Schools (CBITS)) are among the most used and effective interventions for individuals and groups who have experienced some kind of trauma.TF-CBT is one of the basic and most used modalities of CBT intervention for trauma issues. This method is based on Humanistic, Cognitive-Behavioral, and Family Theory. Evaluation of TF-CBT includes several randomized controlled trials. Studies of the effectiveness and ongoing studies have shown that this method of therapy is useful for cases who have experienced sexual abuse, domestic violence, traumatic grief, terrorism, disaster, and multiple trauma (Isaac, 2015). In addition, TF-CBT was used to treat victims of the Hurricane Katrina, the Sandy Hook Shooting, the Boston Bombing, and the earthquakes in Nepal and after the 2004 tsunami (Isaac, 2015). The current paper offers a perspective suggesting that CBT approaches to social trauma can be an area framework that helps facilitate the experience of social trauma.

9.2 Learning Outcome Related to Trauma-Specific CBT Interventions to Social Trauma

Traumatic experiences are diverse and can produce traumatic effects that resonate for several generations, affecting perspectives, hopes, cognitive styles, and personalities. It is important to understand the facts of the traumatic event, ways of coping, and lessons about life and survival conveyed consciously and subconsciously.

The learning outcome related to Trauma-Specific CBT interventions to social trauma in this chapter will be:

- To explain aspects of social trauma in terms of Trauma-Specific CBT (TSCBT) interventions.
- To become familiar with the TSCBT interventions model of social trauma.
- To learn about practical implications of TSCBT in the field of social trauma.

9.3 Trauma-Specific CBT Intervention Approaches to Social Trauma

Western psychology has primarily viewed the term trauma through the diagnostic category of post-traumatic stress disorder. CBT offers effective methods for treatment of disorders associated with trauma and promotes healing. There are different modalities of intervention within CBT (i.e., TF-CBT, CBITS, TGCT) that speak about access to trauma at both the individual and social levels. TF-CBT is modality of CBT intervention derived from the General CBT and which will be described in this chapter. Besides that, clinicians are speaking about good effects of CBITS and TGCT as well. CBITS was originally designed for trauma-impacted communities. Other CBT models of intervention are in manner similar to TF-CBT and include the common elements for Trauma-Specific CBT interventions. It is recommended to the reader to explore them independently.

TF-CBT offers different methods, as well as family therapy component, in the approach to trauma. It is an empirically supported treatment model that has been evaluated and refined over the past 20 years. The model can be adapted for use with individuals and groups who have suffered a variety of traumatic experiences. It is highly structured and relatively short-term (up to 16, 90-min weekly sessions). During these sessions, the client gradually moves through eight components as follows: psychoeducation, relaxation techniques, affective expression and regulation, cognitive coping, development and processing of a trauma narrative, gradual exposure, conjoint sessions, and safety review and future development (Isaac, 2015). The following sections briefly describe these individual stages of treatment.

Psychoeducation: The therapist will provide information regarding the nature of PTSD or other diagnoses and impacts of trauma on family members, as well as information to help normalize the current situation.

Relaxation techniques: These may include demonstration of techniques such as deep breathing, progressive muscle relaxation, meditation, mindfulness, music, sports, knitting, singing, etc.

Affective expression and regulation: The therapist may then start working on the expansion of a range of affective expressions and continues to work on the development of affective modulation skills. The therapist will assist the client with strengthening these skills, encouraging them to practice them in between sessions.

Cognitive coping skills: The therapist will support clients to identify thoughts related to upsetting events, determine the feelings and behaviors they have associated with those thoughts, and then evaluate whether or not these thoughts are accurate or helpful to them. Clients can generate alternative thoughts for each of the situations which they can use while experiencing trauma reminders.

Trauma narrative and cognitive processing of traumatic experiences: The client develops a trauma narrative using a medium of their choice (writing, dictation, art, poem, song, dance). The narrative should include thoughts, feelings, body sensations, and the worst moments of the traumatic experience. Creation of this trauma narrative helps the client to overcome avoidance of traumatic memories, identify their cognitive distortions, and contextualize their traumatic experience into a larger framework of their life by telling the story in a context with time frames. This helps them recognize that they are more than merely a victim of trauma.

Graduated exposure: It is for clients who have developed generalized avoidance of unavoidable social cues/situations, leading to functional impairment. This section follows the same general principles as other graduated exposure programs.

Conjoint sessions: They are an important focus of the model as they allow for a family member to participate in the treatment, making the family member's role a reliable source for trauma-related information. During these joint sessions, clients and their family members build their ability to communicate openly about other aspects of the traumatic experience.

Enhancing safety and future developmental trajectory: It means the implementation of safety skills, tailored to a particular situation, that are practiced during the last few sessions. Clients are encouraged to apply the skills learned during the treatment to other difficult situations after termination of the therapy.

It is important to note, however, that this type of treatment is not optimal for everyone. It is not ideal for those whose primary issues are not trauma-related. In these cases, the individual should be referred to the alternative-evidence-supported treatment model.

9.4 Practical Implications in the Field of Social Trauma

The historical memory of social trauma can last for millennia, with groups reminiscent of traumatic events that can be traced back to antiquity and even to biblical times. Memories of victimization beg the question: Why do these people not want to move on instead of indulging in the past? One answer goes to the basic evolutionary level. At the basic evolutionary level, remembering trauma promotes alertness that can enhance the group's actual survival and restore a sense of effectiveness (Shnabel, Nadler, Ullrich, Dovidio, & Carmi, 2009; Vollhardt, 2012). The memory of trauma and the existential threat motivate a desire to construct a meaning around the experience of extreme adversity. In this process of meaning-making, a transgenerational collective self is pieced together so that it provides a sense of continuity between past, present, and future members of the group and promotes the group cohesion, a sense of group importance, and a strong commitment to the group identity (Kahn, Klar, & Roccas, 2017). To let go of the trauma is highly aversive and costly; it is akin to abdicating the collective meaning, and societies mobilize against this threat to the meaning in order to keep the trauma alive as a lesson from the past.

The 2004 Indian Ocean tsunami caused significant devastation and high mortality rate—up to 90%. In 1930, a tsunami of a similar magnitude struck Papua New Guinea with only a fraction of the death toll—less than 1% of the population. According to a study on cultural responses to tsunamis (Mercer et al., 2012), this curious discrepancy in the lethality of two similar natural disasters can be attributed to an implausible cause: oral traditions. These traditions have been passed down from generation to generation for hundreds of years, including even the instructions to run to the hills when the sea goes down. Papuans who did not question this tradition successfully escaped almost a certain death. An analysis of the communities that were most hit in the 2004 tsunami reveal that these were mostly recent immigrants to coastal regions that had no collective memory about tsunamis and no tradition on how to identify this threat and defend against it (Mercer et al., 2012). This comparison of two tsunamis provides a glimpse into how the memory of social trauma may directly influence group survival by promoting life-saving efficacy. The social memory of natural disasters and the social memory of traumas intentionally caused by humans have much in common—they serve as guidelines for future generations on how to identify the threat and respond to it effectively (Hirschberger 2018).

Remembering and scrutinizing disasters helps to increase risk awareness and builds resilience to future events. In addition, remembering a disaster and sharing memories is a cathartic experience for survivors. Through memory, disasters become a shared past and can form a group identity. Memories can be expressed through different forms. Storytelling, myth, and dialogue are examples of narrative practices that are crucial for remembering. More formally organized disaster commemorations are coordinated in a number of ways. All are key in creating a social memory. But what happens if survivors are not allowed to remember a disaster? Or when they are only allowed to remember certain aspects? Or they show signs of trauma and traumatic experience? What about when social memory becomes social trauma?

In the last two decades, the treatment of trauma, both individual and group, as well as community trauma has been significantly discussed. Understanding the ways of responding to social trauma through known mechanisms within psychotherapy portrays the attempt of practical implication in the field of social trauma.

Different research has demonstrated that CBT is one of the most beneficial treatments for trauma survivors, with the exposure component, or imaginal exposure to the event itself, thought to be a large factor in its success (Foa et al., 1999; Foa, Keane, & Friedman, 2000; Foa, Rothbaum, Riggs, & Murdock, 1991). Furthermore, studies show that CBT typically has the best outcomes when it begins 2–6 weeks following the trauma and is completed in five to nine sessions (Devilly, Gist, & Cotton, 2006). Hamblen, Norris, Gibson, and Lee (2008) conducted a study investigating the effectiveness of Cognitive Behavioral Therapy for Postdisaster Distress (CBT-PD) following Hurricane Katrina, a ten-session CBT intervention provided at least 90 days post-disaster to address the client's cognitive, behavioral, and emotional reactions to trauma. The use of CBT-PD was related to significant reductions in participants' distress and worked equally well for individuals suffering from both moderate and severe stress levels. The percentage of participants experiencing severe distress decreased from 61% (pre-treatment) to 14% (post-treatment). This reduction in stress was maintained at 5 months post-treatment when researchers followed-up with participants.

Trauma-Specific CBT interventions and research are available on the existing and relatively new CBT approaches to trauma treatment that continues to accumulate. CBT treatments for trauma include both individual and group approaches. Interventions included in this review demonstrated improvements in trauma symptoms with treatment, and many of these gains were sustained over time. Many such practices combine common elements of CBT approaches to treating trauma with other CBT interventions, or aspects of other interventions to explicitly address system-related issues or common comorbid conditions. Several of these treatments are currently being evaluated, and as research continues to accumulate, these treatments may supplement our menu of options and understanding of how to effectively treat communities in terms of treating social trauma.

Future directions for the CBT in social trauma setting include continuing to conduct research on promising practices and their ability to remediate a trauma symptom, examining issues related to cultural applicability and responsiveness, ensuring effective implementation and dissemination (e.g., treatment reach), and sustaining treatment gains over time.

9.5 Suggested Reading

Allen, J. G. (2001). *Traumatic relationships and serious mental disorders*. New York, NY: John Wiley & Sons, Ltd.

Dattilio, F. M., & Freeman, A. (2000). *Cognitive behavioral strategies in crisis intervention.* New York, NY: The Guilford Press.

Feather, J. S., & Ronan, K. R. (2009). Trauma-focused CBT with maltreated children: A clinic-based evaluation of a new treatment manual. *The Australian Psychologist*, *44*(3), 174–194.

References

Alexander, J., Eyerman, R., Giesen, B., Smelser, N., & Sztompka, P. (Eds.). (2004). *Cultural trauma and collective identity: Toward a theory of cultural trauma.* Berkeley, CA: University of California Press.

Canetti, D., Hirschberger, G., Rapaport, C., Elad-Strenger, J., Ein-Dor, T., Rosenzveig, S., Pyszczynski, T., & Hobfoll, S. E. (2017). Collective trauma from the lab to the real world: The effects of the holocaust on contemporary Israeli political cognitions. *Political Psychology, 39*(1), 3–21. https://doi.org/10.1111/pops.12384

Devilly, G. J., Gist, R., & Cotton, P. (2006). Ready! Fire! Aim! The status of psychological debriefing and therapeutic interventions: In the work place and after disasters. *Review of General Psychology, 10*, 318–345. https://doi.org/10.1037/1089-2680.10.4.318

Erikson, K. T. (1976). *Everything in its path.* New York, NY: Simon and Schuster.

Foa, E. B., Dancu, C. V., Hembree, E. A., Jaycox, L. H., Meadows, E. A., & Street, G. P. (1999). A comparison of exposure therapy, stress inoculation training, and their combination for reducing posttraumatic stress disorder in female assault victims. *Journal of Consulting and Clinical Psychology, 67*, 194–200. https://doi.org/10.1037/0022-006X.67.2.194

Foa, E. B., Keane, T. M., & Friedman, M. J. (2000). Guidelines for treatment of PTSD—Introduction (reprinted from effective treatments for PTSD, 2000). *Journal of Traumatic Stress, 31*, 539–588. https://doi.org/10.1023/A:10078020314

Foa, E. B., Rothbaum, B. O., Riggs, D. S., & Murdock, T. B. (1991). Treatment of posttraumatic stress disorder in rape victims: Comparison between cognitive-behavioral procedures and counseling. *Journal of Consulting and Clinical Psychology, 59*, 715–723. https://doi.org/10.1037/0022-006X.59.5.715

Hamblen, J., Norris, F., Gibson, L., & Lee, L. (2008). Training community therapists to deliver cognitive behavioral therapy in the aftermath of disaster. *Journal of Traumatic Stress, 30*, 539–588.

Hirschberger G. (2018). Collective Trauma and the Social Construction of Meaning. *Frontiers in Psychology, 9*, 1441. https://doi.org/10.3389/fpsyg.2018.01441

Isaac, L. (2015, July 29). *The origins and practice of trauma-focused cognitive behavioral therapy (TF-CBT)*. Retrieved September 20, 2019, from http://www.socialjusticesolutions.org/2015/07/29/origins-practice-trauma-focused-cognitive-behavioral-therapy-tf-cbt/

Kahn, D. T., Klar, Y., & Roccas, S. (2017). For the sake of the eternal group: Perceiving the group as trans-generational and endurance of ingroup suffering. *Personality and Social Psychology Bulletin, 43*, 272–283. https://doi.org/10.1177/0146167216684123

Lifton, R. J. (2005). Americans as survivors. *The New England Journal of Medicine, 352*, 2263–2265. https://doi.org/10.1056/NEJMp058048

Mercer, J., Gaillard, J. C., Crowley, K., Shannon, R., Alexander, B., Day, S., & Becker, J. (2012). Culture and disaster risk reduction: Lessons and opportunities. *Environmental Hazards, 11*, 74–95. https://doi.org/10.1080/17477891.2011.609876

Park, C. L. (2013). Trauma and meaning making: Converging conceptualizations and emerging evidence. In J. A. Hicks & C. Routledge (Eds.), *The experience of meaning in life* (pp. 61–76). New York, NY: Springer.

Shnabel, N., Nadler, A., Ullrich, J., Dovidio, J. F., & Carmi, D. (2009). Promoting reconciliation through the satisfaction of the emotional needs victimized of members perpetrating group: The needs-based model of reconciliation. *Personality and Social Psychology Bulletin, 35*, 1021–1030. https://doi.org/10.1177/0146167209336610

Vollhardt, J. R. (2012). Collective victimization. In L. Tropp (Ed.), *Oxford handbook of intergroup conflict* (pp. 136–157). New York, NY: Oxford University Press.

Yehuda, R., Halligan, S. L., & Bierer, L. M. (2002). Cortisol levels in adult offspring of holocaust survivors: Relation to PTSD symptom severity in the parent and child. *Psychoneuroendocrinology, 27*, 171–180. https://doi.org/10.1016/S0306-4530(01)00043-9

Chapter 10
A Dialogical-Humanistic Approach to the Treatment of Complex Trauma Sequelae in Social Trauma

Thomas Maurer and Willi Butollo

10.1 Introduction

Gestalt therapy is subsumed with other approaches (client-centered therapy, body psychotherapy, psychodrama, transactional analysis and existential analysis) under the term humanistic psychotherapy. They share the assumption that people have a fundamental ability to be conscious, to introspect and reflect,that people have a potential freedom of perception and action, and an attitude of responsible relating to others and to life in society. Self-realization and personal growth are possible if the existing potential is not blocked by restrictive expectations and norms and if this personal growth is supported by benevolent resource-oriented others.

On the other hand, however, there is also the freedom to take such actions that violate the boundaries, integrity and dignity of others. Unprocessed, pathogenic interaction experiences (neglect, disregard for personal boundaries, suppression and coercion and chronically confusing relationship patterns) are postulated as causes for the development and maintenance of mental disorders. Such biographical conditions can result in fragmentation of the self, which is cognitively represented as unconnected self-conceptual parts as well as in behavior and experience. Such intrapersonal breakdowns of the ability and/or willingness to dialogue are intertwined with corresponding limitations of the interpersonal capacity for dialogue.

Translated from German by Dr. Boris Drenkov

T. Maurer (✉)
MIT—Munich Institute for Trauma Therapy, Munich, Germany

W. Butollo
Department of Clinical Psychology, Ludwig Maximilians Universität München, München, Germany

MIT—Munich Institute for Trauma Therapy, Munich, Germany
e-mail: willi@butollo.de

© Springer Nature Switzerland AG 2021

A. Hamburger et al. (eds.), *Social Trauma – An Interdisciplinary Textbook*,
https://doi.org/10.1007/978-3-030-47817-9_10

Such limitations can reach the extent of lasting traumatizing experiences. The breaking off of relationships by a group of people (family, classmates, fan clubs up to ethnic groups, majority populations, religious groups) will additionally burden the implications for self processes and the ability to engage in dialogue in a way that is difficult to grasp (Rosner, Powell, & Butollo, 2003).

Therapeutic offers from the field of humanistic psychology aim at establishing a secure working relationship that is also experienced as trustworthy, in which growth-oriented new possibilities for can be explored and tested that correct and potentially compensate for previous experiences. As a rule, the aim of therapy is not to change a person, but to expand the range of choices for his or her experience, thinking and acting.

Gestalt therapy (Francesetti, Gecele, & Roubal, 2016; Maragkos & Freyberger, 2016; Polster & Polster, 2001; Votsmeier-Röhr & Wulf, 2017) in the narrower sense is what we understand with Lore Perls (1988) as an experimental, experiential, existential approach and supplemented by the defining characteristic "dialogical-humanistic". Its approach is phenomenological and resource-oriented, and its goal is to(re)take responsibility for one's own experience and behaviour. It is about experiencing oneself as a decisive person, not at the mercy of learned automatisms and/or submitting oneself to the unchecked attributions and expectations of others. The dialogic-humanistic Gestalt therapy approach takes up Buber's thoughts on the dialogic (Buber, 2008); in the theory and practice of Gestalt therapy, it was also developed in connection with PTSD (Butollo and Karl, 2012/2019, 27 ff.). It is based on the assumption that, on the one hand, important diagnostic insights can be gained from the specifics of contact shape; on the other hand, the therapeutic relationship represents a field of experimentation for learning and practicing new options of contact and regaining vitality in the form of encounters with oneself and others.

At the relationship level, resources and competencies as well as impairments of interpersonal-interactive behaviour are evident. The symptomatology for which a patient comes has usually also a correspondence on the relationship level; the impaired ability to engage in dialogue is reflected in projections and transmission processes as well as in the individual way of establishing or breaking off contact.

Of course, the resumption of the dialogical relationship is made more difficult if the "partner" of interaction experienced as threatening is a large number of more or less anonymous people, a group whose members cannot be identified and addressed individually. How does one speak, for example, to a group of people who are mutually reinforcing in their rejection of each other? Even contact with football fans of the opposing team in a crowded subway can feel life-threatening. And what does this mean for the configuration of the self in the acting or thinking person, if the interaction partner is a hostile crowd from which the individuals can no longer be identified? A dialogical attitude is characterized by presence, as an attitude of focusing on the particularities of the present, common relationship (shaping). Confirmation of the other in the sense of a validating look at his or her currently lived and already invested, but still to be discovered potential. This does not mean that one should indiscriminately approve of everything that one perceives in the other – of course it should be seen in the sense of a "what is, is" as the present reality of the other. It can thus serve as a starting point for joint work and facilitate processes of change on the basis of a joint clarification of tasks. The dialogue-phenomenological attitude is an offer to resume dialogues that were broken off early on and aims at the reintegration of split personality parts and the gradual "de-tabooing" of behaviour and feelings that were frowned upon or forbidden in the course of the biography. Patients are accompanied on the way to reconcile isolated fragments of their self and to release those forces that have been invested in defending and maintaining the divisions. New patterns of interaction can be practised in dialogue, and this refers both to individual characteristics of the exchange between patient and therapist and in the form of exercises of expression with the "empty chair".

But who do you put on the "empty chair" when your counterpart is a nation, a state, or more recently a completely anonymous group of drones sitting thousands of kilometres away in a bunker, transporting devastatingly explosive material to fire it at your own relatives?

10.2 Learning Outcome Related to Social Trauma

The specificity of social trauma as violence perpetrated by and against groups requires a therapeutic approach for individual victims that focuses on the level of the relationship, as opposed to individual-oriented therapeutic approaches. Dialogical-humanistic therapy represents such a relationship-oriented therapeutic approach (Butollo, Karl, König, & Hagl, 2014).

This is particularly relevant against the background of man-made traumatization, both on an individual level and in the case of systematic and organized persecution and murder. (Sequential) traumatization(s) must be regarded as a complex event with a number of influencing factors at biographical, transgenerative (Huber & Plassmann, 2012; Wardi, 2014) and societal level. Treatment approaches should do justice to these variables in their breadth.

Biographically (and consequently also clinically) significant is the time of traumatization and the available ego structures (see Hancheva, 2020), as well as the confirmations made (or not made) before the trauma and sustain-validating relationship and attachment experiences, both in the family and with other people. Furthermore, the question of whether or not contact persons were available post-traumatically to deal with the horror experienced, the losses, the shattered hopes and perspectives is also of importance—or whether, for example, the surroundings were equally affected (Hamburger, 2020) and were in a state of agony because of helplessness and powerlessness?

At the level of society, questions arise such as was it an individual who was unexpectedly and massively excluded from an apparently cohesive community, robbed of his dignity, whose inviolability of life and limb was called into question, or was a whole group affected by people of the "wrong" religion, ethnicity, skin colour defined as "different" and without a right to exist? In the latter case, beyond the individual, a population and its entire culture is defined as extinguishable and, on this basis, a correspondingly horrific action is taken. Its members are robbed of their identity and lose the support of the group, the experience of belonging and the potential support that provides stable and trustworthy relationships. Relevant for life and experience in the post-traumatic phase are (role) attributions to the children of the survivors as symbols of victory and of overcoming the violent regime and the perpetrators, if this role can be accompanied by the fading out of all those feelings, sensations and impulses to which nothing victorious is attached (cf. Wardi, 2014).

The consequences of persecution, inflicted suffering, torture and death of relatives are evident and documented (only a selection, Benz & Distel, 1996; Jokl, 1997; Keilson, 2005; Niederland, 1980; Wardi, 2014, and for the war in the Balkans, Butollo, Krüssmann, & Hagl, 1998, 168 ff; as vignette Höfer, 1995).

10.3 Suggested Model: The Dialogical-Humanistic Therapy

What consequences do traumatizations of individuals have for the social system in which they live, e.g. for group cohesion or the change of values? Are there secondary trauma consequences for the community? But are there also secondary trauma consequences in the individual still directly affected as a result of collective trauma? Finally, traumatization triggers lasting shocks on several levels. It confronts us with the fragility of apparent certainties beyond all previously imaginable, on the psychological, physical, material and religious-spiritual levels. Nothing is the same as before; the experience cannot be placed in a previously valid frame of reference (Butollo, 2000, 2002; Zvizdic & Butollo, 2000) The acute and massive real threat of the situation determines peritraumatically the present experience and post-traumatically the subsequent perception and evaluation of the world and of oneself in the world. Peritraumatic experiences of fear, powerlessness, helplessness, humiliation and overwhelming can lead to an attitude of imposed bearing. During this phase, such forced acts of subjugation have the quality of a survival and coping strategy, combined with symptoms of stiffening, dissociation and numbing in the face of a counterpart experienced as overpowering, from whom it is impossible to distinguish oneself. There is a lack of response possibilities beyond the collapse or fragmentation of the self. The latter is defined as the totality of the mental functions that are in interactive exchange with the environment and represent a set of cognitively represented relational experiences. These are called up in new contacts and determine the experience and behaviour through the way one presents oneself and is consistently accepted or rejected by others.

If the violent counterpart is a group, a political movement or a warring state, the processes become considerably more complex in the course of collapsing self-processes with possibly fragmented self-parts. If even an aggressive counterpart still offers a certain chance to position itself in efforts to distance itself from the torturer, e.g. in the course of a torture, the self sinks into a bottomless fog of impending destruction from nowhere in the face of anonymous, incomprehensible, quasi-impersonally organized violence. It may be that many a survivor tries to help himself here by carrying out a kind of anthropomorphization of the masses ("The Russian, the German, the American is coming"). Similar things may be used to help with physical processes in illness: "The cancer", "the heart attack", etc. Post-traumatic self-processes without a tangible enemy lead to the expectation that a later treatment of chronic fainting reactions to organized collective aggression is considerably more difficult. A concretization of the enemy, an attempt to make him a tangible counterpart by configuring its cognitions, can be helpful here as an intermediate step. In the long term, however, the confrontation with the unfathomable anonymity of the perpetrator will remain indispensable, but then again thanks to the intermediate steps from a strengthened self (Hagl, Powell, Rosner, & Butollo, 2015).

During individual and collective experiences of violence, the formed representations of "Me" and "the other(s)" are, so to say, "overwritten". Previously tenable assessments of one's own value, of being suspended in the world and of the fundamental possibility of trusting oneself and others dissolve. Now a shift takes place and self-experience is characterized by helplessness, powerlessness and worthlessness, whilst the representation of the other(s) is attributed the powerful and overwhelming aspects. On the basis of this relationship experience, a trauma self with the described characteristics is formed, which is subsequently further solidified in the event of renewed assaults and injuries. This limits the range of self-options in the form of ideally finely graded responses to the current situational conditions.

Of particular importance is witnessing violence against others, especially close ones. Watching the abuse of relatives helplessly is more traumatizing than being a victim yourself. In principle, this also applies to other life situations, not only to social traumatization. It deepens the experience of powerlessness and pain and leads to an abyss of agony, which proves to be extremely resistant to later therapeutic efforts.

Exceptions are only reported if the surviving witnesses of the violent excesses experienced social support immediately afterwards, or at least remember a supportive attitude in retrospect ("perceived social support": Lueger-Schuster et al., 2015).

The peritraumatically understandable self-configuration, which may make survival possible, determines post-traumatic interpersonal contacts in the sense of a polarity "at the mercy" versus "overpowering". On the side of the maltreated person, this can lead to a chronic gesture of subjugation, a mode of enduring and bearing, accompanied by processes of dissociation, fragmentation of the self and reduced self-esteem. Changes of the self processes themselves, not only of their contents, can also be the result. Instead of an inferior, submissive self being configured, the result would then be the absence of a self, experienced as inner confusion, without a configured counterpart and without a configured self.

When liberated from the concentration camp, one young woman was to recover in a community to regain her strength. She refused because she did not want to be perceived in her psychic "no longer existing" and did not want to have to answer questions because subjectively there was no one who could have answered. As quickly as she could she disappeared to Canada, avoided Jewish offers of help and took a simple job in a very rural area, far away from the better organized civilization. She married a forestry worker, gave birth to three children and remained a woman without a story all her life. Only when the children grew up, daring to ask the tabooed questions about the mother's origin, did the memories of horror, which had never disappeared even in Canada, demand attention and treatment. She told her children her story, then decided to return to the place of deepest humiliation and found a Jewish travel group with whom she set off for Germany and Poland to heal her divided self through confrontation with memory, supported by direct contact with the places of her agony.

It was very important for her to meet and talk to "Germans" on this trip. She came across an Austrian (W.B.). She wanted to hear if her suffering was acknowledged, feared to be rejected with her wish and was very happy to experience that this did not happen. After the trip she reported that she can finally feel again as a "whole" person who has managed to unite all the extreme experiences of her life.

The pure "endurance" of the experience in the memory had an end. So did the trauma-specific functions corresponding to "enduring". Peritraumatically, such patterns had the quality of an appreciable coping and survival strategy. However, they acquire a dysfunctional quality if they are maintained post-traumatically and, under appropriate conditions, can be the starting point for retraumatization and revictimization. However, solving these problems can take a long time, and the splitting off of memory can be quite protective and important in these intermediate stages. Forced remembrance or forced revelation of what has been experienced can be retraumatizing.

The post-traumatic symptoms found in the form of acute or complex PTSD can be interpreted as a habitual "freezing" of this attitude, even though there is no longer an acute actual threat. What has been lost (at least in part) is the ability to relate both internally (to certain now rejected self-parts) and interpersonally externally. Correspondingly, this shows itself as a tendency to approach others in the same way, not differently, fearfully, suspiciously and insecurely, and at the same time no longer to communicate "on a par". If the social environment is experienced as aggressive-hostile, potentially overwhelming and arbitrary due to the peritraumatic experiences (and their over-generalizing continuation), constant vigilance and excessive controlling is consistent, as is an avoidance-oriented attitude towards one's fellow human beings. A perception oriented towards signals of insecurity and an interpretation of what is perceived that generates insecurity deepens and fixes the fear more. Avoidance also makes intrusions more probable, which, according to the principle of negative reinforcement, strengthen impulses to control more and avoid (even) earlier. This maintains a self-representation formed in this way. Looking at oneself as a powerless, chronically vulnerable and vulnerable person is incompatible with real vitality, lightness and trust. It is also incompatible with the experience of self-efficacy and self-esteem and with an attitude from which respect and attention can be adequately demanded at clearly expressed boundaries. The acquired and so far (still) lived attitude of the victim, which this person actually was, may become a signal for the environment: If the definition is adopted, overprotection on the one hand or revictimization on the other hand can be a consequence—appearing as relationship disorders in partnership, sexual and professional contacts. The understandable need for at least temporary rest may result in abuse of medication, alcohol or drugs. A persistence of peritraumatic helplessness can correspond to anxiety and depression, i.e. a chronic feeling of ineffectiveness and chronic insufficiency. An (see below) impaired relationship to power, strength and clarity may become visible in contact as a swinging between submission and aggressive breakthroughs.

10.4 Practical Application

The dialogic-humanistic approach of a multi-phase trauma therapy (Butollo and Karl, 2012/2019; Butollo et al., 1998, 2016, Butollo, Hagl, & Krüssmann, 2003) offers the therapeutic working relationship as a field in which it is possible to experiment with other, more functional than peritraumatically acquired patterns, in which new options for contact shaping can be identified, tested and practised. According to Perls' image of "peeling onions", the working steps proceed from the outside inwards to the core of the trauma.

A combination of stabilizing and confronting interventions within a programme that includes cognitive-behavioural therapeutic interventions with a focus on symptom reduction and Gestalt therapeutic interventions, emphasizing on relationship formation (focus: ability to engage in intra- and interpersonal dialogue), has empirically proven to be helpful and indispensable (cf. Fig. 10.1).

The fundamental aim is to bring peritraumatically fragmented self-parts back into contact. Processing a traumatization means accepting it as an indelible part of life, to deal with the consequences, to look at the now existing possibilities in order to at least create conditions for a calming of the soul, for steps out of a frozen persistence in grief and out of the mourning for irretrievably lost things as a basis for new response possibilities of a completed self.

It is methodologically important to pay attention to forms of peritraumatically learned subordination in the therapeutic contacts. If patients tend to"slip" into the mode of powerlessness and refrain from more mature options for co-determination of the working relationship, appropriate advice is given. This allows awareness of the trigger stimuli, the accompanying cognitions and experimentation with alternative options for freezing with fear, where up to now neither escape nor attack seemed possible and only "giving up" and dissociation remained as possibilities. Experience has shown that this requires the therapist to take responsibility in those moments when the patient is not yet able to do so.

The social perspective should emphasize the particularities that arise in the face of a collective aggressor and membership of a supportive or compassionate community—a perceived or constructed belonging that can also shift continuously under the pressure of threatening events.

The approach based on the Gestalt therapy aims at (re)activating pre-traumatically existing resources and competencies that have been peritraumatically "frozen" and quasi-overwritten. The ability to reactivate peri- and post-traumatic social support that has actually been experienced, but also (re-)constructed as memory, plays a special role in this process. In therapy, this reconstruction or memory can be supported and thus the traumatized person will get help to appreciate the"perceived" support at the time, which is so essential for the present state of well-being (Butollo, 2014). A sustainable therapeutic working relationship and a therapist with an empathic view, potential orientation and a hope for development based on a realistic assessment, on the other hand, creates the conditions for this in the best case through well-coordinated support from outside.

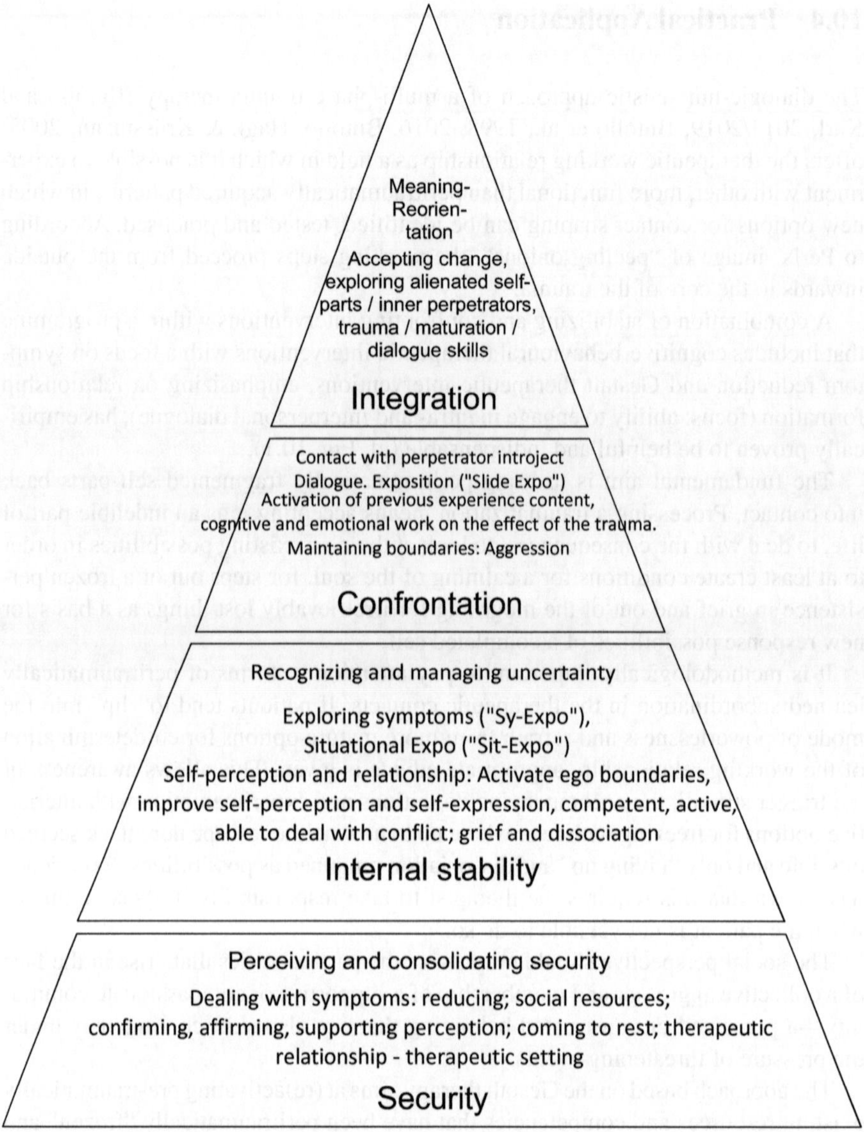

Fig. 10.1 Four phases od Dialogical Trauma Therapy. Butollo and Karl (2012/2019, 4th ed.)

10.4.1 The Four-Phase Dialogic-Humanistic Trauma Therapy for PTSD

After a preliminary diagnosis, appropriate decisions regarding the indication and contraindications for the implementation of the programme and psychoeducation, the work can begin in the form of a four-phase dialogic-humanistic trauma therapy in patients with PTSD as the main diagnosis.

10.4.1.1 The Phase of Safety

The following objectives will be pursued in a first phase of safety:

- Activate and regain safety and trust by creating an outer stable framework of the therapeutic working relationship with appropriate mourning for the experience of the irretrievable loss. Leading symptoms of PTSD are seen as a (natural or "normal") survival strategy during traumatic experiences.
- First steps towards overcoming peritraumatic agony and conditioned submission reaction by teaching social skills and contact skills by linking up with pre-traumatic resources and relationships and development of the ability to control inner psychological processes (ability to verbalize, differentiation of perception, imagination, evaluation, avoidance, affect-tolerance, gradual readjustment of relationship possibilities). Regulation of emotional processes in case of intrusions.
- Re-establishing the foundations for a sense of belonging to a community with culturally significant values, especially amongst victims of collective violence and disassociation from intrusive helpers and their organizations.

10.4.1.2 The Phase of Stabilization and Stability

The second phase serves to promote the inner psychological prerequisites for working on the traumatic experience by:

- Development of the ability to endure aversive states and feelings, differentiation of emotional perception and awareness of the moments and methods of contact loss.
- Strengthening of the ability to contact and deal with conflict, initially in everyday conflicts that are not trauma-prone, also in the therapeutic working relationship as a field of experimentation, e.g. by perceiving one's own wishes and limits as well as by promoting the ability to express oneself—awareness of inner processes that promote and minimize self-confidence.
- Work on the ability to take more responsibility for your own well-being and behaviour.
- Symptomatic area: Work on the ability to express oneself with regard to intrusions and the reduction of avoidance behaviour in this respect, e.g. in the form of trivializing and tabooing.

10.4.1.3 The Phase of Trauma Confrontation

In the third phase, on the one hand, *object-oriented* confrontation takes place as a gradual "dialogical exposure". In sensu and, if possible, also in vivo, the sites of the action are visited and mental and physical reactions are processed. The aim is to restore inner contact and to correct over-generalizing self-destructive consequences, an experience of collapsed self-efficacy.

Secondly, the content of this phase is an *imaginary confrontation with the perpetrator(s), people involved in the accident or aspects of the surviving natural disaster*. The focus of the treatment is now on the configuration of the self that appears as a result.

The objectives are therefore, amongst other things:

- Contact with inner images of the threat and the (probable) re-actualization of submission, supporting emotional processes (confrontation with feelings) and standing firm.
- Reconstruction of contact boundaries, of self-perception and of self-expression with exploration of new ways of expressing emotions.
- Closing the "gap" between pre- and post-traumatic self: Promotion of self-acceptance for post-traumatic (experience) life.

An object-related and interactive-dialogical confrontation can take on different emphases (Butollo and Karl, 2012/2019; Butollo et al., 2003). An essential component is an examination of the contents of the trauma and a joint exploration of the attitude of subjection that has become habitual; this creates inner space for alternatives for action and subsequently post-traumatic growth (Powell, Rosner, Butollo, Tedeschi, & Calhoun, 2003). This means in more detail:

- Investigation of ideas about the circumstances and the experience during the trauma.
- Confrontation with places, people and feelings connected with the memory of the trauma.
- Confrontation with attempts to cope, after the traumatic experience.
- Confrontation with the certainty of a fundamental uncertainty of individual, human existence in connection with the possibility of accepting the traumatic event within oneself.
- Confrontation with the possibility of renewed injuries.

During these confrontations it is always important to pay attention to the dialogical self-response: In terms of content, the patient approaches the memory of the overwhelming interaction in dialogue. He confronts himself with thoughts, ideas and feelings that have been avoided so far. Basic feelings of traumatization should be taken into account: Guilt and shame could explain an emerging resistance against the confrontation or lead to a higher resistance to therapy.

In the phases of confrontation, the signs of a tendency to dissociation should be observed. If they occur, the confrontation is reduced or terminated. The therapist pays attention to signs of excessive demands, creates a safe atmosphere and brings the patient back to the reality he or she is now experiencing. The aim of the confrontation is to expose feelings of fear, shame, guilt, etc. within the framework of the psychological forces (self-support) and to deal with the contents of the trauma and its effects on the whole life in a measured manner. This includes that the affected persons also confront themselves with their evaluation of the trauma and its consequences.

10.4.1.4 The Phase of Integration

In the phase of integration, in contrast to a sheer "endurance" of fear, the following should be achieved:

- The emphasis on the present.
- Developing of the ability to perceive the differences to the past traumatic experience and to stay in contact with the present whilst remembering and reporting the past.
- Promotion of self-responsibility and a realistic assessment of one's own resources.

During this phase the focus is on the emphasizing of the here and now as opposed to a then and there. With this differentiation, the close connection between trigger stimuli and re-memorizing and re-actualizing a trauma mode can be gradually decoupled. The new information, perspectives and experiences acquired can be integrated into the dream story, which corresponds to an elaboration of the traumatic memory and corresponds to a new view of oneself and one's surroundings, visible in a more complete narrative.

Section IV of the *integration* is a phase of mourning for the lost and starting anew: the patient and, in the worse case, the surviving members of his or her community are survivors of trauma and they are more than that. It is therefore a matter of acknowledging what has happened and what has been suffered and at the same time of gradually re-forming and expanding one's identity, including the violence and powerlessness suffered, in such a way that these do not remain at the core of the self.

The following are the contents and objectives during these meetings:

- Acceptance of changes, some of which are irrevocable, in conjunction with the acceptance of one's own limits and the ability to nevertheless perceive and check new contact possibilities.
- Identification with hitherto alienated self-parts, i.e. the promotion of contact between traumatized and healthy self-parts for the purpose of integration.
- Forms of a new self-concept with a corresponding repertoire including the (re-) integration of own aggressive parts: This includes the approach to the perpetrator's way of being.
- Development of future perspectives on the basis of realistic confidence, in connection with relapse prevention: In addition to the skills practised in dealing with flashbacks, intrusions and moments of dissociation, part of the work will also be steps towards an acceptance of the insecurity that in principle belongs to life and possible new vulnerability.

Criteria for an imminent end of therapy are:

- Affect tolerance.
- Restoration of the ability to contact and intra- and interpersonal dialogue.
- Appropriate significance of the own trauma biography.

10.5 Recommended Literature

Butollo, W. & Karl, R. (2019). *Dialogische Traumatherapie—Manual zur Behandlung der Posttraumatischen Belastungsstörung* (4. Aufl.). Stuttgart: Klett-Cotta. (Original work published 2012)

Butollo, W., Hagl, M., & Krüssmann, M. (2003). *Kreativität und Destruktion posttraumatischer Bewäl-tigung. Forschungsergebnisse und Thesen zum Leben nach dem Trauma*. Stuttgart: Pfeiffer bei Klett-Cotta.

Butollo, W., Karl, R., König, J., Hagl, M. (2014). Dialogical exposure in a gestalt-based treatment for posttraumatic stress disorder. *Gestalt Review, 18*, 112–129.

References

Benz, W., & Distel, B. (Eds.) (1996). *Überleben und Spätfolgen*. München: dtv (= Dachauer Hefte 8)

Buber, M. (2008). In V.J. Buber-Agassi (Ed.), *Schriften zur Psychologie und Psychotherapie*. Gütersloh: Gütersloher Verlagshaus

Butollo, A. (2014). *Wahrgenommene soziale Unterstützung und posttraumatische Folgestörungen nach Missbrauch durch Täter aus der Katholischen Kirche Österreichs*. Univ. Wien: Diplomarbeit.

Butollo, W. (2000). Therapeutic implications of a social interaction model of posttraumatic stress. *Journal of Psychotherapy Integration, 11*(4), 357–374.

Butollo, W. (2002). War traumatization—A social interaction model. *European Psychotherapy, 3*(1), 41–63.

Butollo, W., Hagl, M., & Krüssmann, M. (2003). *Kreativität und Destruktion posttraumatischer Bewältigung. Forschungsergebnisse und Thesen zum Leben nach dem trauma*. Stuttgart: Pfeiffer bei Klett-Cotta.

Butollo, W. & Karl, R. (2019). *Dialogische Traumatherapie—Manual zur Behandlung der Posttraumatischen Belastungsstörung* (4. Aufl). Stuttgart: Klett-Cotta. (Original work published 2012)

Butollo, W., Karl, R., König, J., & Hagl, M. (2014). Dialogical exposure in a gestalt-based treatment for posttraumatic stress disorder. *Gestalt Review, 18*, 112–129.

Butollo, W., Karl, R., König, J., & Rosner, R. (2016). A randomized controlled clinical trial of dialogical exposure therapy versus cognitive processing therapy for adult outpatients suffering from PTSD after type I trauma in adulthood. *Psychotherapy and Psychosomatics, 85*, 16–26.

Butollo, W., Krüssmann, M., & Hagl, M. (1998). *Leben nach dem trauma—Über den therapeutischen Umgang mit dem Entsetzen*. Stuttgart: Pfeiffer bei Klett-Cotta.

Francesetti, G., Gecele, M., & Roubal, J. (2016). *Gestalt therapy in clinical practice: From psychopathology to the aesthetics of contact*. Siracusa, Italy: Instituto di Gestalt (=Gestalt Therapy Book Series).

Hagl, M., Powell, S., Rosner, R., & Butollo, W. (2015). Dialogical exposure with traumatically bereaved Bosnian women: Findings from a controlled trial. *Clinical Psychology and Psychotherapy, 22*, 604–618. (Published online 24 September 2014). https://doi.org/10.1002/cpp.1921

Hamburger, A. (2020). Social trauma—A bridging concept. In A. Hamburger, C. Hancheva & V. Volkan (Eds.), *Social trauma. An Interdisciplinary Textbook* (pp. 3–16). New York: Springer.

Hancheva, C. (2020). Developmental trauma and society. In A. Hamburger, C. Hancheva & V. Volkan (Eds.), *Social trauma. An Interdisciplinary Textbook* (pp. 141–154). New York: Springer.
Höfer, T. (1995). *Als Therapeut in Bosnien. Im Gespräch mit W. Butollo*. Flensburg: Flensburger Hefte.
Huber, M., & Plassmann, R. (Eds.). (2012). *Transgenerationale Traumatisierung*. Paderborn: Junfermannsche Verlagsbuchhandlung.
Jokl, A. M. (1997). *Zwei Fälle zum Thema Bewältigung der Vergangenheit*. Jüdischer Verlag: Frankfurt a.M.
Keilson, H. (2005). *Sequential traumatization in children: A clinical and statistical follow-up study on the fate of the Jewish war orphans in the Netherlands*. Jerusalem: Magnes Press.
Lueger-Schuster, B., Butollo, A., Moy, Y., Jagsch, R., Gluck, T., & Kantor, V. (2015). Aspects of social support and disclosure in the context of institutional abuse—Long-term impact on mental health. *BMC Psychology, 3*(1), 19.
Maragkos, M. & Freyberger, H. (2016). *Gestalttherapie (Psychotherapie kompakt)*. Stuttgart: Kohlhammer.
Niederland, W., & G. (1980). *Folgen der Verfolgung: Das Überlebenden-Syndrom, Seelenmord*. Suhrkamp: Frankfurt/M.
Perls, L. (1988). Leben an der Grenze—ein Gespräch mit M. Sreckovic. *Gestalttherapie, 2*, 5–11.
Polster, E., & Polster, M. (2001). *Gestalttherapy integrated*. New York: Vintage Books.
Powell, S., Rosner, R., Butollo, W., Tedeschi, R., & Calhoun, L. (2003). Posttraumatic growth after war: A study with former refugees and displaced people in Sarajevo. *Journal of Clinical Psychology, 59*(1), 71–83.
Rosner, R., Powell, S., & Butollo, W. (2003). Posttraumatic stress disorder three years after the siege of Sarajevo. *Journal of Clinical Psychology, 59*(1), 41–55.
Votsmeier-Röhr, A., & Wulf, R. (2017). *Gestalttherapie*. München: Reinhardt.
Wardi, D. (2014). *Memorial candles: Children of the holocaust*. New York: Routledge.
Zvizdic, S., & Butollo, W. (2000). War-related loss of one's father and persistent depressive reactions in early adolescents. *European Psychologist, 5*(3), 204–214.

Chapter 11
Psychodynamic Imaginative Trauma Therapy in the Treatment of Patients with Social Trauma

Luise Reddemann and Ljiljana Joksimović

11.1 Introduction

Since 1985, Luise Reddemann has worked with severely traumatised persons, particularly with older persons suffering from the effects of their experiences during World War II, thus from so-called social trauma. In addition, Ljiljana Joksimović has gathered considerable expertise in her work with refugees from war and crisis zones who likewise suffer from the sequelae of social trauma. They have worked together on this subject for over 20 years.

11.2 Learning Outcome Related to Social Trauma

We define compassion as the *behaviour* shown by the therapist to (at least) mitigate pain and suffering. This leads in turn to greater perception of a patient's need to retain their dignity. Only when patients have the experience of their dignity being respected can they make real progress in therapy. It is our hypothesis that psychotherapy with refugees can only be effective when we therapists accept the traumatisation precipitated by an experience of degradation or humiliation, whether in the homeland or in country of refuge.

In addition to an empathetic exchange about a patient's painful experiences both now and in the past, we also invite patients to examine the moments of peace, joy,

L. Reddemann (✉)
University of Klagenfurt, Klagenfurt, Austria

Kall, Germany

L. Joksimović
LVR Klinik Viersen, Viersen, Germany

Düsseldorf, Germany

© Springer Nature Switzerland AG 2021

A. Hamburger et al. (eds.), *Social Trauma – An Interdisciplinary Textbook*,
https://doi.org/10.1007/978-3-030-47817-9_11

freedom and safety in their lives. This is what we call querying about "survival skills", which can be done only once the sufferings have been sufficiently acknowledged. In other words, we take great care that any questions concerning the patient's "survival skills" occur as part of our recognising the social, cultural and political circumstances of the traumatised individual. Failure to ask about these aspects might trigger or prolong feelings of irreality and fragmentation closely connected to the traumatic experiences (Varvin, 2017, p. 156).

We do not force patients to do anything; rather, we show our curiosity and openness towards their solutions to their own problems. Though we must necessarily concentrate on social traumas, we must not lose sight of the fact that patients are and remain individuals moved by their desire to survive—whether consciously or unconsciously. Thus, as it were we invite patients to create a so-called good place in their imagination, in order to confer to this inner world a measure of stability, strength and comfort—inasmuch as patients are agreed to this procedure. In fact, many bring along their own images to therapy (Reddemann, 2016, 2020; see also Roth & Stüber, 2018, p. 430).

We should emphasise that focusing on resources can never justify not attending sufficiently to the patient's suffering.

11.3 The Concept of Psychodynamic Imaginative Trauma Therapy (PITT)

Psychodynamic schools of thought recognise that the therapeutic relationship forms the basis of all good therapeutic cooperation. The consequence is to avoid creating stress through the therapeutic process.

We proceed from the premise that a feeling of external security is a basic prerequisite for a desired internal security and that especially refugees who have fled their country to another country experience this situation as precarious and often extremely traumatising. For this reason, we consider it necessary to determine paths to (re)establishing the inner counterbalances these patients often have available to them, for example, pleasant memories of their childhood or other such resources. First and foremost, there is the need for a compassionate therapist who can assist these patients to become compassionate towards themselves. This we understand especially as a loving and consoling approach by their current egos towards their "younger ego states". Our concept foresees a relative stable current ego, helping ego states, damaged ego states as well as hurtful ego states (Federn, 1952). In the context of these younger ego states, *it is important to note that we are not only and always concerned with childhood or childlike parts*. In fact, we often work with older individuals who have had to flee their home countries taking their very recent traumatised ego parts with them. Examples are a man who fled or a woman who was a victim of rape. Luise Reddemann considers the care and treatment of such "younger states" as the centrepiece of this therapeutic approach—which, of course, does not mean, as is sometimes expressed, that she pleads for completely doing without trauma reconstruction.

During the treatment of traumatised persons from war and crisis zones, it is paramount to create a feeling of security within the therapeutic relationship or the therapeutic situation. This is valid as well for imaginative psychotherapy. In order to establish a safe environment and provide sufficient nonverbal signals, the therapist must possess a corresponding consciousness (Joksimović, Bergstein, & Rademacher, 2019; Reddemann, Joksimović, Kaster, & Gerlach, 2019).

A patient from Bosnia who declared feeling safe after being greeted in a friendly manner by the therapist expressed it as follows: "Suddenly my neighbour began greeting me differently. Instead of a smile on his face and a wave from the other side of the street, he would greet me with a rather stern nod. I felt an inner coldness go through my body. He greeted me differently because I had a different nationality than he did, something that up until then had not been important to us. Even his children stopped coming up to me. They stopped asking whether they could come by to play. They held tightly onto his leg as though I were some scary being. From that point on all I could think about was getting out. Within days the city was under siege. My neighbour became a soldier, and I, like many other men of my nationality, was put in a camp where I experienced living hell. That's how I became a camp survivor. And now I'm here, in your therapy".

We addressed this man's problems with PITT, with compassionate comments and, after gathering the proper information, with the offer to use love to directly perceive and take care of his younger ego who had experienced all this woe (Reddemann, 2016).

Our basis is the three-phase model of Pierre Janet, as taught by Onno van der Hart, who discovered many decades ago the value of using compassion to guide our actions.

Often pain and suffering can be accepted only after contact with someone who is compassionate and empathetic. This means also providing information on the trauma and the consequences of trauma especially at the beginning of therapy.

We recommend that patients with social trauma receive specific psychoeducation. Such patients feel great relief when they hear a therapist say that they very well know that unimaginable horrors occur during war. Psychoeducation in this context comprises elements of soothing enlightenment (Ottomeyer, 2011); it serves to strengthen the therapeutic alliance, since patients often suffer from the feeling of being responsible for the fate they and their family have suffered. The very fact of a therapist's acknowledgement that the patient and the social group they belong to were subjected to traumatising circumstances that were damaging to the health and mental status of the patient and others in their surroundings may reassure them. This can play a major role in the alleviation of strain in groups whose persecution, traumatisation and discrimination may have been denied or rejected by others, for example, during asylum procedures. But even a social group that has been traumatised can still provide protection from social isolation, dehumanising treatment and, above all, stigmatisation.

People who have been subjected to structural and political violence, persecution, marginalisation and discrimination often experience the routine social procedures of the host country as strange and stressful situations—sometimes even as purposeful harassment. We thus try to explain such situations in detail and provide transparency. We should be open to the fact that these procedures may trigger feelings of ignorance, rejection, emotional coldness and discrimination in people who have been socially traumatised. It is important to avoid giving them the feeling that they are victims of arbitrary institutional behaviour, which may retraumatise them (Joksimović et al., 2019; Schröder & Joksimović, 2017).

We always attempt to present the necessity of adhering to certain routine procedures in a way that is sensitive to their cultural and social trauma. If irritations do occur, we give repeated honest but easily understandable feedback, for example, "Please always tell me if you have the feeling of being discriminated based on the colour of your skin. I would like to create an atmosphere of equality in our relationship".

It can be damaging to patients' health—in addition to be hurtful and painful—when traumatic fears are triggered in traumatised patients and social groups. For this reason, we always attempt to reassure and soothe, the goal being that patients eventually become able to soothe themselves by having access to information, friendliness and compassion. We want to foster open, understanding and friendly interactions concerning the complex and intricate nature of group events (Reddemann, 2012, 2016; Zehetmair et al., 2019).

An example: A 40-year-old single mother and English teacher from Iraq suffers tremendously from her chronic headaches as well as from depressive states. She tends to withdraw from society, captive to her pain and depression. Her husband was killed, so she fled with her (then) 10-year-old daughter to Germany. In Iraq, her family had belonged to the intellectual middle class for many generations. Yet her attempts there to emancipate herself were caught up in the ambivalence and conflicts present in the family and its surroundings.

Her own parents, her in-laws and the youngest brother of her husband with his family are all presently living as refugees in Turkey. They feel ashamed and stigmatised there and receive little support from the state and no consideration from their environment. They are unable to provide each other with the necessary consolation and understanding. They all look to the patient for help, with her education and language skills, to quickly get a job in Germany; they expect financial support from her, so that they can rent a house for the entire family in Turkey. She does not tell them, herself full of shame and despair, that she is living in a refugee house and has little hope of ever taking up her profession in Germany and being able to settle down there.

So how to help her?

If we are to offer a true measure of help and companionship, it is important that we first become familiar with the life and trauma of the social groups of our patients. What is their attitude towards gender? How do they deal with authorities? What is their innate family structure? Which religious or spiritual background or beliefs must be attended to? Patients often reveal to us that they have found their own creative ways of feeling safe and secure. The question of course is whether these ways are still active and helpful.

It can be disastrous to think that we know better than our patients what is good for them—or anything else about them for that matter. Thus, we consider humility to be one of the most important basic attitudes. Our patients know particularly more than we do about what they have experienced and how they felt. We must learn that value and meaning systems change in the face of war and persecution, that previous social ties that provided meaning and identity may have been destroyed in the process and that new allegiances and group loyalties arise as well as new demands of the group members resulting from social trauma.

That was the case with the teacher from Iraq: Her husband, a doctor, had functioned as the upholder of the (in fact rather brittle) family identity as "educated middle-class" citizens. His violent death robbed the family of its central element of identity.

Now the woman had to assume the role of supporting her family, despite the fact that her previous attempts at emancipation had not received much support from both families. This contradiction was then iterated in her relationship to her new home: Her expected integration into the new social group (German society) stood in stark contrast to the political and administrative conditions regarding her accommodations, asylum procedures and laws regulating the access of refugees to the German job market (Joksimović et al., 2019). Thus, the social traumatisation of this woman was extended.

Our understanding of humility is that, regardless of their high level of competence and willingness to cooperate, therapists must always be aware of the fact that in the end we generally know very little about the social and political life in the home countries of refugees—their family structures, their social ties and conditioning, their historical background, their present situation and the true losses and discomforts they had to endure.

If we are able to bear all of these in mind to at least a reasonable degree, then our compassion will prompt us to motivate our patients to listen to their inner wisdom (Wampold & Imel, 2015).

Whenever patients have the experience that therapists trust them and have confidence in them, then they too will be able to develop a way to console themselves.

It is our priority to enable trust to ensue and to create an atmosphere that provides patients with a feeling of security. That in turn permits moments of safety as well as the feeling of being accepted. We use the term "stabilisation" from the perspective of psychodynamics and relationships to describe the act of empowering ego functions.

Our credo: Therapists treat human beings, not social traumas, not diagnoses.

The concept of working with ego states serves to create self-regulation and compassion for oneself and to strengthen the therapeutic collaboration.

Ever since we began working with traumatised people, a major goal was to discover ways to pursue trauma reconstruction (some say trauma confrontation) which are as little detrimental as possible. For this we have often been criticised, but our clinical experience with this method confirms our approach. We work with the construct of the inner observer, which renders experiences conscious but retains the patients' control over how much they can and want to reveal about painful emotions (Reddemann, 2012).

For this reason, we tell patients: "People have the ability to observe themselves—including you! If you like, you can ask this observing part of yourself whether it can convey or show what occurs inside you when you become excited or fearful". We work through the traumatising incident using the BASK model according to Bennett Braun; the inner observer helps to calibrate the distance patients require. After the traumatising experience has been worked through, it is particularly important to take sufficient time to offer what we call "inner consolation". We, as supporters of this process, attach particular importance to the current ego consoling the (younger) damaged parts and acknowledging their sufferings (Reddemann, 2012, 2016).

11.4 Practical Implications in the Field of Social Trauma

What can we support, and where are the limits?

A single woman from Srebrenica (in former Yugoslavia, where in 1995 nearly all male Muslim Bosnians were abducted and murdered in what has come to be known as the Massacre of Srebrenica) was looking to obtain psychotherapeutic support for the first time when she got a notice of her immediate need to leave Germany. The therapist wondered why the clearly very afflicted woman had not sought out psychological help earlier. As it turned out, the patient had lived in a refugee centre with many other women from Srebrenica. She thought her suffering did not match up to that of the fate of the other women. She did not have children; she had lost "only" her fiancé and not her "husband" or the "father of her children". So, she helped the other women and took care of her widowed sister's children. Then she received notice that she would have to leave the country, the reason given that it was considered not unreasonable that as a single adult she would adapt to returning to Srebrenica. She became desperate, was plagued by nightmares and panic attacks and pondered committing suicide. Faced with expulsion, she could no longer avert the previously repressed and menacing feelings of anxiety, abandonment, loneliness and forlornness and had to be admitted to a psychiatric clinic to stabilise her condition. She said she could no longer stand living in the refugee centre: The other women there were in no danger of being expelled since they had children, and she did not want to become a burden. But the idea of being separated from the community also frightened her. The solidarity amongst the women there was the only thing that had kept her alive over the years. She had lost all male relatives: her father, brother, brother-in-law, a 15-year-old nephew, three maternal uncles, a paternal uncle and his two sons. Now there was no one left, including her fiancé. "It feels like I died a little myself. It's so awful because I have no idea how I can live on if I'm partially dead. How does that work? Who can show me how to survive in a place where there was so much death if I myself am half-dead"?

Did the threat of expulsion cause this woman's "social death"? And how can we assist her? Surely not just with an individual therapy, but rather with significant compassion and tangible support in her dealings with authorities. "Social trauma" to us means raising our voice against public injustice, inequity and degradation. We do not see trauma therapy solely as an individual event, no less than we see psychotherapy solely in the realm of social trauma. We consider it imperative that we, as citizens, raise our voices to mobilise for human dignity and human rights.

11.5 Suggested Reading

http://www.luise-reddemann.de/home/english-version/

Reddemann, L. (2020). *Who you were before trauma: Use your imagination and reclaim buried strengths to heal from within*. New York: The Experiment.

Joksimovic, L., & Kruse, J. (2017). Stabilisierende psychodynamische Traumatherapie für Flüchtlinge—ein Leitfaden für das therapeutische Vorgehen bei PTBS und Somatisierung. Psychotherapie Psychosomatik Medizinische Psychologie Journal, 1, 5–48.

Kruse, J., Joksimović, L., Cavka, M., Wöller, W., & Schmitz, N. (2009). Effects of trauma-focused psychotherapy upon war refugees. Journal of Traumatic Stress, 22, 585–592.

References

Federn, P. (1952). *Ego psychology and the psychoses*. New York: Basic Books.

Joksimović, L., Bergstein, V., & Rademacher, J. (2019). *Mentalisierungsbasierte Psychotherapie und Beratung von Geflüchteten Grundlagen und Interventionen für die Praxis*. München: Kohlhammer.

Ottomeyer, K. (2011). *Die Behandlung der Opfer. Über unseren Umgang mit dem Trauma der Flüchtlinge und der Verfolgten*. München: Klett-Cotta.

Reddemann, L. (2012). *Psychodynamisch imaginative Traumatherapie—das manual*. Stuttgart: Klett-Cotta.

Reddemann, L. (2016). *Imagination als heilsame Kraft*. Stuttgart: Klett-Cotta.

Reddemann, R., Joksimović, L., Kaster, S. D., & Gerlach, C. (2019). *Trauma ist nicht alles. Ein Mutmach-Buch für die Arbeit mit Geflüchteten*. Stuttgart: Klett-Cotta.

Reddemann, L. (2020). *Geflüchtete würdeorientiert begleiten:Ethische und psychosoziale Annährungen*. Vandenhoeck & Ruprecht.

Roth, G., & Stüber, N. (2018). *Wie das Gehirn die Seele macht*. Stuttgart: Klett-Cotta.

Schröder, M., & Joksimović, L. (2017). Institutionelle Einflüsse auf die psychotherapeutische Arbeit mit geflohenen Menschen. In M. Borcsa & C. Nikendei (Eds.), *Psychotherapie nach Flucht und Vertreibung: Eine praxisorientierte und interprofessionelle Perspektive auf die Hilfe für Flüchtlinge* (pp. 65–72). Stuttgart: Georg Thieme Verlag.

Varvin, S. (2017). Psychoanalytische Arbeit mit traumatisierten Flüchtlingen. In M. Leuzinger-Bohleber, U. Bahrke, T. Fischmann, S. Arnold, & S. Hau (Eds.), *Flucht, Migration und Trauma: Die Folgen für die nächste Generation* (pp. 153–175). Göttingen: Vandenhoeck & Ruprecht.

Wampold, B., & Imel, Z. E. (2015). *The great psychotherapy debate: The evidence for what makes psychotherapy work* (2nd ed.). New York: Routledge.

Zehetmair, C., Tegeler, I., Kaufmann, C., Klippel, A., Reddemann, L., Junne, F., ... Nikendei, C. (2019). Stabilizing techniques and guided imagery for traumatized male refugees in a German state registration and reception center. A qualitative study on a psychotherapeutic group intervention. *Journal of Clinical Medicine, 8*(6), 894–910.

Chapter 12
Music Therapy and Social Trauma

Susanne Metzner

12.1 Introduction: Methods of Music Therapy under Consideration of the Treatment for Posttraumatic Disorder

In music therapy, music listening or active music playing is used to initiate those affective, communicative and (co-)creative processes that contribute to the improvement of psychological, psychosomatic and/or psychosocial disorders by stimulating sensual-aesthetic and semiotic abilities (Metzner, 2018, p. 223). In receptive music therapy, pieces of music are listened to from a sound carrier. This serves patients with posttraumatic disorders in one case as relaxation, distraction, calming or stabilization in the sense of a so-called safe inner place. In yet another case, pieces of music are based on a guided imagination (Guided Imagery and Music (GIM)) for the purpose of dosed dream exposition and processing (Maack, 2012; Rudstam, Elofsson, Søndergaard, Bonde, & Beck, 2017).

In active music therapy, the patients play music themselves. In group music therapy, for example, people sing or drum together to promote the experience of community and solidarity and to activate resources. In individual music therapy, for example, songs are written and composed (Coulter, 2000), which serves the articulation of inner experiences and self-efficacy during trauma processing. Probably the most common form is improvisational music therapy, which is offered in a group or individual setting in a room with a variety of instruments. When making music spontaneously, sensual and affective perception, expressive and interactive action,

---

Translated from German by Dr. Boris Drenkov

S. Metzner (✉)
Faculty of Philosophy and Social Sciences, Augsburg University, Augsburg, Germany
e-mail: susanne.metzner@phil.uni-augsburg.de

© Springer Nature Switzerland AG 2021

A. Hamburger et al. (eds.), *Social Trauma – An Interdisciplinary Textbook*,
https://doi.org/10.1007/978-3-030-47817-9_12

remembrance and fantasy are continuously related to each other. Therapeutic processes of updating and solving intrapsychic and interpersonal problems intertwine.

12.2 Essential Learning Content on Music Therapy and Social Trauma

Music therapy differs from approaches that use music to promote health in that, like trauma psychotherapy, it is linked to a therapeutic relationship. The use of music therapy in the treatment of social trauma requires the reflection of individual, social and societal functions of music (Sect. 12.3.1). In improvisations, the atonal or arrhythmic forms of contemporary music build a matrix for scenic understanding (Sect. 12.3.2). This contribution is based not only on a psychodynamic understanding of disorders and on treatment and clinical experience (Sect. 12.3.3) but also on empirical evidence (Sect. 12.3.4).

12.3 Explanatory Approaches to Music, Music Therapy and Social Trauma

12.3.1 Some Reflections on Music, Political Violence and Social Trauma

From an anthropological point of view, the emergence and function of art is associated with the awareness of the risks of survival: The human being needs a medium that enables him or her to cope with their emotions. Even the elementary aesthetic practice of early man, as well as that of a baby's rattling game, is based on the fact that human beings are in need of a concrete exterior in order to be aware of themselves and to orientate themselves in the surrounding world, i.e. time, space and social interaction. Amongst the arts, it is music that is used worldwide in all cultures to regulate emotional states. It has a positive connotation as a carrier of knowledge about the challenges in human existence, conveys a sense of community and is a messenger of hope for a better world. However, it must not be concealed here that music can be misused for political manipulation or military purposes as well as for the execution of violence in form of non-touch torture, so that music does not only appear in the context of treatment but also in the context of causing traumatization.

The potentials of music to express, play with and transform inner movements and forms of relationship independently from language are almost infinite. Musical means are used to bring tension-filled exaggerations, micro-fine misunderstandings, overwhelming or drifting apart, fragmentation, endless extension, stereotypical repetition, fusion, dissolution as well as a harmonic entanglement, a resonance with each other, lustful rapture and narrative or dialogical structures.

Musical works of art contain individual as well as collective experience and function as bastions against the unbearable (Metzner, 2015). In relation to the phenomena of war and political violence, the most diverse musical forms can be found, depending on the epoch and region, from a Freedom Lied to a Peace Motet and from a Liberation Opera to contemporary music and popular songs.

12.3.2 Musical-Scenic Understanding

The sound events in improvisatory music therapy sometimes seem like experimental music. Not the harmonious but the true expression is the goal of the musical doing, even if it sounds at times unbalanced, dissonant or confused. It was Tronick who pointed out that "reparation of messiness rather than synchrony might be a key change-inducing process in therapy" (Tronick, 2007, 14, cited after Fonagy, 2015, p. 364). In other words, the use of music in therapy allows disharmony. Feelings of threat, irritation or intolerability do not have to be excluded (cf. Strehlow, 2010, p. 245), but are articulated and preserved in music with the potential of being transformed. When treating posttraumatic disorders, however, the risks of retraumatization must be kept in mind, because patients can feel lost or not heard in the midst of such music. They may fail to find their own voice, or unpleasant memories may be triggered by sounds (cf. Metzner, 2018, p. 39). Consequently, situations occur in music therapy to which it is necessary to react immediately:

Vignette I.[1]

Music therapist Sandra Wallmeier talks to 80-year-old Heinz, who survived the Holocaust as a child, about his musical life before, during and after this time. Before the actual conversation begins, Heinz suggests to sing the song "Weißt Du wieviel Sternlein stehen?" ("Can you count the stars that brightly…"*). He recently learnt it during rehearsal of the elderly choir. Heinz begins to sing the first verse with a powerful voice, but he does not quite hit the intonation and melody. Sandra tunes in with a lower dynamic and holds the melody. Consequently the song temporarily sounds bitonal but the two singers try to attune softly in order not to fall apart. At the end Heinz' voice remains—harmonically seen—unclear. Sandra as well doesn't end on the tonic, but intuitively decides for a half-end on the dominant.*

From a normative point of view, one could say that the attempt to sing together was not very successful. But the message, which lies in the drifting apart of the voices, can be understood psychologically. For Heinz the song is one that he has learned in his old age; for Sandra it belongs to the song repertoire of her childhood. The song connects the old man

[1] Unpublished material.

and the young music therapist and builds a bridge between his approaching end of life and the beginning of her life. But it is clearly not a bridge to the beginning of his life, because in his childhood Jewish songs were sung in the family and his sheltered life was suddenly destroyed by the Nazi's persecutions. The song serves as connection and gives orientation, but scenically its realization marks an unbridgeable gap.

12.3.3 Psychodynamic Music Therapy for Social Trauma

The theoretical reference framework for psychodynamic music therapy (Metzner, 2016) consists of several complementary explanatory approaches. These are, in particular, the theory of the development of the self (Stern, 2000, 2010), the theory of attachment and mentalization (Gergely & Unoka, 2011; Fonagy, Gergely, Jurist, & Target, 2002), psychotraumatology (Fischer & Riedesser, 1999; Hamburger, 2016; Reddemann, 2004), symbol theory (Langer, 1942) and analytical social psychology (Lorenzer, 1983).

The following case illustration serves to exemplify processes from an improvisational individual music therapy. In order to underline the importance of the social in relation to traumatization, the story of a young man in the context of German-German history who was not diagnosed with PTSD was chosen. This appears probable only after reconstruction of the life story including socio-historical knowledge.

Vignette II.[2]

In the 1990s, the 23-year-old patient, Mr. X., was an inpatient in psychiatric treatment for multiple psychological and somatic symptoms: social anxiety and avoidance, suicidal behaviour, depersonalization, dizziness and sweating and substance dependence. As a teenager he had moved from the GDR to the West together with his mother after the fall of the Wall and the sudden death of his father. It was the social climate in their neighbourhood that had cooled because his father had been an employee of the Ministry of State Security. The patient was a single child, received infant and child care and attended regular school and GDR youth organizations. Except for a late speech development, he was inconspicuous.

With the move to the West, the then 15-year-old had to cope with the change of school and transfer to a completely different social and societal environment. He remained an outsider, was "the Ossi"[3] and withdrew more and more. After finishing school, he attempted suicide for first time. He had to abandon his training as a medical laboratory assistant due to health problems. After that he stayed at home without training or work and wandered through the city for hours, taking the subway and increasingly developing the feeling that he was not "in the world".[4] This was followed by another suicide attempt and a short stay in the psychiatric ward and an outpatient behavioural therapy. Despite this his (social) fear increased. It was centred around the complex that other people would recognize his origins by his language and humiliate him, or at least avoid him, which he tried to numb with

[2] Abbreviated from Metzner (2012).

[3] "Ossi" is the offensive nickname East Germans were given by West Germans after the unification of the country (note by transl.).

[4] The term "To be in the world" was coined and elaborated by Martin Heidegger, meaning as much as feeling comfortable in the reality due to its familiarness (note by transl.).

increased consumption of medication and alcohol. The insight into the necessity of an addiction detoxification was finally the reason for the current admission.

In addition to the standard psychiatric treatment, he received individual music therapy. Wide passages of the improvisations could be described as grey zones: uneventful, consistent, soundless playing, repeated actions without recognizable intentions and little musical or interpersonal references. Apart from this there were moments in which feelings of horror occurred when realizing own actions and the unprotectedness in the encounter with one another. An instance to this was a scene from the seventh session:

After a short conversation and the agreement to make music, the patient approaches the bass slit drum, sits down and picks up mallets. A pause follows in which it is not clear how to proceed. The therapist takes the children's carillon off the shelf and begins to jingle in little. Seemingly as if of its own, the well-known melody of the Sandman on the TV of the GDR starts sounding.

A fright chases both through, but there seems to be no turning back; the melody is irreversible. When the music ends, neither of them says a word. When the therapist turns around, she sees that the patient has turned his gaze to the window. She mentions that she grew up in Berlin, where one could watch GDR television, and that as a child she had always seen both Sandman programmes, first East and then West, and always liked the East Sandman better. Doubts rage in her about the effects that the melody might have caused. Her personal remark seems chummy to her. Actually, she would have loved to drop the carillon. Instead, she expresses her feelings in words: that everything is quite intense and hardly bearable and whether it is right to end the session for today in this moment. The patient rises, walks to the door and simply says "Thank you" as he walks out, without the therapist knowing what he is referring to.

Comment:

It is noticeable that little is spoken in this music therapy which is symptomatic. The fear of being recognized and exposed by the language is related to the fact that Mr. X. was socialized in a society in which an unconsidered spoken word could have serious negative consequences. He had also grown up in a parental home where it was not allowed to talk about his father's professional activities and experienced the unspoken reservations of neighbours after the fall of the Iron Curtain. As already known from Holocaust research (e.g. Grünberg, 1997), secrecy is highly effective.

Through the possibility of making music in therapy, the speechless is not avoided, but can take shape, even as an uneventful game. Letting these "grey zones" happen may have been a relief for those involved. For the music therapist, it is because she gained time to get to know "not being in the world" (see above) first of all without pressure to act; for the patient, it is because he could feel that he was accepted. Nevertheless, this music points to unrepresented or even dissociated experience, which diagnostically increases the probability of a traumatic effect of deprivation and social upheaval.

In the scenes such as those depicted, however, symbolizations began to emerge. In the Sandman scene, something good from the past appears for the first time. At the same time, the realization opens up that there can be a contact between unknown people with different biographies across the walls between political systems. This realization leads far beyond this subtle individual case from the 1990s, considering extensive forms of state violence in the GDR. Germany is still concerned with the question of how social traumata from the time of the GDR dictatorship and the subsequent radical upheaval of reunification continue to have an effect and how they can be processed (Frommer, 2002).

12.3.4 State of Scholarly Knowledge

The (international) sources on music therapy for posttraumatic disorders in the context of individual and collective experiences of violence are extensive (Landis-Shack, Heinz, & Bonn-Miller, 2017). Particular attention is currently paid to theoretical considerations on psychological (Garrido, Baker, Davidson, Moore, & Wasserman, 2015) and neurological (WFMT, 2019) interrelations in the use of music therapy. Publications on music therapy with survivors of (civil) war, terror, flight and expulsion were mainly collected in (former) crisis areas (e.g. Bosnia-Herzegovina, South Africa, Israel, Northern Ireland, USA).

Scholarly studies are predominantly based on qualitative research methodology, less often on quantifying methods. This is related to the difficulty of implementing ethically justifiable study designs. The current overview of the scientific evidence of music therapy for posttraumatic disorders is published in the study protocol by Beck et al. (2018). As a result, effects on PTSD symptoms, depression, anxiety, somatization, hyperactivity, sleep quality, etc. were demonstrated in small samples. Changes in hearing ability were also found in the form of an increased hearing threshold with reduced volume tolerance (Metzner, 2018).

12.4 Practical Implications of Music Therapy for Social Trauma

Theoretical and methodological concepts as well as goals of music therapy for posttraumatic disorders vary depending on the context and institutional framework. Common characteristics are that:

1. Music therapy is linked to a therapeutic relationship and is performed by trained music therapists.
2. Part of the therapeutic work is the mediation of musical ideas and preferences of the participants. This shows—not only in intercultural music therapy—that music is not a universal language.
3. Music therapy is part of a multi-professional overall treatment concept and is not a one-sided resource-oriented offer, but participates in all phases of trauma therapy (Keller, Strehlow, Wiesmüller, Wolf, & Wölfl, 2018). The flexible adaptation of the methods to the individual needs of the clientele and to the respective time in the therapeutic process limits contraindications to (a) the acute danger of flashbacks, (b) an extremely unstable psychophysical state and (c) the patient's aversion to music.

In music therapy, patients are not urged to tell anything about what has happened to them. But the music therapist conveys their unrestricted willingness to listen, whether in conversation or in music.

Especially in the context of social trauma, the therapeutic relationship is seen as an equal work alliance. More than usual, social values such as honesty, integrity, sensitivity to others and efforts towards equality, justice and truthfulness play a role in the discussions. The therapist is prepared for the fact that trauma leads to a loss of trust in people and that those affected have to assess whether they can trust for a longer period of time. Unusual actions, traumatic reactions, impulsiveness, retreat and sometimes even ruthlessness are regarded as fundamentally understandable. Especially in a group, it is the task of the music therapist to carefully mediate between the needs of expression and protection with structuring offers, so that making music together can unfold its special development potentials.

12.5 Suggested Reading

Sutton (2002), Wolf (2007), Stewart (2010) and Wiesmüller (2014) can be listed as standard works on music therapy for posttraumatic disorders. A collection of all publications up to 2016 can be found at https://www.nordoff-robbins.org.uk/research-projects/evidence-bank/#Section%206%20-%20Trauma%20and%20Abuse.

References

Beck, B. D., Lund, S. T., Søgaard, U., Simonsen, E., Tellier, T. C., Cordtz, T. O., et al. (2018). Music therapy versus treatment as usual for refugees diagnosed with posttraumatic stress disorder (PTSD): Study protocol for a randomized controlled trial. *Trials, 19*, 301–321.

Coulter, S. (2000). Effect of song writing versus recreational music on posttraumatic stress disorder (PTSD) symptoms and abuse attribution in abused children. *Journal of Poetry Therapy, 13*, 189–208.

Fischer, G., & Riedesser, P. (1999). *Lehrbuch der Psychotraumatologie*. München: Reinhardt.

Fonagy, P. (2015). Mutual regulation, mentalization, and therapeutic action: A reflection on the contributions of Ed Tronick to developmental and psychotherapeutic thinking. *Psychoanalytic Inquiry, 35*(4), 355–369.

Fonagy, P., Gergely, G., Jurist, E. L., & Target, M. (2002). *Affect regulation, mentalization and the development of the self*. New York: Other Press.

Frommer, J. (2002). Psychische Störungen durch globale gesellschaftliche Veränderungen. Zur politischen Traumatisierung der Bevölkerung in den neuen Bundesländern. *Fortschritte der Neurologie-Psychiatrie, 70*, 418–428.

Garrido, S., Baker, F. A., Davidson, J. W., Moore, G., & Wasserman, S. (2015). Music and trauma: The relationship between music, personality, and coping style. *Frontiers in Psychology, 6*, 977. https://doi.org/10.3389/fpsyg.2015.00977

Gergely, G., & Unoka, Z. (2011). Bindung und Mentalisierung beim Menschen. Die Entwicklung des affektiven Selbst. Psyche – Z Psychoanal, *65*, 862–890.

Grünberg, K. (1997). Schweigen und Ver-Schweigen. NS-Vergangenheit in Familien von Opfern und von Tätern oder Mitläufern. *Psychosozial, 20*(68), 9–22.

Hamburger, A. (2016). Soziales Trauma. *Forum Psychoanal, 32*, 151–164.

Keller, J., Strehlow, G., Wiesmüller, E., Wolf, H.-G., & Wölfl, A. (2018). Methodische Modifikationen für die musiktherapeutische Behandlung von Patienten mit Traumfolgestörungen. *Musiktherapeutische Umschau, 39*(1), 23–32.

Landis-Shack, N., Heinz, A. J., & Bonn-Miller, M. O. (2017). Music therapy for posttraumatic stress in adults: A theoretical review. *Psychomusicology: Music, Mind, and Brain, 27*(4), 334–342.

Langer, S. K. (1942). *Philosophy in a new key: A study in the symbolism of reason, rite and art*. New York: New American Library of World Literature.

Lorenzer, A. (1983). Sprache, Lebenspraxis und szenisches Verstehen in der psychoanalytischen Therapie. *Psyche—Zeitschrift für Psychoanalyse und ihre Anwedungen, 37*, 97–115.

Maack, C. (2012). *Outcomes and processes of the bonny method of guided imagery and music (GIM) and its adaptations and psychodynamic imaginative trauma therapy (PITT) for women with complex PTSD*. Retrieved October 27, 2019, from http://gim-therapie.de/Thesis.pdf

Metzner, S. (2012). Ein Fall von Zimmerlautstärke. Musiktherapie und soziale Angst. *Musiktherapeutische Umschau, 33*(3), 238–253.

Metzner, S. (2015). Musik als Brennglas. Ein Essay zur ästhetischen Transformation von kollektiver Gewalt in zeitgenössischen Kompositionen. *Musiktherapeutische Umschau, 36*(4), 342–351.

Metzner, S. (2016). Psychodynamic music therapy. In J. Edwards (Ed.), *The Oxford handbook of music therapy* (pp. 448–471). Oxford: Oxford University Press.

Metzner, S. (2018). Über Einstimmungen. Erkenntnisse musiktherapeutischer Prozessforschung aus leibphänomenologischer Perspektive. *Psychodynamische Psychotherapie, 4*, 222–231.

Reddemann, L. (2004). *Psychodynamische-imaginative-Traumatherapie (PITT). Das Manua.* Stuttgart: Pfeiffer bei Klett-Cotta.

Rudstam, G., Elofsson, U., Søndergaard, H. P., Bonde, L. O., & Beck, B. D. (2017). Trauma-focused group music and imagery with women suffering from PTSD/complex PTSD: a feasibility study. *Approach, 9*, 202–216.

Stern, D. N. (2000). The interpersonal world of the infant. New York: Basic Books. (Original work published 1985)

Stern, D. N. (2010). *Forms of vitality. Exploring dynamic experience in psychology, the arts, psychotherapy, and development*. Oxford: Oxford University Press.

Stewart, K. (Ed.). (2010). *Music therapy and trauma: Bridging theory and clinical practice*. New York, NY: Satchnote.

Strehlow, G. (2010). *Töne an der Grenze. Interaktionsmuster in der musiktherapeutischen Begegnung mit Patientinnen, die unter einer Borderline-Persönlichkeitsstörung leiden*. Inaugural-dissertation, Hochschule für Musik und Theater Hamburg, 300 Seiten. Retrieved December 20, 2014, from http://ediss.sub.uni-hamburg.de/volltexte/2011/4968/pdf/Strehlow,_Dissertation.pdf

Sutton, J.P. (Ed.). (2002). Music, Music Therapy and Trauma. International Perspectives (pp. 193–207). London, Philadelphia: J. Kingsley Publishers.

Tronick, E. (2007). *The Neurobehavioral and Social-Emotional Development of Infants and Children*. New York: W.W. Norton & Company.

WFMT—World Federation of Music Therapy. (2019). Music therapy and trauma. Special edition by A. Heiderscheit, G.A. Ann Behrens. *Music Therapy Today, 15*, 1. Retrieved from https://www.wfmt.info/music-therapy-today/

Wiesmüller, E. (2014). *Traumaadaptierte Musiktherapie. Musiktherapie mit Erwachsenen, die an (komplexen) Traumafolgestörungen leiden*. Wiesbaden: Reichert.

Wolf, H. G. (2007). *Musiktherapie und Trauma*. Wiesbaden: Reichert.

Chapter 13
Dance/Movement Therapy and Social Trauma

Beatrix Weidinger-von der Recke

13.1 Introduction: Dance/Movement Psychotherapy (DMP)

DMP recognises body and movement as both implicit and expressive instruments of communication and expression. In a relational process between client/clients and therapist, both engage in a creative empathic exchange using movement and dance to promote the integration of emotional, cognitive, physical, social and spiritual aspects of the self. DMP is used in both individual and group settings (see admp.uk).

In other words, DMP focuses on the experience of sensing movement and the meaning of that movement. The dance therapist empathically brings him- or herself into this intersubjective experience, which is rooted in the body (Best, 2010).

A frequently used term in this context is "body memory". Koch, Caldwell, and Fuchs (2013) state: "The term body memory refers to all the implicit knowledge, capacities and dispositions that structure and guide our everyday being-in-the-world without the need to deliberately think of how we do something, to explicitly remembering what we did, or to anticipate what we want to do" (Koch et al., 2013, p. 82). "This knowledge is acquired in the course of our embodied experiences – mainly in early childhood – and then modified, and changed throughout our entire life" (Koch et al., 2013, p. 82).

DMP consists primarily of two approaches: the "movement analysis according to Rudolf von Laban" (cf. Laban, 1981) and psychodynamic psychotherapy, which investigates the experience and behaviour of the individual as a combination of conscious and unconscious mental processes (cf. Ermann, 2004). Rudolf v. Laban (1879–1958) developed a scientific system for the observation, precise recording and written description of body movements. The specific qualities of any movement

Translated from German by Dr. Boris Drenkov

B. Weidinger-von der Recke (✉)
München, Germany
e-mail: kontakt@praxis-weidinger.de

© Springer Nature Switzerland AG 2021

A. Hamburger et al. (eds.), *Social Trauma – An Interdisciplinary Textbook*,
https://doi.org/10.1007/978-3-030-47817-9_13

are categorised in the following movement factors: weight/force, space, time and flow. Each of these four movement efforts is defined as a continuum; for example, a hand gesture can be recorded in its temporal duration from gradual and slow to fast and abrupt. All human movements take place in three planes: horizontal (also called “table” plane), vertical (also called “door” plane) and sagittal (also called “wheel” plane). Communication with an infant takes place primarily in the horizontal plane, the erection of humans in the course of evolution requires the vertical plane, and locomotion such as walking, running, jumping, etc. is performed in the sagittal plane. A person’s body awareness can be captured by observing the movements in the surrounding space, in the way he or she interacts with one or more others and in the execution of gestures or whole-body movements. Repeated patterns of movement can be understood as everyday or professional activities, for example, or give indications of the person’s psychophysical condition. With the help of this precise system, both conscious and unconscious movements (so-called shadow movements, cf. North, 1975) can be recorded in posture and gestures.

The psychodynamic understanding of the human being makes it possible to classify the observed movements and postures and thus to derive hypotheses on the intra- and interpsychic state of the person (cf. Kestenberg, 1975).

13.2 DMP and Social Trauma

In the following, the meaning of body and movement is explained in order to awaken curiosity about this non-verbal dimension of our being as well as to promote knowledge, perception and understanding of it.

The personal suffering of people who have been victims of trauma in a social context, e.g. a raped woman, must be appreciated and recognised in the social context of their culture, ethnicity and gender. Mass rape of women is part of patriarchal warfare, with the intention of humiliating both the woman and the male enemy. This social context, in turn, often leads to an increase in the already serious suffering of the individual woman, since helplessly watching how others are mistreated without being able to intervene is a massive traumatisation, which can manifest itself, for example, in the phenomenon of survival guilt (cf. Leuzinger-Bohleber, Bahrke, Fischmann, Arnold, & Hau, 2017). Feelings of guilt and shame often cause speechlessness, which in turn affects the next generation as a taboo. Fromm describes this as “the intertwining of parental trauma with a child’s development” (cf. this volume).

Traumatised people suffer from physical and psychological pain, dissociation, memory problems, overexcitation, avoidance, anxiety and feelings of overload, of shame and of guilt. Research, especially in the English-speaking world, emphasises the effective use of DMP in working with traumatised people, be they refugees, veterans or Holocaust survivors (cf. Callaghan, 1993; Moore & Stammermann, 2009).

13.3 Selected Explanatory Model

Experiences from dance/movement psychotherapy with traumatised female refugees within the framework of outpatient psychotherapy in Refugio—the counselling and treatment centre for traumatised refugees and torture victims in Munich—clearly illustrate the specific approach and the special effect of DMP on social trauma (cf. Koch & Weidinger-von der Recke, 2009).

The idea of offering verbal psychodynamic psychotherapy with DMP in work with traumatised refugees as combination therapy for groups arose as a result of the war in former Yugoslavia, especially after the war in Kosovo, when many so-called contingent refugees came to our treatment centre in Munich. Many Kosovar women had had both individual and collective traumatic experiences in this war, either as direct victims of violence or as witnesses of acts of violence against others. In order to adequately counter their painful experiences psychotherapeutically, it was necessary to include the social, cultural and political dimensions of their experiences, to think about them and to reflect on them. As Hamburger writes: "The concept of Social Trauma describes the individual and inter-individual mental consequences of a traumatic experience in the frame of societal occurrences, where a social group is the target of planned persecution" (Hamburger cf. this volume p. 175).

For illustration purposes, excerpts from individual and group therapy are described by the author in her role as the psychotherapist.

13.3.1 Individual Therapy

In the presence of a French-speaking interpreter a woman from Togo in her mid-40s, married with four children, was seen by the therapist. She had attended school in her home country for 4 years. She suffered from anxiety, panic attacks and a post-traumatic stress disorder with massive intrusions. The observation of her everyday movements showed her clear preference for rhythm (triple beat) in her upper extremities. We identified her Christian religiosity as a resource. The patient complained about an intrusive image that frightens and terrifies her and causes feelings of guilt in her: She sees soldiers tearing a baby out of a pregnant woman's body and how the woman dies shortly afterwards.

Together we develop two interventions:

1. How can she associate her deep faith in God with the intrusive image? She takes up this impulse verbally and says that God takes away the feelings of guilt from religious people. She stands up spontaneously, folds her hands, lowers her head and begins to mumble to pray. Interpreter and therapist also stand up and accompany these physically emotional movements with inner empathy and non-verbal mirroring of the observed movement qualities, consisting of tense flow, direct posture in space and synchronized calm.

2. In order to focus on her current self-experience and to support her psychological and somatic stability, we work on three sentences: "Here in Germany people talk about the past to make it easier". "The past is gone". "The woman's image is the past". In order to make these sentences physically perceptible, we develop a simple rhythmic dance, in which the patient determines the qualities of movement with her swinging arms and hands. She pronounces the practised sentences one after the other loudly and moves to them. On suggestion she speaks French and Ewe (her mother tongue). She repeats this dance several times. Interpreter and therapist accompany her by incorporating the patient's movement qualities into their own rhythmic movements. The patient becomes visibly more relaxed in terms of her affective state. At the end of this session, she expresses joy about her dance. After further sessions, the intrusive image dissolves, the patient feels strengthened and relieved, and her sleep improves significantly.

13.3.2 Group Therapy

Ten Kosovar women, an Albanian-speaking interpreter and the psychotherapist meet once a week for a double session at the treatment centre. All women come from rural areas and as housewives cared for siblings, parents and their own families. All have a basic education, some are Muslim, and none is strictly religious.

There is a ritualised procedure that was more or less followed in each group session: At the beginning we listen to music (mostly Mozart) and then each one briefly reports what is important to her and what topic she wants to work on. We agree on topics and work for about 60 min. We then take a 20-min walk in the immediate vicinity of the treatment centre, before exchanging views and saying goodbye for further 20 min in the group room. This therapy is humorously called "the walking group".

After 1 year of therapy, at the beginning of one of the group sessions, a woman spontaneously decides to tell about the sixth anniversary, which "destroyed me". The therapist asks the women present whether they agree. From the individual preliminary talks at the beginning of the group therapy, it is known that all women have experienced violence and rape on their own and/or have become witnesses to such.

The women agree and draw the circle of chairs narrower. There is intense concentration and silence. The word "rape" has not yet been pronounced in the course of the group so far, but has rather been turned into a taboo. The woman says in tears: "I was raped". Immediately afterwards she freezes physically. A short verbal intervention of the therapist causes her to turn her head and look at the therapist directly. Her initially empty gaze gives way to a recognition of the person, and she is again able to answer the following question in the here and now: "Do you see this experience now in the moment?" "Yes". At this instant the whole group moves, the narrowness of the chair circle is dissolved, some patients move away with their chairs, most cry loudly or quietly, some wipe away tears and others let them flow.

What has happened? At first, the women sit almost motionless in the circle of chairs, many with their arms folded in front of their breasts, their eyes either on the floor or on the narrator. After the word "rape", non-verbal changes can be observed, the so-called shadow movements (North, 1975). These unconscious gestures and minimal changes in sitting posture show women's emotional involvement in what is happening. In my physical-emotional countertransference, I feel feelings of fear, sadness and shame. This sensitive moment confronts me with an anticipated challenge not yet experienced in this group: What do I decide now in order to be able to keep the group as a "safe place" (container), on the one hand, and to protect the patient from slipping into further dissociation or re-traumatisation, on the other? At the "horizontal level", the dedicated "oral" communication seems to me to be the appropriate intervention. I address the narrator and encourage her to look at the others in the group. At this moment she looks as if emerging from the depth of her experience; she moves her eyes and her head in slow motion and then looks at a woman of similar age. The woman looks back at the patient and cries openly. The patient moves on with her gaze and captures several of those present. What can be observed in this movement are shape flow (i.e. its use of form) and postural shift (i.e. how it changes its position), which enable the narrator to make contact with the others. In this brief moment, I am pretty sure that she is not flooded with inner images and that she will not slide into further dissociations. In correspondence with the narrator's movement, some of the women begin to move. From the general physical rigidity with the "shadow movements", clear non-verbal movement impulses develop, e.g. turning to the neighbour, arbitrary active movements to change the sitting posture and in facial expressions and gestures. Spontaneously, typical Albanian lamentation sounds are ejected with simultaneous crossing of the hands in front of the breast accompanied by a slight swinging back and forth of the upper body. This sequence of movements is repeated several times by some women. Others show increased self-touching by placing both palms on their cheeks, pressing and holding. There's crying and sighing. The narrator cries violently.

I use these changes to ask the narrator if she would like to hear from the others. She looks at me and nods. Several women speak spontaneously at the same time and then let the eldest take the lead. This one expresses her sympathy softly mumbling. Neighbours of the narrator put their hands on her arm with light effort and at a gradual pace, saying it was bad. Meanwhile the narrator cries less sobbing, cleans her nose and slowly raises her eyes, straightens up and looks around. This looking happens above all in the movement factor time; she looks "gradually" from one to the next. With a calm voice, she thanks the women, which they reciprocate with their own expressions of sympathy. Then the narrator looks at the therapist and says it was good.

Now I turn to the three women who had neither moved nor participated verbally. I turn my upper body in their direction and open an arm in the quality of movement that I had previously perceived as the primary quality of movement in the group (light force, bound flow with gradual time). The two women, addressed by name, express their sympathy in a soft voice and verbally indicate that they have experienced something similar. The third woman, the youngest in the group, begins to cry violently and moves her head back and forth to say "No". I decide to tell the group what I as the psychotherapist am experiencing right now, my being touched as a woman, my respect for the narrator and her courage to talk about her rape. I also connote the different behaviour of women in a positive way and stress that each expresses her compassion, their presence in different ways, with words, with movement and in silence. The youngest woman tells after a few moments that she has only "heard" about it, but not yet directly from a woman who has been raped. The interpreter also wants to express her sympathy; she first tells me her words in German and then in Albanian to the group. At my suggestion, everyone stands up and hands on spontaneously. The narrator says once again that it was so good, everyone looks at each other, and after a moment of silence the hands come loose and everyone sits down. At the end of the session, the women exchange views on the difficulty of talking about stressful topics and crying.

In the following group meetings, the patients share their long-suppressed feelings of shame, guilt and powerlessness, which refer both to their self-confidence with their own bodies and to living together with their husbands and families. The communal social experience of being able to express oneself as a victim of rape in a safe therapeutic setting brought about a healing change in the narrator as well as in the collective of the group participants; the spell of the unspeakable had been broken. As a result, the joint walk became livelier with more differentiated movement qualities, and in the group discussions, individual marriage problems were increasingly discussed and worked on.

13.4 Practical Implications for the Area of Social Trauma

In clinical practice, it is often observed that therapeutic work with body and movement has a particularly anxiety-inducing and unsettling effect on adults. Therefore we developed a psychotherapeutic approach for individual and group work with the following components: verbal psychoeducation about typical symptoms of trauma disorder, about resources or the rediscovery of one's own resources (cultural, individual) and about resilience; building a fixed group with binding rules (e.g. confidentiality, regular participation, etc.); constant and attentive checking of verbal and non-verbal communication between the patient, the interpreter and the psychotherapist; one-third of the therapy time consisting of simple movements such as walking and sensual perception exercises of hearing, smelling and touching the surface of the skin, the feet and legs as well as everyday movements; and our therapeutic attitude consisting of free-floating sympathy and benevolent curiosity about the foreign culture, language, non-verbal communication and the developing psychodynamics.

The implementation and success of this approach are highly dependent on the cooperation between the respective language and culture mediator and the psychotherapist. In addition to personal sympathy, professional preparation and follow-up are required after each group meeting.

This approach, consisting of DMP and psychodynamic psychotherapy, proved itself in the treatment centre Refugio in the long-term treatment of traumatised women and complemented the therapeutic spectrum meaningfully. What is decisive here is that it is not a matter of construing or interpreting the individual movements. Rather, this approach makes it possible to observe and record small and large movements in detail and precisely, which a person has available in his or her individually and culturally formed movement repertoire.

Trauma-specific symptoms, such as avoidance behaviour, can be understood in their individual expression for diagnostic classification. The movement therapeutic adjustment and recording and mirroring of the individual movement qualities enable a direct non-invasive access to the patient. The resulting movement therapeutic interventions are often not particularly spectacular and support the person in his or her search for suitable solutions and adequate coping strategies.

The concept of "social trauma" encompasses events that have been done to a specific group of people, i.e. a group of feeling bodies that move. The application of DMP complements both the grasping and understanding of what happened to this specific group and the processing of the trauma consequences both for the individual and as part of one's own social group.

13.5 Suggested Reading

www.admp.org.uk

References

Best, P. A. (2010). Observing interactions being shaped. In S. Bender (Ed.), *Bewegungsanalyse von Interaktionen* (pp. 257–266). Berlin: Logos Verlag.

Callaghan, K. (1993). Movement psychotherapy with adult survivors of political torture and organized violence. *The Arts in Psychotherapy, 20*, 411–442.

Ermann, M. (2004). *Psychosomatische Medizin und Psychotherapie. Ein Lehrbuch auf psychoanalytischer Grundlage*. Stuttgart: Kohlhammer.

Kestenberg, J. S. (1975). *Children and parents. Psychoanalytic studies in development*. New York: Jason Aronson.

Koch, S., Caldwell, C., & Fuchs, T. (2013). On body and embodied therapy, body. *Movement and Dance in Psychotherapy, 8*(2), 82–94.

Koch, S., & Weidinger-von der Recke, B. (2009). Traumatisierte Flüchtlinge: Tanz-und Gesprächspsychotherapie im Zusammenspiel. In C. Moore & U. Stammermann (Eds.), *Bewegung aus dem Trauma. Traumazentrierte Tanz- und Bewegungstherapie* (pp. 121–143). Stuttgart: Schattauer.

Laban, R. V. (1981). *Der moderne Ausdruckstanz*. Wilhelmshaven: Heinrichshofen.

Leuzinger-Bohleber, M., Bahrke, U., Fischmann, T., Arnold, S., & Hau, S. (Eds.). (2017). *Flucht, Migration und Trauma: Die Folgen für die nächste Generation*. Göttingen: Vandenhoeck & Ruprecht.

Moore, C., & Stammermann, U. (Eds.). (2009). *Bewegung aus dem Trauma.Traumazentrierte Tanz- und Bewegungspsychotherapie*. Stuttgart: Schattauer.

North, M. (1975). *Personality assessment through movement*. London: Macdonald and Evans.

Chapter 14
Using Psychodrama and Sociodrama to Overcome Social Trauma

Konrad Schnabel

14.1 Introduction

Psychodrama is an experiential method that supports participants to explore their inner and outer world through direct actions in the here and now (e.g., Carnabucci, 2014). It was developed by Jacob Levi Moreno in the first half of the twentieth century and uses role-play techniques as a principal method. Importantly, psychodrama goes beyond ordinary role-play with respect to three main differences (e.g., Carnabucci, 2014). First, psychodrama thoroughly considers the processes and experiences involved in role-playing. This applies to playing own roles but also to assuming roles of other persons. Special attention is paid to the insights that result from changing back from the role of another person into the own role (i.e., role exchange or role reversal). This also includes an explicitly stated detachment after the psychodramatic play from roles that were played for other persons (i.e., de-roling). Second, psychodrama uses doubling techniques in order to verbalize the inner thoughts and feelings of the protagonists and to develop the actions on the psychodrama stage. During doubling, the psychodrama director stands next to the protagonist and speaks out, as if she or he was the protagonist, what is supposedly happening inside the protagonist. This could be realized by using an empathic doubling, for instance: "When I hear all your unfair criticism, I feel so angry!" Another possibility, especially for moving onward with the psychodramatic scene, is starting a sentence that is then completed by the protagonist, for instance: "When I hear you shouting at me, I would like to…" Doubling allows to get a deeper insight into the emotions and thoughts of the protagonist and to further develop the dramatic scene without interrupting the role-play and the course of action. Third, psychodrama usually embraces three different phases. The initial warming-up phase helps participants to get familiar with each other and to develop an atmosphere of trust and

K. Schnabel (✉)
IPU Berlin, Stromstr, Berlin, Germany
e-mail: konrad.schnabel@ipu-berlin.de

© Springer Nature Switzerland AG 2021
A. Hamburger et al. (eds.), *Social Trauma – An Interdisciplinary Textbook*,
https://doi.org/10.1007/978-3-030-47817-9_14

safety. This could be realized in multiple ways and includes singing a song or using action sociometry (e.g., participants put themselves on different places of the stage that represent their different origins). The second phase is the action phase where the actual role-play or enactment takes place. Finally, the third phase is a feedback phase where the participants can speak about their experiences during the role-play. An important part of the feedback phase is the sharing where participants share experiences from their own lives that they have in common with the scene that has just been presented on stage.

While psychodrama deals with the enactment of topics from individual participants, sociodrama deals with topics from groups of participants and uses group enactments. In this regard, sociodrama is a group-as-a-whole procedure that allows groups to explore their social context and to transform their intergroup conflicts (cf., Kellermann, 2007). Sociodrama puts the focus on the collective aspects of a problem and deals with intergroup relations and collective ideologies. Similar to psychodrama, it uses role reversal as a principal method.

Psychodrama as well as sociodrama can be conceptualized as mentalization-based intervention methods that use enactment tools in order to change mentalization processes (cf. Krüger, 2015). Mentalization (Bateman & Fonagy, 2012) describes a cognitive activity that enables human beings to perceive and interpret their behavior in terms of mental states (e.g., needs, desires, feelings, beliefs, and goals). Mentalization allows us to understand our behavior as a result of our inner thoughts and feelings. As a consequence, we become able to separate external behavior from internal drives (e.g., feelings, desires, and wishes) and internal interpretations of that behavior. The ability to mentalize is closely linked to psychological well-being, and different psychological disorders can be attributed to specific mentalization deficits (Bateman & Fonagy, 2012). Psychodrama and sociodrama techniques help to reorganize damaged mentalization processes by offering a stage that directly puts into action and implements the various tools and steps of mentalization (Krüger, 2015). First, scene developing deals with the questions of space and context of a respective problem. Second, enactments retrace the dynamics of a scene and help to understand questions of time and chronology. Third, role exchange (i.e., adopting the role of an antagonist and later changing back in the own role) allows to clarify the causalities and origins of our own behavior and the reactions of our social environment. Mirroring, a technique where others play the scene while the protagonists can observe the scene from outside, also helps to better understand the causal chain of events of a specific scene. Finally, sharing our painful experiences with others in the feedback phase supports our self-esteem, decreases our feelings of loneliness, and helps us to generate meaning and an integrated self-concept. In a similar vein, by generating new, alternative scenes with more desirable outcomes, we can develop and pursue our own view of meaning and purpose in life.

14.2 Learning Outcome Related to Social Trauma

Sociodrama supports spontaneity and creativity, fosters psychological health, and renews community life (Leveton, 2010). While creativity provides inspiration to develop new ideas, spontaneity translates these ideas in real action. In this sense, individuals can learn to be more self-reliant and active, and develop an understanding of how their actions have an impact on social life. More importantly, groups start to realize that they are collectively responsible for how they deal with themselves, others, and this planet. In this light, sociodrama may result in strong interpersonal support networks. Reenacting intergroup conflicts, working on representations of different groups, and role reversals with one another provide new perspectives that lead to new understanding, peace, and reorganized social order. *Sociodrama allows to validate experiences of victims, to ease emotional pain, and to strengthen feelings of not being alone*. It uncovers origin, process, and extent of social traumas and offers ways to rehabilitate the victims for what they had to experience. In that way, sociodrama may reunite conscious and unconscious meanings and affects and supports to develop a more coherent narrative of what one has experienced (cf. Bateman & Fonagy, 2012). Sociodrama can initiate a truth recovery process that offers ways to forgiveness and reconciliation, even if this process may require continuous effort and may proceed at a slow pace (cf., Volkas, 2009). Sociodramatic work with folk or fairy tales can support resiliency, well-being, and survival skills even of traumatized children and child victims of war (Veronese & Barola, 2018; Walters, 2017).

14.3 Preferred Model of Explanation

An important prerequisite for successful sociodrama work is that warming-up techniques are used to develop a necessary degree of trust between the participants (Leveton, 2010). This may be realized by action sociometry (see above), by establishing safe places on stage, by communicating realistic goals, and by short initial exercises in smaller groups or couples of participants that start by putting a focus on strengths and resources. In the action phase, participants have the opportunity to understand social situations more deeply through spontaneous enactment and to gain action insight into what has happened. Understanding is supported by techniques such as role reversal, doubling (the sociodrama director or another participant stands next to the person and speaks out inner thoughts, contains emotions, and develops new ideas or alternative reactions), future projection (envisioned interactions in future), and mirroring (opportunity to observe an interaction from outside like in a mirror in order to get some detachment from a terrifying event). Sociodrama enactments uncover the wider social, economic, cultural, political, and religious contexts of a problem. Finally, the feedback or debriefing phase allows participants to share feelings, to express what has been learned, to focus on the collective aspects of the roles, and to develop an emotional distance from their own roles.

A main aspect of social trauma is that traumatized individuals often keep suffering individually and in isolation. Traumatized individuals may be caught in a vicious circle of guilt, shame, and anger and may pass their unexpressed and unresolved collective pain on to the next generation (Leveton, 2010). Sociodrama allows to overcome isolation and alienation, to share similar emotions, to transform shame and rage into constructive action, and to collectively experience comfort and support from others. As a consequence, the interdependence between individuals and groups can be strengthened and hope may be restored. Since every group member is kept in action during sociodrama, embarrassments from being in the spotlight as a single individual can be avoided and tendencies of group members to become passive bystanders may be prevented.

With regard to a mentalization-oriented understanding, mentalization processes in traumatized people may be seen as frozen in a state of shock (cf., Bateman & Fonagy, 2012; Krüger, 2015). Individuals may react aggressively or show tendencies to self-injury during flashbacks. Additionally, dissociations may occur in order to distance oneself from the traumatic situation and the devastating affects. Dissociations further impede memories to be processed adequately and flashbacks may lead to re-traumatization in a vicious circle. *Sociodramatic work allows to re-integrate the fragmented memories of collective trauma events and to incorporate them as a regular part of memory.* In this way, sociodrama aims to liberate from the hidden and unconscious agenda of collective trauma (e.g., self-blame, feelings of guilt and shame, social isolation). The main target is to develop a more consistent mentalizing self that actively mediates between feelings and action.

As an example, crisis sociodrama after a catastrophic event (e.g., earthquakes, wars, terrorist attacks) according to Leveton (2010, p. 67 ff.) is described. As a warm-up, participants could introduce themselves to each other as an imaginative plant. The purpose is to create a secure and safe environment and to sensitize participants to their resources and healing forces. In the action phase, the traumatic event is reenacted. Here, participants are given opportunities to show what they have experienced during the traumatic events. If trauma survivors are still overwhelmed by events and unable to reenact, playback theatre offers an alternative (Fox, 1991). In playback theatre, trained actors improvise the happenings that are told by participants. The action phase helps participants to express through action what may be impossible to be expressed in words. Enactment helps to cognitively reprocess the events and to develop a deeper understanding of what had happened. Facts and events can be presented in a structured manner within a safe atmosphere and the emotional support of the group. Emotions (grief, shame, anger) can be expressed openly and alternative ways of coping can be explored. Realizing that others had to go through similar experiences and suffered similar pains offers social comfort and reduces feelings of loneliness and isolation. Enactment allows to openly show emotions that may have been brushed under the carpet and offers opportunities for emotional catharsis. Importantly, a suitable balance between confrontation and emotional support needs to be found, which respects the particular emotional needs of the participants who may long have avoided their feelings. Enactment allows participants to no longer see themselves as objects only but also as active and responsible creators of their lives while they are on the way of finding trauma resolution. The final feedback phase provides room for communal sharing and interpersonal support. Participants can once more develop a deep understanding that their feelings are shared with numerous others. During this phase, sociodramatists should offer individual consultations to participants who indicated need for further support. The sociodrama should end with a closure ritual where participants explicitly de-role from roles if they also played other roles than themselves during the enactment.

14.4 Practical Implications in the Field of Social Trauma

Sociodramatists should be well informed about the history and background of the communities in which they work (Kellermann, 2007). In conflicts, the different parties tend to ignore their own misbehaviors, view themselves as victims, and blame others as aggressors. Therefore, sociodramatists should focus on the shared central issues of the whole group (e.g., search for peace, striving for freedom) and communicate this perspective to the group. Also, sociodramatists need to start their group work by explaining what is going to happen and need to get explicit consent from the participants for their participation. At no time, sociodramatists should try to be manipulative or directive. In contrast, they should rather follow their participants and should make themselves available as catalysts who help their participants to present and develop their own stories. Sociodramatists should be realistic and develop an understanding that conflicts and trauma may never be resolved completely. However, healing of emotional wounds is possible and every sociodrama should balance between emotional ventilation of individual issues on one side and dealing with interpersonal aspects of the group as a whole (e.g., reconciliation) on the other side. In some cases, preparatory individual interventions or separate meetings with more homogenous subgroups may be necessary to do some basic intrapsychic work, which does not require participants to be responsive to the feelings of other groups and that may prepare them for the subsequent reciprocal reconciliation process.

Every sociodrama should start with a warm-up that creates a safe atmosphere and supports the development of trust between the participants (cf., Guglielmin, Gola, Basilicò, Gorinova, & Nikolova, 2012). Warm-ups can include action sociometry, expressions of current feelings, short introductory tasks in small groups, etc. Before the action phase, it is also recommended to establish a safe place with pillows or comfortable chairs where participants may withdraw to and get some rest if they are overwhelmed by the enactment. Giving participants the opportunity to choose an ally participant for mutual support contributes to a safe environment and also helps participants to engage in spontaneous action. In the end, there should be enough time for participants to recompose themselves, to calm down their emotions, and to understand what has just happened. It is essential for participants to have the opportunity to reduce their arousal in order to be able to think again of other perspectives and to repair their mentalization processes (cf. Bateman & Fonagy, 2012).

Sociodrama is not recommended during or immediately after a catastrophic event, when individuals are still overwhelmed by fear (Leveton, 2010). In this case, debriefing activities, fear reduction, and measures to secure physical safety should be seen as principal interventions. Sociodrama participants need a little distance from the real drama, which gives them time to process the events cognitively and emotionally. Every sociodrama has the power to heal but also the power to harm and may therefore cause retraumatization. If a setting cannot offer the necessary protection to participants, reenactments of traumatic events should be avoided. As an alternative, playback theater (see above) may be used. In this regard, sociodrama needs to find a balance between preventing denial and avoiding intrusive flashbacks. Participants who have been abused or hurt by others should not be invited to reverse roles with these people. A request for role reversal in this case may be misinterpreted as an invitation to empathize with these others and to understand their motifs (Kellermann, 2007). Participants should first get in touch with their own emotions (e.g., anger, sadness, shame) before they may be willing to develop an understanding of the position of others.

14.5 Suggested Readings and Further Information

Information about playback theatre according to Peter Fox can be found at www.playbacktheatre.org.

Information about the therapeutic spiral model by Kate Hudgins, a psychodramatic approach primarily developed for the therapy of PTSD in individual settings that can be applied also to collective trauma, can be found at www.therapeuticspiralmodel.com.

Information about the work of Peter Felix Kellermann, author of Sociodrama and Collective Trauma (Kellermann, 2007), can be found at www.peterfelix.weebly.com.

Information about the drama therapy approach by Armand Volkas, an approach that combines psychodrama techniques with art therapies, can be found at www.livingartscenter.org.

References

Bateman, A. W., & Fonagy, P. (Eds.). (2012). *Handbook of mentalizing in mental health practice*. Arlington, VA: American Psychiatric Publishing.

Carnabucci, K. (2014). *Show and tell psychodrama: Skills for therapists, coaches, teachers, leaders*. Racine, WI: Nusanto Publishing.

Fox, J. (1991). Die inszenierte persönliche geschichte im playback-theater [dramatized personal story in playback theater]. *Psychodrama: Zeitschrift für Theorie und Praxis, 4*, 31–44.

Guglielmin, M. S., Gola, N., Basilicò, L., Gorinova, M., & Nikolova, T. (2012). Classic Morenian psychodrama as a therapeutic tool in support of women victims of violence and victims of trafficking in Albania and Bulgaria. *Interdisciplinary Journal of Family Studies, 17*, 137–152.

Kellermann, P. F. (2007). *Sociodrama and collective trauma*. London: Jessica Kingsley.

Krüger, R. T. (2015). *Störungsspezifische Psychodramatherapie: Theorie und praxis [disorder-specific psychodrama therapy: Theory and praxis]*. Göttingen: Vandenhoeck & Ruprecht.

Leveton, E. (2010). *Healing collective trauma using sociodrama and drama therapy*. New York, NY: Springer Publishing Company.

Veronese, G., & Barola, G. (2018). Healing stories: An expressive-narrative intervention for strengthening resilience and survival skills in school-aged child victims of war and political violence in the Gaza strip. *Clinical Child Psychology and Psychiatry, 23*, 311–332.

Volkas, A. (2009). Healing the wounds of history: Drama therapy in collective trauma and intercultural conflict resolution. In D. R. Johnson & R. Emunah (Eds.), *Current approaches in drama therapy*. Charles C Thomas: Springfield, IL.

Walters, R. (2017). Fairytales, psychodrama and action methods: Ways of helping traumatized children to heal. *Zeitschrift für Psychodrama und Soziometrie, 16*, 53–60.

Part III
Developmental Psychology of Social Trauma

Chapter 15
Developmental Trauma and Society

Camellia Hancheva

15.1 Introduction

The term trauma when applied to psychological functioning carries three implicit ideas—about certain events, about their immediate subjective experience by the individuals, and about the long-term effects over the personality organization and the overall functioning. Laplanche and Pontalis (1985) include in the definition of trauma the idea of a violent shock, causing a wound in the psychic, and thus affecting the structure of the self and leading to impairments in functioning.

Events and experiences that present ultimate threats to survival cause extreme pain or overwhelming terror have the potential to result in trauma. Disregarding the nature of threat—natural disasters (earthquakes, tsunamis, flooding, etc.), accidents (car crashes, injuries, etc.) or man-made (kidnapping, violence, armed conflicts, war, genocide, etc.)—when it exceeds physical and/or mental capacity, it could seriously hinder further adaptation. If strong affects accompanying trauma cannot be processed, contained, or regulated, the experience has an overwhelming impact on emotional functioning, resulting in an intense fear, helplessness, and hopelessness (Teicholz, 2012).

Traumatic consequences of a single event or prolonged periods of uncontrollable (as in war) and incomprehensible (as in nationalistic or totalitarian regimes) threats and the effect of both on the internal world is deeply destabilizing. Subsequent traumatization encompasses a wide continuum of psychological states, ranging from mild to severe, and results in acute or chronic conditions (Lanyado, 1999).

People differ significantly in their capacity to face challenges and process experiences. The degree, the scope, and the form of the traumatic consequences are the result of the following key factors: (1) the character of the external event (suddenness, witnessed or experienced life treats, etc.); (2) the meaning ascribed to the

C. Hancheva (✉)
Department of Psychology, Sofia University "St. Kliment Ohridski", Sofia, Bulgaria

© Springer Nature Switzerland AG 2021

A. Hamburger et al. (eds.), *Social Trauma – An Interdisciplinary Textbook*,
https://doi.org/10.1007/978-3-030-47817-9_15

event (by important others, attachment figures or community, during and after the event); (3) personality factors (the stage of psychological development, coping strategies and defenses developed at the certain stage; and (4) available support from the environment (quality of external and internal relationships). Thus, children and adults perceive and react differently to potentially traumatic experiences (Kaplan & Hamburger, 2017).

15.1.1 Developmental Trauma and the Concept of the Average Expectable Environment Revisited

The starting point of psychological development is the experience of being in the world that is shaped in an intuitively found balance between terror (early anxieties) of annihilation and a hope that everything would be in order. It forms a fluid sense of the basic trust (Erikson, 1968). The accumulation of positive experiences enhances hope that what is out there—no matter how powerful—could be perceived, understood, and, eventually, tamed. Traumatic experiences have the potential to estrange the person from the world and from oneself, attacking the sense of safety and security and bringing a constant threat of annihilation. For adults, the traumatic event becomes a focal point dividing time and creating a sense of "before" and "after," changing self-perceptions, and bringing about the feeling that one could never be the same again (Lanyado, 1999). During early developmental stages, when the time dimension of past, present, and future is not integrated into the form of autobiographical self, the traumatic experience is disorganizing the cognitive and emotional functioning. Thus, the traumatic experience makes every attempt to create structures of knowledge meaningless and every form of emotional containment or regulation unachievable (Bion, 1959). The experience of being flooded with affects—nameless, endless, and uncontrollable—could only be acted-out in chaotic destructive and/or self-destructive ways. Children with their limited capacity for emotional regulation depend on responsible adults to help them survive the horror of an immediate experience and later ascribe a meaning to the events and recover from the emotional shock.

Hartmann's concept of the *average expectable environment* describes variables such as resources and care, people and emotional exchanges that are a precondition for the development and maturation (Hartmann, 1958). The meaning and usage of the term has shifted more in the direction of the impact of human relations as in Winnicott's concepts of the *ordinary devoted mother* and *facilitating environment* (Winnicott, 1965b). Predictability and safety of the environment are equally important for child development (e.g., abusive relationships are predictable, but with devastating consequences). The process of social traumatization resembles the dynamics of abusive relationships where a failure of the environment might be a long process of deterioration of emotional ties and distortion of meanings resulting in the trading of freedom and spontaneity for (questionable) safety and survival. In such cases, to paraphrase Laub and Lee (2003), the normality (not abruptly, but slowly and steadily) ceases to exist.

15.1.2 The Impact of Loss on Child Development

15.1.2.1 Attachment Theory

There are single events with a high potential for a traumatic impact even though they seldom go alone. Events like an early loss of attachment figures or prolonged and/or multiple separations with the main caregiver at an early age tend to result in various psychopathological conditions, behavioral problems, and social difficulties (Bowlby, 1980). There is evidence from retrospective and prospective studies, as well as epidemiological data, to support the negative impact of childhood separation and loss (Main & Hesse, 1990). The effect of separations and losses was significant, irrespective of violence and other traumatic exposure (Briggs-Gowan et al., 2019).

In the situation of social turmoil like civil wars, armed conflicts, and political oppressions, loss is an everyday experience. The attempted banalization of events like losses and witnessing violence rarely succeeds as a maneuver of psychic defense: it usually leads to dissociation of certain parts of the experience. Multiple unmourned losses—real (of people) and symbolic (of home, motherland, ideals, etc.)—are another path to later psychopathology. When an important person is lost, that shatters both children and adults to the core of their existence and a supportive environment is vital for the recovery process. Children depend on adults for emotional support to help them through the process of grieving. When the remaining adults are experiencing the same traumatic influence, they are often unable to provide comfort and support. Even when there are shared rituals of grieving in the culture and society, children are often excluded and their inner experiences remain unrecognized. Main and Hesse (1990) warn against the danger of the unresolved loss and its role for disorganization of emotional and relational systems in the next generation. For children left alone in their naïve attempts to grasp the irreversibility and finality of loss, it is easy to take upon oneself the unrealistic responsibility for the loss and consciously or unconsciously spend considerable efforts in attempted atonement or compensations.

15.1.2.2 Object Relations Theory

The psychoanalytic understanding of loss differs considerably from the attachment theory; it refers to internal vs. external relations. Object relations' theory hypothesizes another connection of loss, trauma, and psychopathological functioning. Psychic trauma evokes past trauma and loss, and, irrespective of age, commences a regression where every person is connecting to the earliest experience of loss of the first good object (Laub & Lee, 2003). The first good object (the "good breast" in

Kleinian terms) stands for every goodness, generosity and life, and, through internalization and identification, it is becoming a center of self. Fear and anxiety over the loss of the external good object is a fear that the internalized goodness will also be lost (Klein, 1935). Defenses against anxieties and pain of loss range from denial and omnipotent undoing to a manic triumph. The dynamics of many social processes and individual psychopathologies could be traced to these defensive transformations. The manic defense creates an omnipotent belief that one is in control of good and bad and could keep them separate—this ideological frame is notoriously known from dictatorships and totalitarian regimes. In a movie *Eastern Plays* (see below), the main character—the elder brother—is a drug addict. His desperate monologue at the psychiatrist's office is almost a literal illustration of the inner conflicts described by Klein as fears of annihilation and *pining* for the good objects (Klein, 1940). The young man is revealing his desperate need of truth to hold on to and reluctance to take again the needle in a fruitless and doomed attempt to *pin* the particle of goodness left and inject it back to his heart and soul. The loss of something external is resonating with doubts that internal goodness will diminish and disappear. A person in doubt of his/her own goodness is inclined to self-destruction, as a person who has lost faith in the goodness of the surrounding world is becoming violent and destructive.

15.1.2.3 Mentalization and Regulation Theory of Attachment

Fonagy and Target are giving another point of view on the traumatic impact of separation and loss on development—"what is lost in a separation is not the bond but the opportunity to generate a higher order regulatory mechanism" (Fonagy & Target, 2002, p. 325). The loss of the meta-cognitive mechanisms for reorganization and reframing of contents of thoughts and experiences as a vital part of emotional maturity results in inhibitions, rigidity and possibly estrangement, and alienation of one's inner life. A mother figure has to be there not only to compensate and regulate the current state of arousal but also to provide a symbolized version of the experience. If caregivers can contain the internal, chaotic experience of the infant, mirror it contingently and markedly and return it in a metabolized form to the infant, the experience will become contoured and slowly growing into patterns that are comprehensible and close to awareness (Fonagy & Target, 2002). Highly disturbing inner states that have not been consistently mirrored and represented seek discharge only in nonsymbolic modes like behavioral outbursts or symptoms. This clinical psychoanalytic hypothesis meets developmental neuropsychoanalysis in Allan Schore's Regulation Theory (2001). The loss of a caregiver carries as much potential threat for impairment of mental functioning as inappropriate care, and both risk factors are mediated by the effect of prolonged, unregulated episodes that cut the way to the development of reflective functioning and regulative capacity (Ensink, Bégin, Normandin, Godbout, & Fonagy, 2017; Schore, 2001).

15.1.3 Violence in Development

Another characteristic of human relations contributing to trauma is violence. Domestic violence, community violence, directly experienced or witnessed, is harmful in many different ways. The developmental psychopathology perspective suggests complex models of the causes and consequences of child maltreatment and traumatic or resilience outcomes (Cicchetti & Toth, 2013). The widely accepted framework for research on child maltreatment emphasizes the interrelatedness of social and cultural influences on individual development (Belsky, 1980). Child maltreatment as a social-psychological phenomenon is determined by family dynamics, community processes, and cultural norms. Understanding of violence against children could not be achieved if regarded as an isolated perpetrator-victim phenomenon.

Maltreatment as "a severe deviation from the average expectable environment" (Cicchetti & Valentino, 2006, p. 161) is defined in the following categories: (1) sexual abuse; (2) physical abuse; (3) neglect; and (4) emotional maltreatment. Social trauma context often confronts children with different forms of community violence. Witnessing harm or humiliation of parents or other close figures has a devastating impact on the child's mind. Fear and helplessness bond together to form a mental representation of self as either a perpetrator or a victim (Lieberman & Amaya-Jackson, 2005). Witnessing violence when the caregivers are involved shatters the child's trust in protective powers of the attachment figures and induces fears of pain and injury.

Another prototypical traumatic situation is when the child victim is also dependent on the adult aggressor. Children who fear their caregivers are facing the paradox of "fright without solution" (Hesse & Main, 2000, p. 484), where the attachment figure is "at once the source of and the solution to its alarm" (Main & Hesse, 1990, p. 163). Neither anger towards the aggressor nor fear of abandonment could be expressed, and that results in a deep disorganization of experience and behavior. The origin of a negative self-image could be traced to the defensive presumption that the aggressor is having "the right" to "punish" the child for his/her "wrongdoings." This maneuver helps ascribing meaning (even though altered) to these relations. Laub and Lee (2003) conceptualize identification with the aggressor as another consequence to a string of losses—first, the loss of an empathic bond with the object, then the good external object, and the good internal one. Identification with the bad external object is at the core of the negative identity. The process of identification with the aggressor is the main mechanism forming the vicious cycle of violence where a traumatic experience is transformed into a traumatizing behavior: "It is a combination of a defense against overwhelming anxiety and distress due to the traumatic event, and the tendency that traumatic events have of repeating themselves in an uncanny way in traumatized people's lives" (Lanyado, 1999, p. 286).

Another defensive strategy with regard to abuse is avoidance of thinking of the minds of others (Allen, 2013; Fonagy & Target, 2002). Children experiencing abuse are frightened by the acts and suspected malevolent intentions in the mind of the abuser, and they are reluctant to explore their own and mental states of others. Abusive caregivers, precluding recognition of the suffering inflicted on the child, discourage the development of coherent discourse about mental states and thus prevent the development of mentalization and affect regulation (Allen, 2013). Long-term consequences of poorly developed mentalizing abilities prevent the integration of the traumatic experience and working through it.

15.1.4 Clinical Perspective on Developmental Trauma: Disorders of Extreme Stress Not Otherwise Specified (DESNOS) and Developmental Trauma Disorder (DTD)

Epidemiological studies and clinical observations on symptoms and sufferings of different groups of people draw attention to certain recurring events, incidents, or conditions in their developmental history, and set the beginning of a systematic exploration of what could be summarized under the term of multiple traumatic influences early in life. Traumatic experiences, most often of an interpersonal nature (e.g., sexual or physical abuse, war, community violence), constitute a high developmental risk. In the late 1990s, a taskforce group (Luxenberg, Spinazzola, & Van der Kolk, 2001) introduced the concept of Disorders of Extreme Stress Not Otherwise Specified (DESNOS). The etiology of diagnoses is rooted in traumatization of a persistent nature, and disruption of biological and socio-emotional systems is summarized into the following broad spheres of impairments: (1) the regulation of affect and impulses, (2) attention or consciousness, (3) self-perception, (4) relations with others, (5) systems of meaning, and (6) somatization (Luxenberg et al., 2001). Bessel van der Kolk (2005) defined a set of diagnostic criteria for developmental trauma disorder (DTD). Despite evidence presented from a numerous prospective and retrospective studies, DTD did not make it into the DSM-5. The idea that there is a general common factor in psychopathology is raised also by another group of researchers and the so-called p-factor is also closely related to the traumatic impact of different nature (Caspi et al., 2014). Acceptance of childhood trauma as a diagnosis is important for it might change mental and physical health policy and stimulate public discussion on the long-term traumatic impact of social processes and conflicts.

15.2 Learning Outcome Related to Social Trauma

The social environment in terms of caregivers, communities, and institutions has a direct impact on child psychological development. The levels of tolerated aggression in society, cultural norms, and practices for raising and educating children differ significantly and form a unique constellation of factors for every child. The bigger the deviation from the *average expectable environment* and *good-enough* caregivers (Hartmann, 1958; Winnicott, 1965a), the greater the predispositions for psychopathology, behavioral, and social problems. Caregivers' influence on development follows two distinct, but not always separable lines: (1) violent relations destabilizing profoundly the personality organization and (2) insensitive, unavailable, emotionally misattuned, and low mentalizing parenting that hinders the development of the capacity for regulation and integration of experience.

Bowlby has explicitly made a connection between the quality of care the attachment figures are able to provide for their children and the support and provision that they receive from the society. In his report for WHO he states: "If a community values its children it must cherish their parents" (Bowlby, 1951, p. 84). Maturity required by the parents and responsible adults in performing this task presupposes extensive work on their behalf with their own past and current stressors. If a traumatic history of any kind is part of the caregiver's experience, the working through and integrating traumatic experiences is a key determinant for the adaptive development of their children. The choice to protect the next generation by being silent about the past provides short-term solutions with long-term negative impact. In the case of social trauma, the *conspiracy of silence* is a symptom. But silence is also a symbol, a representation of the missing words for the traumatic experience. If a parent is silent for certain parts of outer or inner reality, the segments would stay nameless but present in the child's mind in a form of the *unthought known* (Bollas, 1987). Experiences that are not put in words do not disappear, but seek manifestation in nonverbal forms, and are often represented in social symptoms of postwar and post-totalitarian societies.

Quality of the early attachment relationship is a key protective factor in the development. Adults guide and support children to go through horrible experiences by meaning making and contextualizing, externally regulating, and symbolizing the shared terror. Social inequality, injustice, and totalitarianism prevent meaningful, productive, and creative participation of some adults in the society and thus plunder the future of their children. As Bretherton (1992) eloquently puts it:

> When powerful groups in society promote their own control over life circumstances by subordinating and marginalizing others, they make it less possible for these groups to offer and experience security in their own families. Valuing of attachment relations thus has public policy and moral implications for society, not just psychological implications for attachment dyads. (p. 770)

15.3 Preferred Model of Explanation

The following assumptions help to understand the impact of social trauma on child development: (1) cumulative developmental trauma is a relational phenomenon, (2) social trauma "is contagious, that is, it is transmitted interpersonally" (Renn, 2012, p. 107), and (3) traumatic impact is possibly mediated and mitigated by the quality of attachment relationships and mentalization capacity of the responsible adults and the whole society.

Processes of traumatization and recovery are to be studied within the attachment and relational psychoanalytic paradigm. Social trauma is a severe attack on connection—a person is losing the link to his/her own past, to other people, and to the world. The traumatized individual is alienated from herself/himself, unable to involve in deep intimate relationships, to share and empathize with others, and trapped in a paranoid position toward the world. From a relational psychoanalytic perspective, being "psychologically alone in unbearable emotional states" is the quintessence of trauma (Allen, 2013, p. 255). Cumulative developmental trauma results in severe disorganization of internal and external relations, inability to handle and regulate affect, inability to reflect on the experience, and act in a constructive way. Suggested *relational diathesis* (Lyons-Ruth, Bronfman, & Atwood, 1999) provides an explanatory model of interrelatedness of trauma, early attachment relations, and subsequent behavioral and mental dysfunctions. *Relational diathesis* stands for accounting multiple factors over long time periods influencing the attachment dyad and providing insights over mechanisms of transgenerational transmission of both traumatization and resilience. If fear is an organizing principle of representational models of the caregiver, it is shaping frightening-frightened or helpless caregiving interactions with the child. The uncontrolled and often unconscious qualities of the emotional presence, be it in a pervasive, continuous manner, or in strong but isolated instances, have a disorganizing effect on the child's functioning (Lyons-Ruth, 2003; Lyons-Ruth et al., 1999). If the caregiver consistently fails to recognize and compensate for these moments of rupture, then the traumatic impact of the parents' past is transmitted to the next generation. Frightened or frightening caregiver's behaviors are proven to be connected to unresolved traumatic experiences such as individual history of abuse, or community violence, significant loss and social trauma (Laub & Lee, 2003). It is the "unresolved loss or trauma, not loss or trauma per se" (Lyons-Ruth et al., 1999, p. 35) that is predictive to children's disorganized behaviors. Unresolved states of mind and/or dissociated parts of the experience are often consequences of a massive trauma, which "has an amorphous presence, not delimited by place, time, or agency" (Laub & Lee, 2003, p. 448).

The quality of attachment figure depends on her/his history of development and actual experience. If a caregiver is in the process of deep mourning, overwhelmed by current emotions, or past experiences, he/she is unavailable for the child. The effect of severely depressed, unresponsive adult is described by Andre Green (1986) in the "dead mother" phenomenon and verified by Ed Tronick in the *still face* experiment. The disorganizing effect of the "psychically dead" mother figure on the child is devastating. In the case of social trauma, the attachment figure is unable to help because he or she may be traumatized by the same events or reminded of past traumatic experiences (Hamburger, 2020, this volume). Mother figures who were victims are apt to respond with compliance to the discipline and violence inflicted by the father figure or other authorities. Caregivers motivated by fear or self-delusive belief in the idealized prototype (true Arian, communist, etc.) fail to respond to the child's creativity and initiative and foster obedience and thus development of False self (Winnicott, 1965b). The further away the caregiver is from her authentic experience—ambivalent but human—the more intolerant she is toward acknowledging her limits and vulnerabilities. Maternity has a special place in totalitarian ideology—a perfect mother of a hero. The pretended perfection of the mother requires a perfect child in accordance with the totalitarian ideal—always happy, strong, strict, unemotional or showing only "correct" emotions of exaltation when in touch with the symbols of the narcissistic ideal. Children master a defensive structure of the False self in compliance with the requirements of the authoritative figures. Alienation from the True self is reflected in apathy, compulsion, destructiveness, and a lack of vitality and creativity.

Understanding of the impact of social trauma on child development is only possible when contextualizing the attachment relations within the family, community, and particular sociohistorical moment. "Ghosts in the nursery" (Fraiberg, Adelson, & Shapiro, 1975) originate not only from the individual history of the caregivers but also bear resemblance to the traumatic past of the whole society. In case of social trauma, when traumatic events are inflicted on one group of people to the other (Hamburger, 2020, this volume), parental self-reflective capacity and resilience are vital mediators of children's development and coping with traumatizing circumstances. *Holding* capacity of the parents (Winnicott, 1965b) is inextricably linked to the capacity of the community and society to provide support and *containment* (Bion, 1962) of emotional experiences in a time of inescapable ordeals. And even more important is the capacity to reflect (Allen, 2013; Fonagy, 1999) and involve in the process of thinking and trying to know (Bion, 1959). Studies of descendants of Holocaust survivors (van IJzendoorn, Bakermans-Kranenburg, & Sagi-Schwartz, 2003) prove the importance of social support and collective mourning in the mitigation of symptoms and integration of a traumatic experience. One of the important presumptions in clinical trauma theory is that the trauma precludes its knowing (Laub & Lee, 2003, p. 449) but, at the same time, fuels individual and social processes of acting out, unconscious repetitions and transmission of terrifying unsymbolized psychic contents. Traumatic memory studies (Hancheva, 2020, this volume) reveal how extreme emotionally charged memories are brought back and relived at the present moment when distress and feelings of betrayal and abandonment prevail (Allen, 2013). The perception of a constant threat is activating unceasingly the alarm mode of functioning. Strong negative affects and complete inability to recognize, communicate, or regulate them often result in destructive acting-out or somatization.

A movie example illustrates processes in post-totalitarian society and consequences of social trauma on two generations. A cluster of phenomena conceptualized in psychoanalytic literature when implied to social trauma conveys the picture of psychic dynamic and interpersonal relations revealed in the movie: the lack of authenticity and False self, pretend mode vs. mentalization, destruction and repetition instead of creativity.

Eastern Plays is the story of two brothers, an artist woodcarver, on methadone therapy, and a teenager who is involving in a neo-Nazi gang. The initiation of the younger brother in the gang is an attack on a Turkish family, who are spending a night in Sofia *en route* to Germany. The elder brother, who happens to be around, intervenes. He is also beaten, but that puts an end to the fight and he calls an ambulance for the injured man. On the next day, he visits his brother at their father's home. The boys' mother is barely mentioned; it is clear that she is alive but in a remote and disconnected way, one might suspect mental illness and institutionalization. The feeling of shame shared by the brothers is conveyed by the setting—they are turning their backs to people and houses, facing the empty field and speaking without looking to each other, half seen by the camera. The stepmother is physically present but staring at the TV, uttering some clichés for greeting without even looking up. The boys' father is a grotesque-tragic figure holding his pseudo transitional object—a radio—always emitting news. False political promises are hiding ethnic intolerance and violence. But corruption and gang fights at football games that are financially supported and used for political interests are only visible for the spectators. The father's desperate attempt to be informed reveals only a deep confusion and inability to comprehend the surrounding world. His only modus of connecting with the children is through harsh language (addressing his son as "a piece of shit") and rigid rules. The father is only able to look at his children at the skin-deep level: bruises or haircut. He is scolding the elder brother, "how dare he to show his smashed face like that and what an example he sets for his younger brother," and the story behind, as spectators know, confirms again the inadequacy of the father. The elder brother has come in the act of care and concern for his sibling. Incapacity of the father to tell right from wrong, good from bad, puts the children in high risk. The risk is partly compensated for the younger boy by his elder brother, taking parental responsibilities. The end of the movie gives a hint on some solutions. The elder brother attempts to involve in a relationship where sharing and creative play are possible and much more fulfilling then the pretend-play-intimacy with the student-actress (ex-girlfriend). The younger brother gets over destruction, body mutilation (tattoo), imitation (making after, conforming to the gang) to choosing the creative part of his brother for a role model. But ways to those solutions are still to be invented.

15.4 Practical Implications in the Field of Social Trauma

The psychic landscape of social trauma "survivors" resembles a postwar zone, something that could be called the *minefield of the mind,* where every move is bringing about a potential threat of explosion. The unconscious knowledge (Bowlby, 1979) for the existence of the *mind mines* looms behind the state of hypervigilance, causing stillness and numbness in the inner landscape. Identity diffusion is often the symptom of survivors and their descendants, for whom not the aftermaths of war but indigestible experiences create wounds in the psychic web, thereby destroying the individual's sense of personal sameness and historical continuity (Erikson, 1968). The loss of sense of agency is an important part of personal consequences of social trauma. Creativity and spontaneity are impossible and every inviting gesture from the outside is perceived with epistemic mistrust (Fonagy & Campbell, 2017) and blockage of communication. Severe interpersonal trauma results also in ego-destructive shame. A person treated as a physical object doubts the possibility of ever being recognized in his/her subjectivity and valued as a human being. Destroyed internal agency and self-respect and mistrust toward the initiatives coming from the outside form the main paradox of social trauma consequences—being in a desperate need but incapable of either giving or receiving.

Erikson's epigenetic model of psychosocial development can be applied to social trauma recovery: first, facing the problems of trust, then shame, doubt and autonomy; and only then creative capacity and initiative to be spontaneous can be taken; and responsibility in the form of guilt can be accepted. Restoration of trust is the starting point of every rehabilitation or therapeutic initiative. Adaptation to the ever-changing social and cultural context depends on critical levels of epistemic trust to enables social learning (Fonagy & Campbell, 2017). Trust in the capacity to connect (Bion, 1959) and in the potential to meet in a *transitional space* (Winnicott, 1971) and cocreate and restore dialogue is a critical prerequisite for development.

In a developmental process, the modus of "being" comes before "doing" (Winnicott, 1965b). Social trauma recovery process follows the same sequence—the experience of *being*, in terms of being safe in existing and safe in trying to know, and reflecting on mental content should precede the attempts of doing—repairing. Postwar and post-totalitarian societies often value performance before experience and are organized around doing as an escape of thinking and contemplating. The major challenge of creating and cocreating the shared meaning of the traumatic past could be met by daring to ask and approach the *unthought known*, and to communicate and create new forms of togetherness and being alone in the presence of the other.

15.5 Suggested Readings and Further Information

Information about therapeutic approach and practice informed by attachment and mentalization theories https://beaconhouse.org.uk/trauma-and-attachment/ and video channel of Beacon House https://www.youtube.com/channel/UCW4MyzYmJ1Kg7NTQMmWKXlw

Information about the movie Eastern plays (dir. Kalev) on https://www.imdb.com/title/tt1426361/?ref_=nv_sr_srsg_0

References

Allen, J. G. (2013). *Mentalizing in the development and treatment of attachment trauma*. London: Karnac Books.

Belsky, J. (1980). Child maltreatment: An ecological integration. *American Psychologist, 35*(4), 320–335.

Bion, W. R. (1959). Attacks on linking. *International Journal of Psycho-Analysis, 40*, 308–315.

Bion, W. R. (1962). *Learning from experience*. London: William Heinemann. [Reprinted London: Karnac Books].

Bollas, C. (1987). *The shadow of the object*. New York: Columbia University Press.

Bowlby, J. (1951). Maternal care and mental health. *Bulletin of the World Health Organization, 3*.

Bowlby, J. (1979). On knowing what you are not supposed to know and feeling what you are not supposed to feel. *Canadian Journal of Psychiatry, 24*(5), 403–408.

Bowlby, J. (1980). *Attachment and loss* (Loss: Sadness and depression) (Vol. 3). New York: Basic Books.

Bretherton, I. (1992). The origins of attachment theory: John Bowlby and Mary Ainsworth. *Developmental Psychology, 28*(5), 759–775.

Briggs-Gowan, M. J., Greene, C., Ford, J., Clark, R., McCarthy, K. J., & Carter, A. S. (2019). Adverse impact of multiple separations or loss of primary caregivers on young children. *European Journal of Psychotraumatology, 10*(1), 1646965.

Caspi, A., Houts, R. M., Belsky, D. W., Goldman-Mellor, S. J., Harrington, H., Israel, S., … Moffitt, T. E. (2014). The p factor: One general psychopathology factor in the structure of psychiatric disorders? *Clinical Psychological Science, 2*(2), 119–137.

Cicchetti, D., & Toth, S. L. (2013). A developmental psychopathology perspective on child maltreatment. *Child Maltreatment, 18*(3), 135–139.

Cicchetti, D., & Valentino, K. (2006). An ecological transactional perspective on child maltreatment: Failure of the average expectable environment and its influence upon child development. In D. Cicchetti & D. J. Cohen (Eds.), *Developmental psychopathology* (Vol. 3, 2nd ed., pp. 129–201). New York, NY: Wiley.

Ensink, K., Bégin, M., Normandin, L., Godbout, N., & Fonagy, P. (2017). Mentalization and dissociation in the context of trauma: Implications for child psychopathology. *Journal of Trauma Dissociation, 18*(1), 11–30.

Erikson, E. H. (1968). *Identity: Youth and crisis*. New York: W.W. Norton Company.

Fonagy, P. (1999). The transgenerational transmission of holocaust trauma. Lessons learned from the analysis of an adolescent with obsessive-compulsive disorder. *Attachment in Human Development, 1*(1), 92–114.

Fonagy, P., & Campbell, C. (2017). Mentalizing attachment and epistemic trust how psychotherapy can promote resilience. *Psychiatria Hungarika, 32*(3), 283–287.

Fonagy, P., & Target, M. (2002). Early intervention and the development of self-regulation. *Psychoanalytic Inquiry, 22*(3), 307–335.

Fraiberg, S., Adelson, E., & Shapiro, V. (1975). Ghosts in the nursery. A psychoanalytic approach to the problems of impaired infant-mother relationships. *Journal of the American Academy of Child & Adolescent Psychiatry, 14*(3), 387–421.

Green, A. (1986). The dead mother. In *On private madness* (pp. 142–173). London: Hogarth Press. (Original, La Maire morte, 1980)

Hamburger, A. (2020). Social trauma—A bridging concept. In A. Hamburger, C. Hancheva & V. Volkan (Eds.), *Social trauma. An Interdisciplinary Textbook*. (pp. 3–16). New York: Springer.

Hancheva, C. (2020). Social trauma memory construction. In A. Hamburger, C. Hancheva & V. Volkan (Eds.), *Social Trauma. An Interdisciplinary Textbook*. (pp. 191–200) New York: Springer.

Hartmann, H. (1958). *Ego psychology and the problem of adaptation*. New York: International Universities Press, Inc. (First edition published in 1939)

Hesse, E., & Main, M. (2000). Disorganized infant, child, and adult attachment: Collapse in behavioral and attentional strategies. *Journal of the American Psychoanalytic Association, 48*(4), 1097–1127.

Kaplan, S., & Hamburger, A. (2017). The developmental psychology of social trauma and violence—The case of the Rwanda genocide. In D. Laub & A. Hamburger (Eds.), *Psychoanalysis, social trauma, testimony: Unwanted memory and the holocaust* (pp. 104–124). London: Routledge.

Klein, M. (1935). A contribution to the psychogenesis of manic-depressive states. *The International Journal of Psychoanalysis, 16*, 145–174.

Klein, M. (1940). Mourning and its relation to manic-depressive states. *The International Journal of Psychoanalysis, 21*, 125–153.

Lanyado, M. (1999). The treatment of traumatisation in children. In M. Lanyado & A. Horne (Eds.), *The handbook of child psychotherapy. Psychoanalytic approaches* (pp. 275–291). London: Routledge.
Laplanche, J., & Pontalis, J. B. (1985). *The language of psychoanalysis*. London: Hogarth Press.
Laub, D., & Lee, S. (2003). Thanatos and massive psychic trauma: The impact of the dead instinct on knowing, remembering, and forgetting. *Journal of the American Psychoanalytic Association, 51*(2), 433–463.
Lieberman, A. F., & Amaya-Jackson, L. (2005). Reciprocal influences of attachment and trauma: Using a dual Lens in the assessment and treatment of infants, toddlers, and preschoolers. In L. J. Berlin, Y. Ziv, L. Amaya-Jackson, & M. T. Greenberg (Eds.), *Duke series in child development and public policy. Enhancing early attachments: Theory, research, intervention, and policy* (pp. 100–124). New York: Guilford Press.
Luxenberg, T., Spinazzola, J., & Van der Kolk, B. A. (2001). Complex trauma and disorders of extreme stress (DESNOS) diagnosis, part one: Assessment. *Directions in Psychiatry, 21*, 373–394.
Lyons-Ruth, K. (2003). Dissociation and the parent-infant dialogue: A longitudinal perspective from attachment research. *Journal of the American Psychoanalytic Association, 51*, 883–911.
Lyons-Ruth, K., Bronfman, E., & Atwood, G. (1999). A relational diathesis model of hostile-helpless state of mind. Expressions in mother-infant interactions. In J. Solomon & C. George (Eds.), *Attachment disorganization* (pp. 33–69). New York: Guilford Press.
Main, M., & Hesse, E. (1990). Parents' unresolved traumatic experiences are related to infant disorganized attachment status: Is frightened and/or frightening parental behavior the linking mechanism? In M. Greenberg, D. Cicchetti, & E. M. Cummings (Eds.), *Attachment in the preschool years: Theory, research and intervention* (pp. 161–184). Chicago: University of Chicago Press.
Renn, P. (2012). *The silent past and the invisible present*. New York: Routledge.
Schore, A. N. (2001). The effects of early relational trauma on right brain development, affect regulation, and infant mental health. *Infant Ment Health J, 22*(1–2), 201–269.
Teicholz, J. G. (2012). Forward. In P. Renn (Ed.), *The silent past and the invisible present*. New York: Routledge.
van der Kolk, B. A. (2005). Developmental trauma disorder: Towards a rational diagnosis for children with complex trauma histories. *Psychiatric Annals, 35*(5), 401–408.
van IJzendoorn, M. H., Bakermans-Kranenburg, M. J., & Sagi-Schwartz, A. (2003). Are children of holocaust survivors less well-adapted? A meta-analytic investigation of secondary traumatization. *Journal of Traumatic Stress, 16*, 459–469.
Winnicott, D. W. (1965a). A clinical study of the effect of a failure of the average expectable environment on a child's mental functioning. *International Journal of Psychoanalysis, 46*, 81–87.
Winnicott, D. W. (1965b). *Maturational processes and the facilitating environment*. New York: International Universities Press.
Winnicott, D. W. (1971). *Playing and reality*. London: Tavistock.

Chapter 16
Complex and Sequential Traumatic Stress Disorders

Annette Streeck-Fischer

16.1 Introduction: Background and Main Theoretical Concepts

A psychological trauma is an event that both overwhelms a person's psychological and biological coping mechanisms, and that is not responded to by outside help to compensate for the inability of *the organism* itself to cope (van der Kolk & Streeck-Fischer, 2002/2003, p. 818). A trauma is thus not an objective event whose effects would be the same for all human beings, but an experience which is overwhelming because of the personal interpretation of the victim, his or her stage of development, constitutional preconditions, and individual social environment.

In the case of traumatization in development, the (traumatic) environmental conditions take on a special significance. They influence how the traumatic stress is processed and whether chronification occurs.

16.1.1 From the Historical Perspective

Already in the 1950s–1960s, studies by Spitz (1969) showed that traumatizations lasting for years can have serious consequences. Spitz was one of the first researchers to draw attention to the consequences of emotional neglect in infants. Around 1974, Burgess and Holström (1974) examined the symptoms of rape victims and described them as *Rape Trauma Syndrome. In* the following years, Bryers, Nelson, Miller, and Krol (1987) published a study that showed a connection between child-

Translated from German by Dr. Boris Drenkov

A. Streeck-Fischer (✉)
IPU Berlin, Berlin, Germany
e-mail: annette.streeck-fischer@ipu-berlin.de

© Springer Nature Switzerland AG 2021
A. Hamburger et al. (eds.), *Social Trauma – An Interdisciplinary Textbook*,
https://doi.org/10.1007/978-3-030-47817-9_16

hood trauma and the development of mental disorders in adulthood. They underlined the finding that repeated and man-made traumatizations have more serious consequences than one-off acute traumatizations.

On this basis, the American psychiatrist Leonore Terr (1991) was able to make the following differentiation on the basis of her investigations: *Type 1 traumatizations,* which include one-time, time-limited and public events such as accidents, natural disasters, war experiences, and *Type 2 traumatizations,* which occur repeatedly over a longer period of time, sometimes secretly or sequentially, such as complex traumatizations due to consequences of war, migration and flight, sexual abuse, family violence, abuse, violence at school, surrounding situation, subcultural milieu, neglect, separation, serious experiences of loss, traumatization due to medical interventions, serious illnesses with pain experiences. On the basis of her research (1975, 1981, 1991), she has defined a distinction between the consequences of Type 1 and Type 2 trauma, which refer to various disturbance patterns (Fig. 16.1).

Judith Herman (1992) warned that post-traumatic stress disorder (PTSD) does not adequately capture the complexity of the symptoms after many years of trauma, which is why she coined the term complex post-traumatic stress disorder.

During the development of the DSM IV, Bessel Van der Kolk, Roth, Pelkowitz, Sunday, and Spinazzola (2005) were commissioned to develop a diagnostic concept to describe the symptom picture after chronic interpersonal traumatization. This concept was called *disorder of extreme stress not otherwise specified* or DESNOS. Literature research and field studies have revealed changes in the following symptom areas: regulation of affects and impulses, attention and consciousness, self-perception, perception of the perpetrator, relationship to others, somatization and attitudes towards life. DESNOS was included as an additional descriptive feature of PTSD in the Annex to DSM IV.

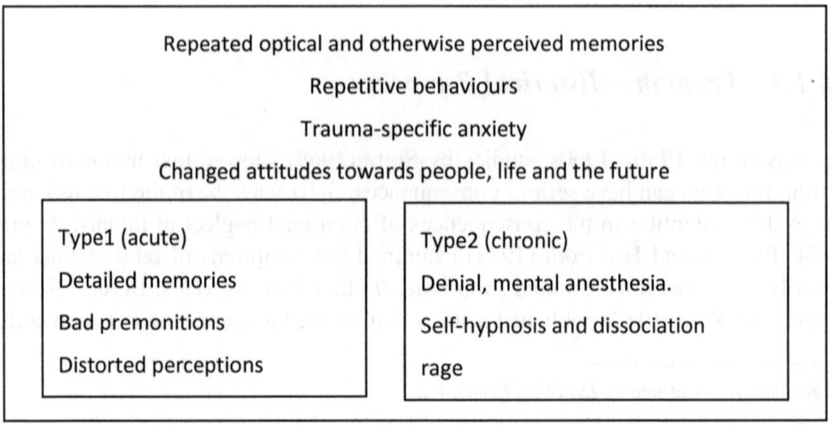

Fig. 16.1 Consequences of childhood trauma (after Terr, 1991)

Another concept developed by van der Kolk (2009), among others, due to the lack of developmental sensitivity of the PTSD concept, is *developmental trauma disorder* (DTD). However, due to insufficient empirical evidence, this concept was not included in DSM 5.

The forthcoming ICD 11 has integrated a second diagnosis of PTSD, with its core symptoms of re-experience, avoidance and vegetative overexcitation, which includes complex PTSD with further impairment areas such as emotional regulation, negative beliefs of the self and persistent difficulties in maintaining relationships. The DSM 5, on the other hand, attempts to incorporate the complex symptoms into the PTSD diagnosis, which thus becomes broader.

Young and older people can now be diagnosed with trauma related to social and societal conditions.

16.1.2 From the Perspective of Development

There is now overwhelming evidence that childhood stresses such as trauma from war, migration and flight, family violence, abuse and neglect lead to psychiatric disorders and are responsible for serious behavioural problems in children and adolescents (e.g. Gilbert et al., 2009).

Gordon and Wraight (1993) used a follow-up study on trauma disorders in children and adolescents to illustrate how trauma is processed. States become traits. The traumatic stress is woven into the personality development. General signs of stress become apparent, and there is an increased tendency to somatization. The attitudes towards relationships change in connection with a recognizable social retreat, loneliness, or antisocial tendencies. Self-destructive behaviour and destructive behaviour towards others can occur. Previous developmental paths are lost and school failure can be also a part of the picture. Alcohol and drugs are used as self-help measures. Youth groups with destructive rituals support the continuation of traumatization. There are changes in identity. The personality changes are increasingly becoming chronic in connection with distorted perceptions in relationships, in thinking, a hostile and distrustful attitude towards the world, feelings of emptiness and hopelessness, increased irritability and feelings of alienation (Gordon & Wraight, 1993; Kiser, Heston, Millsap, & Pruitt, 1991).

The extent of the stress disorder and the premorbid personality development is in a negative relation to the resilience. The lack of social embedding also has an unfavourable influence on resilience. This applies to children, who often have outsider positions, and young people with their aspirations to detach themselves from their families and their previous surroundings. They are therefore particularly vulnerable to traumatic stress disorders, which are often not recognized as such by the environment and are kept hidden. Youth cultures with glorification of violence and Satanic rituals are special places for traumatic new traumatizations or even retraumatizations in the case of traumatic stress disorders that were previously concealed.

16.1.3 From the Analytical Perspective

Freud (1916/1917/1978, 1920/1976) has described two important consequences of traumatic stress that provide important explanatory models for understanding the consequences of trauma in development.

Freud compared the living organism simplistically with a vesicle, which normally develops a shield against irritation from the outside world. He conceives the traumatic neurosis as the consequence of an extensive breakthrough of the stimulus shield (Freud, 1920/1976, pp. 25–30). The task of the mental apparatus is to mobilize all available forces in order to mobilize counter-occupations. Freud thus describes the traumatic destruction of a boundary layer or boundary membrane of the psychological apparatus or the self in the case of traumatic effects, which has consequences for the ability to draw boundaries between the self and others, between the inside and the outside. At this point, he refers to the importance of the protection against irritation or the development of an empathic shield, which the internalized primary object builds and which is emphasized in later concepts.

On the other hand, Freud explains how traumatic neuroses fixate on the moment of the traumatic accident: 'It is as though these patients had not finished with the traumatic situation, as though they were still faced by it as an immediate task which has not been dealt with; and we take this view quite seriously' (1916–1917 p. 275). Although he views this behaviour from a one-person perspective, he also opens up a view of a space filled with reenactments, which are not only shaped by the person concerned but by others as well. Although the compulsion to repeat has often occupied psychoanalysts, the fact that traumatic experiences are restored by acting out does not receive the necessary attention, especially in the clinical practice of adolescent therapy.

It was Ferenczi (1933/1984) who first described the consequences of the 'Beziehungstrauma' (*relational trauma*) and who observed the division of the ego into an observing and an abandoned part, the paralysis of affects, and, in particular, the tendency to identify with the perpetrator as a consequence of trauma. In addition, Ferenczi has described characteristic personality changes in people who have experienced trauma, such as Mimikry-developments, that is, superficial adaptations to the traumatizing person. Later elaborated on this problem in his concept of false self-development.

Others such as Khan (cumulative trauma), Kris (1956, *strain trauma*) and Hoffer (1953, silent trauma), to name but a few, have described traumatizations from different perspectives that will not be discussed here. Important is Keilson (1992) with his description of the '*sequential trauma*'. He describes separation traumas of Jewish children who had intact early relationships and were placed in foster families in the Netherlands during the Nazi occupation. He was able to prove a connection both between the developmental age at the time of traumatization and the severity of the traumatization with the traumatization effects.

Keilson chose the concept of sequential traumatization because he saw the traumatization of developing children as a disturbance of developmental and adaptive processes (1992). Processes of shock and demoralization that take place in various sequences are, on the other hand, mainly described among migrants. The first sequence is the period in the homeland, which may be associated with persecution, states of war, poverty, in the next sequence with the conditions of flight itself, the third sequence of arrival in reception camps, and finally a chronification of provisionality (Becker & Weyermann, 2006).

16.2 Learning Outcome Related to Social Trauma

In psychiatric classification systems, the conditions of the surrounding situation, society's approach, its offers of help and its participation in the process of making certain manifestations chronic receive little attention. Especially, after the Second World War, trauma consequences were hardly perceived as consequences of war in contrast to Holocaust consequences in Germany. As a result, such traumatically caused problems were only realized very late among Germans (in the 1990s).

Social chronic traumatizations have multiple consequences for the individual, his or her environment, and the social coexistence. The resulting personality changes with splitting into different self-states in the affective experience, in the cognitive and linguistic abilities and the somatosensory integration also influence the social togetherness.

Memory gaps can lead to connections not being made. Then what has actually happened is, more or less, not reproduced. Dissociative breaks in perception lead to confusion between fantasy and reality, what was real and what was fantasized. Explanations such as the division of the ego, the paralysis of affects, and the tendency to identify with perpetrator personalities as a consequence of trauma are constantly actual (Ferenzci, 1984). We find such problems, for example, in young people who join militant groups. Characteristic personality changes, such as the development of mimicry ((Ferenzci, 1984), which are superficial adaptations to the traumatizing environment, are also significant. Myers spoke of *apparently normal personality* (Myers, 1940). He has noted these changes in soldiers. These persons adapt reflexively and chameleon-like to external conditions and at the same time remain unattainable and affectively inaccessible due to their dissociative defence. Berry (1997) has also described such superficial assimilation as an identity problem among (traumatized) migrants. Others are unintegratable in social terms due to their aggressive-destructive behaviour. They create interactions that are marked by traumatizing repetitions, whether as victims or perpetrators.

Those affected often lack the ability to clearly distinguish between reality and fantasy, past and present, and to maintain boundaries. This has serious consequences for dealing with reality, especially the lack of ability to separate past and present, as traumatic pasts constantly break into the present.

As a result of the traumatizing experiences, a good–evil confusion develops. The immediate surroundings, individuals do not provide security, but are potentially also dangerous. People, environment and social order are perceived as unreliable. Value systems and norms are corrupt or fragile, such as the behaviour of adults who do not adhere to law and order.

Furthermore, a central problem lies in passing on the problem to children. The absent, dysregulating or traumatized early caregiver cannot take over the tasks of a neuropsychobiological regulator. Lacking ability of stress regulation with recourse to emergency regulations and 'failed' self-help measures of the children are the result, which show themselves self-destructive and foreign-destructive behaviour (hair pulling out, coils, frequent accidents, nail biting in childhood, alcohol and drug abuse, visiting thrill and kicker experiences (e.g. subway surfing in adolescence).

Finally, the duration of traumatization and lack of care influence the extent of cognitive deficits (Arnsten, 1998; Beers & DeBellis, 2002). As a result, attention and concentration disorders occur, especially impairments in cognitive flexibility and planning behaviour. The ability to integrate and coherently organize sensory, emotional and cognitive information can be destroyed.

16.3 Preferred Model of Explanation: Case Example

The complexity of traumatization in the context of the respective social and societal conditions will be illustrated by means of a case study. In this case study, there are also sequential traumatizations in connection with a migration problem.

The 15-year-old A. comes to psychotherapy because of depressive states, compulsive brooding, panic attacks, nightmares, paranoid performances and others. She lives in a youth welfare institution together with her younger sister, whom she constantly monitors, controls and restricts her and reacts with violent aggressive breakthroughs. A. comes from an Arab country, but has lived in Germany with her family and three siblings for many years. She is a very good student and was socially well integrated until the time when her father suddenly died under unexplained circumstances of heart failure in his country of origin. The mother returned to Germany with the children—A. was 12 years old at the time. Apparently helpless and unable to cope with the new situation, she very quickly married a much younger relative who had only recently arrived in Germany on the escape route and hoped for the right to stay in the country through the marriage. This man—a Muslim with strict beliefs—oppressed and terrorized the mother and the girls who had grown up with a European orientation. They now had to wear headscarves, stay at home and make no contacts. They were draconically punished and beaten if they did not adhere to the prescribed rules. The mother was also subjugated. So this new stepfather shaved her head as a punishment when she did not submit immediately. The children were treated like his property. Towards A. he showed sexually assaulting behaviour. Because the mother made no attempt to change the situation, A. turned to the Youth Welfare Office, whereupon the three girls were placed in an accommodation of the Youth Welfare. All the girls and especially A. were relieved, but strengthened by the mother's accusations, A. felt guilty and as a destroyer of the family. Even though her life before her father's death was apparently inconspicuous—the extent to which her father had been assaulted remained in the dark—she had since been traumatized in many ways: by sudden death, violence, the strictly religious lifestyle, the sexual assaults and the radical break with her mother or the loss of her family. The diagnoses she received—depressive episode, panic disorder, temporary psychotic experience etc.—did not do justice to her problems.

The recent diagnosis of complex PTSD in the ICD-11 could better grasp the problems of young people and convey to them that they are not affected by their internal neurotic conflicts, but that they are survivors of multiple traumatizations in their development, which are complex and sequential in character. Due to the apparently favourable conditions of development despite migration until the death of her father, which were destroyed abruptly and then by sequential trauma (loss of her father, new stepfather, accommodation in youth welfare facilities), she was able to develop well after finding lasting social conditions.

16.4 Practical Implications for the Field of Social Trauma

The psychiatrization or medicalization of mental disorders, which are more or less socially and socially caused, can be observed in various places. Such an example can also be found in dealing with ADHD (attention deficit disorder, hyperactivity disorder and impulsivity disorder) or prolonged grief, but especially in complex traumatization. ADHD, originally a pedagogical problem, has become part of child psychiatric care, as this disorder appears treatable with psychotropic drugs. In this respect, it will first be important to point out the perspective of social trauma and to give it more weight in the future.

16.5 Suggested Reading

Herman, J. L. (1992). Complex PTSD. A syndrome in survivors of prolonged and repeated trauma. *Journal of Traumatic Stress,* 5, 377–391.

Streeck-Fischer, A. (2014). *Trauma und Entwicklung—Folgen in der Adoleszenz* (2. Auflage). Stuttgart: Schattauer.

Streeck-Fischer, A. (2019). Borderland and borderline: Understanding and treating adolescent migrants in crisis. *Adolescent Psychiatry*, *9*, 3.

References

Arnsten, A. F. (1998). The biology of beeing frazzled. *Science, 280,* 711–712.

Becker, D., & Weyermann. (2006). *Toolkit: Gender, conflict transformation and psychosocial approach.* Bern: Swiss Development Cooperation.

Beers, S. R., & DeBellis, M. M. (2002). Neurophysiological function in children with maltreatment-related post-traumatic stress disorder. *American Journal of Psychiatry, 159*, 483–486.

Berry, J. W. (1997). Immigration, acculturation, and adaptation. *International Journal of Applied Psychology, 46*, 5–34.

Bryers, J. B., Nelson, B. A., Miller, J. B., & Krol, P. A. (1987). Childhood sexual and physical abuse as factors in adult psychiatric illness. *American Journal of Psychiatry, 144*, 1426–1430.

Burgess, A. W., & Holström, L. L. (1974). Rape trauma syndrome. *American Journal of Psychiatry, 131*, 981–986.

Ferenzci S. (1984). Sprachverwirrung zwischen den Erwachsenen und dem Kind. Die Sprache der Zärtlichkeit und der Leidenschaft. In: Ferenczi S. (Ed.). *Bausteine der Psychoanalyse* (Bd. 3, pp. 511–525). Frankfurt a. M.: Fischer. (Original work published 1933)

Freud, S. (1917). Introductory lectures on psycho-analysis. In *Vol: XVI: The Standard Edition of the complete psychological works of Sigmund Freud* (pp. 241–463). London: Hogarth Press.

Freud, S. (1920). Beyond the pleasure principle. In *Vol: XVIII: The STANDARD edition of the complete psychological works of Sigmund Freud* (pp. 1–64).

Gilbert, R., Spatz-Widom, C., Brown, K., Fergusson, D., Webb, E., & Janson, S. (2009). Burden and consequences of child maltreatment in high-income countries. *Lancet, 373*(9657), 68–81.

Gordon, R., & Wraight, R. (1993). Responses of children and adolescents to disasters. In J. P. Wilson & B. Raphael (Eds.), *International handbook of traumatic stress* (pp. 561–575). New York: Wilson and Beverley Raphael Plenum Press.

Herman, J. L. (1992). Complex PTSD. A syndrome in survivors of prolonged and repeated trauma. *Journal of Traumatic Stress, 5*, 377–391.

Hoffer, W. (1953). The mutual influences in the development of ego and id: Early stages. *Psychoanalytic Study of the Child, 7*, 31–41.

Keilson, H. (1992). *Sequential traumatization of children*. Jerusalem: Magnes Press. (Original work published 1979).

Kiser, I. J., Heston, J., Millsap, P. A., & Pruitt, D. B. (1991). Physical and sexual abuse in childhood: Relationship with post traumatic stress disorder. *Journal of the American Academy of Child & Adolescent Psychiatry, 30*, 776–783.

Kris, F. (1956). The recovery of trauma in psychoanalysis. *PSA Study Child, 11*, 54–88.

Myers, C. S. (1940). *Shell shock in France 1914–1918*. Cambridge: Cambridge University Press.

Spitz, R. A. (1969). *Vom Säugling zum Kleinkind*. Stuttgart: Klett-Cotta.

Terr, L. (1975). Children of chowchilla. *The Psychoanalytic Study of the Child, 34*, 547–623.

Terr, L. (1981). Forbidden games. *Journal of the American Academy of Child and Adolescent Psychiatry, 20*, 741–760.

Terr, L. (1991). Childhood traumas: An outline and overview. *American Journal of Psychiatry, 27*, 96–104.

van der Kolk, B. (2009). Entwicklungstrauma-Störung. *Praxis der Kinderpsychologie und Kinderpsychiatrie, 58*(8), 572–586.

van der Kolk, B., & Streeck-Fischer, A. (2003). Trauma and violence in children and adolescents: A developmental perspective. In W. Heitmeyer & J. Hagan (Eds.), *International handbook of violence research* (pp. 817–833). Dordrecht: Springer Science & Business Media. (Original work published 2002).

Van der Kolk, B. A., Roth, S., Pelkowitz, D., Sunday, S., & Spinazzola, J. (2005). Disorders of extreme stress. The empirical foundation of a complex adaptation of trauma. *J Trauma Stress, 16*, 389–399.

Chapter 17
Attachment and Mentalization in Social Trauma

Julia Holl and Svenja Taubner

17.1 Introduction

Attachment and mentalization are crucial for the individual's psychological development and well-being, and particularly in the face of adversity, our responding and adaptation rely significantly on attachment and mentalization. We will present three forms of association between impairments in attachment/mentalization and experience of social trauma. First, experiencing social trauma might affect parental mentalizing capacities inhibiting them to serve as a secure base for their infants and therefore promoting the development of insecure attachment representations in infants. Second, adult individuals can directly be affected by social trauma resulting in impaired mentalizing capacities, as well as altered attachment representations due to the overwhelming experience of social trauma. Third, parental traumatization itself can influence an infant's development of attachment and mentalizing.

According to Bowlby's theory, the early infant–caregiver relationship plays a significant role in the development of a child's attachment representation (Bowlby, 1973). Attachment representations shape the basis for future relationships with significant others by determining a representation of self and others on relationships, for example, how lovable am I, how helpful are others. It is assumed that repeated early experiences with primary caregivers generate inner working models of attachment. In fear-inducing or stressful situations (e.g., loss and separation but also danger), a child's attachment system is activated, which means a deactivation in exploration and proximity seeking to achieve safety through the caregiver. If caregivers provide safety in a reliable, consistent, and reassuring way, the child develops a "secure" pattern of attachment. Unreliable, inconsistent, or neglectful responses from the caregiver are thought to lead to an "insecure" attached pattern with anxious and/or avoidant behavioral styles of coping with attachment-related fears. Abusive

J. Holl · S. Taubner (✉)
Institute for Psychosocial Prevention, University Hospital Heidelberg, Heidelberg, Germany
e-mail: julia.holl@med.uni-heidelberg.de; Svenja.Taubner@med.uni-heidelberg.de

© Springer Nature Switzerland AG 2021

A. Hamburger et al. (eds.), *Social Trauma – An Interdisciplinary Textbook*,
https://doi.org/10.1007/978-3-030-47817-9_17

or threatening behavior by the attachment figure is thought to induce disorganized attachment representations because the child is confronted with an unsolvable situation of seeking proximity with a threatening person. Using the experimental procedure of the strange situation test with 1- to 2-year-old infants (Ainsworth, Blehar, Waters, & Wall, 1978), it is possible to differentiate between secure, insecure-avoidant, insecure-ambivalent, and disorganized attachment patterns. Caregiver's different ways of responding to a child's proximity seeking are thought to depend on the parents' current mental representations of their own childhood attachment experiences (Main, Kaplan, & Cassidy, 1985), although other factors may contribute to the transgenerational transmission of attachment as paternal mentalizing capacities (Bohmann et al., 2014). Hence, attachment and mentalizing capacities are strongly related (Fonagy, Gergely, Jurist, & Target, 2002).

Mentalization can be defined as the imaginative ability to consider own mental states, as well as the mental states of others (emotions, thoughts, desires, intentions, and beliefs) in order to understand the behavior (Fonagy et al., 2002; Taubner, 2015). Therefore, mentalizing capacities play a significant role in the understanding of behavior beyond the observable and shape social interactions especially in close relationships. Impaired mentalizing capacities—failed perception or inaccurate understanding of oneself and others in terms of feelings, beliefs, intentions, and desires—show associations with psychopathology such as severe personality disorders (Katznelson, 2014). The capacity to mentalize is dependent on contextual variables, for example, surrounded persons, emotions, and level of arousal. Especially, anxiety and mentalizing are highly related—experiencing distress can interfere with mentalizing capacities leading to a temporary loss of the ability to mentalize about the thoughts and emotions of others and the self in a balanced way (Fonagy & Luyten, 2009). In high intense emotional states, an individual's' capacity to mentalize is at risk, resulting in misunderstandings and interpersonal problems, encouraging a vicious cycle with further impairments in mentalizing. From a developmental perspective, the capacity to mentalize evolves from the experience of being mentalized by caregivers and is strongly associated with the quality of the early infant–caregiver relationship (Fonagy et al., 2002). Hence, early caregivers have a significant role in the development of mentalization, and impairments can lead to a developmental vulnerability in mentalizing. Secure attachment relationships are seen as the optimal frame to establish mentalizing. From a secure base, the child is able to explore mental states of the caregiver, to experience being mentalized itself by the caregiver, and, finally to learn to mentalize itself. Indeed, effects of parental mentalizing on caregiving can be found empirically: effective mentalizing capacities are positively associated with more sensitive perception of child' signals (Farrow & Blissett, 2014), more accurate mirroring and co-regulation of child's affective states (Rutherford, Goldberg, Luyten, Bridgett, & Mayes, 2013), child's development of mentalizing capacities (Ensink, Bégin, Normandin, & Fonagy, 2016), infant secure attachment, as well as child's social-cognitive development (Laranjo, Bernier, Meins, & Carlson, 2010). Hence, attachment and mentalization are strongly interrelated and can both be tremendously affected by the experience of traumatic events within or outside the family.

17.2 Learning Outcome Related to Social Trauma

Attachment and mentalization are crucial for psychological well-being and can be affected by social trauma resulting in impaired mentalizing abilities, as well as altered attachment representations.

Traumatic experiences are overwhelming in nature, leaving the individual with a failure in normal coping strategies and a sustainable shock of the self and the worldview (Fischer & Riedesser, 2009). Experiencing traumatic events represents a relevant risk factor for a psycho-pathological development and is negatively associated with physical as well as mental well-being (Felitti et al., 1998). Furthermore, repeated and prolonged traumatic events may lead to major personality changes, including significant alternations in relationships and identity (Terr, 1991), conceptualized as complex posttraumatic stress disorder (Streeck-Fischer, this volume). Taking place in a social context, the concept of social trauma combines psychological and social aspects of traumatic events (Hamburger, 2016, this volume) and traumatic experiences of war, persecution, dictatorship, and the loss of attachment figures of significant others can have massive enduring effects. Furthermore, social trauma can affect the caregiving qualities of parents when caregivers themselves are constantly threatened or traumatized, they are impaired in their ability to serve as a mentalizing secure base for their children (Bateman & Fonagy, 2008). Hence, experiencing social trauma involves tremendous consequences on an individual (e.g., severe psychopathological symptoms), as well as collective (e.g., influencing group identities) level and especially on an interpersonal level. Complex interactions of all levels can be seen in the phenomena of transgenerational transmission of social trauma—with enduring traumatic effects targeting the following generations (e.g., offspring (second and third generations) of holocaust survivors) (Bar-On et al., 1998). The phenomenon of transgenerational transmission of trauma describes long-term effects of trauma persisting into the following generations. Attachment, as well as mentalization, appears to be useful for understanding the interindividual differences in reactions to social trauma, as well as the intergenerational effects.

Thus, attachment and mentalization can be directly affected by the experience of social trauma resulting in impaired mentalizing abilities, as well as altered attachment representations in both caregivers and their offspring. First, experiencing traumatic events goes along with overwhelmingly emotional reactions as intense fear in adult individuals. In the face of social trauma, impairments in parents' mentalizing capacities might occur inhibiting them to serve as a secure base for their infants and consequently limiting them in their parental mentalizing capacities. In fact, traumatization affects the ability of mothers in dealing with the child's internal states (Bateman & Fonagy, 2008), as well as other cognitive and emotional regulatory functions (Jennissen, Holl, Mai, Wolff, & Barnow, 2016). More specifically, maternal psychopathological alternations as a result of social trauma affect the maternal participation in the mutual regulation of emotions and tension during the infant's early important developmental phases (Schechter et al., 2008) promoting an impaired development of infant's mentalizing capacities. Accordingly, the capacity to mentalize is considered to be central to the transmission of attachment patterns and might lead to insecure attachment representations in infants (Ensink et al., 2016).

Second, even adult survivors of social trauma can be massively affected. A prospective study examined the stability of veterans' attachment orientations over time and the association between changes in attachment orientations and the course of posttraumatic stress symptoms 18 and 30 years after the 1973 Yom Kippur war (Solomon, Dekel, & Mikulincer, 2008). The veterans experienced war captivity, a series of repeated and prolonged traumatic events. Even 30 years after the veterans' release from captivity, the veterans reported more posttraumatic stress symptoms than a matched control group (war veterans without the experience of captivity) with a significant increase of posttraumatic stress symptoms. Further, the attachment style of the war veterans changed over time with an increase in attachment avoidance and anxiety. These findings demonstrate the tremendous cumulative effects of social trauma that can alter attachment styles. Lastly, posttraumatic stress symptoms were identified as a more powerful predictor for attachment style, as attachment style served as less powerful predictor for an increase in posttraumatic stress symptoms. Specifically, the level of posttraumatic stress symptoms at the first timepoint predicted the subsequent increases in attachment anxiety and avoidance over time. Hence, traumatic events and posttraumatic reactions have the potential to impact individuals' sense of attachment security, meaning having an impact on representations of self and others in relationships. Experiencing social trauma might have an enduring impact on individuals' basic trust in others in a way that undermines their ability to maintain secure attachments in the future. Hence, even survivors of social trauma who have had secure attachments may become more anxious and defensive. In turn, such alterations may affect the attachment development of their offspring through the early child–caregiver relationship and, therefore, may illustrate a potential pathway of the enduring effects of social trauma. Also, mentalizing capacities can be affected by an experience of social trauma resulting particularly in the impaired capacity to mentalize regarding the trauma (Ensink, Berthelot, Bernazzani, Normandin, & Fonagy, 2014). Specifically, women with experience of social trauma do not manifest a generic inhibition of mentalization, but a temporary loss of the ability to mentalize specific to the trauma. This context-dependent mentalization specifically about trauma was associated with the difficulty in investment in the pregnancy and lack of positive feelings about their children and motherhood. Furthermore, the ability to mentalize about trauma served as the best predictor of investment in pregnancy and couple functioning. These findings highlight the importance of mentalization specifically about trauma and suggest that the absence of mentalization regarding trauma may have an influence on close relationships, as well as the transition to parenthood.

Lastly, parental traumatization itself can influence an infant's development of attachment and mentalizing. Traumatized parents may be triggered by infants' highly affective states (e.g., distress), exhibiting posttraumatic stress symptoms (flashbacks etc.). In turn, traumatized parents confront the infant with fear-inducing situations and, therefore, might cause traumatic effects on infants' development through the parents' frightening behavior due to the posttraumatic stress symptoms

(Fraiberg, Adelson, & Shapiro, 1975). Accordingly, there is consistent evidence for the relationship between parental unresolved trauma and disorganized infant–caregiver attachment relationships (van IJzendoorn, 1995). More specifically, unprocessed parental trauma experience contributes to the development of a disorganized attachment style in infants, which, in turn, leads to incoherent and inconsistent strategies for coping with stress and anxiety in children (Fonagy, 2001). Although, parenthood holds the opportunity for reorganizing attachment representations and, therefore, interrupting the transgenerational transmission of trauma. Taken together, the developmental psychological perspective of social trauma provides an explanatory model by identifying possible transmission pathways via attachment and mentalization. Simultaneously, attachment and mentalization can be conceptualized as protective factors in the context of social trauma.

17.3 Preferred Model of Explanation

In the context of transgenerational transmission of social trauma, attachment and mentalization might function as transmission pathways for the enduring traumatic effects targeting even the following generations. Focusing on strengthening mentalizing capacities, as well as supporting a secure attachment in survivors of social trauma, might have an impact on the effect of transgenerational transmission of social trauma. Hence, attachment and mentalization can be understood as protective factors that might influence the tremendous individual as well as transgenerational effects of social trauma.

Empirically, there is an association between attachment styles and posttraumatic stress disorder (PTSD) symptoms. A recent meta-analysis found that secure attachment style was associated with fewer PTSD symptoms, whereas an insecure attachment style was associated with more PTSD symptoms (Woodhouse, Ayers, & Field, 2015). Hence, adult attachment plays a role in the development and maintenance of PTSD symptoms and secure attachment seems to function as a protective factor. Further, trauma severity and social support seem to mediate the relationship between PTSD symptoms and attachment (Marshall & Frazier, 2019), shedding light on implications for interventions after the experience of social trauma to interrupt further psychopathological development as well as the transgenerational transmission effect of social trauma.

Expecting parents represent a vulnerable population for the transgenerational transmission of social trauma. Investigating the relationship between social trauma, mentalizing, and psychological symptoms in expecting parents, it was found that mentalizing partially mediated the relationship between trauma history and psychopathology, therefore providing empirical evidence of the protective role of mentalizing during the prenatal period in parents with trauma histories (Berthelot, Lemieux, Garon-Bissonnette, Lacharité, & Muzik, 2019). Hence, strengthening the mentalizing capacities of traumatized parents can have a buffering effect on a later psychopathological development after trauma exposure. More specifically, Borelli et al.

(2019) focused in their recent study on the intergenerational link of traumatic experiences investigating the associations between mothers' and children's histories of childhood sexual abuse, and the influence of maternal mentalizing capacities. A key result was that among trauma-exposed mothers, higher maternal mentalizing capacities regarding their own trauma history were related to a lower likelihood of child trauma exposure of their own offspring. This finding highlights the protective potential of mentalization in the context of transgenerational transmission of social trauma. Considering the fact that also attachment insecurities play an important role in maintaining psychopathological symptoms (Solomon et al., 2008), survivors of social trauma and their infants may also benefit from pre- and intervention programs focusing on supporting attachment security.

17.4 Practical Implications: Mentalization and Attachment as Protective Factors

Mentalization, as well as attachment, can be provided as a helpful framework for developing effective intervention programs to reduce the psychopathological and intergenerational risk of trauma. Our research focuses on the development of mentalization-based as well as attachment-orientated intervention programs for psychopathology of children at risk. Within a major research project on the transgenerational transmission of trauma, we adapted the mentalization-based Lighthouse Parenting Program for the implementation in psychiatric settings for mentally ill parents. This program aims to support parents with psychiatric conditions in their parenting skills while strengthening their mentalizing capacities, and, additionally, to improve the parent–child relationship, to reduce parental stress, and in the long-term to promote the child's development. The Lighthouse Parenting Program constitutes a promising approach, which can easily be trained and implemented in existing mental healthcare systems. A randomized controlled trial to evaluate the program's effectiveness is currently running (Volkert et al., 2019).

Furthermore, we developed a mentalization-based early prevention program for daycare professionals that promotes positive effects to the psychosocial development of children in daycare centers (Bark, Baukhage, & Cierpka, 2016). Due to the worldwide refugee movements, approximately a quarter of all individuals arriving in Germany is under the age of 4 years old and, therefore, at a particular risk of a psychopathological development as a consequence of traumatic experience in the country of origin, during flight or during stressful admission procedures. Therefore, we developed a mentalization-based and attachment-orientated supplementary training focusing on cultural sensitivity and psychological traumatization in refugee children and their families to reduce daycare professionals' emotional distress and support their mentalizing capacities (Mayer, Taubner, Bark, & Holl, 2019). Considering daycare institutions as the first possibility for integrating refugees into the host society, the successful attachment of refugee children to the daycare professionals is essential. At the same time, interacting with traumatized children from diverse cultural backgrounds might cause emotional distress for the daycare professionals, impairing their mentalizing capacities, and, lastly, impede an attachment relationship. Funded by the German Federal Ministry of Education and Research (BMBF), we are currently investigating the effectiveness of this one-day training program. The program provides information on psychotraumatology and cultural differences, as well as strengthening the daycare professionals' mentalizing capacities via self-reflective practices. Taken together, attachment-orientated and mentalization-based prevention programs integrating both psychological as well as social aspects might imply the potential to influence the transgenerational transmission of social trauma. Strengthening the mentalizing capacities of survivors of social trauma and individuals at risk for a psychopathological development and supporting the development of a secure attachment relationship might represent a potential protective and preventive mechanism in the transgenerational transmission of social trauma intervening the enduring effects of social trauma.

17.5 Suggested Readings and Further Information

Allen, J. G. (2013). *Mentalization in the development and treatment of attachment trauma.* London: Routledge.

Bateman, A. W., & Fonagy, P. (2019). *Handbook of mentalizing in mental health practice* (2nd edition). Washington, DC: American Psychiatric Association Publishing.

Fonagy, P., Gergely, G., Target, M., & Jurist, E. L. (2005). *Affect regulation, mentalization and development of the self.* New York: Other Press.

Jurist, E. (2018). Minding Emotions: *Cultivating Mentalization in Psychotherapy.* New York: Guilford Press.

Further information on our projects can be found on our institute homepage: https://www.klinikum.uni-heidelberg.de/zentrum-fuer-psychosoziale-medizin-zpm/institut-fuer-psychosoziale-praevention as well as on the homepage of the German National Centre for Early Assistance: www.fruehehilfen.de

References

Ainsworth, M. D. S., Blehar, M. C., Waters, E., & Wall, S. (1978). *Patterns of attachment: A psychological study of the strange situation.* Mahwah: Lawrence Erlbaum.

Bark, C., Baukhage, I., & Cierpka, M. (2016). A mentalization-based primary prevention program for stress prevention during the transition from family care to day care. *Ment Health Prev, 4*(1), 49–55.

Bar-On, D., Eland, J., Kleber, R. J., Krell, R., Moore, Y., Sagi, A., … van Ijzendoorn, M. H. (1998). Multigenerational perspectives on coping with the holocaust experience: An attachment perspective for understanding the developmental sequelae of trauma across generations. *International Journal of Behavioral Development, 22*(2), 315–338.

Bateman, A., & Fonagy, P. (2008). *Psychotherapie der Borderline-Persönlichkeitsstörung. Ein mentalisierungsgestütztes Behandlungskonzept.* Gießen: Psychosozial Verlag.

Berthelot, N., Lemieux, R., Garon-Bissonnette, J., Lacharité, C., & Muzik, M. (2019). The protective role of mentalizing: Reflective functioning as a mediator between child maltreatment, psychopathology and parental attitude in expecting parents. *Child Abuse & Neglect, 95*, 104065.

Bohmann, J., Fritsch, S., Luck, M., Stumpe, A., Taubner, S., & Vesterling, C. (2014). [Mentalization and attachment transmission]. *Praxis der Kinderpsychologie und Kinderpsychiatrie, 63*(9), 699–722.

Borelli, J. L., Cohen, C., Pettit, C., Normandin, L., Target, M., Fonagy, P., & Ensink, K. (2019). Maternal and child sexual abuse history: An intergenerational exploration of Children's adjustment and maternal trauma-reflective functioning. *Frontiers in Psychology, 10*, 1062–1062.

Bowlby, J. (1973). *Attachment and loss: Vol. 2. Separation: Anxiety and anger*. London: Hogarth Press.

Ensink, K., Bégin, M., Normandin, L., & Fonagy, P. (2016). Maternal and child reflective functioning in the context of child sexual abuse: Pathways to depression and externalising difficulties. *European Journal of Psychotraumatology, 7*, 30611–30611.

Ensink, K., Berthelot, N., Bernazzani, O., Normandin, L., & Fonagy, P. (2014). Another step closer to measuring the ghosts in the nursery: Preliminary validation of the trauma reflective functioning scale. *Frontiers in Psychology, 5*, 1471.

Farrow, C., & Blissett, J. (2014). Maternal mind-mindedness during infancy, general parenting sensitivity and observed child feeding behavior: A longitudinal study. *Attachment & Human Development, 16*(3), 230–241.

Felitti, V. J., Anda, R. F., Nordenberg, D., Williamson, D. F., Spitz, A. M., Edwards, V., … Marks, J. S. (1998). Relationship of childhood abuse and household dysfunction to many of the leading causes of death in adults. The adverse childhood experiences (ACE) study. *American Journal of Preventive Medicine, 14*(4), 245–258.

Fischer, G., & Riedesser, P. (2009). *Lehrbuch der Psychotraumatologie*. München, Basel: Reinhardt.

Fonagy, P. (2001). *Bindungstheorie und psychoanalyse*. Stuttgart: Klett-Cotta.

Fonagy, P., Gergely, C., Jurist, E. L., & Target, M. (2002). *Affect regulation, mentalization and the development of the self.* New York, NY: Other Press.

Fonagy, P., & Luyten, P. (2009). A developmental, mentalization-based approach to the understanding and treatment of borderline personality disorder. *Development and Psychopathology, 21*(4), 1355–1381.

Fraiberg, S., Adelson, E., & Shapiro, V. (1975). Ghosts in the nursery: A psychoanalytic approach to the problems of impaired infant-mother relationships. *Journal of the American Academy of Child Psychiatry, 14*(3), 387–421.

Hamburger, A. (2016). Soziales Trauma. *Forum der Psychoanalyse, 32*, 151–164.

Hamburger, A. (this volume). Social trauma: A bridging concept. In A. Hamburger, C. Hancheva, and V. Volkan (Eds.), *Social trauma. An interdisciplinary textbook* (pp. xx–xx). New York: Springer.

Jennissen, S., Holl, J., Mai, H., Wolff, S., & Barnow, S. (2016). Emotion dysregulation mediates the relationship between child maltreatment and psychopathology: A structural equation model. *Child Abuse & Neglect, 62*, 51–62.

Katznelson, H. (2014). Reflective functioning: A review. *Clinical Psychology Review, 34*(2), 107–117.

Laranjo, J., Bernier, A., Meins, E., & Carlson, S. M. (2010). Early manifestations of Childrens theory of mind: The roles of maternal mind-mindedness and infant security of attachment. *Infancy, 15*(3), 300–323.

Main, M., Kaplan, N., & Cassidy, J. (1985). Security in infancy, childhood, and adulthood: A move to the level of representation. *Monographs of the Society for Research in Child Development, 50*(1/2), 66–104.

Marshall, E. M., & Frazier, P. A. (2019). Understanding posttrauma reactions within an attachment theory framework. *Current Opinion in Psychology, 25*, 167–171.

Mayer, A., Taubner, S., Bark, C., & Holl, J. (2019). Herausforderungen in der frühpädagogischen Arbeit mit geflüchteten Familien mentalisierungsbasiert begegnen. *Praxis der Kinderpsychologie und Kinderpsychiatrie, 68*(8), 711–727.

Rutherford, H. J., Goldberg, B., Luyten, P., Bridgett, D. J., & Mayes, L. C. (2013). Parental reflective functioning is associated with tolerance of infant distress but not general distress: Evidence for a specific relationship using a simulated baby paradigm. *Infant Behavior and Development, 36*(4), 635–641.

Schechter, D. S., Coates, S. W., Kaminer, T., Coots, T., Zeanah, C. H., Jr., Davies, M., … Myers, M. M. (2008). Distorted maternal mental representations and atypical behavior in a clinical sample of violence-exposed mothers and their toddlers. *Journal of Trauma and Dissociation, 9*(2), 123–147.

Solomon, Z., Dekel, R., & Mikulincer, M. (2008). Complex trauma of war captivity: A prospective study of attachment and post-traumatic stress disorder. *Psychological Medicine, 38*(10), 1427–1434.

Streeck-Fischer, A. (this volume). Complex and sequential traumatic stress disorders. In A. Hamburger, C. Hancheva, and V. Volkan (Eds.), *Social trauma. An interdisciplinary textbook* (pp. xx–xx). New York: Springer.

Taubner, S. (2015). *Konzept Mentalisieren. Eine Einführung in Forschung und Praxis*. Gießen: Psychosozial-Verlag.

Terr, L. C. (1991). Childhood traumas: An outline and overview. *American Journal of Psychiatry, 148*(1), 10–20.

van IJzendoorn, M. H. (1995). Adult attachment representations, parental responsiveness, and infant attachment: A meta-analysis on the predictive validity of the adult attachment interview. *Psychological Bulletin, 117*(3), 387–403.

Volkert, J., Georg, A., Hauschild, S., Herpertz, S. C., Neukel, C., Byrne, G., & Taubner, S. (2019). Strengthening attachment competencies in parents with mental illness: Adaptation and pilot testing of the Mentalization-based lighthouse parenting program. *Praxis der Kinderpsychologie und Kinderpsychiatrie, 68*(1), 27–42.

Woodhouse, S., Ayers, S., & Field, A. P. (2015). The relationship between adult attachment style and post-traumatic stress symptoms: A meta-analysis. *Journal of Anxiety Disorders, 35*, 103–117.

Chapter 18
Age Differences in Childhood Trauma

Aleksandra Hadžić

18.1 Introduction

Trauma is a unique individual experience of an event or enduring conditions in which the individual's ability to integrate his/her emotional experience is overwhelmed and the individual experiences (either objectively or subjectively) pose a threat to his/her life, bodily integrity, or that of a caregiver or family (Saakvitne, Gamble, Pearlman, & Tabor Lev, 2000). According to DSM V, childhood traumatic experiences include exposure to actual or threatened death, a serious injury, or sexual violence in one or more of the following ways: directly experiencing the traumatic event(s), witnessing, in person, the event(s) as it occurred to others, especially primary caregivers, learning that the traumatic event(s) occurred to a parent or a caregiving figure, an experience of an event or enduring conditions which (either objectively or subjectively) present a threat to one's life, bodily integrity, or that of a caregiver or family (Substance Abuse and Mental Health Services Administration, 2016).

18.1.1 Developmental Differences in Reacting to Stressful and Traumatic Experiences

Due to the basic characteristics of the developmental process, children are more flexible in some respects than adults, but are also more fragile and sensitive to both positive and negative influences. The coping strategies and resilience capacity of children are limited due to their scarce experience in life. Their ability to perceive

A. Hadžić (✉)
Faculty of Philosophy, Department of Psychology, University of Banja Luka, Banja Luka, Bosnia and Herzegovina
e-mail: aleksandra.hadzic@ff.unibl.org

© Springer Nature Switzerland AG 2021

A. Hamburger et al. (eds.), *Social Trauma – An Interdisciplinary Textbook*,
https://doi.org/10.1007/978-3-030-47817-9_18

and ascribe a meaning to different experiences depends on the current level of their cognitive and emotional development (Kruger & Reddemann, 2013; Muller & Ostojić, 2011; Profaca & Arambaa, 2009; van der Kolk, 2007). Children's reaction to stressful and traumatic experiences is mediated by adults and the emotional, physical, and cognitive support that they can provide (Glaser, 2000). At the same time, inherent vitality of children, along with the support from adults, can allow them to feel joyful again, even in circumstances under which some adults would not be able to accept the suffering and would remain living in the past (Kruger & Reddemann, 2013).

This chapter provides an overview of different reactions to traumatic events that children have, depending on their developmental stage.

Children and young people are often looking back to reactions typical to earlier periods of their lives in cases of trauma. With regard to symptoms, their reaction to trauma is complex, variable, and different from adults'. Reactions on different levels of functioning can be confusing. Typical symptoms of traumatic stress depending on age, observed by Kruger and Reddemann (2013) or Bui et al. (2014), can be observed in the period to up to the first year of life in crying, lack of sleep, eating problems, general lack of development, and attachment. Children from 1 to 3 years have issues with attachment (Stefanović - Stanojević 2011), demonstrate anxiety, hypervigilance or apathy, fear, twitching, mutism. Preschool period (children from 3 to 6 years of age) show somatization (stomachache, headaches), "traumatic play" (repetition of the scene with peers and toys), dissociative symptoms, and tics. Many children from 6 to 10 years of age clearly show recognizable PTSD symptoms or other symptoms as described in ICD-10 (reliving, avoidance, oversensitivity/sensory alertness) (Pynoos, Steinberg & Goenjian, 1996), learning difficulties, attention problems (including ADHD), altered, pessimistic view of the world, feelings of guilt, depressive symptoms, risky behavior, self-infliction, suicidal tendencies, conversion symptoms (pseudo-psychotic episodes), and compulsive symptoms. Early adolescents (10–14 years of age) show the classic triad of PTSD symptoms (Davidson, 1993), which are characterized, in cases of relational trauma, by relations stress symptoms, risky behavior, self-infliction, suicidal tendencies, conversion symptoms, increased suicidal tendencies, early consumption of psycho-active substances (PAS), and psychotic symptoms. Late adolescents (14–18 years of age) show signs of the circle of failure: they experience social failure, abandon educational system, they are unsuccessful at first relationships, they consume PAS, and have massive existential fears concerning the future.

18.2 Learning Outcome Related to Social Trauma

Most studies are based on a single traumatic event, while repetition of those events increases the negative impact on overall functioning (Muller & Ostojić, 2011; Profaca & Arambaa, 2009; Pynoos, 1993). A traumatic experience happens when a child is not able to assimilate an event or a series of events to its basic structures of the knowledge of the world. Those understandings are shaken in such circumstances, and the child is forced to change them or create new ones (Cook et al., 2005). The difference between a stressful situation and a traumatic event is in its intensity and nature (Shalev, 2007; van der Kolk, 2005). The type of reaction will depend on the age, the nature of the trauma, and the meaning ascribed to the event or the encounter. The traumatic experience will cause strong reactions, which can inflict lasting consequences in the development, should the child not be provided with adequate help (Hadžić, 2019; Lieberman, 2008).

The concept of social trauma describes the individual and inter-individual consequences of a traumatic experience in the frame of social processes, where a social group is the target of planned persecution (Hamburger, 2017). Children are also affected by social trauma, but the ways in which they experience the situation and their reactions will depend on their developmental characteristics and the ability of important adults to provide protection. Some techniques applicable to dealing with traumatized children will be discussed.

18.3 Preferred Model of Explanation

18.3.1 Concept of "Developmental Resourceology"

Vast differences in children's reactions to stress pose the question how some children overcome stressful and traumatic situations unscathed, while others overreact even to low-intensity stressors (Lazarus & Folkman, 1984). Resource-oriented work provides some answers to the needs of many children and young people, while also taking into account neurological findings concerning the nature of stress processing (Smith & Werner, 2001, cited in Kruger & Reddemann, 2013). Different resources exist in different developmental phases and can be reactivated or suspended. For example, shame with regard to "childish behavior" might prevent the adult to reach out for support and resources that are fully available. Spontaneous self-care and care for others of the child, as well as turning toward him/herself with love, act as an antidote to traumatic helplessness.

Children's reactions to stressful and traumatic experiences depend on their age and available support and reactions from adults, especially their attachment figures (Bui et al., 2014; Byng-Hall, 1995; Profaca & Arambaa, 2009). Children react differently to stressful events. For example, being held hostage would cause considerable distress and anxiety in an older child who can understand the danger of the situation, compared to the younger one, who if in a presence of attachment figure, would tend to feel safe and perhaps in an adventure.

If in potentially traumatic situations, attachment figures are capable of controlling their own reaction of fear and anxiety, and they provide a safe haven for the child. In many situations, children mirror or resonate with the emotional reactions of important adults.

Some of these examples might sound a bit naive, and we could ask what happens to the parents who cannot rebuild their homes or are unable to buy new toys for their children? Or maybe the experiences they went through are beyond comprehension and exceed their abilities to cope? It seems that, although adults face the same difficult and potentially traumatic situations, with the child they could manage to convey the message that there would always be a benevolent significant other who is going to be there for us. A good example of a father's supportive reaction to an extremely traumatic situation can be seen in Roberto Benini's film *La vita e bella*.

Children often go through many stressful and traumatic experiences spontaneously reorganizing their resources. Many families are also able to reorganize and overcome difficulties. The quality of attachment is an important mediator of the traumatic impact of stressful events. Secure attachment functions as a protective shield (Byng-Hall, 1995; Carter & McGoldrick, 1988; Milojković, Srna, & Mićović, 1997), whereas unsecure attachment system hinders spontaneous recovery (Išpanović Radojković, 2007; Lieberman, 2008).

18.4 Practical Implications in the Field of Social Trauma

Various psychotherapeutic modalities offer evidence-based interventions for traumatized people. Most of the techniques can easily and efficiently be adjusted for children (Fridman & Combs, 2009; Lieberman, 2008; Muller & Ostojić, 2011; Stallard, 2010; Višić, 2019). However, most professionals have individual preferences for certain interventions/techniques/approaches, which they see as the closest to them and in a lot of ways, "their own." In the following section, some of the interventions of choice will be presented. As Salvador Minuchin puts it nicely: "When a professional/councilor/helper/therapist know the direction they want to go, they will easily find a transportation" (Minuchin & Fishmen, 1981).

- *Working with imagination*
  - Using imagination with children of different ages for *creating a potential space for working with symbols,* alternative roles, symbolization of the experience in play.
  - Using an imaginary time machine—evoking *different states of ego from different developmental stages* ("How do I see my younger self? Would my older self (e.g., 8 years) be able to protect my younger self (e.g., 5 years.)?")
  - "A safe place," "Prison/box of fears"—*creating a safe environment* for the first periods of work, as well as a *place where difficult experiences and unpleasant emotions can be left behind.* Creating an imaginary space, which the child can access in its thoughts to rest and regain strength before meeting with new challenges
  - "Frozen film"—*observation of traumatic experience from a distance*—with the idea that you can watch a film that can be paused at any moment (a child is holding a remote controller), and the child controls the situation.

- *Deconstruction of a dominant story*
  - Providing an alternative narrative where not only negative stories exist.
  - Application of externalization.
  - Searching for unique outcomes—searching for aspects of the story which go against the dominant flow: "Has something happened that made you think/feel/see something else, even for a single moment? When? How? How did that make you feel? What was different then? Did you like it? How could we have that feeling/thought more often?"
  - Family inclusion—including the child's point of view in order for important others to react—the perspective of family and important others (in case we are working only with the child), inclusion of actual significant others given that they are available and engaged.
- *Affirmation and working on one's strengths*
  - Highlighting the child's (and the family's) capacity to overcome obstacles—finding examples of reaction, thoughts, feelings which indicate strength, caring for self, and support. It is important, in the case of a child not being able to think of themselves like this, for a professional to discover such an experience (e.g., an 8-year-old who feels even more badly because they have started to cry—they are brave because they are expressing emotions we all experience).
  - Trust, positive image of oneself—developing a sense of not being defined by a single moment or a reaction, no matter how intense and uncomfortable it was.
  - Encouraging thinking and seeing oneself in multiple layers (I'm not just one thing I did, neither negative nor positive).
  - Finding ways to learn from the experience—acquiring good strategies—What have I learned? How could I use this on some other occasion (e.g., searching for powers which were helpful in the situation of floods that happened in May 2014 and connecting them to various everyday situations.

Witnessing a child's suffering and working with traumatized children is challenging for every professional. Children's experiences and reactions can be rather provocative to our "incomplete stories" and "gray" unknown areas. At the same time, the incompleteness of the developmental process, flexibility, and resiliency of children and young people show us that it is possible to overcome many difficulties and integrate them into strengths for the future. Meaning that working with traumatized children and young people can be seen as a space in which the adults can also learn and discover their own strengths and vitality.

18.5 Suggested Readings and Further Information

Mirović, T., & Tomašević, M. (2019). *Trauma—Our story*. Belgrade: Schema Therapy Center. Especially the chapters: (1) Introduction: about trauma—Aleksandra Hadžić, (3) The cultural context of trauma—Irena Stojadinović & Isidora Živić, (30) Child psychotherapy and trauma—Katarina Višić.

Two short films:

Beacon House. (2018, January 6). *The window of tolerance* [Video file]. Retrieved from https://www.youtube.com/watch?v=Wcm-1FBrDvU

Beacon House. (2017, August 7). *The repair of early trauma: A bottom up approach* [Video file]. Retrieved from https://www.youtube.com/watch?v=FOCTxcaNHeg

References

Bui, E., Ohye, B., Palitz, S., Olliac, B., Goutaudier, N., Raynaud, J. P., … Stoddard, F. J. Jr. (2014). Acute and chronic reactions to trauma in children and adolescents. In J.M. Rey (Ed.), *IACAPAP e-Textbook of child and adolescent mental health* (pp. 1–29). Geneva: International Association for Child and Adolescent Psychiatry and Allied Professions. Retrieved from https://www.researchgate.net/publication/263010920_Acute_and_chronic_reactions_to_trauma_in_children_and_adolescents

Byng-Hall, J. (1995). Creating a secure family-base: Some implications of attachment theory for family therapy. *Family Process, 24*(1), 45–68.

Carter, B., & McGoldrick, M. (1988). *The changing family life cycle: Framework for family therapy*. Boston, MA: Allyn & Bacon.

Cook, A., Spinazzola, J., Ford, J., Lanktree, C., Blaustein, M., Cloitre, M., … van der Kolik, B. (2005). Complex trauma in children and adolescents. *Psychiatric Annals, 35*(5), 390–398.

Davidson, J. (1993). Issues in the diagnosis of posttraumatic stress disorder. In J. M. Oldham, M. B. Riba, & A. Tasman (Eds.), *American Psychiatric Press review of psychiatry* (Vol. 12, pp. 141–155). Washington, DC: American Psychiatric Press.

Fridman, J., & Combs, G. (2009). *Narativna terapija. Socijalna konstrukcija omiljenih stvarnosti* (Lj. Miočinović, Transl.). Novi Sad, Serbia: Psihopolis Institut.

Glaser, D. (2000). Child Abuse and neglect and the brain—A review. *Journal of Child Psychology and Psychiatry, 41*(1), 97–116.

Hadžić, A. (2019). Uvod: O traumi [Introduction: About trauma]. In T. Mirović & M. Tomašević (Eds.), *Trauma—Naša priča [Trauma—Our story]* (pp. 19–43). Belgrade, Serbia: Schema Therapy Center.

Hamburger, A. (2017). Genocidal trauma. Individual and social consequences of assault on the mental and physical life of a group. In D. Laub & A. Hamburger (Eds.), *Psychoanalysis and holocaust testimony: Unwanted memories of social trauma psychoanalysis, social trauma, testimony: Unwanted memory and the holocaust* (pp. 66–91). London: Routledge.

Išpanović Radojković, V. (2007). Mentalno zdravlje I afektivno vezivanje u djetinjstvu [Mental health and attachment in childhood]. In N. Hanak & A. Dimitrijević (Eds.), *Attachment, theory, research, psychotherapy* (pp. 67–81). Belgrade, Serbia: Fakultet za specijalnu rehabilitaciju i edukaciju, Centar za izdavačku djelatnost.

Kruger, A., & Reddemann, L. (2013). *Psihodinamska imaginativna terapija traume za djecu i mlade. PITT-KID—priručnik* (E. Ostojić, Transl). Goražde, BiH: Kuća SEKA, Ženska asocijacija SEKA.

Lazarus, R. S., & Folkman, S. (1984). *Stres, procjena i suočavanje* (M. Krizmanić, Transl). Jastrebarsko, Croatia: Naklada Slap.

Lieberman, A. F. (2008). *Psychotherapy with infants and young children: Repairing the effects of stress and trauma on early attachment*. New York: The Guilford Press.

Milojković, M., Srna, J., & Mićović, R. (1997). *Porodična terapija [Family therapy]*. Belgrade, Serbia: Centar za brak i porodicu.

Minuchin, S., & Fishmen, H. C. (1981). *Family therapy techniques*. Cambridge, MA: Harvard University Press.

Muller, G., & Ostojić, E. (2011). *Vratiti svoju efikasnost i samopoštovanje. Terapija traume metodom psihodrame [Restore your effectiveness and self-esteem. Trauma therapy using the Psychodrama method]*. Goražde, BiH: Kuća SEKA, Ženska asocijacija SEKA.

Profaca, B., & Arambaa, L. (2009). Traumatic events and trauma in children and young people. *Clinical Psychology, 2*(1–2), 53–74.

Pynoos, R. S. (1993). Traumatic stress and developmental psychopathology in children and adolescents. In J. M. Oldham, M. B. Riba, & A. Tasman (Eds.), *American Psychiatric Press review of psychiatry* (Vol. 12, pp. 205–238). Washington, DC: American Psychiatric Press.

Pynoos, R. S., Steinberg, A. M., & Goenjian, A. (1996). Traumatic stress in childhood and adolescence—Recent developments and current controversies. In B. A. van der Kolk, A. C. McFarlane, & L. Weisaeth (Eds.), *Traumatic stress—The effects of overwhelming experience on mind, body and society* (pp. 331–358). New York: The Guilford Press.

Saakvitne, K., Gamble, S., Pearlman, L., & Tabor Lev, B. (2000). *Risking connection: A training curriculum for working with survivors of childhood Abuse*. Baltimore, MD: Sidran Press.

Shalev, A. Y. (2007). Stress versus traumatic stress: From acute homeostatic reactions to chronic psychopathology. In B. A. van der Kolk, A. C. McFarlane, & L. Weisaeth (Eds.), *Traumatic stress: The effects of overwhelming experience on mind, body, and society* (pp. 77–102). New York: The Guilford Press.

Stallard, P. (2010). *Misli dobro, osjećaj se dobro: kognitivno-bihejvioralna terapija u radu sa djecom i mladim ljudima. Vodič za kliničare* (R. KRAMAR, TRANSL.). JASTREBARSKO, CROATIA: NAKLADA SLAP.

STEFANOVIĆ-STANOJEVIĆ, T. (2011). *Afektivno vezivanje. Razvoj, modaliteti i procjena [Attachment. Development, modality and assessment]*. NIŠ, SERBIA: FILOZOFSKI FAKULTET.

SUBSTANCE ABUSE AND MENTAL HEALTH SERVICES ADMINISTRATION. (2016). *DSM-5 changes: Implications for child serious emotional disturbance. CBHSQ methodology report*. ROCKVILLE. MD: CENTER FOR BEHAVIORAL HEALTH STATISTICS AND QUALITY, SUBSTANCE ABUSE AND MENTAL HEALTH SERVICES ADMINISTRATION.

Van der Kolk, B. A. (2005). Developmental trauma disorder. *Psychiatric Annals, 35*(5), 401–408.

Van der Kolk, B. A. (2007). The complexity of adaptation to trauma: Self-regulation, stimulus discrimination and characterological development. In B. A. van der Kolk, A. C. McFarlane, & L. Weisaeth (Eds.), *Traumatic stress: The effects of overwhelming experience on mind, body, and society* (pp. 182–214). New York: The Guilford Press.

Višić, K. (2019). Dečija psihoterapija i trauma [Child psychotherapy and trauma]. In T. Mirović & M. Tomašević (Eds.), *Trauma—Naša priča [Trauma—Our story]* (pp. 533–549). Belgrade: Centar za shema terapiju.

Part IV
Memory Studies

Chapter 19
Neurobiology of Memory in Trauma Survivors

Maida Koso-Drljević and Dženana Husremović

19.1 Introduction

In everyday life, we are often exposed to traumatic experiences which can lead to diagnosis of posttraumatic stress disorder (PTSD). In *Diagnostic and Statistical Manual of Mental Disorders* (DSM)-5 (2013), PTSD, as part of trauma and stressor-related disorders, is defined by diagnostic criteria which include: (1) Exposure to actual or threatened death which, in the new version of DSM-5, compared to DSM 4, includes not only directly experiencing or witnessing the traumatic event but also learning that the traumatic event occurred to a close friend or family member. Also, experiencing repeated or extreme exposure to aversive details of the traumatic event can be criteria for the diagnosis of PTSD: (2) Presence of intrusion symptoms associated with the traumatic event (memories, dreams, dissociative reactions, distress, and physiological reactions); (3) Persistent avoidance of stimuli associated with the traumatic event; (4) Negative alterations in cognition and mood, which include the inability to remember an important aspect(s) of the traumatic event(s) often due to dissociative amnesia. Also, distorted cognitions, feelings of detachment, and persistent inability to experience positive emotions are described, among other symptoms, within these criteria.

19.1.1 Biological Correlates

The main biological correlates in PTSD patients are most often described within the hypothalamic–pituitary–adrenal (HPA) axis. Stressors cause activation of HPA axis, which leads to secretion of glucocorticoids and mobilization of energy reserves for

M. Koso-Drljević (✉) · D. Husremović
Faculty of Philosophy, University of Sarajevo, Sarajevo, Bosnia and Herzegovina
e-mail: maida.koso@ff.unsa.ba; dzenana.husremovic@ff.unsa.ba

© Springer Nature Switzerland AG 2021

A. Hamburger et al. (eds.), *Social Trauma – An Interdisciplinary Textbook*,
https://doi.org/10.1007/978-3-030-47817-9_19

stress response (Herman et al., 2011). Stress levels of glucocorticoids affect multiple bodily systems to maintain homeostasis including limbic brain structures: hippocampus, prefrontal cortex, amygdala, septum, and midline thalamus, which we know are connected to emotional responses and memory functions (Myers, McKlveen, & Herman, 2012). Excessive exposure to glucocorticoids during stressful experiences over the course of several weeks reversibly causes atrophy of the hippocampal dendrites, while glucocorticoid exposer for months (or years, as it was present in Bosnian war veterans) can cause a permanent loss of hippocampal neurons (Sapolsky, 1996). Neuroanatomical studies show that hippocampus volume can be smaller in PTSD victims (reviewed by Hull, 2002). Using the MRI, Bremner et al. (1995) found that US-combat veterans having served in Vietnam have a 6% decrease in right hippocampal volume in PTSD compared to control subjects and no significant decreases for left hippocampus. In a research conducted by Gurvits et al. (1996), right and left hippocampal volumes in PTSD combat vietnam were significantly smaller than those in the control group and hippocampal volume was correlated with combat exposure, after adjusting for age, total brain volume, and lifetime months of excessive drinking. Longer durations of combat were associated with smaller hippocampi. The connection of brain areas affected by stress response and cognitive functioning was the basis for two research studies that we conducted with Bosnian war veterans.

19.1.2 Cognitive Functioning in the Bosnian Sample of PTSD Patients

In a two separate research on a sample of Bosnian war veterans, we applied a battery of cognitive tests including the test of memory functions. The PTSD group, in comparison to healthy controls, had significantly lower results on the two tests used for memory assessment (Koso & Hansen, 2006; Koso, Sarač-Hadžihalilović, & Hansen, 2012). All cognitive functions in both samples, including memory functions, were severely impaired. What should be noted as a very interesting result is that cognitive functioning of PTSD patients in both studies was compared to the results of the control group of ex-soldiers, also Bosnian war veterans with similar war-related experiences, who did not have the PTSD diagnosis. Considering that we had ex-soldiers without the PTSD diagnosis in the control group, we can conclude that the extreme cognitive dysfunction is connected to the PTSD diagnosis, not to the exposure to stressful experiences per se. Also, Bosnian veterans in comparison to the results in similar studies on PTSD war veterans from, for example, the United States had greater cognitive dysfunction. Multivariate modeling that we applied to the whole sample of PTSD participants in these two research studies showed that memory function is one of the main predictors in explaining the PTSD symptom severity (Koso et al., 2012). The severity of cognitive dysfunction of the Bosnian PTSD subjects can be related to the specificity of the Bosnian sample. If we go back to diagnostic criteria described in the beginning of this text, we can notice that witnessing, and learning of, not only directly experiencing the traumatic events, can be diagnostically important. What we have experienced very often in direct contacts with PTSD participants during testing is that they have described multiple and lengthy traumatic experiences, some of them not able to choose one traumatic experience as it was demanded by the questionnaire that we used. We know from literature that multiple traumas, which was present in all of our participants, are connected to the PTSD symptom severity, and with less improvement after psychotherapy (Priebe et al., 2018). Some of the subjects stated that the main concern during their war experience was the constant worry about the family members who were in everyday life-threatening situations in the city of Sarajevo while they were at the frontline often not able to get in touch with them for days. All those factors, including multiple traumas, worries about family members, traumatic events that occurred in our participants on- and off-duty, and postwar environment of political, social, and economic instability in today's Bosnia and Herzegovina, can be the reason for difficulties the PTSD patients experience in everyday life. The results obtained in our research about the connection between PTSD and cognition mean also that the care for PTSD patients should not solely be focused on the clinical emotional problems but also on the cognitive impairments.

19.2 Learning Outcome Related to Social Trauma

Memory function in ex-soldiers and other victims of extreme traumatic experiences would be presented in this text, but it would be discussed in a broader context. Individual processes of memory and mostly remembering are viewed as determined and shaped by the current and passed environmental and social traumas.

19.3 Preferred Model of Explanation

There is no simple answer to the question: How do we remember a traumatic event? While, for most people, the memory of a traumatic event fades over time, the situation is completely different for the people with PTSD. In some cases, the memory may be so fresh even years after the traumatic event that a person listening to a person with PTSD describing a traumatic event has the feeling that event occurred yesterday, not a few or many years ago. Memories of traumatic events in the group of PTSD-diagnosed Bosnian war veterans (Koso & Hansen, 2006) were extremely vivid and full of details. It is very well described in the DSM-5 (2013) where PTSD patients may have a symptom of persistently re-experiencing a traumatic event with the presence of unwanted upsetting memories, nightmares, flashbacks, emotional distress, and physical reactivity after exposure to traumatic reminders. Also, in the literature, we can find the concept of flashbulb memories which we can notice in

PTSD patients. Those memories are described by Brown and Kulik (1977) as a special form of autobiographical memories, memories that are hard to forget, very vivid, detailed, and elaborate, usually involving the circumstances of a public event (Brown and Kulik used the example of John F. Kennedy assassination to explain the concept of flashbulb memories).

On the other hand, it is possible that the person is unable to describe the traumatic event. From personal communication with PTSD subjects during the research described before and from a witness support psychologist working in the court of Bosnia and Herzegovina, we learned about different examples of remembering a traumatic event. In one case, we witnessed a vivid memory of a traumatic event with all specific details. In another case, a witness, a sexual torture victim with the PTSD diagnosis, after being prepared to testify on several occasions, was unable to describe the events related to the experience of repeated rape situations while she was captured during the war. She was described in the situation of witnessing as a person with physical manifestations of full-body tremor, increased sweating, and dry mouth manifested by frequent drinking of water. Cognitively, her attention was very unstable with difficulties in focusing. Speech was intermittent, and sentences were unfinished, often losing its connection with reality. The witness support psychologist described her as a person who seemed to have a hard time remembering the details and even addresses herself with questions why she could not remember certain moments. We can consider these two examples within PTSD criteria where, in the first example, the dominant symptom is intrusive distressing memories of a traumatic event, while, in the other case, there are persistent efforts to avoid distressing memories associated with a traumatic event. We can speculate that the case of the woman described before is connected to the symptom described in the DSM-5 (2013) where, within negative alterations in cognitions, the main symptom can be inability to remember an important aspect of the traumatic event due to dissociative amnesia and that persistent distorted cognitions, negative emotions, and feelings of detachment can lead to inability to testify about the events. From the literature (e.g., Nöthling, Lammers, Martin, & Seedat, 2015), we also know that victims of extreme sexual violence are more vulnerable to develop PTSD and the traumatic dissociation has been identified as a precursor of PTSD.

19.4 Practical Implications in the Field of Social Trauma

19.4.1 From Individual to Collective

Individual trauma is widespread in the postwar Bosnia and Herzegovina. The consequence of severe traumatic experiences of war survivors is the presence of PTSD symptoms in a large part of the population. Such persons, with their personal traumatic experiences, are living in the present society, a society that can encourage a person or a symptom. Consequences that the individual traumas of ex-soldiers and civilians have left on their mental health can only be explained if we also consider the society in which such persons live now. The Bosnian society today, almost 25 years after the end of the war, is still under a significant influence of war. Constant political and socioeconomic insecurity, a considerable number of people leaving the country, and the society that is still deeply divided can be obstructing factors in recovering of ex-soldiers suffering from PTSD. The "survivors" are in constant relation with those who have died. Reminder of the war and war victims as, for example, the annual commemoration at the Potočari memorial center on July 11, are something which is hard to integrate especially for the traumatized Bosnian population. There is a Peace March each year where participants trace the reverse path of the mostly Bosniak men and boys who tried to escape massacre that happened in July 1995. More than 8000 men and boys were killed by Serb forces in Srebrenica, and each year on July 11, the victims, whose remains were removed from mass graves, are reburied. So far, 6643 victims of the Srebrenica genocide have been buried in Potočari.

We can also give an example of the Tomašica mass grave. It was discovered in 2013, very near to the village where people were living next to it for almost 20 years. Is the silence which lasted for around 20 years the result of ignorance? If some of the people who lived in the village knew that the remains of around 400 victims were buried near, what does it mean now for them?

Or, as it was presented in the book of photographs "*Behind the Seven Camps: From Crimes of Culture to Culture of Crime*" (Stjepanović, Polan, & Ivančić, 2019) where cultural buildings in Croatia and Bosnia were used as places where people were tortured and killed during the 1990s (and the examples presented in the book are from all three armies). Some of those buildings still exist but have mostly been abandoned in the central parts of small cities in Bosnia and Herzegovina, where inhabitants are passing by on a daily basis. If the reader will be interested in such a paradox, we can recommend the book with a text by Viktor Ivančić as the comment to the photographs within the book.

In the context of these examples, we can ask ourselves how to overcome the influence of stress-related memories and build social cohesion? This is a question to which there is no easy answer. Societies where such difficult events have occurred are trying to find ways, more or less successful, to build social cohesion and to somehow cure the climate in which the society is developing or trying to develop. There are examples, not so present in the mainstream media, within the projects of few nongovernmental organizations (NGOs), such as the Centre for Peacebuilding or Centre for Civic Initiatives (CCI) where we find rare attempts to work together to build peace. As stated on the website of an NGO (http://unvocim.net/eng/): the mission of the organization is: "… rebuild trust and foster reconciliation among the people of Bosnia—Croats, Serbs, Bosniaks, and others—as well as support peace processes in other countries that have suffered violent conflict." As one of the activities, ex-soldiers from different armies get together for workshops on peace and reconciliation. It was a basis for a movie *Men Don't Cry* by Bosnian director Alen Drljević where personal stories in a workshop of ex-soldiers from different armies were presented through the process of psychodrama therapy, which we can be also recommended for the reader to see.

19.4.2 Conclusion

Memory function in PTSD patients can be described as very poor in everyday situation with two different patterns of remembering a traumatic event. One, with vivid and detailed memory of traumatic event which can be explained by biological mechanisms of storing the memories connected to traumatic experiences and which the DSM-5 recognizes as intrusion symptoms. The other, having trouble to remember important details of the traumatic event which can be connected to symptoms of dissociation.

Such a severe clinical picture and significant cognitive dysfunction can be linked to a society living with social trauma. Awareness about social trauma within post-war societies, where collective mainstream beliefs and narratives are still under great influence of war and where individual trauma meets collective trauma, can be a factor which makes it significantly more difficult for individuals to successfully cope with individual traumatic experiences.

19.5 Suggested Reading

We would recommend the book *The Body Keeps the Score: Brain, Mind, and Body in the Healing of Trauma* by Professor Bessel van der Kolk (2015), one of the most cited and most influential authors in the field of trauma and stress. Years of dedicated work and a number of publications are contained in the aforementioned book, which is a comprehensive and, to an extent, a personal reflection of the author to different aspects of stress and trauma.

References

American Psychiatric Association. (2013). *Diagnostic and statistical manual of mental disorders (DSM-5®)*. Arlington, VA: American Psychiatric Pub.

Bremner, J. D., Randall, P., Scott, T. M., Bronen, R. A., Seibyl, J. P., Southwick, S. M., … Innis, R. B. (1995). MRI-based measurement of hippocampal volume in patients with combat-related posttraumatic stress disorder. *The American Journal of Psychiatry, 152*(7), 973.

Brown, R., & Kulik, J. (1977). Flashbulb memories. *Cognition, 5*(1), 73–99.

Gurvits, T. V., Shenton, M. E., Hokama, H., Ohta, H., Lasko, N. B., Gilbertson, M. W., … Pitman, R. K. (1996). Magnetic resonance imaging study of hippocampal volume in chronic, combat-related posttraumatic stress disorder. *Biological Psychiatry, 40*(11), 1091–1099.

Herman, J. P., McKlveen, J. M., Ghosal, S., Kopp, B., Wulsin, A., Makinson, R., et al., (2011). Regulation of the hypothalamic-pituitary-adrenocortical stress response. *Comprehensive Physiology, 6*(2), 603–621.

Hull, A. M. (2002). Neuroimaging findings in post-traumatic stress disorder. *British Journal of Psychiatry, 181*, 102–110.

Koso, M., & Hansen, S. (2006). Executive function and memory in posttraumatic stress disorder: A study of Bosnian war veterans. *European Psychiatry, 21*(3), 167–173.

Koso, M., Sarač-Hadžihalilović, A., & Hansen, S. (2012). Neuropsychological performance, psychiatric symptoms, and everyday cognitive failures in Bosnian ex-servicemen with posttraumatic stress disorder. *Review of Psychology, 19*(2), 131–139.

Myers, B., McKlveen, J. M., & Herman, J. P. (2012). Neural regulation of the stress response: The many faces of feedback. *Cellular and Molecular Neurobiology, 32*(5), 683–694.

Nöthling, J., Lammers, K., Martin, L., & Seedat, S. (2015). Traumatic dissociation as a predictor of posttraumatic stress disorder in South African female rape survivors. *Medicine, 94*(16), e744.

Priebe, K., Kleindienst, N., Schropp, A., Dyer, A., Krüger-Gottschalk, A., Schmahl, C., … Bohus, M. (2018). Defining the index trauma in post-traumatic stress disorder patients with multiple trauma exposure: Impact on severity scores and treatment effects of using worst single incident versus multiple traumatic events. *European Journal of Psychotraumatology, 9*(1), 1486124.

Sapolsky, R. M. (1996). Why stress is bad for your brain. *Science, 273*(5276), 749–750.

Stjepanović, N., Polan, H., & Ivančić, V. (2019). *Iza sedam logora; od zločina kulture do kulture zločina*. Buybook: Sarajevo.

Van der Kolk, B. A. (2015). *The body keeps the score: Brain, mind, and body in the healing of trauma*. New York: Penguin Books.

Chapter 20
Social Trauma Memory Construction

Camellia Hancheva

20.1 Introduction

In the late nineteenth century and long before the introduction of posttraumatic stress disorder (PTSD) into psychopathology, Sigmund Freud, Joseph Breuer (Breuer & Freud, 1895, cited in Renn, 2012), and Pierre Janet (1919/1925, cited in van der Kolk, 1994) have independently suggested the connection between psychological symptoms, trauma, and memory. When Freud and Breuer first stated that hysterics (and later extrapolated that to other mental conditions) suffer mainly from reminiscences, that was a summary of their clinical observations. In this chapter, these aphoristic and controversial statements will be taken only as a reminder of the links between human sufferings and memory processes. The temptingly simple first model of "talking cure" very soon proved wrong or at least insufficient in both explanation power and treatment technique. The presupposed healing is not a simple consequence of remembering the traumatic content. Memory is an active process of construction and reconstruction. Freud's notion of deferred action (Nachträglichkeit) is a reminder of the constant possibility for rearranging and revising of memory traces. Keeping in mind the clinical relevance of the repression mechanism, forgetting, and symptom formation in psychotherapy, the increasing number of practitioners second Fonagy's claim that "therapies focusing on the recovery of memory pursue a false god" (Fonagy, 1999, p. 219). It is more the process of reflection and reintegration of sensory-affective and semantic aspects of memories that matters for the overall psychological functioning and well-being.

The leading questions in this chapter would be: (1) What is known about memory construction, in general, and memories of social trauma, in particular? and (2) How knowledge and research on memory from cognitive psychology, psychoanalysis,

C. Hancheva (✉)
Department of Psychology, Sofia University "St. Kliment Ohridski", Sofia, Bulgaria

© Springer Nature Switzerland AG 2021

A. Hamburger et al. (eds.), *Social Trauma – An Interdisciplinary Textbook*,
https://doi.org/10.1007/978-3-030-47817-9_20

and neuroscience could inform practices in prevention, therapy, and rehabilitation of long-term consequences of social trauma?

Memory system and processes: In accordance with computer metaphors in cognitive psychology, memory is often thought of as storage of information and experience. But memory is, at the same time, a cognitive process of encoding, consolidating, keeping, and, eventually, using (voluntarily or involuntarily) this information in all kinds of other cognitive processes and overall personality functioning. Within the contemporary computer and data metaphor, it is well known that data are vulnerable entities and their usage and storage is subjected to many kinds of "threats." Memory traces are not copies of experiences and initial information; they are complex formations with high plasticity at every stage of memory process and every moment in time.

Explicit and implicit memory systems: A well-known and widely accepted distinction of two memory systems was proposed by Endel Tulving (1985). Explicit (declarative) memory consists of two types of information: first, episodes of personal experience, some of which are organized into autobiographical life story; and second, semantic memory, which refers to organized, acquired knowledge of the world. This general factual knowledge is usually shared with large group of people and independent of personal experience, and thus, it is often lacking the spatial and temporal context. Autobiographical memory is closely interlinked with the sense of self, providing the content of experience of self-sameness and continuity. Recent conceptualizations include also the sense of *mineness* as a second component necessary for identity (Klein & Nichols, 2012). Ownership of internal experiences is often lacking in patients with PTSD.

Implicit memory operates through a different mental process; it is automatic, principally perceptual, nonreflective, out of awareness, and not accessible to verbal report. In daily life, implicit memory in the form of procedural memory is responsible for the vast majority of performed activities (Schacter, 1996). Unlike explicit memories, implicit memories could persist, even in the face of brain damage and disease (Renn, 2012; Schacter, 1996).

Implicit memory, repression, and the dynamic unconscious: The implicit memory differs markedly from psychoanalytic conceptualization of the dynamic unconscious (BCPSG, 2008). The dynamic unconscious contents are a result of repression. And repression is aimed at diminishing or removing the negative experience memories from conscious awareness. Implicit memories are constructed from repetitive everyday actions or interactions and, as a rule, are functioning out of awareness. Implicit memories of practical and/or emotional nature are performed in behavioral terms in the form of emotional procedural memories. In this respect, a certain similarity between primal repression, formulated by Freud, and implicit memories is observed, but more recent psychoanalytic constructs like Bollas' "unthought known" (Renn, 2012) and "implicit relational knowing" (Lyons-Ruth, 1998) convey more relevantly the idea of memory traces that have never been part of language, semantic, or other symbolic structures and are represented in the mind in different phenomenological terms.

Traumatic experience and implicit–explicit memory: Traumatic experiences might be repressed, dissociated, or distorted, which leaves qualitatively and structurally different memory traces in the form of flashbulb memories, implicit memories, screen memories, and verbalized narratives. Often, some parts of terrifying experiences are remembered vividly, whereas other parts are missing temporally or permanently (Rubin, 2011; Rubin et al., 2016; Rubin, Berntsen, Ogle, Deffler, & Beckham, 2016; van der Kolk, 1998, 2014; Yovell, Bannett, & Shalev, 2003). Memory traces for ordinary events disintegrate in clarity over time opposite to some memories (usually in nonverbal, visual modality) where the same traumatic scenes could be vividly recalled even after decades. Vividness and emotional intensity of the memory do not guarantee its accuracy (Laney & Loftus, 2008). Researchers that introduced the term "flashbulb" also explicitly noted that flashbulb memories are not photograph-like, and in that, many details of the context scene are not recalled later (Brown & Kulik, 1977). Van Der Kolk (1996, 1998) summarizes the results of studies on different kinds of traumatization on explicit and implicit memory. Individual clinical cases, huge groups of war veterans, children experiencing abuse and maltreatment, and many other examples of conditions involving traumatic memories show that: (1) articulated narratives or otherwise symbolized experience may coexist with sensory imprints and those two declarative and implicit memory traces might be of contradicting nature. Trauma narratives are more prone to distortions, interpretations, and modifications, whereas sensory experiences remain more stable over time and might be triggered by reminders and re-experienced at the present moment with a frightening vividness and overwhelming affect; (2) traumatic memories demonstrate discrepancies in detailed and overgeneralized accounts of the traumatic experience.

Encoding and role of the emotions: The first stage of memory formation is the encoding process. The information perceived is converted into traces of different modalities—visual, tactile, audio, semantic, etc. Emotional events—either positive or negative—tend to be remembered differently from neutral events. Under conditions of threat and high levels of emotional arousal, attention narrowing is causing strong encoding of information closely connected to the source of emotional arousal and vague traces of peripheral details accompanied by the false subjective appraisal that the whole picture is clearly remembered. Some data support the idea that not level of arousal but the perception of a threat is causing the unnoticed and involuntary narrowing of attention (van Steenbergen, Band, & Hommel, 2011). Personally relevant autobiographical memories of emotional experiences seem to be recalled more often and with more clarity and details but with changed emotional intensity. There is bias in memory for overestimation of experienced emotions (especially negative) interpreted in terms of an adaptive evolutionary mechanism that motivates avoidance of potentially threatening situations (Urban, Charles, Levine, & Almeida, 2018). Paradoxically, memory for aggravated negative emotion might have a survival value, but it also changes cognitive appraisal of events over time. Understanding bias in the remembered emotions is critical because behavior is better predicted by memory about the emotional experience than of the actually experienced (Levine, Lench, & Safer, 2009). Still negative, unpleasant, and even threatening events are something different from traumatic experience.

Memory consolidation is the processes of creating networks or embedding and stabilizing a memory trace into an available schema. At this stage, memory traces are also susceptible to suggestions, especially if the information helps to fill in the gaps or to ascribe a meaning through labeling the experience. After the initial consolidation of memories, every recall initiates a new process of reconsolidation which could either strengthen and/or modify memories that are already stored. The very act of reconsolidation may change the initial memory through reactivating neural connections or activating new associative strings relevant to emotional or environmental conditions of the present moment. The actual experience, new information, and expectations at the moment of the retrieval may be incorporated into the memory, causing significant distortions of information regarding the initial event. Research into false memory pioneered by Elizabeth Loftus in the 1970s is providing insights on memory construction and raises ethical questions highly relevant to trauma studies (Ceci & Loftus, 1994). False memories are actively constructed to include actual memory contents, suggestions, and misinformation. Loftus has explicitly warned that "although experimental work on the creation of false memories may raise doubt about the validity of long-buried memories, such as repeated trauma, it in no way disproves them" (Loftus, 1997, p. 75).

20.2 Learning Outcome Related to Social Trauma

Recent findings from neuroscience and theoretical cognitive models of memory support Schacter's formulation that memory is composed of a variety of distinct and dissociable processes and systems (Schacter, 1996). At the level of individual memory construction, there is a complex relationship between memory, fantasy, and reality. Memory deals more with meaning than with facts. Contextualization of certain events and experiences, forgetting them, or recovered remembering and re-experiencing them, like traumatizing, retraumatizing, or neutral, depend on the intensity of affect at the time of the event, emotional and relational context at the time of retrieval, preexisting cognitive schema, and age at the moment of experience.

1. Emotional context of memory, stress at the time of memory encoding, consolidation, and retrieval can influence memory function.
2. Context and "political agenda" at the process of retrieval could redefine the emotional tone and/or the factual frame of the experience. To whom the memories are told strongly interferes with the contents of the memory.
3. Age of the person is a significant moderator of the traumatic impact of the experience. Amnesia of emotional and cognitive material is age- and dose-related. Young age and repeated or long-lasting traumatic experiences have multiple consequences in altering memory functioning, self-perception, and relation to the world.

As Schacter (1996) warns, memory research is not just an "exercise in intellectual curiosity," it has a serious challenge to meet by providing a better understanding of social processes and human sufferings.

20.3 Preferred Model of Explanation

Life Is Beautiful (La vita è bella) is a 1997 film directed by Roberto Benigni. The plot revolves around a family in a concentration camp. The father is creating a pretense play to his 5-year-old son, convincing him that the camp is a complicated game, and performing various tasks earns points and whoever gets to 1000 points first will win a tank. The father is playing his part up to the walk to his execution, and the boy fulfilling his last task of hiding is "winning" a Sherman tank that arrives at the liberation of the camp.

Questions, hypothesis, and speculations on how would this experience be later recollected by the boy would help the reader through next paragraphs.

The debate around memory and forgetting, motivational issues, and phenomena of recovered memories has two main opposite positions (Iyadurai et al., 2019): autobiographical memory researchers' version and clinical (psychoanalytic) view. The chosen model of explanation of memory processes in regard with social trauma is within the clinical framework. The observations and research on psychological consequences of trauma on memory is presenting a complicated picture characterized with disruption and fragmentation of some memory traces resulting in different levels of disturbance in functioning—from disorder conditions like PTSD or acute stress disorder (ACD) to less salient but tentatively more significant changes in identity, self-perception values, goals, and views of the self in relation to others and the world (Berntsen & Rubin, 2007; Brewin, 2016; Rubin, Berntsen, et al., 2016; van der Kolk et al., 1996).

At the center of the debate on memory and trauma are the questions of whether a traumatic experience: (1) strengthens or weakens the memories; (2) motivates forgetting; and (3) influences the content of remembered and memory functioning as a whole (what is remembered disregarding of true or false motivates behavior).

The first question creates difficulties in reconciling two phenomena of contradictory nature—flashbulb and intrusive memories and traumatic amnesia. Events with high emotional valence (either positive or negative) of surprising nature and of special personal importance are believed to enhance memory. A variety of research data supports this view (Lorenzzoni, Silva, Poletto, Kristensen, & Gauer, 2014). The event might be regarded fundamental in personal and/or community history (like "chosen trauma" see Volkan, 1991) and integrated as an essential and central part of individual or national narrative. This phenomenon is known as a "centrality of event," organizing the experience into life history (Berntsen & Rubin, 2007). If centrality is assigned to a negative event that is influencing the process of meaning attribution to other events, it might cause distortion of perceptions and rumination (Lorenzzoni et al., 2014). Through a process of integration into the sense of self, this event might become essential to personal identity (Brewin, 2011, 2016). Variations of the same event are presented in narratives, and different versions depend on time and context of their recollection (Habermas & Bluck, 2000). In the revised version of his theory of dual representation, Brewin (2016) is clarifying that a coherent memory narrative of a traumatic or turning point event is coexisting with more subtle markers of fragmentation. Discrepancies between well-rehearsed, detailed, and accessible narrative version of the traumatic event (usually developed for communication with the outside world) and omission of "hot spots"—the most painful moments that are liable to trigger vivid images or flashbacks—are diagnostically and clinically differentiating the risk of PTSD and other disturbances in functioning. The debate about coherence vs. fragmentation and well-remembered vs. forgotten (and eventually recovered) highly emotional traumatic memories has to consider a multilayered memory process and a possibility of discrepancies in autobiographical (semantic) memories, episodic memories, and implicit memories of the same event. General narratives and global accounts could be well coordinated or completely forgotten; at the same time, episodic memories of the most frightening moments might be either missing or fragmented with an involuntary memory in mainly visual modality (flashbacks) reoccurring.

The second question about motivational factors behind traumatic amnesia is pointing at the psychoanalytic concept of repression. Memory gaps of irreversible nature are common in all trauma survivors but "longer, progressive, and potentially reversible amnesia occurs among survivors who develop PTSD" (Yovell et al., 2003, p. 676). Difficulties in voluntary recall together with conscious or unconscious avoidance of the traumatic contents speak for motivation behind forgetting. The three core characteristics of PTSD (Karatzias et al., 2018) are: (1) avoidance of the most painful moments, (2) reexperiencing in the form of nightmares or flashbacks, and (3) the feeling of constant threat. Intrusive memories with a particular distortion of sense for time and space and experience that everything is happening here and now are constant reminders of a traumatic experience. At the level of narratives, markers of fragmentation and loss of sense of time are feasible in spontaneous shifts in the verb tense. Social processes of reenactment of the past, confusion of the history and actual moment, and sense of being under a constant threat are symptoms of disintegrated, fragmented historic memories. One could not even state that the history is repeating itself because of the lost time perspective and complete emersion into the emotional experience. Overcoming of repression and integration of the traumatic contents has a high clinical relevance in recovery of both individuals with PTSD and societies with social trauma. Time matters! Re-living of trauma is not bringing relief unless tendencies of avoidance are overcome and past is revisited for reflection. Memories—recovered, traumatic, and/or collective—need to be contextualized and, thus, integrated into personal (and social) historical narrative.

The third question of overall influence of trauma on memory is approached through the phenomenon of overgeneralized memories. Williams and Broadbent (1986) introduced the hypothesis that trauma could result in significant changes in recollections, possibly explained by the tendency to avoid emotional distress. When asked about life events, some people respond with vague or unspecific accounts.

This overgeneralization tendency is related to several disorders in psychopathology and connected to decreased ability in solving problems and an increased feeling of hopelessness (Sumner, Griffith, & Mineka, 2010). In their evaluative review, Moore and Zoellner (2007) question the notion of a direct link between trauma and overgeneralization of autobiographic memory but agree that more research is needed to explore the mediating mechanisms of trauma-related memory impairment for both cultural and autobiographical events.

20.4 Practical Implications in the Field of Social Trauma

Elizabeth Loftus is citing Harold Pinter and his definition of the past as compiled of what is remembered, imagined to be remembered, of what people could convince themselves they remember or pretend to remember (Loftus, 2017). Memory construction is dependent on personal past and history and memories influence present and future individual and social acts.

Cognitive psychologists formulate models of memory which seek verification in neuroscience and neuroimaging, bringing an advanced understanding of the encoding, storage, and retrieval processes. One influential rule dates back to 1949 when Donald Hebb (1949) formulated the principle that "neurons wire together, if they fire together," implying that, through a repeated use, connections between neurons are established and, therefore, mechanics of memory consolidation and potential for change are an open opportunity.

What is happening if a lie is told a 1000 times? Reformulation of the application of Hebb's rule to recovered memories, false memories, and childhood trauma memories justifies Steven Rose's formulation of the "historical" vs. "biological reality" (cited in Bone, 2006). The active nature of remembering opens possibilities for creating neurochemical traces in the brain, which are "biologically real" for the person but that tells nothing about their nature—real events or induced constructions. What seems like a danger of falsification brings also a hope for recovery. Memory traces might not be deleted, but their network of associations could be shifted. Several key factors are to be observed in the process of memory retrieval, critical reflection, and reintegration into a new contextual scheme. One possibility for false memory construction is the confusion of the source of information. When the content and source are dissociated, memories are more prone to distortion. Another risk is the social contagion effect (Meade & Roediger, 2002) proven in experimental settings where the effect is significant even when people are explicitly warned. These findings support the claim that false memories may be transmitted between people and reveal critical factors in the social trauma memory constructions in the society.

Fergus Craik and Robert Lockhart (1972) proposed the levels-of-processing theory of memory which states that recall is a function of the depth of mental processing, dependent on sets of connections with the preexisting memory, time spent in processing the stimuli, and cognitive effort. Clinical reconceptualization of processing (or work with the repressed) presupposes contextualization of memories and second order of reflection to enhance understanding and integration of emotional experience in relation to traumatic memories (Fonagy & Target, 1997; Karatzias et al., 2018).

Constructions of individual and social life history are a mixture of subjective interpretations of objective facts and events. Interwoven memories, wishes, and fantasies are hard, if not impossible to be disentangled (Fonagy & Target, 1997). A difficult balance between relief of suffering and truth recovery is needed when doing research, making therapy or forming an expert position in regard of recovered memories of individual or social trauma.

20.5 Suggested Readings and Further Information

More on new formulations of memory in PTSD diagnoses available at:

Brewin, C. (2016, June). *Understanding post-traumatic stress disorder.* Presentation part of the Academy of Medical Sciences New Fellow's Admissions Day 2016, held on 29 June. [Video file]. Retrieved from https://www.youtube.com/watch?v=bjHCoGDn9Dk&t=309s

More on the false memory and its legal and ethical implications available at:

Loftus, E. (2013, June). *How reliable is your memory?* [Video file]. Retrieved from https://www.ted.com/talks/elizabeth_loftus_how_reliable_is_your_memory?language=en

More on the work Bessel van der Kolk on memory trauma and recovery available at: http://www.besselvanderkolk.net/index.html

References

Berntsen, D., & Rubin, D. C. (2007). When a trauma becomes a key to identity: Enhanced integration of trauma memories predicts posttraumatic stress disorder symptoms. *Applied Cognitive Psychology, 21*(4), 417–431.

Bone, J. D. (2006). Steven Rose's 21st century brain: Explaining, mending and manipulating the mind. *Body & Society, 12*(1), 121–122.

Boston Change Process Study Group (BCPSG). (2008). Forms of relational meaning: Issues in the relations between the implicit and reflective-verbal domains. *Psychoanalytic Dialogues, 18*, 125–148.

Brewin, C. R. (2011). The nature and significance of memory disturbance in posttraumatic stress disorder. *Annual Review of Clinical Psychology, 7*, 203–227.

Brewin, C. R. (2016). Coherence, disorganization, and fragmentation in traumatic memory reconsidered: A response to Rubin et al. (2016). *Journal of Abnormal Psychology, 125*, 1011–1017.

Brown, R., & Kulik, J. (1977). Flashbulb memories. *Cognition, 5*, 73–99.

Ceci, S. J., & Loftus, E. F. (1994). "Memory work": A royal road to false memories*? Applied Cognitive Psychology, 8*, 351–364.

Craik, F. I. M., & Lockhart, R. S. (1972). Levels of processing: A framework for memory research. *Journal of Verbal Learning and Verbal Behavior, 11*(6), 671–684.

Fonagy, P. (1999). Memory and therapeutic action [editorial]. *The International Journal of Psychoanalysis, 80*(2), 215–223.
Fonagy, P., & Target, M. (1997). Perspectives on the recovered memories debate. In J. Sandler & P. Fonagy (Eds.), *Recovered memories of abuse: True or false?* (pp. 183–216). London: Karnac Books.
Habermas, T., & Bluck, S. (2000). Getting a life: The emergence of the life story in adolescence. *Psychological Bulletin, 126*(5), 748–769.
Hebb, D. O. (1949). *The organization of behavior: A neuropsychological theory*. New York: John Wiley and Sons.
Iyadurai, L., Visser, R. M., Lau-Zhu, A., Porcheret, K., Horsch, A., Holmes, E. A., & James, E. L. (2019). Intrusive memories of trauma: A target for research bridging cognitive science and its clinical application. *Clinical Psychology Review, 69*, 67–82.
Karatzias, T., Cloitre, M., Maercker, A., Kazlauskas, E., Shevlin, M., Hyland, P., … Brewin, C. R. (2018). PTSD and complex PTSD: ICD-11 updates on concept and measurement in the UK, USA, Germany and Lithuania. *European Journal of Psychotraumatology, 8*(7), 1418103.
Klein, S., & Nichols, S. (2012). Memory and the sense of personal identity. *Mind, 121*(483), 677–702.
Laney, C., & Loftus, E. F. (2008). Emotional content of true and false memories. *Memory, 16*, 500–516.
Levine, L. J., Lench, H. C., & Safer, M. A. (2009). Functions of remembering and misremembering emotion. *Applied Cognitive Psychology, 23*, 1059–1075.
Loftus, E. (1997). Creating false memories. *Scientific American, 277*(3), 70–75.
Loftus, E. (2017). Eavesdropping on memory. *Annual Review of Psychology, 68*, 1–18.
Lorenzzoni, P. L., Silva, G. L. T., Poletto, P. M., Kristensen, H. C., & Gauer, G. (2014). Autobiographical memory for stressful events, traumatic memory and post traumatic stress disorder: A systematic review. *Avances en Psicología Latinoamericana, 32*(3), 361–376.
Lyons-Ruth, K. (1998). Implicit relational knowing: Its role in development and psychoanalytic treatment. *Infant Mental Health Journal, 19*(3), 282–289.
Meade, M. L., & Roediger, H. L. (2002). Explorations in the social contagion of memory. *Memory & Cognition, 30*, 995–1009.
Moore, S. A., & Zoellner, L. A. (2007). Overgeneral autobiographical memory and traumatic events: An evaluative review. *Psychological Bulletin, 133*(3), 419–437.
Renn, P. (2012). *The silent past and the invisible present: Memory, trauma, and representation in psychotherapy*. New York: Routledge.
Rubin, D. C. (2011). The coherence of memories for trauma: Evidence from posttraumatic stress disorder. *Consciousness and Cognition, 20*(3), 857–865.
Rubin, D. C., Berntsen, D., Ogle, C. M., Deffler, S. A., & Beckham, J. C. (2016). Scientific evidence versus outdated beliefs: A response to Brewin (2016). *Journal of Abnormal Psychology, 125*, 1018–1021.
Rubin, D. C., Deffler, S. A., Ogle, C. M., Dowell, N. M., Graesser, A. C., & Beckham, J. C. (2016). Participant, rater, and computer measures of coherence in posttraumatic stress disorder. *Journal of Abnormal Psychology, 125*, 11–15.
Schacter, D. (1996). *Searching for memory: The brain, the mind, and the past*. New York: Basic Books.
Sumner, J. A., Griffith, J. W., & Mineka, S. (2010). Overgeneral autobiographical memory as a predictor of the course of depression: A meta-analysis. *Behaviour Research and Therapy, 48*, 614–625.
Tulving, E. (1985). How many memory systems are there? *American Psychologist, 40*(4), 385–398.
Urban, E. J., Charles, S. T., Levine, L. J., & Almeida, D. M. (2018). Depression history and memory bias for specific daily emotions. *PLoS One, 13*(9), e0203574.
van der Kolk, B. A. (1994). The body keeps the score: Memory and the emerging psychobiology of post traumatic stress. *Harvard Review of Psychiatry, 1*, 253–265.

van der Kolk, B. A. (1996). Trauma and memory. In B. A. van der Kolk, A. C. McFarlane, & L. Weisaeth (Eds.), *Traumatic stress: The effects of overwhelming experience on mind, body, and society* (pp. 279–302). New York: Guilford Press.
van der Kolk, B. A. (1998). Trauma and memory. *Psychiatry and Clinical Neurosciences, 52*(1), 52–64.
van der Kolk, B. A. (2014). *The body keeps the score: Brain, mind, and body in the healing of trauma*. New York: Viking.
van der Kolk, B. A., Pelcovitz, D., Roth, S., Mandel, F. S., McFarlane, A., & Herman, J. L. (1996). Dissociation, somatization, and affect dysregulation: The complexity of adaptation of trauma. *American Journal of Psychiatry, 153*, 83–93.
van Steenbergen, H., Band, G. P., & Hommel, B. (2011). Threat but not arousal narrows attention: Evidence from pupil dilation and saccade control. *Frontiers in Psychology, 2*, 1–5.
Volkan, V. D. (1991). On "chosen trauma". *Mind and Human Interaction, 3*, 13–38.
Williams, J. M. G., & Broadbent, K. (1986). Autobiographical memory in suicide attempters. *Journal of Abnormal Psychology, 95*, 144–149.
Yovell, Y., Bannett, Y., & Shalev, A. Y. (2003). Amnesia for traumatic events among recent survivors: A pilot study. *CNS Spectrums, 8*, 676–680.

Chapter 21
Development of Autobiographical Narrating: Possible Implications for Coping with Social Trauma

Tilmann Habermas and Eleonora Bartoli

21.1 Introduction

In this chapter, we provide a brief overview of the development of remembering and narrating and hypothesize their relevance for coping with social trauma. Two separate fields of research deal with memory and with narrating. We believe that both contribute to everyday remembering.

The development of basic memory skills (Bauer & Fivush, 2013) begins in infants with the building up of expectations that show in directing attention and surprise reactions, as well as in the learning of motor actions. These are memory faculties termed procedural (knowing-how) and implicit, that is, these memories cannot be explicated verbally before the advent of language. As soon as children begin to acquire language, they explicitly communicate memories in a highly contextualized way. Memories of personal experiences and of self-defining facts from one's life are termed autobiographical episodic and semantic memories to differentiate them from nonpersonal memories. They are declarative and explicit. The amount and correctness of autobiographical memories improves in the course of childhood. Adults tend to not remember anything from their first 2–3 years of life. This childhood amnesia, however, does not mean that young children cannot remember. Rather, nonverbal memories for events that occurred before the acquisition of language are hardly transferrable in a verbal form (Simcock & Hayne, 2002). After language acquisition, memories become increasingly elaborated with age, and strategies for remembering become more refined. Thus, during the first 10 years of life, children increasingly learn to retain and find their memories (Bauer, 2015).

T. Habermas (✉) · E. Bartoli
Goethe University Frankfurt, Frankfurt a.M., Germany
e-mail: tilmann.habermas@psych.uni-frankfurt.de

© Springer Nature Switzerland AG 2021

A. Hamburger et al. (eds.), *Social Trauma – An Interdisciplinary Textbook*,
https://doi.org/10.1007/978-3-030-47817-9_21

Autobiographical memories can only be communicated to others by narrating them. The ability to narrate events, both fictional and based on one's or others' experience, also develops during the first decade of life. An early predecessor of narrating is understanding and enacting scripts for specific social situations, that is, knowledge of the sequence of events that should normally happen when, for example, going to the restaurant (Nelson & Gruendel, 1979). In their foundational study, Peterson and McCabe (1983) used three ways of analyzing narrations to demonstrate that a basic ability to narrate is reached by grade school which continues to be refined up to late childhood (cf. Bamberg, 1997).

21.2 Learning Outcome Related to Social Trauma

We will argue in the following sections that the development of autobiographical narrating helps children and adolescents understand and contextualize the experience of collective violence. However, this depends to a large degree on the narrative input by parents, who are themselves exposed to collective violence.

21.3 The Sociocultural Model of the Development of Autobiographical Narrating: The Possible Impact on the Experience and Consequences of Collective Violence

Telling stories is a central human ability. Whereas we explain natural events causally by reference to natural laws, we explain human actions by reference to motives and through embedding them in a story. Putting experiences in a narrative form organizes them, relates our own with others' perspectives, and forces us to explicate what they mean to us (Bruner, 1991). Memory and narrative come together in the activity of explicit autobiographical remembering, the development of which is best modeled by Lev Vygotsky's sociocultural theory of development. It posits that the development of skills is rooted in social interaction with a competent member of a given culture. The adult adapts the quality of interaction to the child's zone of proximal development, that is, to the level of abilities that the child has not yet acquired but which it can already use if it is scaffolded by an adult.

This can be shown for narrating fictional stories as well as memories. The adult expert's feedback helps the inexperienced child narrator to grasp the relevant information of a story and to re-narrate it (Nelson, 2009). Dialogic reading in which parents prompt preschoolers with questions and encourage further elaborations of the story fosters the development of narrative skills (Lever & Sénéchal, 2011; Reese, 2013). Studies using wordless pictures to elicit children's narratives highlighted improvements in children's narratives after conversational interventions (e.g., Veneziano & Hudelot, 2006).

Also autobiographical narrating is learned in the shared narrating of past events between adults and children (Nelson & Fivush, 2004). Reese, Haden, and Fivush (1993) studied two styles of mothers' co-narrating past events with their 3-year-old children. The elaborative style motivates children to elaborate the bits they have provided before by complementing information, asking open questions, or encouraging the child, depending on the developmental level of the child, whereas the repetitive reminiscing style focusses on details and does not motivate the child to continue and elaborate narrating. Children whose mothers used the two different reminiscing styles at ages 2–4 later differed in their abilities to explicitly remember and narrate past events. Moreover, children whose mothers reminisce elaboratively in early childhood tend to excel those whose mothers use repetitive reminiscing in many socio-cognitive and social–emotional areas such as language, perspective-taking, emotion understanding, and attachment (Fivush, 2019).

By the time children start school, they are more or less able to narrate personal experiences by themselves. A new quality of autobiographical remembering that goes beyond single stories develops when remembering becomes more closely intertwined with the sense of self in adolescence. This new and truly autobiographical ability is to narrate coherently entire lives. When children are asked to tell their life story, up to age 10, they produce a collection of unrelated stories about interesting positive and negative memories, but do not arrange them into a life (Habermas, 2006). Only in preadolescence do they begin to learn to manage calendar time and acquire a cultural concept of biography. This includes the cultural life script, a sequence of normative transitional events with normative ages attached to them as a basic grid that structures any individual life story, as well as knowledge that life stories begin before individual memory sets in, that is with birth or earlier, and that the relevance of the past for present self-understanding needs to be spelled out (Habermas, 2007). When telling their entire lives, early adolescents succeed in creating temporal coherence. In mid-adolescence, episodes are imbued with autobiographical meaning through autobiographical reasoning by linking past experiences to personal development, beginning to motivate personality change and directions taken in life. Young adults add thematic coherence by discovering repeated patterns of experience and acting (Köber, Schmiedek, & Habermas, 2015).

However, telling an entire life is not something we do in everyday life. Nevertheless, acquiring the ability to construct coherent life stories changes the way we understand and remember others and ourselves. The life story helps to biographically embed memories and actions. So even if only a local event is remembered and narrated, it may be embedded in the life story via autobiographical arguments that link it to distant events and to the individual's personal development.

Like the ability to narrate memories, also the ability to reason autobiographically and to construct a life story is acquired in social interaction. When mothers and their children co-narrate the child's life, mothers adapt their scaffolding to the child's or adolescent's zone of proximal development by supporting those elements of the life story that the child is about to learn next (Habermas, Negele, & Mayer, 2010). The life story is used by adolescents to construct a mature psychosocial identity that selectively intertwines attributions by and identifications with parents and family with later identifications with roles and social groups.

This encompasses identification with political and ethnic groups and their collective histories of selected traumas and triumphs (Volkan, 1997). However, we would surmise that the acquisition of a narrative, life story identity might protect against too essentialist social identities. Continuing with this line of reasoning, the finding that less individualized, more family-oriented societies with an interdependent self-definition has less coherent life narratives because they include more of their family in them (Hatiboğlu Altunnar & Habermas, 2018) might seem to imply that members of individualistic societies are better protected against simplified collective identities that pitch them against other groups. But, alas, recent political developments in individualized societies speak strongly against this generalization.

21.4 Practical Implications in the Field of Social Trauma

The clinical field tends to assume that traumatic experiences lead to a fragmentation of the life story and of narratives of the traumatic experience itself, so that self-continuity is interrupted and the traumatic event is not narrated in an oriented and sequential manner. However, there are no systematic studies of fragmentation of entire life narratives of traumatized individuals, and the studies of narratives of traumatic events do not confirm that they are generally fragmented (Crespo & Fernández-Lansac, 2016). However, studies suggest that narratives of extremely threatening experiences are more immersed in the protagonist's perspective, reflecting a reliving of the past (Fohn et al., 2017; Römisch, Leban, Habermas, & Döll-Hentschker, 2014). Thus, it is generally assumed that narrativizing a traumatic experience helps put it into perspective, elaborate emotions, and modulate the arousal connected to the remembering. Once narrated, the memory becomes a cultural product negotiated in a social context (Vygotsky, 1934) and its internal representation is externalized in a "language for others" (cf. Bartoli & Smorti, 2019; Smorti, 2011). In addition, integrating biographical ruptures into the life story through autobiographical reasoning helps re-establish the sense of self-continuity (Habermas & Köber, 2015).

Now, how may child and adolescent development of autobiographical narrating influence the experience and psychological consequences of potentially traumatic collective violence by dictatorial states or through war? Children rely in their interpretation of extra-familial events largely on their parents' interpretations and evaluations, picking up both emotional signals and explicit judgments. The ability to construct stories enables them to understand human actions, but not necessarily more abstract social and societal processes, leave alone historical processes. The understanding of societal (Furnham, 1991) and historical (Seixas, 2017) processes develops mainly between late childhood and late adolescence. A more abstract understanding of social processes may help adolescents reduce personal implications of the experience of violence and understand them in a wider context.

These cognitive developments show in changes in autobiographical remembering, specifically in life narratives. First, between ages 8 and 20, life narratives become less agentic, reflecting a growing realization of wider contexts that limit and determine one's scope for acting (de Silveira & Habermas, 2011). Second, across adolescence, life narratives increasingly contextualize the individual life in family history and in a socioeconomic context (Köber & Habermas, 2017). Historical events, however, are usually not mentioned in life narratives in our longitudinal *MainLife* study, except for war experiences such as from the civil war in Yugoslavia and from WWII. This is corroborated by studies of events people use to date their autobiographical memories, among which personally experienced war memories are highly prevalent (Brown, Schweickart, & Svob, 2016).

This seems to imply that the younger children are, the less they may remember social violence in a distancing way, and the more traumatizing these events may be. However, children rely heavily on their parents in coping with menacing events. And collective violence affects not only children and adolescents but also entire communities. Therefore, the degree to which their parents have been affected does play a crucial role in how much children are affected by collective violence (Lindblom et al., 2017). This is mediated by psychological factors such as a secure attachment and a sense of security in family and community (Cummings et al., 2013), and possibly also by the parents' potentially reduced ability to scaffold narrative emotion regulation abilities in their children (Graneist & Habermas, 2019).

Finally, the willingness of parents and others to talk about potentially traumatic experiences does play a decisive role in how experiences of collective violence are processed by children. Being able to co-narrate negative experiences in a trusting relationship certainly helps protect children against negative consequences (Salmon & Reese, 2015). However, it is not merely the fact that these experiences are being talked about, but that they are talked about in a way that parents contain their own distress and empathize with their child's needs (Dalgaard, Diab, Montgomery, Qouta, & Punamäki, 2019). In addition, the cultural interpretation of collective violence does play an important role in how parents talk about it and how children and adolescents remember it. The cultural and familial framing may stress the experience of collective violence to be part of collective identity (Muldoon, 2013), either as heroic or traumatic past (Lomsky-Feder, 2004; Volkan, 1997), sometimes drawing positive lessons from it (Dalgaard et al., 2019).

21.5 Suggested Reading

Dalgaard, N. T., Diab, S. Y., Montgomery, E., Qouta, S. R., & Punamäki, R. L. (2019). Is silence about trauma harmful for children? Transgenerational communication in Palestinian families. *Transcultural Psychiatry*, *56*, 398–427.

Salmon, K., & Reese, E. (2015). Talking (or not talking) about the past: The influence of parent–child conversation about negative experiences on children's memories. *Applied Cognitive Psychology*, *29*, 791–801.

References

Bamberg, M. G. (Ed.). (1997). *Narrative development: Six approaches*. London: Routledge.
Bartoli, E., & Smorti, A. (2019). Facing the language-memory problem in the study of autobiographical memory. *Integrative Psychological and Behavioral Science, 53*, 374–396.
Bauer, P. J. (2015). A complementary processes account of the development of childhood amnesia and a personal past. *Psychological Review, 122*, 204–231.
Bauer, P. J., & Fivush, R. (2013). *The Wiley handbook on the development of children's memory*. New York: Wiley.
Brown, N. R., Schweickart, O., & Svob, C. (2016). The effect of collective transitions on the organization and contents of autobiographical memory: A transition theory perspective. *American Journal of Psychology, 129*, 259–282.
Bruner, J. (1991). The narrative construction of reality. *Critical Inquiry, 18*, 1–21.
Crespo, M., & Fernández-Lansac, V. (2016). Memory and narrative of traumatic events: A literature review. *Psychological Trauma: Theory, Research, Practice, and Policy, 8*, 149–156.
Cummings, E. M., Taylor, L. K., Merrilees, C. E., Goeke-Morey, M. C., Shirlow, P., & Cairns, E. (2013). Relations between political violence and child adjustment: A four-wave test of the role of emotional insecurity about community. *Developmental Psychology, 49*, 2212–2224.
Dalgaard, N. T., Diab, S. Y., Montgomery, E., Qouta, S. R., & Punamäki, R. L. (2019). Is silence about trauma harmful for children? Transgenerational communication in Palestinian families. *Transcultural Psychiatry, 56*, 398–427.
De Silveira, C., & Habermas, T. (2011). Narrative means to manage responsibility in life narratives across adolescence. *Journal of Genetic Psychology, 172*, 1–20.
Fivush, R. (2019). *Family narratives and the development of an autobiographical self.* London: Routledge.
Fohn, A., Bouhmidi, S., Bushati, E., Mba, D., Yesilgöz, E., & Habermas, T. (2017). Given up by parents for survival: Separation narratives by formerly persecuted elderly Belgian Jews. *Journal of Applied Research on Memory and Cognition, 6*, 74–81.
Furnham, A. (1991). *Young people's understanding of society*. London: Routledge.
Graneist, A., & Habermas, T. (2019). Beyond the text given: Studying the scaffolding of narrative emotion regulation as a contribution to Bruner and Feldman's cultural cognitive developmental psychology. *Integrative Psychological & Behavioral Science, 53*, 644–660.
Habermas, T. (2006). "Kann ich auch ganz, ganz am Anfang anfangen?" Wie Jugendliche lernen, Lebenserzählungen zu eröffnen und beenden. In H. Welzer & H. J. Markowitsch (Eds.), *Warum Menschen sich erinnern* (pp. 256–275). Stuttgart: Klett-Cotta.
Habermas, T. (2007). How to tell a life: The development of the cultural concept of biography across the lifespan. *Journal of Cognition and Development, 8*, 1–31.
Habermas, T., & Köber, C. (2015). Autobiographical reasoning in life narratives buffers the effect of biographical disruptions on the sense of self-continuity. *Memory, 23*, 564–574.
Habermas, T., Negele, A., & Mayer, F. B. (2010). "Honey, you're jumping about"—Mothers' scaffolding of their children's and adolescents' life narration. *Cognitive Development, 25*, 339–351.
Hatiboğlu Altunnar, N., & Habermas, T. (2018). Life narratives are more other-centered, more negative, and less coherent in Turkey than in Germany: Comparing provincial-Turkish, Metropolitan-Turkish, Turkish-German, and native German educated young adults. *Frontiers in Psychology, 9*, 2466.
Köber, C., & Habermas, T. (2017). The development of temporal macrostructure in life narratives across the lifespan. *Discourse Processes, 54*, 143–162.
Köber, C., Schmiedek, F., & Habermas, T. (2015). Characterizing lifespan development of three aspects of coherence in life narratives: A cohort-sequential study. *Developmental Psychology, 51*, 260–275.
Lever, R., & Sénéchal, M. (2011). Discussing stories: On how a dialogic reading intervention improves kindergartners' oral narrative construction. *Journal of Experimental Child Psychology, 108*, 1–24.

Lindblom, J., Peltola, M. J., Vänskä, M., Hietanen, J. K., Laakso, A., Tiitinen, A., ... Punamäki, R. L. (2017). Early family system types predict children's emotional attention biases at school age. *International Journal of Behavioral Development, 41*, 245–256.

Lomsky-Feder, E. (2004). Life stories, war, and veterans: On the social distribution of memories. *Ethos, 32*, 82–109.

Muldoon, O. T. (2013). Understanding the impact of political violence in childhood: A theoretical review using a social identity approach. *Clinical Psychology Review, 33*, 929–939.

Nelson, K. (2009). *Young minds in social worlds: Experience, meaning, and memory*. Cambridge, MA: Harvard University Press.

Nelson, K., & Fivush, R. (2004). The emergence of autobiographical memory: A social cultural developmental theory. *Psychological Review, 111*, 486–511.

Nelson, K., & Gruendel, J. M. (1979). At morning it's lunchtime: A scriptal view of children's dialogues. *Discourse Processes, 2*, 73–94.

Peterson, C., & McCabe, A. (1983). *Developmental psycholinguistics: Three ways of looking at a child's narrative*. New York: Plenum.

Reese, E. (2013). *Tell me a story: Sharing stories to enrich your child's world.* New York: Oxford University Press.

Reese, E., Haden, C. A., & Fivush, R. (1993). Mother-child conversations about the past: Relationships of style and memory over time. *Cognitive Development, 8*, 403–430.

Römisch, S., Leban, E., Habermas, T., & Döll-Hentschker, S. (2014). Evaluation, involvement, and fragmentation in narratives of distressing, angering, and happy events by traumatized and non-traumatized women. *Psychological Trauma: Theory, Research, Practice and Policy, 6*, 465–472.

Salmon, K., & Reese, E. (2015). Talking (or not talking) about the past: The influence of parent–child conversation about negative experiences on children's memories. *Applied Cognitive Psychology, 29*, 791–801.

Seixas, P. (2017). Historical consciousness and historical thinking. In M. Carretero, S. Berger, & M. Graver (Eds.), *Palgrave handbook of research in historical culture and education* (pp. 59–72). London: Palgrave Macmillan.

Simcock, G., & Hayne, H. (2002). Breaking the barrier? Children fail to translate their preverbal memories into language. *Psychological Science, 13*, 225–231.

Smorti, A. (2011). Autobiographical memory and autobiographical narrative: What is the relationship? *Narrative Inquiry, 21*, 303–310.

Veneziano, E., & Hudelot, C. (2006). Etats internes, fausse croyance et explications dans les récits: Effets de l'étayage chez les enfants de 4 à 12 ans. *Langage et l'Homme, 41*, 117–138.

Volkan, V. (1997). *Bloodlines: From ethnic pride to ethnic violence*. Boulder, CO: Westview.

Vygotsky, L. S. (1934). *Thinking and speech* (p. 1987). New York: Plenum Press.

Lindblom, J., Peltola, M. J., Vänskä, M., Hietanen, J. K., Laakso, A., Tiitinen, A., … Punamäki, R.-L. (2017). Early family system types predict children's emotional attention biases at school age. *International Journal of Behavioral Development, 41*, 245–256.

Lomsky-Feder, E. (2004). Life stories, war, and veterans: On the social distribution of memories. *Ethos, 32*, 82–109.

Muldoon, O. T. (2013). Understanding the impact of political violence in childhood: A theoretical review using a social identity approach. *Clinical Psychology Review, 33*, 929–939.

Nelson, K. (2007). *Young minds in social worlds: Experience, meaning, and memory*. Cambridge, MA: Harvard University Press.

Nelson, K., & Fivush, R. (2004). The emergence of autobiographical memory: A social cultural developmental theory. *Psychological Review, 111*, 486–511.

Nelson, K., & Gruendel, J. M. (1979). At morning it's lunchtime: A scriptal view of children's dialogues. *Discourse Processes, 2*, 73–94.

Peterson, C., & McCabe, A. (1983). *Developmental psycholinguistics: Three ways of looking at a child's narrative*. New York: Plenum.

Reese, E. (2013). *Tell me a story: Sharing stories to enrich your child's world*. New York: Oxford University Press.

Reese, E., Haden, C. A., & Fivush, R. (1993). Mother-child conversations about the past: Relationships of style and memory over time. *Cognitive Development, 8*, 403–430.

Römisch, S., Leban, E., Habermas, T., & Döll-Hentschker, S. (2014). Evaluation, involvement, and fragmentation in narratives of distressing, angering, and happy events by traumatized and non-traumatized women. *Psychological Trauma: Theory, Research, Practice, and Policy, 6*, 465–472.

Salmon, K., & Reese, E. (2015). Talking (or not talking) about the past: The influence of parent-child conversation about negative experiences on children's memories. *Applied Cognitive Psychology, 29*, 791–801.

Seixas, P. (2017). Historical consciousness and historical thinking. In M. Carretero, S. Berger, & M. Grever (Eds.), *Palgrave handbook of research in historical culture and education* (pp. 59–72). London: Palgrave Macmillan.

Simcock, G., & Hayne, H. (2002). Breaking the barrier? Children fail to translate their preverbal memories into language. *Psychological Science, 13*, 225–231.

Smorti, A. (2011). Autobiographical memory and autobiographical narrative: What is the relationship? *Narrative Inquiry, 21*, 303–310.

Veneziano, E., & Hudelot, C. (2009). Étayage et explications: fausse croyance et explications dans les récits chez les enfants de 4 à 12 ans. *Langage et l'Homme, 44*, 119–128.

Volkan, V. (1997). *Bloodlines: From ethnic pride to ethnic terrorism*. Boulder, CO: Westview.

Vygotsky, L. S. (1934). *Thinking and speech* (Vol. 1, 1987). New York: Plenum Press.

Chapter 22
Trans-Generational Transmission of Trauma

Sue Grand and Jill Salberg

22.1 Introduction: Background and Main Theoretical Concepts /Discussions

Trans-generational trauma transmission has been studied and researched in psychoanalysis and clinical psychology throughout the last decades. Clinical and epidemiological studies show that children of parents who experienced trauma are at risk of developing emotional, cognitive, and behavioral problems including post-traumatic symptoms, depression, anxiety, hyperactivity, and conduct disorders (see Aviad-Wilchek & Cohenca, 2013; Felsen, 1998; Scharf, 2007; Schwab, 2010), especially if the traumatic experience is connected to social trauma (see Hamburger, 2020, this volume).

In psychoanalysis, increasing attention to massive trauma has inspired a trans-generational perspective which incorporates ethics, history, politics, social justice, as well as a broader acknowledgment of a familial unconscious (see, e.g., Fromm, 2012). Trans-generational trauma studies entered psychoanalysis mainly through the work of Selma Fraiberg, Adelson, and Shapiro (1975). Fraiberg pointed to parents' unremembered past and to the transmission of fear, anxiety, and violent behavior. The multi-generational sequelae of the Holocaust alerted us to the effect of "Big History" on multiple generations (see Bergmann & Jucovy, 1982; Felman & Laub, 1992; Grubrich-Simitis, 1984; Kestenberg, 1980; Krystal, 1985; Laub, 1993, 1998; Laub & Hamburger, 2017). Eventually, new work on childhood sexual abuse (Alpert, 2017) became linked to these trends.

Major *theoretical shifts in psychoanalytic theory and practice* contributed to the conceptualization of trans-generational trauma transmission. First, a shift from a one-person to a two-person psychology and to a more co-constructed understanding

S. Grand · J. Salberg (✉)
New York University Postdoctoral Program in Psychotherapy and Psychoanalysis, New York, NY, USA

© Springer Nature Switzerland AG 2021

A. Hamburger et al. (eds.), *Social Trauma – An Interdisciplinary Textbook*,
https://doi.org/10.1007/978-3-030-47817-9_22

of the analytic process. Simultaneously, the rediscovery of Ferenczi's work on trauma and alteration of technique, along with the explosion of attachment research. These theoretical changes fostered a paradigm shift from solely focused on internal conflict to acceptance of the effects of external trauma on the mind and of an intersubjective model of mind and technique.

Abraham and Torok (1975) began writing about internalized memorialization that they referred to as a phantom and crypt. Rich work in this field continues (Gerson, 2009; Grand, 2010; Grand & Salberg, 2015; Guralnik, 2014; Richman, 2006). In the past 20 years, that scholarship on witnessing, testimony and trans-generational transmission have extended beyond the Holocaust, to other political and social traumas and genocides. Recently, psychoanalysis has examined the legacies of African–American slavery and the legacy on subsequent generations; (Apprey, 2003; Grand, 2000; Gump, 2010; Leary, 1997), the Armenian genocide and the legacy of Native American "vanishing" genocide in the United States (Davoine & Gaudillière, 2004; Grand, 2000, 2018) linked the inchoate memory of WWII with psychosis in subsequent generations; and Kaplan (2013) wrote on the Tutsi genocide and its impact on trans-generational linking.

22.2 The Trans-Generational Model

The psychoanalytic look at three generations started with Faimberg's (2005) idea of "telescoping of generations." Most early formulations were grounded in several bedrock psychoanalytic assumptions, which are now undergoing critique. The trauma transmission was presumed to occur, exclusively within what we previously thought of as the "psychoanalytic family:" maternal dyads and Oedipal triangles. This is a hierarchical model absent of siblings (Mitchell, 2003) and multiple generations. The effects were presumed to be intrapsychic and/or interpersonal, without attending to the collective and social effects. This perspective sustained an individualized insularity that separated applied and clinical psychoanalysis. In addition, our emphasis was exclusively on victimization, and failed to include aspects of generational trauma that included acts of perpetration and an inattention to ethical dimensions. The effect has been a very limited awareness of our need to make repair toward the other. With rare exception (Frie, 2011; Grand, 2000, 2010; Guralnik, 2014), the wounded Other remained invisible in clinical process.

In a more contemporary view, the trans-generational perspective understands the psyche as constituted by a multi-generational object world, including siblings and peer cohorts. The social/political/cultural markers of collective trauma link global violence and social justice to psychoanalytic thought, thus interpenetrating applied and clinical psychoanalysis. Ethics and social justice are being incorporated into clinical practice and in the definition of "mental health" (Grand, 2000, 2010, 2014; Layton, 2009, 2015; Orange, 2016). Empathic capacity is understood as a necessary part of healthful functioning and the engagement with others as an outgrowth of this developed capacity. In this rewriting, the psychoanalytic family can become the more fully developed *human family.*

Radical change in psychoanalysis and in our social world: This requires a departure from classical models of the psychoanalytic family. To continue adhering to old models of psychoanalytic family—this would be a retreat from radical change and from being affected by the violence of collective wounds. This lack of radical change would continue to fixate us in the individualized insularity that has long separated applied and clinical psychoanalysis. In the earlier work on trans-generational transmission, analytic processes expected to move individualized wounds toward a more reflective narrative (see Meares, 1998) in the context of empathic witnessing. However, with rare exception (Frie, 2011; Grand, 2000; Guralnik, 2014), the *Other* in this healing trajectory remains absent, a fixed alienated ghost in psyche and culture. In our contemporary trans-generational model, the alienated, objectified *Other* must enter into a healing conversation. In any heritage of persecution, there will always be some persecutory object left inside of us. This is always problematic, for individual minds and for cultural collectives–even if our efforts at splitting and projection are sanctioned by normative culture. Thus, psychoanalytic work with trans-generational trauma must converse with the alienated Other whom we have internalized and we must speak to the alienated *Other who is actually outside of us.* As psychoanalysts, we sense that we cannot avoid the alienated *Other* of our pre-history. *And we cannot avoid being the alienated Other in someone else's pre-history.* Most of us hold multiple positions within multiple histories, and possibly host a persecutory ghost that shape-shifts through the generations. Within our psyches, our lives, and in our global politics, we discover that we are fighting or fleeing, our ancestors' war, as we carry out our transgenerational errands (Apprey, 2003). And many of us are still fighting over or fleeing from our ancestors' *culpability* for that war.

22.3 Attachment and Trauma Transmission

Trauma transmissions have been written about as projections from one mind to another while the mode of transmission remained mysterious. Family traumas and social traumas are now being understood as transmitted transgenerationally through the attachment system (Salberg, 2015) based on a greater knowledge of procedural knowing and micro-relational communications from mother to child (Schechter, 2003, 2017). Ruptures in attachment relationships that occur in trauma become one of the key mechanisms of how it is transmitted to the next generation. The scars from traumas that are inside of people who become parents often affect directly their capacity to be consistent and engaged in their caregiving. Unresolved mourning, persistent states of anxiety, depression, and terror interfere with attaching and trusting new relationships. Grand (2000) has also written about the child's search to find an intimate connection to their parent only possible in the parent's traumatized state.

While many survivors of trauma also transmit resiliency and want to create loving families and communities, more often trauma survivors carry both resiliency and the scars of trauma. It is the imprint of the dehumanizing aspects of trauma; the violent victimization of one's integrity as a person, as well as surviving when others perished, that continues to haunt survivors. These ghosts of their past get transmitted and can be seen in the successive generations. The transmission of resiliency is what allows many survivors to form friendships, new families, and seek out psychotherapy and/or psychoanalysis so as to improve their social functioning. It is important to understand that the attachment system is more nuanced and expansive than currently conceptualized in a dyadic formation. Attachment studies, (Lyons-Ruth, 2003; Schechter, 2003, 2017) mother–infant research (Beebe & Lachmann, 2013), and neuroscience have expanded our understanding to see attachment as a mutually intersubjective self-other emotion-regulating system. Talk therapies often work well because of the intersubjective possibilities at helping trauma survivors to learn self-regulation, empathy, and self-care.

22.4 Practical Implications in the Field of Social Trauma

Clinically, this shift of scope requires a change in the psychoanalytic position. We privilege the telling and listening of stories with empathic witnesses, and an "imaginative witness" (Grand, 2010; Reis, 2015) who engage the story's aesthetic while containing its aggression, knowing that aggression keeps escaping this container.

The Transgenerational Model Connects to Major Findings in Developmental Psychology:

- *Attachment* functions play a major role in trans-generational transmission (Salberg, 2015). The violence of trauma pulls at the fabric of attachment, our intrinsic way of feeling safe. When a child's parent has had a trauma, we can assume that some part of their mind will not be accessible. If a parent's inaccessibility is great, the child, in a desperate search to be found in the parent's mind (Fonagy, 1999), will attune to the parent's absence as well as their presence. The texture of traumatic attachment (Salberg, 2015) is woven from the demands placed upon the child's mind while she is searching for a safe base of attachment, oftentimes entering a role reversal and emotionally regulate and 'parent/take care of' their parent (Lyons-Ruth, 2003).
- Drawing upon Fonagy (1999), Holmes (1999), and the work of Lyons-Ruth (2003) on disorganized attachment, Reis (2015) concludes that it is not trauma but the mental state of the caregiver, the fragmentation that is transmitted via the attachment relationship that is causative of problems.
- Biological factors also seem to play a role in trans-generational trauma transmission, as epigenetic studies show. Cortisol levels, receptor site alterations, and myelinization changes are found to affect gene expression and are inheritable by the next generation (see Bowers & Yehuda, 2016; Yehuda et al., 2014, 2016 on

Holocaust intergenerational transmissions; Perroud et al., 2014, on the Tutsi genocide). If children inherit altered biochemistry, then traumatized mothers are raising children with these more fearful propensities. Trans-generational trauma transmission, then, works through an alteration in both the biology and the attachment systems.

- Extending earlier work of Sullivan (1953), Schechter (2003, 2017) finds that mothers with a post-traumatic stress history will turn their priority in emotional regulation "to survival and self-regulation rather than affiliation and mutual regulation" (p. 265). The mother's post-traumatic stress disorder (PTSD) state triggers an alarm in the child without any link to an actual fearful situation, creating a new traumatizing dynamic (p. 267).

However, traumatic states are not the only transmissions that are occurring. It has rightly been criticized to leave the impression, as a great deal of the Holocaust literature does, that trauma and damage pervade all of the survivor's life and their children's mind (see Ornstein, 1985; Richman, 2006). The transmission of strength, resourcefulness, and resilience that operates in tandem with the transmission of wounds is widely missing from trans-generational literature. There is a dual edge of history's legacy: the ways it can take shape in an ethos of *care,* as well as in varieties of (self/other) destruction. Besides the disintegrative effects of trauma on attachment bonding, we also can find the miracle of *enduring attachment* that is also threaded through encounters with trauma. This familial unconscious is shaped through stories and relational patterning, by both resiliency *and* wounds (Salberg & Grand, 2017).

22.5 Suggested Reading

Grand, S. (2010). *The hero in the mirror: From fear to fortitude.* New York: Routledge/Taylor & Francis Group.

Salberg, J., & Grand, S. (2017) *The wounds of history: Repair and resilience in the transgenerational transmission of trauma.* New York: Routledge.

References

Abraham, N., & Torok, M. (1975). *The Shell and the kernel: Renewals of psychoanalysis*. Chicago, IL: University of Chicago Press.

Alpert, J. (2017). Enduring mothers, enduring knowledge: on rape and history. In: The wounds of history: repair and resilience in the trans-generational transmission of trauma. Eds: Salberg, J. and Grand, S. New York: Routledge. 2017.

Apprey, M. (2003). Repairing history: Reworking transgenerational trauma. In D. Moss (Ed.), *Hating in the first person plural* (pp. 3–29). New York: Other Press.

Aviad-Wilchek, Y., & Cohenca, D. (2013). The effects of the survival characteristics of parent holocaust survivors on offsprings' anxiety and depression symptoms. *Israel Journal of Psychiatry, 50*(3), 210–216.

Beebe, B., & Lachmann, F. M. (2013). *The origins of attachment: Infant research and adult treatment*. London: Routledge.

Bergmann, M., & Jucovy, M. (1982). *Generations of the holocaust*. New York: Columbia University Press.

Bowers, M. E., & Yehuda, R. (2016). Intergenerational transmission of stress in humans. *Neuropsychopharmacology Reviews, 41*, 232–244.

Davoine, F., & Gaudillière, J. M. (2004). *History beyond trauma: Whereof one cannot speak, thereof one cannot stay silent*. New York: Other Press.

Faimberg, H. (2005). *The telescoping of generations: Listening to the narcissistic links between generations*. London: Routledge, Taylor & Francis Group.

Felman, S., & Laub, D. (1992). *Testimony: Crises of witnessing in literature, psychoanalysis, and history*. New York: Routledge.

Felsen, I. (1998). Transgenerational transmission of effects of the holocaust: The north American research perspective. In Y. Danieli (Ed.), *International handbook of multigenerational legacies of trauma* (pp. 43–68). New York: Plenum Press.

Fonagy, P. (1999). The transgenerational transmission of holocaust trauma: Lessons learned from the analysis of an adolescent with obsessive-compulsive disorder. *Attachment & Human Development, 1*(1), 92–114. https://doi.org/10.1080/14616739900134041

Fraiberg, S., Adelson, E., & Shapiro, V. (1975). Ghosts in the nursery: A psychoanalytic approach to the problems of impaired infant–mother relationships. *Journal of the American Academy of Child and Adolescent Psychiatry, 14*, 387–421.

Frie, R. (2011). Irreducible cultural contexts: German-Jewish experience, identity and trauma in a bilingual analysis. *International Journal of Psychoanalytic Self Psychology, 6*, 136–158.

Fromm, M. G. (Ed.). (2012). *Lost in transmission: Studies of trauma across generations* (pp. 5–19). London: Karnac.

Gerson, S. (2009). When the third is dead: Memory, mourning, and witnessing in the aftermath of the holocaust. *International Journal of Psychoanalysis, 90*, 1341–1357.

Grand, S. (2000). *The reproduction of evil*. Hillsdale, NJ: Analytic Press.

Grand, S. (2010). *The hero in the mirror: From fear to fortitude*. New York: Routledge/Taylor & Francis Group.

Grand, S. (2014). Skin memories: On race, love and loss. *Psychoanalysis, Culture and Society, 19*(3), 232–250.

Grand, S. (2018). The other within: White shame, native-American genocide. *Contemporary Psychoanalysis, 54*(1), 84–102.

Grand, S., & Salberg, J. (Eds.). (2015). The evolution of witnessing: Emergent relational trends in holocaust studies [Special issue]. *Contemporary Psychoanalysis, 51*(2), 185–194.

Grubrich-Simitis, I. (1984). From concretism to metaphor: Thoughts on some theoretical and technical aspects of the psychoanalytic work with children of holocaust survivors. *The Psychoanalytic Study of the Child, 39*, 301–319.

Gump, J. (2010). Reality matters: The shadow of trauma on African-American subjectivity. *Psychoanalytic Psychology, 27*(1), 42–54.

Guralnik, O. (2014). The dead baby. *Psychoanalytic Dialogues, 24*(2), 129–145.

Hamburger, A. (2020). Social trauma as a bridging concept. In A. Hamburger, C. Hancheva & V. Volkan (Eds.), *Social Trauma. An Interdisciplinary Textbook*. (pp. 3–16). New York: Springer.

Holmes, J. (1999). Ghosts in the consulting room. *Attachment & Human Development, 1*(1), 115–131.

Kaplan, S. (2013). Child survivors of the 1994 Rwandan genocide and trauma-related affect. *Journal of Social Issues, 69*, 92–110.

Kestenberg, J. S. (1980). Psychoanalyses of children of survivors from the holocaust: Case presentations and assessment. *Journal of the American Psychoanalytic Association, 28*, 775–804.

Krystal, H. (1985). Trauma and the stimulus barrier. *Psychoanalytic Inquiry, 5*(1), 131–161.

Laub, D. (1993). Knowing and not knowing massive psychic trauma. *The International Journal of Psycho-Analysis, 74*, 287–302.

Laub, D. (1998). The empty circle: Children of survivors and the limits of reconstruction. *Journal of the American Psychoanalytic Association, 46*(2), 507–529.

Laub, D., & Hamburger, A. (Eds.). (2017). *Psychoanalysis and holocaust testimony: Unwanted memories of social trauma*. London: Routledge.

Layton, L. (2009). Who's responsible? Our mutual implication in each other's suffering. *Psychoanalytic Dialogues, 19*(2), 105–120.

Layton, L. (2015). Beyond sameness and difference: Normative unconscious process and our mutual implication in each other's suffering. In D. Goodman & M. Freeman (Eds.), *Psychology and the other* (pp. 168–188). Oxford: Oxford University Press.

Leary, K. (1997). Passing, posing and 'keeping it real'. *Constellations, 6*(1), 85–96.

Lyons-Ruth, K. (2003). Dissociation and the parent-infant dialogue: A longitudinal perspective from attachment research. *Journal of the American Psychoanalytic Association, 51*, 883–911.

Meares, R. (1998). The self in conversation: On narratives, chronicles, and scripts. *Psychoanalytic Dialogues, 8*, 875–891.

Mitchell, J. (2003). *Siblings, sex and violence*. Cambridge, UK: Polity Press.

Orange, D. (2016). *Nourishing the inner life of clinicians and humanitarians: The ethical turn in psychoanalysis*. New York: Routledge.

Ornstein, A. (1985). Survival and recovery. *Psychoanalytic Inquiry, 5*(1), 99–130.

Perroud, N., Rutembesa, E., Paoloni-Giacobino, A., Mutabaruka, J., Mutesa, L., Stenz, L., ... Karege, F. (2014). The Tutsi genocide and transgenerational transmission of maternal stress: Epigenetics and biology of the HPA axis. *World Journal of Biological Psychiatry, 15*(4), 334–345.

Reis, B. (2015). How deep the sky: Discussion of special issue on the evolution of witnessing: Emergent relational trends in holocaust studies. *Contemporary Psychoanalysis, 51*(2), 333–347.

Richman, S. (2006). Finding one's voice: Transforming trauma into autobiographical narrative. *Contemporary Psychoanalysis, 42*, 639–650.

Salberg, J. (2015). The texture of traumatic attachment: Presence and ghostly absence in transgenerational transmissions. *Psychoanalytic Quarterly, 84*(1), 21–46.

Salberg, J., & Grand, S. (2017). *The wounds of history: Repair and resilience in the transgenerational transmission of trauma*. New York: Routledge.

Scharf, M. (2007). Long-term effects of trauma: Psychological functioning of the second and third generation of holocaust survivors. *Development and Psychopathology, 19*, 603–622.

Schechter, D. (2003). Intergenerational communication of maternal violent trauma: Understanding the interplay of reflective functioning and posttraumatic psychopathology. In S. Coates, J. Rosenthal, & D. Schechter (Eds.), *September 11: Trauma and human bonds* (pp. 115–142). Hillsdale, NJ: The Analytic Press.

Schechter, D. (2017). On traumatically skewed Intersubjectivity. *Psychoanalytic Inquiry, 37*(4), 251–264.

Schwab, G. (2010). *Haunting legacies. Violent histories and transgenerational trauma*. New York: Columbia University Press.

Sullivan, H. S. (1953). *The interpersonal theory of psychiatry*. New York: W.W. Norton & Company.

Yehuda, R., Daskalakis, N. P., Bierer, L. M., Bader, H. N., Klengel, T., Holsboer, F., & Binder, E. B. (2016). Holocaust exposure induced intergenerational effects on FKBP5 methylation. *Biological Psychiatry, 80*(5), 372–380.

Yehuda, R., Daskalakis, N. P., Lehmer, A., Desarnaud, F., Bader, H. N., Makotkine, I., ... Meaney, M. J. (2014). Influences of maternal and paternal PTSD on epigenetic regulation of the glucocorticoid receptor gene in holocaust survivor offspring. *American Journal of Psychiatry, 171*(8), 872–880.

Part V
Social Psychology of Trauma

Chapter 23
Social Trauma: A Socio-Psychological Perspective

Phil C. Langer and Alina Brehm

23.1 Introduction

The paradigmatic understanding of social trauma that is developed transdisciplinarily in this textbook assumes that phenomena of collective and collectively mediated violence must always be understood in the social contexts in which they occur and in which they have consequences (see the contribution by Andreas Hamburger (2020) in this book; see also Hamburger, 2016; Hamburger & Hancheva, 2018). In this sense, violence that members of one group *as* members of that group exercise against members of another group *as* members of that group must always be seen in the context of a historically concrete, culturally anchored, and politically supported horizon of events that determines these groups and sets them in relation to each other. In this respect, violence is experienced in different ways and the experience is interpreted or made accessible for individual and collective processing. Despite its inherent situational dynamics and logic, violence can be understood both as a social action and as a communicative act (see Reemtsma, 2008). In this regard, social psychology, which by definition studies the experience and actions of subjects in their social contexts, can make a significant contribution to the comprehension of social trauma. The present contribution is to be seen in the tradition of a critical and interdisciplinary social psychology (see Keupp, 1993; Kühn, 2014; Langer, 2019). Theoretical approaches and empirical findings in the academically dominant tradition of psycho-

P. C. Langer (✉)
International Psychoanalytic University Berlin, Berlin, Germany
e-mail: phil.langer@ipu-berlin.de

A. Brehm
University of Vienna, Vienna, Austria

© Springer Nature Switzerland AG 2021

A. Hamburger et al. (eds.), *Social Trauma – An Interdisciplinary Textbook*,
https://doi.org/10.1007/978-3-030-47817-9_23

logical social psychology (see Fiske, 2018; Gilovich, Keltner, Chen, & Nisbett, 2016) will nevertheless be referred to and made useful for the development of an understanding of social trauma.

Despite all the vagueness of the concept of violence, it seems necessary for a constitutive ambivalence to be emphasized: In the act of violence, the experiences of perpetrator and victim are inextricably linked, while the very experiences of violence and the different ways of understanding, interpreting, integrating, processing or even dealing with them, separate victims and perpetrators in the sharpest possible way. With reference to the Shoah, Lyotard (1989) notes that the sentences of the victims and the sentences of the perpetrators, which refer to the same shared event that he marks with the cipher Auschwitz, cannot be translated into each other, that to "give the differend its due is to institute new addresses, new addressors, new significants, and new referents in order for the wrong to find an expression and for the plaintiff to cease being a victim" (p. 13). From a socio-psychological point of view, this refers to three perspectives in which social trauma in its experience and action of the subjects can be considered: the perspective of the perpetrators, that of the victims and that of a subsequent social interaction.

To date, the academically dominant psychological social psychology has mainly dealt with the perspective of the perpetrators. This has to do with a specific narrowing of the concept of violence as a subcategory of aggression. Bushman and Bartholow (2010) define aggression as "any behavior that is intended to harm another person who does not want to be harmed" (p. 304) and violence as "aggression that has extreme physical harm, such as injury or death, as its goal" (p. 305). The supposed precision of these definitions is, of course, accompanied by a recognizable vagueness, since—illustrated only by extreme examples—it remains unclear when damage is to be understood as extreme damage. It is clear, however, that it is a matter of intentional behaviour—of the perpetrator—whose causal and effect factors must subsequently be determined and investigated. At the same time, considerations based on this individual conception of aggression remain rather unproductive for an understanding of collective violence in the sense of social traumatization. In the present article, therefore, social-psychological studies and theories will be presented that address aspects of conformity, authority and obedience, group influence, group behaviour and deindividuation as well as prejudice, dehumanization and social identity. They provide new insights for investigation of the perpetrator's perspective in collectively occurring and collectively related violent actions.

Approaches to addressing the victims' perspectives and a collaborative approach to social trauma in its manifold consequences are available above all in the tradition of interdisciplinary social psychology. Among other things, they deal with questions of collective and cultural memory, the associated memory politics and blueprints of identity, the negotiation of collective trauma narratives and the dynamics of transgenerational transmission of extreme traumatizations, the ambivalent possibilities of reappraisal, reparation and forgiveness and the challenges of pedagogical memory work. Many of these topics are included in other contributions to this book.

Social psychology, however, fails to systematically link the perspectives of victims and perpetrators in the sense of Lyotard's demand. Here it could learn from an engagement with programmatic approaches to an "integrated history," as Friedländer (1998), for example, has done in his work "The Third Reich and the Jews."

Social psychology attempts to make collective violence understandable and to explain it in two thematic strands. The first emphasizes the power of the social situation and the group behaviour that unfolds in this situation; while the second, in contrast, emphasizes the importance of historically and socioculturally anchored prejudices and enemy images and the resulting patterns of attitude.

23.1.1 The Power of the Situation

The emphasis on the power of the situation results, on the one hand, from research of conformity, authority and obedience. They are regularly discussed in social psychology as forms of social influence through which people influence other people (in their attitudes, feelings and behaviours by the actual, imagined or implied presence of others). To investigate conformity, Asch (1956) conducted a classical experiment in the early 1950s, which involved a simple optical comparison task. He was able to show that the majority of the research group exerts a normative social influence (by urging the only test subject in a group of confederates to choose an obviously wrong answer that all others claimed to be the right one). Deviant behaviour was linked with the fear of being criticized, ridiculed or excluded. Individual resistance to social norms, even if they may seem rather abstruse, is quite difficult. Research subsequent to Asch has also shown that the conformity effect is already deployed in three to four people (e.g. Campbell & Fairey, 1989).

In the early 1970s, a research group led by Zimbardo, in an experiment in a prison simulation in the basement of Stanford University, randomly assigned 24 students the role of either a "prisoner" or a "guard" and wanted to investigate over a period of 2 weeks which dynamics unfolded within and between the groups (Haney, Banks, & Zimbardo, 1973). The study had to be terminated after less than a week, because of the strongly antisocial and sometimes cruel-sadistic behaviour of the "guards" towards the "prisoners" and extreme emotional reactions among the "prisoners": "Despite the fact that guards and prisoners were free to engage in any form of interaction (e.g. positive or negative, supportive or affrontive, etc.), the characteristic nature of their encounters tended to be negative, hostile, affrontive and dehumanizing" (Haney et al., 1973, p. 80). Notwithstanding numerous ethical and methodological criticisms, the study points out how quickly and with few preconditions "normal" people can assume the roles assigned to them and, in line with these, behave unethically, illegitimately and violently. The tendencies of aggressive victimization that quickly became visible were apparently facilitated and reinforced by the uniformization of the "guards" and the deindividualization of the "prisoners," who among other things had to put on prisoner clothing and were addressed with numbers, which mimicked respective social identities.

Milgram's (1963, 1964, 1965, 1974) famous experiments on obedience behaviour have similarly shown that people in authoritarian-structured situations also follow orders that can harm other people. In a laboratory, test persons were instructed to give simulated electric shocks in their role as "teachers" to the "pupils" (who were instructed about the conditions of the experiment) if they gave a wrong answer. Not a small proportion of the test subjects went up to the level that had previously been marked as "life-threatening." Any hesitation was usually overcome after an explicit order from the facilitator to continue. In more than 18 different variations of the experiment conducted by Milgram with over 1000 subjects and dozens of follow-up studies by other researchers* even in different cultural contexts (cf. Miller, 1986), it became clear that a very high proportion (of up to 90% of the subjects) showed obedience in such situations of authority. It is noteworthy that the willingness to obey was highest when the test subjects observed other peers following the orders. The willingness to obey was also changed by psychological closeness: If "teacher" and "pupil" were in the same room, the readiness decreased, but it decreased even more when the "teacher" had to press the hand of the "pupil" on the (supposed) electrode. Bauman (1992) has described the effect that physical distance is accompanied by social and ultimately moral distance as "adiaphorization" (see also Marshman, 2008). Migram's studies are regarded as "a paradigm for understanding evil" (Fiske, 2018, p. 533), pointing out how easily "normal" people can become perpetrators if they find themselves in a corresponding situation in which they are asked or even encouraged to do so.

On the other hand, the emphasis on the power of the situation results from research on group processes. The clear social influence in the mentioned studies of Asch and Zimbardo is not conceivable without the group context. Freud (1964) had already vividly described and tried to explain the fact that people in groups change their behaviour, in his reflections on mass psychology. Through the identification of the individual people in the masses with a common object (e.g. the leader, the nation) as a collectively shared ego-ideal, an identification of the people with each other occurs, which is carried by libidinous bonds: "*A primary group of this kind is a number of individuals who have put one and the same object in the place of their ego ideal and have consequently identified themselves with one anothe[r in their ego*" (Freud 1964, p. 116; emphasis in original). According to Freud, this goes hand in hand with the projection of aggressive elements onto an external enemy, while within the masses regressive tendencies take hold, leading to an "oceanic" feeling of omnipotence. In these considerations, aspects are already mentioned that were taken up in later approaches in classical and psychoanalytical social psychology. Festinger, Pepitone, and Newcomb (1952) have described as deindividuation the state in which people no longer act as individuals and in which inner resistance, for example, willingness to use violence, disappears. The standards developed in a group and the extent to which they are accepted as a characteristic of membership play a major role. What Freud understood as the externalization of difficult feelings is described in theories of social identity (e.g. Reicher, 2001; Reicher, Spears, & Postmes, 1995; Tajfel, 1981; Tajfel & Turner, 1979) as a tendency to upgrade one's own group ("ingroup favoritism") and at the same time to devalue other groups—perceived as more homogeneous and stereotypical—in order to achieve a positive self-image and an increase in self-esteem through a sense of belonging to a positively filled group. If the group identity is threatened, these tendencies are reinforced and can lead to antisocial behaviour such as violence towards members of the other group. In this context, Kühner (2011) points out from a psychoanalytically informed perspective that it is experiences of hurt and devaluation that favour the instrumentalization of collective traumas.

23.1.2 Prejudices

Prejudices play an important role in the construction of the outgroup that is indispensable for the facilitation and stabilization of a positive social identity. In psychological social psychology, the arbitrariness of the formation of prejudices is marked as a "minimal group paradigm" (see Diehl, 1990; Lemyre & Smith, 1985). The arbitrary assignment of people to random and only temporary groups alone leads (at least in the laboratory) to people seeing themselves as members of this group (self-categorization) and to valorizing and favouring their own group, while prejudices against the other group arise and legitimize their disadvantage or even exclusion and more.

The special significance of prejudices for violent action lies in their historical and socio-cultural anchoring. From this perspective, the social conditions of their emergence or manifestation and their psychosocial dynamics are examined. Representatives of the first generation of the later Frankfurt School of Critical Theory already pointed out the importance of prejudices, structures of prejudice and enemy images in American emigration in the early 1930s in view of the increasing spread of National Socialist ideology in Germany and then more systematically during the Nazi era and World War II.

The starting point was the assumption of a historically specific disposition, which had to be rooted in a corresponding character structure. Fromm (1936) was the first to formulate the basic features of the "authoritarian character" as it was later taken up again by Adorno (1950) in his *studies on the authoritarian character.* This character, that is, a certain life-historical orientation of wishes, fears and needs is based on arbitrary, authoritarian educational experiences in the family as an "agency of society." It is characterized by a lustful occupation of subjugation and domination. It is the character of the "cyclist's nature"—bucking up, kicking down. The underlying psychic processes are structured by splitting the experience of authority. The desire for authoritarian leadership with a strong hand and insertion into a selfless community is contrasted with the "conformist rebellion" against supposed authorities "up there" and failures "down there." In education, the tyrannical power of external identities has prevented the formation of a strong self. A rationally predictable authority can be internalized, contribute to the formation of superego and ego and enable autonomous self-reflection and self-control. Under the arbitrary rule, however, only a "dress at superego" thrives, which worships power itself and despises (its own) powerlessness (cf. Fromm, 1936, p. 84).

The concern of Adorno and his colleagues was to find out how and why people are responsive to fascist propaganda. Their "Studies on Authoritarian Character"are set in the context of the 1940s in the USA. They focused on a relatively homogeneous group of researchers, namely mainly members of the white urban West Coast middle class born in the USA between 1910 and 1925. The result is the development of the so-called "F-scale," a questionnaire instrument designed to measure the susceptibility of certain character structures to anti-democratic tendencies (Adorno, 1950, p. 1). The items are not aimed at attitudes, but at nine dimensions of authoritarian character: conventionalism, authoritarian subservience, authoritarian aggression, anti-intraception, superstition and stereotypy, power thinking and "power struggle," destructiveness and cynicism, projectivity and sexuality (p. 45).

Several long-term studies in Germany—e.g. by Heitmeyer (2012), Zick, Küpper, and Berghan (2019) and Decker, Kiess, and Brähler (2015)—not only refer in part explicitly to the studies, but also focus on the statistical recording of the spread of authoritarian attitudes. In doing so, they rely on Heitmeyer's concept of the "Group-Focused Enmity" (GFE). The GFE concept follows the insight of the social psychologist Allport that various prejudices are interconnected (Heitmeyer, 2012, p. 15). In this syndrome, which at its core is an ideology of inequality, the following aspects come together: Sexism, homophobia, established privileges, xenophobia, racism, Islamophobia, anti-Semitism, devaluation of the disabled, homeless, Sinti and Roma, asylum seekers and the long-term unemployed (cf. Heitmeyer, 2012, p. 17). Empirical evidence confirmed the assumption of such a syndrome, by demonstrating that different types of prejudice are significantly inter-related: A group or person who expresses negative prejudices towards a certain group is more likely to devalue other groups. (cf. Zick et al., 2019, p. 57) The role of the previously presented character concept fades into the background in the GFE concept. The motivation to take over the GFE is not explained by educational experiences, but much more situationally as a reaction to social changes such as the advancing neoliberalism and related crises and safeguards (cf. Heitmeyer, 2012, pp. 19–25; Zick et al., 2019, pp. 27–33).

Haubl has developed a different perspective on the role of the accompanying emotional life and its connection to earlier experiences and the character structures that developed within it. He understands hate as a perpetuation of aggressive emotions such as anger, rage or fury, which chronifies into a character trait. Haubl locates the function of hate in this character within the maintenance of one's own subjectivity: I hate therefore I am (cf. Haubl, 2007, p. 34). The aim of this hatred, which preserves the weak ego, is to destroy the subjectivity of the object of hatred, to destroy its subject status in order to make sure of its own. This can also be applied to hostilities between groups. The individual is always partly identified with certain groups in addition to his or her personal identity. The more unstable, the more threatened the subjectivity of the personal identity feels; the weaker the ego is, the more attractive the expansion of the share of group identity within self-perception becomes (cf. Haubl, 2007, p. 39). Individual differences and behaviour that does not fit the group identity appear threatening. Thus hate can be understood as "the defense of group-centered personal identities" (Haubl, 2007, p. 39). For this group-hatred enemy images have a central function. They serve to focus on a target of hatred. Also the image of the enemy aims at forming and supporting it as negative of one's own self-image (cf. Haubl, 2007, p. 42). In pop-cultural phrasing: *"Fear leads to anger, anger leads to hatred and hatred leads to suffering"* (Master Yoda). Haubl identifies fear as a decisive driving force for hatred as well: "People who hate try to drown out deep-seated fears they cannot bear with their hatred of their hate object and their hate-motivated propensity to violence towards this object. [...] Hatred and hate-motivated violence silence this fear and thus have a calming function" (Haubl, 2007, p. 25). Fear and above all the fear of dissolving oneself as a subject, thus often leads to anger; anger, whose steady form is hatred, whose ultimate goal is always (!) the psychic as well as, in the last consequence, physical extermination of the hated object, ends in destructive violence. (cf. Haubl, 2007, 33 f.)

23.2 Learning Outcome Related to Social Trauma

Social psychology offers two different perspectives for an understanding of perpetrator action in the sense of the initially determined social trauma: The first emphasizes the power of the situation and of the group action that unfolds in it, and points out that anyone can become a perpetrator if the situation allows it, and if neither psychopathological dispositions nor ideological convictions or other socio-cultural backgrounds are necessary. The other perspective focuses on the formation and impact of often deeply rooted prejudices, resentments and hate-occupied stereotypes, which are historically, culturally, socially and politically very specific and have an impact far beyond the situation and motivate and drive violent action.

23.3 Preferred Model of Explanation

Using the example of the acts of violence committed by the German Reserve Police Battalion 101, which was involved in the genocide against the Jews of Europe, especially from the summer of 1942 onwards, the explanatory power of the two perspectives presented can be shown and a model can be proposed that links them together (cf. Newman & Erber, 2002 for further approaches).

The Shoah can be seen as a paradigm of social trauma and as a central reference point for debates on genocidal violence and its consequences. Research with survivors of the Shoah still shapes knowledge about the origins, dynamics and consequences of trauma on an individual, psychosocial, transgenerational and collective level. The attempt to explain how National Socialism and the Second World War, the Shoah and the exclusion and murder of other groups could have come about has long guided the socio-psychological preoccupation not only with authority and obedience, with destructive group dynamics and stereotypes, but also with discrimination and violence. The collective violence of the Reserve Police Battalion 101 is particularly revealing here. It is well documented by extensive empirical material obtained not only in the form of interviews in the course of legal investigations and court cases, but also in the form of photographs taken from the perpetrators' surroundings. More than 500 men of the battalion coming from Hamburg were "normal men," as Browning calls them, many came from the middle or working class, there was no self-selection or institutional selection—in the sense of men who were particularly prone to violence or who were associated with the NSDAP—and they had not undergone any particular ideological indoctrination. After far-reaching personnel and structural changes, the battalion was transferred to the Nazi-occupied eastern Poland in the summer of 1942, after having participated in various temporally and spatially rather limited actions for the deportation of Jews since 1939. One key scene is worthy of note here. It marked the starting point for the acts committed in the following months, to which over 38,000 Jews fell victim and in which more than 45,000 Jews were deported. In the early hours of the morning of July 13, 1942, the battalion was driven to the outskirts of the small village of Josefów, where Commandant Major Trapp "Pale and nervous, with choking voice and tears in his eyes," as Browning notes, issued the order, coming from "the highest commanders," to round up the Jews of the village, to deport able-bodied men to a labour camp and to kill all the remaining Jews, the women, the children and the old people. Major Trapp then first made an offer to the older police officers: if they did not feel ready or able to carry out the assignment, they could step out and be assigned to other tasks. However, the opt-out option was only used by a few. Almost all the men of the battalion subsequently participated in the murder of about 1500 Jews.

The question of how these "perfectly normal men" could have become mass murderers, why they no longer took the option of not participating in the events, and how they could subsequently commit many other excesses of violence, was answered in research—following the two strands of discussion described in the previous section—by two different explanatory approaches.

Goldhagen (1996), in his investigation, programmatically called "Hitler's Willing Executors," proceeded from a specifically eliminatory anti-Semitism of the Germans, which became representative in the Police Reserve Battalion 101: "Germans' anti-Semitism was the basis of their profound hatred of the Jews and the psychological impulse to make them suffer" (p. 584). The non-appreciation of the opt-out option offered by Major Trapp thus appears as an expression of a deep-seated and far-reaching anti-Semitism, which determines the murder of the Jews that is imminent in this situation as just, right and necessary. The emergence of this eliminatory anti-Semitism is assumed on the basis of a specific historical and socio-political constellation, which is fed by the diagnosis of Germany as a "belated nation," a historically consolidated authoritarian mindset of "the Germans," and a version of biological-racist anti-Semitism endemic in Germany. Goldhagen refers not only to the opt-out option at the beginning of the battalion's genocidal violent action, which was not taken up by most men, but also to the special brutality of murder—not necessary for the execution of the mission—a lust for murder that was not only evident in the violence itself, but also in the photographs taken during the mission, which depicted gestures of triumph, of fun, of lust: "Not only did virtually all men of this battalion kill, but they killed with dedication and zeal..." (pp. 261–262). Moreover, the men had not kept their deeds and experiences to themselves as a personal secret, which could suggest feelings of shame and guilt, but had talked about them during their stays in Germany with their families and circle of friends, had bragged about the deeds, shown the photographs and shared them in their social contexts, that is, they had expected and could have required a positive response, precisely because of their shared anti-Semitism. In Goldhagen's words: "[A] demonological anti-semitism, of the virulent racial variety, was the common structure of the perpetrators' cognition and of German society in general. The German perpetrators... were assenting mass executioners, men and women who, true to their own eliminationist anti-semitic beliefs, faithful to their cultural anti-semitic credo, considered the slaughter to be just" (pp. 392–393).

From the point of view of an approach oriented to the power of the situation, one could criticize and counter-interpret every single evidence point of Goldhagen (Browning, 1992). Using the same empirical material and discussing often the same events, Browning comes to a completely different explanation. Both agree that, for example, obedience to the command authority did not play a special role (if any). He also does not assume a specific selection of the men who could have identified them as particularly prone to violence. There had been no ideological indoctrination, nor had there been any previous brutalization by and during the war, since the men had only arrived shortly before the said deployment in the summer of 1942, where the proceedings on the battlefield had not been for a long time. In sharp contrast to Goldhagen, however, Browning understands anti-Semitism at most as a factor that simplifies killing in the isolated situation, but does not make it possible or even urges the men to commit it. While noting that "The Jews stood outside their [the police officers'] circle of human obligation and responsibility," he adds that "Such a polarization between 'us' and 'them', between one's comrades and the enemy, is of course standard in war" (p. 73). Anti-Semitism—or rather, as he writes elsewhere: anti-Semitisms in the various forms it has assumed – he observes as a kind of "background noise" in the German population under National Socialism, a given, but neither a necessary nor a sufficient condition for the actions of the men. Moreover, despite all caution with retrospective statements in legal contexts, which formed a substantial part of the empirical material, not even all men could be assumed to have anti-Semitic attitudes. In an epilogue to his book, Browning summarizes the differences in his assessment of the importance of anti-Semitism in violent behaviour:

> For instance, I agree that anti-Semitism was a strong ideological current in nineteenth-century Germany, but I do not accept Goldhagen's assertion that anti-Semitism "more or less governed the ideational life of civil society" in pre-Nazi Germany. I agree that by 1933 anti-Semitism had become part of the "common sense" of the German right without thereby concluding that all German society was "of one mind" with Hitler about the Jews, and that the "centrality of antisemitism in the Party's worldview, program, and rhetoric… mirrored the sentiments of German culture." I agree that anti-Semitism-negative stereotyping, dehumanization and hatred of the Jews was widespread among the killers of 1942, but I do not agree that this

anti-Semitism is primarily to be seen as a "pre-existing, pent-up" anti-Semitism that Hitler had merely to "unleash" and "unshackle." (p. 222)

But then how does Browning explain the actions of the men from the Reserve Police Battalion? In addition to a division of labour and simultaneous habituation to killing ("cumulative habitualization"), which was introduced more strongly in the course of the following months, he cites two factors that led to the non-use of the opt-out option and the subsequent mass murder: peer pressure and group loyalty on the one hand and banal careerism, on the other. He notes that "the act of stepping out that morning in Jozefow meant leaving one's comrades and admitting that one was "too weak" or "cowardly." Who would have "dared," one policeman declared emphatically, to "lose face before the assembled troops" (p. 72). The argument that pure careerism also played a major role is not easy to postulate and consists rather of circumstantial evidence. The men who admitted to having been involved in the murders did not claim to have acted for career reasons. However, the (already older) men who finally accepted the opt-out stated that they could do so because they no longer had a career at stake. When a senior officer was temporarily relieved of duty due to obvious problems with killing, he complained bitterly about the possible career damage this could cause.

In the tradition of situationist approaches, Browning's analysis emphasizes the factors present in the situation of action: the presence of comrades who exerted an implicit pressure to participate, a group to which one would like to feel a part of precisely in such an extreme situation, the fear of career problems if one withdraws. While Browning's approach was subsequently used to investigate and understand other genocidal violence events such as those in Rwanda or Bosnia (cf. Clark, 2009; Lemarchand, 2002), Goldhagen's analysis inevitably remains related to the Shoah, since it presupposes the uniqueness of the specifically German eliminatory anti-Semitism at that particular time.

Which explanatory approach is more convincing? Do situational factors play the essential role in collective violence in the sense of social trauma, or are the culturally and socially anchored and politically instrumentalizable discourses and structures of prejudice decisive? With regard to the Reserve Police Battalion 101, Goldhagen's thesis of eliminatory anti-Semitism has not been able to assert itself in the scholarly debate. In fact, the reception in scholarly circles to his approach was in the opposite direction: his presumptions were very far-reaching, the analyses of the empirical material based on them were selective and not always sustainable. At the same time, however, Browning seems to underestimate the importance of anti-Semitism even in the specific situation, despite all the explanatory power that the clear and also counter-exampled argumentation unfolds. In the National Socialist perception it was, after all, an anti-Semitism that was aimed at the complete extermination of all Jews. By merely marking the "us" against "them" as the basis of any formation of prejudice, "the Jews" (as a group) and "the male Jew" / "the female Jew" (as a member of this group) were not only devalued, but excluded from the human community; moreover, in the depiction as "parasites," "the Jews" appear as an element destroying the German "Volksgemeinschaft"[1] from within, which in Nazi logic leads to the conclusion that their annihilation was existential for the German "people." In Major Trapp's speech on that day in July 1942, he explicitly asked the men to think about the fate of the family back home. Here this existential aspect must be considered: what they were doing here and now in Josefów enabled them and their families to have a life, a future. Anti-Semitic resentment was not just a "background noise," but first and foremost made the situation possible, framed their perception and influenced the men's actions. How can this be combined with Browning's approach?

"The fundamental problem," writes Browning in his epilogue, "is to explain why ordinary men—shaped by a culture that had its own particularities but was nonetheless within the mainstream of western, Christian, and Enlightenment tradition—under specific circumstances willingly carried out the most extreme genocide in human history" (Browning, 1992, p. 222). Neitzel and Welzer (2012) have made accessible what Browning marks as a challenge here as a frame of reference analysis based on wiretap protocols of Wehrmacht soldiers in captivity. They understand these same frames of reference as the totality of what influences, guides or even determines the perception, interpretation and ultimately the acting appropriation of a situation by a subject. They underlie the human "routines, habits and certainties" and provide answers to the question "what is going on here?" (Neitzel and Welzer 2012 , p. 9). The authors distinguish between

- Frame of the first order ("the broader socio-historical backdrop against which people in a given time operate," Neitzel & Welzer, 2012, p. 10, e.g. the Western modernity Browning speaks of).
- Frame of the second order (already stipulated as "a socio-historical space that, in most respects, can be clearly delimited—for instance, the length of a dictatorial regime or the duration of a historical entity like the Third Reich"; Neitzel & Welzer, 2012)
- Frame of the third order ("a concrete constellation of sociohistorical events within which people act [...], for example, a war in which soldiers fight," Neitzel & Welzer, 2012)
- Frame of the fourth order ("the special characteristics, modes of perception, interpretative paradigms and perceived responsibilities that an individual brings to a specific situation," Neitzel & Welzer, 2012)

Deviating from the authors' focus on the meaning of the third frame, which leads to a strong situationist interpretation of the soldiers' violent actions in war, this analysis scheme allows to focus on the successive shift of the first and second frame during the Nazi era. After years of socio-political shifts in world interpretations and ideas of normality, which Steuwer (2017) has impressively analysed in diary entries, the men of Reserve Police Battalion 101, who murdered in the summer of 1942, were no longer "within the mainstream of western, Christian, and Enlightenment

[1] The German ethno-national community.—B.D.

traditions." The now fundamental NS world view, which was oriented, among other things, on the idea of a "Volksgemeinschaft" and for which a biologic-racist anti-Semitism was constitutive, framed, so it could be concluded, quite substantially and not necessarily consciously, the perception and interpretation of the situation on that morning in the summer of 1942 in Josefów and legitimized an act of violence, the dynamics of which itself can be explained strongly from the situation. By reflecting on the (historically, culturally, socially, politically specific) constitutional conditions of the situation, whose influence on the emergence and course of collective violent events can be well explained with the socio-psychological approaches outlined above, the (contextually different) significance of previous prejudice and resentment structures, social categorization discourses and exclusion practices can be systematically included in the analysis.

23.4 Practical Implications in the Field of Social Trauma

For research on collective violence in the sense of social trauma, social psychology provides rich theoretical approaches and empirical findings, but their respective relevance must be determined contextually. The implications of such a social psychological analysis of perpetrator action for psychoanalysis is outlined by Hohl (2002) with reference to Browning (1992) and Bauman (1992). On one hand, he points out that the psychopathology model, which has a calming effect, has become obsolete, in so far as the perpetrators are not usually psychopathologically conspicuous sadists or fanatics disposed to violence by the personality structure. Two other points seem to be important: On one hand, Hohl states that the affect model of perpetrator action should be reviewed. Affects such as rage and hatred did not play a role as causal factors for the majority of the perpetrators; they had acted largely without affect. On the other hand, he points out that in psychoanalytical considerations of perpetration, there is often talk of guilt and feelings of guilt on the part of the perpetrators, but that in the empirical studies, indications of self-criticism or even feelings of guilt on the part of the perpetrators were largely absent. This coincides with a recent study on former child soldiers of the Islamic state in northern Iraq, whose reports hardly mention this either (Langer & Ahmad, 2020). What this means for therapeutic work with perpetrators (or, in the case of child soldiers, with extremely traumatized young people for whom the differentiation between perpetrators and victims does not help) and socio-political efforts towards "reintegration," forgiveness and reconciliation must remain open at this point. However, the combination of the perspective of the perpetrator presented here with the victim's perspective developed in other contributions to this book still awaits systematic justification. Here, the handling of social trauma in post-conflict societies at the various levels—individual, institutional and social—should be considered and made fruitful for theory development.

23.5 Suggested Readings and Further Information

Miller, A. G. (Eds.) (2004). *The social psychology of good and evil.* New York: Guilford.

Newman, L. S., & Erber, R. (Eds.). (2002). *Understanding genocide: The social psychology of the Holocaust.* Oxford: Oxford University Press.

Reemtsma, J. P. (2008). Vertrauen und Gewalt. *Versuch über eine besondere Konstellation der Moderne.* Hamburg: Hamburger Edition.

References

Adorno, T. W. (1950). *Studien zum autoritären Charakter.* Frankfurt: Suhrkamp. (Original work published 1950).

Asch, S. E. (1956). Studies of independence and conformity: I. A minority of one against a unanimous majority. *Psychological Monographs: General and Applied, 70*(9), 1–70.

Bauman, Z. (1992). *Dialektik der Ordnung: die Moderne und der Holocaust.* Hamburg: Europäische Verlagsanstalt.

Bushman, B. J., & Bartholow, B. D. (2010). Aggression. In R. F. Baumeister & E. J. Finkel (Eds.), *Advanced social psychology. State of the science* (pp. 303–341). New York: Oxford University Press.

Campbell, J. D., & Fairey, P. J. (1989). Informational and normative routes to conformity: The effect of size as a function of norm extremity and attention to the stimulus. *Journal of Personality and Social Psychology, 57*(3), 457–468.

Browning, C. (1992). Ordinary men: Reserve police battalion 101 and the final solution in Poland. New York: Harper Collins.

Christopher, B. (1992). *Ordinary men: Reserve police battalion 101 and the final solution in Poland.* New York: Harper Collins.

Clark, J. N. (2009). Genocide, war crimes and the conflict in Bosnia: Understanding the perpetrators. *Journal of Genocide Research, 11*(4), 421–445.

Decker, O., Kiess, J., & Brähler, E. (Eds.). (2015). *Rechtsextremismus der Mitte und sekundärer Autoritarismus.* Gießen: Psychosozial.

Diehl, M. (1990). The minimal group paradigm: Theoretical explanations and empirical findings. *European Review of Social Psychology, 1*(1), 263–292.

Festinger, L., Pepitone, A., & Newcomb, T. (1952). Some consequences of de-individuation in a group. *The Journal of Abnormal and Social Psychology, 47*(2S), 382.

Fiske, S. T. (2018). *Social beings: Core motives in social psychology.* Hoboken: John Wiley & Sons.

Freud, S. (1964). Group psychology and the analysis of the Ego. In *The standard edition of the complete psychological works of Sigmund Freud , Vol. XVIII (1920–1922): Beyond the pleasure principle, group psychology and other works* (pp. 65–144). London: Macmillan. (Original work published 1921).

Friedländer, S. (1998). *Das Dritte Reich und die Juden.* München: C. H. Beck.

Fromm, E. (1936). Sozialpsychologischer Teil. In M. Horkheimer (Ed.), *Studien über Autorität und Familie. Forschungsberichte aus dem Institut für Sozialforschung.* Paris: Librairie Félix Alcan.

Gilovich, T., Keltner, D., Chen, S., & Nisbett, R. E. (2016). *Social psychology* (4. Auflage ed.). New York: W.W. Norton & Company.

Goldhagen, D. J. (1996). *Hitler's willing executioners.* New York: Alfred A. Knopf.

Hamburger, A. (2016). Soziales Trauma. *Forum Psychoanalyse, 32*, 151–164.
Hamburger, A., & Hancheva, C. (2018). *Trauma and migration. Forced migration and social trauma: Interdisciplinary perspectives from psychoanalysis, psychology, sociology and politics*. London: Routledge.
Haney, C., Banks, C., & Zimbardo, P. (1973). Study of prisoners and guards in a simulated prison. *Naval Research Reviews, 26*(9), 1–17.
Haubl, R. (2007). Gattungsschicksal Hass. In R. Haubl & V. Caysa (Eds.), *Hass und Gewaltbereitschaft* (pp. 7–68). Göttingen: Vadenhoeck und Ruprecht.
Heitmeyer, W. (2012). Gruppenbezogene Menschenfeindlichkeit (GMF) in einem entsicherten Jahrzehnt. In ders. (Hrsg.), *Deutsche Zustände Folge 10*. Frankfurt/M.: Suhrkamp.
Hohl, J. (2002). Zygmunt Bauman und Christopher Browning. Soziohistorische Erklärungsversuche zur nationalsozialistischen Massenvernichtung und ihre Konsequenzen für die Psychoanalyse. In A.-M. Schlösser & A. Gerlach (Eds.), *Gewalt und Zivilisation. Erklärungsversuche und Deutungen* (pp. 383–397). Gießen: Psychosozial.
Keupp, H. (Ed.). (1993). *Zugänge zum Subjekt: Perspektiven einer reflexiven Sozialpsychologie*. Suhrkamp: Frankfurt/M.
Kühn, T. (2014). *Kritische Sozialpsychologie des modernen Alltags: zum Potenzial einer am Lebenslauf orientierten Forschungsperspektive*. Wiesbaden: Springer VS.
Kühner, A. (2011). Nicht Trauma ist gefährlich, sondern Kränkung. Wie Freuds Massenpsychologie helfen kann, die Instrumentalisierbarkeit "kollektiver Traumata" zu verstehen. In J. A. Schülein & H.-J. Wirth (Eds.), *Analytische Sozialpsychologie. Klassische und neuere Perspektiven* (pp. 359–386). Psychosozial: Gießen.
Langer, P. C. (2019). Sozial- als Friedenspsychologie denken. In C. Kirchhoff, T. Kühn, P. C. Langer, & F. Schumann (Eds.), *Psychoanalytisch denken. Sozial- und kulturwissenschaftliche Perspektiven* (pp. 61–138). Gießen: Psychosozial.
Langer, P. C., & Ahmad, A.-N. (2020). *Psychosocial needs of former ISIS child soldiers in Northern Iraq*. Research report. Retrieved from http://www.ipu-berlin.de/professoren/langer-phil-c
Lemarchand, R. (2002). Disconnecting the threads: Rwanda and the holocaust reconsidered. *Journal of Genocide Research, 4*(4), 499–518.
Lemyre, L., & Smith, P. M. (1985). Intergroup discrimination and self-esteem in the minimal group paradigm. *Journal of Personality and Social Psychology, 49*(3), 660–670.
Lyotard, J.-F. (1989). *Der Widerstreit* (2., korrigierte Auflage). München: Fink.
Marshman, S. (2008). Bauman on genocide–modernity and mass murder: From classification to annihilation. In M. H. Jacobsen & P. Poder (Eds.), *The sociology of Zygmunt Bauman: Challenges and critique* (pp. 75–94). Hamshire: Ashgate.
Milgram, S. (1963). Behavioral study of obedience. *Journal of Abnormal and Social Psychology, 67*, 371–378.
Milgram, S. (1964). Issues in the study of obedience: A reply to Baumrind. *American Psychologist, 19*, 848–852.
Milgram, S. (1965). Some conditions of obedience and disobedience to authority. *Human Relations, 18*, 57–76.
Milgram, S. (1974). *Obedience to authority: An experimental view*. New York: Harper & Row.
Miller, A. G. (1986). *The obedience experiments: A case study of controversy in social science*. New York: Praeger.
Neitzel, S., & Welzer, H. (2012). *Soldiers: German POWs on fighting, killing, and dying*. New York: Alfred A. Knopf.
Newman, L. S., & Erber, R. (Eds.). (2002). *Understanding genocide: The social psychology of the holocaust*. Oxford: Oxford University Press.
Reemtsma, J. P. (2008). *Vertrauen und Gewalt. Versuch über eine besondere Konstellation der Moderne*. Hamburg: Hamburger Edition.
Reicher, S. (2001). The psychology of crowd dynamics. In M. A. Hogg & R. S. Tindale (Eds.), *Blackwell handbook of social psychology: Group processes* (pp. 182–208). Malden, MA: Blackwell.

Reicher, S., Spears, R., & Postmes, T. (1995). A social identity model of deindividuation phenomena. *European Review of Social Psychology, 6*, 161–198.
Steuwer, J. (2017). *"Ein Drittes Reich, wie ich es auffasse": Politik, Gesellschaft und privates Leben in Tagebüchern 1933–1939*. Wallstein: Göttingen.
Tajfel, H. (1981). *Human groups and social categories*. New York: Cambridge University Press.
Tajfel, H., & Turner, J. C. (1979). The social identity theory of intergroup behavior. In W. G. Austin & S. Worchel (Eds.), *The social psychology of intergroup relations* (pp. 7–24). Chicago: Nelson-Hall.
Zick, A., Küpper, B., & Berghan, W. (2019). *Verlorene Mitte. Feindselige Zustände. Rechtsextreme Einstellungen in Deutschland 2018/2019*. Bonn: Dietz.

Chapter 24
Organizational Psychology: Traumatic Traces in Organization

Vladimir Hedrih and Dženana Husremović

24.1 Introduction

Trauma and collective memory influence societies in different aspects of life. Those aspects include employment, work, and unemployment. We often believe that work is done in well-regulated systems in which meritocracy rules and in which taking care of workers is focused on achieving high results. We believe that organizational goals are reached by a consensus through the participatory decision-making of all parties involved, that there are clear rules, that the power in an organization comes from authority, that tasks are assigned according to expertise, and that everyone perceives the organization as a common good. However, in real life, there are often hidden and conflicting interests in organizations, and too often unwritten rules are more important than those which are official and written; power is exercised through formal and informal influences, and relationships with people are based on games that may be on the verge of legal or even illegal.

24.2 Learning Outcomes Related to Social Trauma

Organizations are one of the major components of any society. In addition to enabling people to work and make money, they are essentially a reflection of how a society lives, how it treats its citizens, what is important and what is not important to it.

V. Hedrih
Faculty of Philosophy, University of Niš, Niš, Serbia
e-mail: vhedrih@hm.co.rs

D. Husremović (✉)
Faculty of Philosophy, University of Sarajevo, Sarajevo, Bosnia and Herzegovina
e-mail: dzenana.husremovic@ff.unsa.ba

© Springer Nature Switzerland AG 2021

A. Hamburger et al. (eds.), *Social Trauma – An Interdisciplinary Textbook*,
https://doi.org/10.1007/978-3-030-47817-9_24

The main objective of this chapter is to give an overview of some of the basic concepts underlying today's society and how they are broken through the prism of social trauma and the collective memory of a society. We will make a short overview of the most significant existing coercive organizational practices relevant for the topic of social trauma and their psychological consequences. After reading this chapter, readers will see the importance of organizational sciences in defining values of the society and moving it away from social trauma in order to abolish all practices which are harmful and humiliating for any human being.

24.3 Preferred Model of Explanation

In countries that have experienced collective trauma and are dominated by a transitional economy, corrupt governance makes employment and work almost a luxury. Collective trauma leads to the reinforcement of prejudices and stereotypes in the society, which are then reflected on employment and processes within working organizations. On the other hand, today's world is shaped by diversity. The lack of appreciation of diversity leads to discrimination, and consequently, to coercive organizational practices. Discrimination occurs both at the individual and institutional levels. Institutional bias is a social outcome advantage, documented at the institutional level, that favors some groups over others. It may also be a natural consequence of concentrating power among members of a few socially advantaged groups (Jones, Dovidio, & Vietze, 2014). The worst forms of discrimination can be seen through the coercive organizational practices.

Slavery. The practice of slavery is probably as old as human civilization. Although banned in the modern society, it has existed through most of human history and for a significant period in history trading in slaves has represented an important part of international trade (e.g., Lovejoy, 2012). Slavery is commonly defined as a system in which human beings can be owned and traded like a commodity, but this definition is likely too narrow to refer to all the known variants of slavery. Slavery has four distinguishing characteristics:

> the use of violence or the threat of violence to control the person, a lack of payment beyond minimal subsistence, few or no opportunities to escape, and the theft of labor or other qualities of the person for economic gain. (Hyde, Bales, & Levin, 2006, p. 116)

Concepts related to slavery are unfree labor/forced labor and human trafficking. Unfree labor and forced labor include any relationship in which a person is employed against his/her will with a threat of destitution, detention, violence (including death), compulsion, or other forms of extreme hardship to themselves or members of their families (Unfree Labor, 2020). These include slavery, but also a variety of practices similar to slavery. Human trafficking refers to the recruiting or transporting of persons by force, abduction, or deception for the purposes of exploitation (Belser, 2005). Trafficking is typically a starting phase of what is to become a forced/unfree labor relationship or a relationship of slavery. This forced/unfree labor relationship then either comes in the form of forcing the person to work in industry, agriculture, services or within households, or in the form of sexual exploitations (Feingold, 2005). Although illegal, estimates of the number of victims, that is, people currently held in the status of slaves throughout the world run in tens of millions (Belser, 2005; Okech, Howard, & Anarfi, 2018).

An important aspect of modern slavery is the enslavement of children. Children particularly at risk are those living in extreme poverty in societies valuing children for their labor. In such situations, the idea of the family obtaining money for a child sent to work for someone else may mean the difference between life and death (Hyde et al., 2006). Another practice often leading to enslavement of children is the practice of "fostering" or "placement," where families living in extreme poverty give up their children to relatives or other persons with whom they believe the child will have a better life. Researchers have studied such practices in countries such as Côte d'Ivoire, Haiti, and Togo, but they exist in a multitude of countries throughout the world (Hyde et al., 2006).

People living in the status of slaves are sometimes kept in hiding by their holders, but are often employed to work in places where they come in regular contact with other members of the society. For example, exploitation of the enslaved for commercial prostitution by its very nature includes the contact with other people. Maintenance of slavery depends on the conspiracy of silence within the immediate social environment. Another important component in the maintenance of slavery is a traumatic bonding of the slaves to their captors (George, 2015; O'Callaghan, Storey, & Rafferty, 2012).

The experience of slavery typically includes a variety of abuse experiences including both physical abuse such as beatings, rape and other forms of torture, but also living conditions detrimental to the well-being, such as living in crowded spaces, sleeping on the floor, inadequate food, and drinking water, inability to maintain personal hygiene, etc. (Okech et al., 2018). Survivors of slavery, after being rescued, often demonstrate various symptoms such as anxiety, depression, alienation, disorientation, aggression, suicide ideation, attention deficit, and post-traumatic stress disorder (PTSD), and the intensity of these symptoms has been found to be clearly related to the intensity of abuse experienced during slavery (Okech et al., 2018). More recent researchers have proposed that the array of psychopathological symptoms found in the survivors of slavery is much better described by the concept of complex PTSD (Hyde et al., 2006). Children sold or given up for slavery by their parents and relatives may also experience what is referred to as the betrayal trauma (Freyd, Klest, Carolyn Allard, Allard, & Elhai, 2005) with amnesia of traumatic events being a prominent symptom (Freyd, 2016).

Workplace harassment. Referred to also as workplace bullying, aggression, mistreatment or mobbing, it refers to the exposure to persistent or recurrent oppressive, abusive, offensive, intimidating, or insulting behavior by a superior or a colleague (Berge Matthiesen & Einarsen, 2004). These behaviors may be physical, involving physical violence or nonphysical and are systematically directed at one or more colleagues and subordinates leading to their stigmatization and victimization. Zapf proposes five types of workplace bullying behavior (Einarsen, 1999):

- Changing work tasks of the victim or making them difficult to perform.
- Social isolation.
- Attacks on the victim through ridicule, gossip, remarks etc.
- Verbal threats, yelling, or public humiliation, and.
- Physical violence or threats of such violence.

An important feature of this phenomenon is the power difference between the harasser and the victim, making the victim especially vulnerable.

Practices now considered to be workplace harassment have been a well-known fact of life for employees through most of history. However, only in the recent decades has such behavior, even when conducted by superiors in the organization, become criminalized in most parts of the world (e.g., Hedrih, 2017). This change has mostly led to the disappearance of the physical forms of workplace harassment, but nonphysical forms remain a common occurrence today (Berge Matthiesen & Einarsen, 2004; Węziak-Białowolska, Białowolski, & McNeely, 2020). Case studies of situations of workplace harassment often show that the social environment where harassment occurs manifests behavior akin to the conspiracy of silence (Hamburger, 2018), and this along with the social acceptance of harassments behavior and it being based on group membership (superior-employee) makes workplace harassment a social trauma-related situation.

Research has shown that workplace harassment is perceived by the victims as an extreme form of social stress at work, more crippling and devastating then all other forms of work-related stressors put together (e.g., Berge Matthiesen & Einarsen, 2004) leading to psychiatric distress and even PTSD (Berge Matthiesen & Einarsen, 2004; Bonafons, Jehel, & Coroller-Béquet, 2009).

Workplace sexual harassment. Workplace sexual harassment refers to unwelcome sexual advances, requests for sexual favors or other verbal and physical conduct of a sexual nature that happens in situations when cooperation or submission is an explicit or implicit condition of employment or when it is used as a basis for employment-related decisions. It also includes situations when the conduct has the purpose or effect of unreasonably interfering with a person's work performance or creating an intimidating, hostile, or offensive work environment (Avina & O'Donohue, 2002). Literature mentions two types of sexual harassment—when unwanted sexual remarks or advances create a hostile environment and when workplace consequences (e.g.,, continued employment, advancement, better work conditions, etc.) are made contingent upon sexual factors. In a 2007 meta-analysis of antecedents and consequences of sexual harassment Willness, Steel, and Lee (2007) state that 40–75% of women and 13–31% of men in the US experienced some form of sexual harassment in the workplace. An important antecedent for the occurrence of sexual harassment in an organization is a permissive organizational climate. This type of organizational climate is described as having three crucial aspects: the perceived risk to victims for complaining, a lack of sanctions against offenders, and the perception that complaints will not be taken seriously (Hulin, Fitzgerald, & Drasgow, 1996). Organizational climate of this type has been shown to have the single largest effect size of all the antecedent variables examined (Willness et al.,

2007), confirming the crucial role the social environment plays in the occurrence of workplace sexual harassment. When comparing this to the definitions of environments conducive to social trauma, it can be noticed that the described organizational climate also corresponds to social environments conducive to social traumatic events.

Research has described a multitude of negative consequences such as decreased job satisfaction, lower organizational commitment and withdrawal from work, as well as decreased physical and mental health even resulting in the symptoms of PTSD (Avina & O'Donohue, 2002; Willness et al., 2007)

Despite the fact that today's economy is marked by migrations, a surplus of labor in some areas, and a huge deficit in others, and although it may seem that we do our best, discrimination still exists in today's organizations (Tomaskovic-Devey, Thomas, & Johnson, 2005). Many countries import workers from less developed countries and accept migrants fleeing war in their countries. What determines the acceptance of migrants in the economy and their fair treatment? An extensive multilevel study by Dancygier and Donnelly (2013) shows that attitudes toward migrants as a workforce (and therefore workers' willingness to accept migrants in an organization) are partly conditioned by the function of patterns experienced by the indigenous population in the workplace. Migrant preferences are conditioned by the sectoral economy. If the sector develops and arrival of migrants coincides with good economic times, migration is more likely to be linked to economic benefits and support for migrants' integration will be greater. However, if the sectoral economy shrinks and the incomes of the native population decline and layoffs increase migration is likely to be perceived as a negative phenomenon and will produce more resistance.

An important concept for understanding the social environment in which the worst forms of coercive organizational practices exist is the concept of extractive and inclusive economic institutions proposed by Acemoglu and Robinson (2013). Based on the results of their study of the two parts of the city of Nogales, one in the US and the other in Mexico, and an extensive analysis of historical organizations of societies throughout the world, these authors define extractive economic and political institutions of a society as those that "concentrate power in the hands of a narrow elite and place few constraints on the exercise of this power. Economic institutions are then often structured by this elite to extract resources from the rest of the society" (Acemoglu & Robinson, 2013, p. 81). The elite then also uses its power to prevent any changes that would endanger their power and the existing organization and power hierarchy. Such practices, although often effective in the short term, curb economic growth and prosperity in the long term, leading to stagnation, poverty, and eventual collapse of such social systems. As described by many historical examples provided by these authors, infliction of physical and psychological trauma socially accepted by the members of the dominant group against those who are not members of the group, are typical practices in such societies. These practices are often seen as necessary and even crucial for the survival of the society by the social group practicing them.

In transitional countries struggling with ethnic prejudice, unfair privatization and even more unfair political regimes, negative attitudes, and discrimination toward migrants are even more visible. This restrictive view is also publicly supported because of the inadequacy of the fight against discrimination.

It is not just migrants who are affected by negative attitudes and discrimination. Through the re-traditionalization of societies and the shifting of collective values toward the respect for tradition, protection, and security of the social order, many social groups (such as women, national minorities, and people from lower socioeconomic backgrounds) are discriminated against in terms of their employment and promotion within the corporate ladder. Research shows that individuals who report implicit or explicit prejudice against members of a certain social group tend to react negatively to candidates coming from that group in the selection process (Stewart & Perlow, 2001; Ziegert & Hanges, 2005).

If we compare the nature and the psychological consequences of these coercive practices, especially of their worst forms, with the definition of social trauma, we can conclude that psychological trauma resulting from them indeed represents social trauma. These practices also affect the identity and the social environment of the traumatized individual making their social traumatic nature even more clear. While the worst forms of coercive practices in organizations are legally banned today in most world countries, many of them still persist in spite of legal bans or in transformed forms not adequately recognized by law or in places where laws cease to exist or are not enforced—for example, during breakdowns in legal systems (e.g., Amina, 2017).

It is important to note that the described forms of coercive organizational behaviors, although representing situations likely to result in social trauma, occur in "regular," peacetime conditions and do not require necessarily any extraordinary circumstances (such as war, turmoil, and the like), so it is important for psychologists working in practice to recognize them and be familiar with their workings.

24.4 Practical Implications in the Field of Social Trauma

Regardless of how we communicate with modern technology today, we are all in a situation where we have to establish relationships with other people who are different from us. In order to be successful, we must overcome two basic barriers – language and stereotypes. However, like Moran, Harris, and Moran (2011) say, the most important thing is to mentally eliminate the experience associated with the term "stranger" and adopt the view of others as having a background that is different.

Older employees are particularly sensitive to stereotype and older employees tend to more often be those treating diversity as a problem. Therefore, it is important to organize interventions such as trainings and education for older employees in order to accept diversity as an enrichment. A research study shows that a well-organized diversity management also leads to a better organizational performance. However, this study also shows that diverse teams need more time to become familiar with one another (Knippenberg, de Dreu, & Homan, 2004), so it is recommended that organizations extend the time to more diverse teams needed for the task. Patrick and Kumar (2012), in their article "Managing Diversity in the Workplace: Issues and Challenges," made recommendations for activities that increase the acceptance of others and those who are different. Some of them are development of organizational cultures valuing diversity, creativity and openness, equal treatment of all employees regardless of their background, systematic teaching on the benefits of diversity, encouragement of the employees to take on tasks in other countries, and effective and open communication where employees, in a safe and secure environment, can address all their concerns.

24.5 Suggested Reading

Conte, A. (2019). *Sexual harassment in the workplace: Law and practice*. New York: Walter Cluvers.

https://www.antislavery.org/slavery-today/modern-slavery/

https://www.ontario.ca/page/code-practice-address-workplace-harassment

References

Acemoglu, D., & Robinson, J. (2013). *Why nations fail: The origins, of power, Proseprity and poverty*. London: Profile Books.

Amina, M. (2017). *The emergence of the new face of slavery 21st century in Africa case study Libya (2011–2017)*. Algeria: University of Mostaganem.

Avina, C., & O'Donohue, W. (2002). Sexual harassment and PTSD: Is sexual harassment diagnosable trauma? *Journal of Traumatic Stress, 15*(1), 69–75. https://doi.org/10.1023/A:1014387429057

Belser, P. (2005). *Forced labor and human trafficking: Estimating the profits*. Geneva: International Labor Office. Retrieved from SSRN 1838403.

Berge Matthiesen, S., & Einarsen, S. (2004). Psychiatric distress and symptoms of PTSD among victims of bullying at work. *British Journal of Guidance and Counseling, 32*(3), 335–356. https://doi.org/10.1080/03069880410001723558

Bonafons, C., Jehel, L., & Coroller-Béquet, A. (2009). Specificity of the links between workplace harassment and PTSD: Primary results using court decisions, a pilot study in France. *International Archives of Occupational and Environmental Health, 82*(5), 663–668. https://doi.org/10.1007/s00420-008-0370-9

Dancygier, R. M., & Donnelly, M. J. (2013). Sectoral economies, economic contexts, and attitudes toward immigration. *The Journal of Politics, 75*(1). https://doi.org/10.1017/S0022381612000849

Einarsen, S. (1999). The nature and causes of bullying at work. *International Journal of Manpower, 20*(1/2), 16–27. https://doi.org/10.1108/01437729910268588

Feingold, D. A. (2005). Human trafficking. *Foreign Policy, 150*, 26–30.

Freyd, J. (2016). Betrayal trauma: Traumatic amnesia as an adaptive response to childhood abuse. *Ethics & Behavior, 4*(4), 307–329. https://doi.org/10.1207/s15327019eb0404_1

Freyd, J., Klest, B., Carolyn Allard, M. B., Allard, C. B., & Elhai, J. (2005). Betrayal trauma: Relationship to physical health, psychological distress. *Journal of Trauma & Dissociation, 6*(3), 2005. https://doi.org/10.1300/J229v06n03_04

George, V. (2015). *Traumatic bonding and intimate partner violence*. New Zealand: Victoria University of Wellington.

Hamburger, A. (Ed.). (2018). *Trauma, trust, and memory: Social trauma and reconciliation in psychoanalysis, psychotherapy, and cultural memory*. London: Karnac Books Ltd..

Hedrih, V. (2017). Family and work relations at the beginning of the 21st century. In V. Hedrih (Ed.), *Work and family relations at the beginning of the 21st century*. Niš: Filozfski Fakultet.

Hulin, C. L., Fitzgerald, L. F., & Drasgow, F. (1996). Organizational influences on sexual harassment. In M. Stockdale (Ed.), *Sexual harassment in the workplace: Perspectives, Frontiers, and response strategies* (pp. 127–150). SAGE Publications. https://doi.org/10.4135/9781483327280.n7

Hyde, J., Bales, K., & Levin, M. (2006). Physical and mental health aspects of rehabilitating children freed from slavery. In *Linking theory and practice to Elminate worst forms of child labor* (pp. 115–178). US Department of Labor.

Jones, J. M., Dovidio, J. F., & Vietze, D. L. (2014). *The psychology of diversity: Beyond prejudice and racism* (p. 328). Wiley. Kindle Edition.

Knippenberg, D. V., de Dreu, C. K. W., & Homan, A. C. (2004). Work group diversity and group performance: An integrative model and research agenda. *Journal of Applied Psychology, 89*, 1008–1022.

Lovejoy, P. (2012). *Transformations in slavery: A history of slavery in Africa*. Cambridge: Cambridge University Press.

Moran, R. T., Harris, P. R., & Moran, S. V. (2011). *Managing cultural differences: Global leadership strategies for cross-cultural business success*. Amsterdam: Butterworth-Heinemann.

O'Callaghan, P., Storey, L., & Rafferty, H. (2012). Narrative analysis of former child soldiers' traumatic experiences. *Education and Child Psychology, 29*(2), 87–97.

Okech, D., Howard, W., & Anarfi, J. K. (2018). Social support, dysfunctional coping, and community reintegration as predictors of PTSD among human trafficking survivors. *Behavioral Medicine, 44*(3), 209–218. https://doi.org/10.1080/08964289.2018.1432553

Patrick, H. A., & Kumar, V. R. (2012). Managing workplace diversity: issues and challenges. *SAGE Open, 2*, 215824401244461. https://doi.org/10.1177/2158244012444615

Stewart, L. D., & Perlow, R. (2001). Applicant race, job status, and racial attitude as predictors of employment discrimination. *Journal of Business and Psychology, 16*(2), 259–275. https://doi.org/10.1023/A:1011113301301

Tomaskovic-Devey, D., Thomas, M., & Johnson, K. (2005). Race and the accumulation of human capital across the career: A theoretical model and fixed-effects application. *American Journal of Sociology, 111*(1), 58–89. https://doi.org/10.1086/431779

Unfree labor. (2020). In Wikipedia. Retreived from https://en.wikipedia.org/w/index.php?title=Unfree_labouroldid=970848472

Węziak-Białowolska, D., Białowolski, P., & McNeely, E. (2020). The impact of workplace harassment and domestic violence on work outcomes in the developing world. *World Development, 126*, 1–11. https://doi.org/10.1016/j.worlddev.2019.104732

Willness, C., Steel, P., & Lee, K. (2007). A meta-analysis of the antecedents and consequences of workplace sexual harassment. *Personnel Psychology, 60*, 127–162.

Ziegert, J. C., & Hanges, P. J. (2005). Employment discrimination: The role of implicit attitudes, motivation, and a climate for racial Bias. *Journal of Applied Psychology, 90*(3), 553–562. https://doi.org/10.1037/0021-9010.90.3.553

Chapter 25
Understanding Social Trauma in Low-Resource Settings

Shahla M. Eltayeb

The purpose of this chapter is to explore the conceptual model of social trauma in low-resource settings, to identify the contributing factors to social trauma in low-resource settings (LRS), as well as to understand the different individual reactions to trauma, and recognize practical ways to mitigate barriers for providing trauma services in LRS.

25.1 Background and Theoretical Concepts

Postwar societies in low-resource settings (LRS) are marked by the extreme use of violence and massive large group traumatization that is multidimensional, and therefore, we will use an interdisciplinary approach to understand the social trauma in LRS.

There are several challenges that face the understanding of social trauma in low-resource settings (LRS): cultural factors that are different from other settings; a culture that barely recognizes trauma as a dimension that needs health intervention, limitations to financial and human resources, absence of supportive national mental health policies, and a lack of robust health-care delivery systems capable of integrating trauma health-care services (Acharya et al., 2017). Furthermore, LRS are characterized by violence, political instability, poverty, limited funds, and extreme demands on health services that lead to a huge burden on individuals and overall low quality and accessibility to trauma health services (Asgary & Segar 2011; Saraceno et al., 2007).

Hence, social trauma results when LRS communities and their institutions fail to act as support systems against adversities that generate trauma, either by failure to protect vulnerable individuals, or by allowing violence, oppression, and

S. M. Eltayeb (✉)
Ahfad University for Women, Ahfad Trauma Centre, Omdurman, Sudan

© Springer Nature Switzerland AG 2021

A. Hamburger et al. (eds.), *Social Trauma – An Interdisciplinary Textbook*,
https://doi.org/10.1007/978-3-030-47817-9_25

discrimination from governments or social groups against minorities or opposition. Lastly, social trauma occurs when the system is characterized by corruption, stigma, and alienation (Tubert, 2006).

The social trauma factors mentioned above are intensified with war, terrorism, and violence as in several LRS including Sudan, the second-largest country in Africa. Sudan has witnessed 25 years of civil war between North Sudan and South Sudan that ended in 2011, with the South Sudan referendum and the separation of the two countries. During peace negotiations in 2004, violence erupted in the western Darfur region, a region with diverse Arab and African populations and several natural resources including water, minerals, and gold. The Darfur war, led by President Al-Bashir who ordered the army and allied Arab militia (Janjaweed) to kill and drive out entire communities, resulted in mass killing and genocide with a loss of 70,000 lives and over 1.8 million internally displaced (Straus, 2005).

The aftermath of war and conflict has resulted in mass suffering, trauma, and extreme need for services and support. Nevertheless, trauma services in conflict-affected Sudan are few and concentrated in urban centers; they are difficult to access and lack enough adequately trained professionals. Sudan is one of several low-resource settings that are considered "trauma land," whereby several devastating factors exist.

Despite the complexity of trauma-contributing factors (sociocultural and economic–political), the individual's reaction to trauma varies and adds to the complexities. According to Papadopoulos (Trauma Grid Model), the individual reaction to trauma starts from ordinary human suffering and evolves to resilience and beyond (2007). The accommodation of individuals' reaction to traumatic events is critical not only for understanding social trauma, but also for identification and diagnosis of trauma-related disorders and service provision, by widening the scope of the clinical approach in understanding suffering and accommodating aspects of the individual growth and resilience.

25.2 Learning Outcome Related to Social Trauma

- Identify factors that contribute to the complexity of social trauma in LRS.
- Describe the different individual reactions to trauma.
- Recognize practical ways to mitigate barriers for providing trauma services in.

25.3 Model of Explanation Social Trauma in LRS

Models explaining psychological trauma failed to identify specific factors associated with socioeconomic and political functioning in LRS. With time, the models began to explore interactive processes between personal attributes and traumatic events, and associated variables. More complex transactional and developmental pathway models were developed. The Historical Trauma Theory incorporates and builds upon three theoretical frameworks. The first is the psychosocial theory, which links trauma to both physical and psychological stress. Psychosocial stressors not only create vulnerability to traumatization but also directly affect the human brain. The second theoretical framework is political/economic theory, which addresses the political, economic, and structural causes of health and trauma such as unjust power relations and class inequality. The third is social/ecological systems theory, addressing the multilevel dynamics and of present/past, and life course factors in trauma causation (Krieger, 2001).

The historical trauma theory provides four different assumptions: (1) mass trauma is intentionally and systematically committed upon a community by an overpowering, dominant population; (2) trauma is not limited to a single devastating event, but is usually endured over time; (3) traumatic events resonate throughout the affected community, creating a collective experience of trauma; and (4) the extent of the traumatic experience disrupts the community from its natural, historical course leading to a legacy of pain, trauma, and disparities that persist across generations (Brave Heart, 2003). The current chapter will build upon the historical trauma model and explore three factors contributing to social trauma in LRS.

25.3.1 Sociocultural Factors of Social Trauma in LRS

Sociocultural factors influence the individual reaction to traumatic events, individual coping mechanisms, and also the definition of what is traumatic as influenced by sociocultural factors. Different definitions of what constitutes traumatic events have inadvertently emphasized the importance of accounting for the culture-specific aspects of trauma, thus, it is imperative to take into consideration the sociopolitical-cultural context to define social trauma (Caspi, Ghafoori, Smith, & Contractor, 2013).

The type of approach in which trauma service providers are more aware of their worldview and the client is needed. Using a Western definition of trauma that focuses on individual experiences rather than on social and political realities that are often at the root of the traumatizing events is inappropriate in LRS, as different cultures may have different labels of trauma experiences (Wilson & Drožđek, 2007). For example, the case of female genital mutilation is a practice affecting millions of women in Eastern Africa, characterized by extreme assault and pain; it is a traumatic event that a young girl endures in the cultural context of joy, festivity, and celebration. Female Genital Mutilation FGM/C is therefore not only a social convention but also is a social norm—a rule of behavior that members of a community are expected to follow and are motivated to follow through a set of rewards and sanctions. Surviving the traumatic effect of the practice is motivated by expectations of rewards for adherence to the norm and fear of sanctions for nonadherence (Satti et al., 2006).

Defining the events as "traumatic" is often influenced by societal and professional determinants, thus it is crucial to identify the influence of culture on the individual emotional reactions to traumatic exposure in different cultural groups as these symptoms may be influenced by the cultural meaning associated with the traumatic event (Hoshmand, 2007). Furthermore, the perception of the event and its aftermath is also influenced by cultural meanings. The definitions and attitudes toward social trauma can impact the symptoms, assessment, detection, interventions, and resources allocated to prevention and treatment (Caspi, 2009). Looking at how sociocultural factors in LRS impact the definition, exposure, and stigma associated with traumatic events can enrich our understanding of social trauma.

To further understand the sociocultural influence on trauma, one needs to address issues related to trauma and social stigma. Communities in low-resource settings face greater exposure to war and violence including sexual violence which is not only a result of war, but also is used as a deliberate tool of war. Rape has devastating effects on the survivors aside from medical consequences, which may lead to long-lasting trauma and suffering (Hustache et al. 2009). Sometimes this takes the shape of mental health disorders, whereas, at other times, it surfaces in less obvious ways such as shame, guilt, and social stigmatization (Gavey & Schmidt, 2011).

Social stigma is caused by misconceptions and social condemnation-based beliefs or perceptions, which lead to negative stereotyping and labeling of individuals, and can be followed by social marginalization and injustice (Schneider et al., 2018). Stigma is often associated with a traumatic event in LRS, the multiple stigmas construct, whereby cultural, social, and self-perception of stigma exist. For example, women reporting sexual assault in various LRS face cultural rejection and social isolation, in addition to the legal complexity of proving the case of rape; the social stigma that rape survivors face in the criminal justice system, health-care facilities, and/or social service agencies—these triple dimensions only influence the severity of trauma symptoms but also the experiences of women seeking help. Consequently, women are pushed into an emotional dilemma of shame, guilt, silence, and self-stigma, which relates to the negative beliefs an individual holds about her psychological symptoms or help-seeking. One should note that self-stigma is positively related to the trauma symptom severity (Jennings et al., 2015).

Having addressed the rather negative influences of sociocultural factors on social trauma, it is imperative to highlight the positive side related to social support and social cohesiveness, which are too factors that contribute to healing and trauma recovery. Cohen (2004, p. 676) defines social support as: "a social network's provision of psychological and material resources intended to benefit an individual's capacity to cope with stress."

Social support in LRS is usually offered to trauma cases, whereby the victim is considered socially not guilty, such as survivors of road accidents, wars, and natural disasters. In such cases, societal support is enormous including finical aid, visitation, and moral support.

Social support is another relevant component in the belief that health and sickness and traumatic events are from God. Traumatic events could be interpreted as a sanction for wrong deeds, or a test to assess an individual's resilience and belief in God or as a means to eliminate bad deeds in life. Several cultures consider social traumatic events even genocide as a test from (Allah) God. Such beliefs make people tolerate diverse types of traumatic events not only by endurance but also by providing social support to those who accepted God's will; this dynamic process of endurance will eventually boost one's prestige in the community: one gets a heavenly reward and is socially supported.

One can conclude that sociocultural factors have a double-edged effect on trauma. On the one hand, it could crush the trauma survivors through stigmatization and isolation, and on the other hand, social support has a healing effect on the survivors as it promotes resilience, coping, and belonging. The challenge is thus how to mitigate the sociocultural negative factors and promote social support with trauma survivors.

25.3.2 *Economic and Political Factors and Social Trauma in LRS*

The current section will explore how poverty and political factors intersect with social trauma, in particular, in the case of illegal migration and political torture survivors. Individuals in low-resource settings face myriad challenges in maintaining good psychological well-being and receiving mental health treatment. Living in poverty is associated with experiencing extremely high chances of mental illness, particularly depression, anxiety disorders, and post-traumatic stress disorder (PTSD) (Golin et al., 2016).

Poverty not only constitutes a life stressor, but also it increases an individual's vulnerability for being exposed to violence and exploitation. Additionally, having a highly constrained financial status is a major barrier to seeking help for mental illness in general and among trauma survivors in particular (Levy & O'Hara, 2010).

Several economic and political barriers exist in LRS, including structural barriers (e.g., unavailability of mental health service), legislation barriers (e.g., absence of mental health policy), and informational barrier (e.g., not knowing about services). Barriers to accessing mental health services for trauma survivors are a major challenge in LRS whereby individuals experience high levels of unmet basic needs, social isolation, and financial strain. While the importance of addressing the accessibility to mental health services for traumatized groups in low-resource settings is increasingly being recognized, there are many challenges in how this should be done for different categories, as survivors are often excluded from the mainstream policy and decision-making process.

Various structural barriers face refugees and illegal migrants residing in LRS; for example, Sudan has long been a permissive environment for smuggling Eritrean migrants, as corruption, insecurity, and weak borders have enabled human trafficking to flourish. In Sudan's eastern borderlands, smugglers from a nomadic tribe target women and young men in a journey of exploitation and abuse (Ayalew Mengiste, 2018). This vulnerable group of migrants, the majority of whom are women and youngsters, has faced war atrocities in addition to a hazardous border crossing. They are not only traumatized but also face several barriers in accessing mental health services in poor-resource settings like Sudan. They do not speak the language of the host country and lack knowledge on how to access appropriate services. They lack a proper refugee or migration status and hence are threatened to be deported. Further, they struggle to adopt the culture and values of the new host environment, separating from the new environment and maintaining the values and traditions of the culture of origin. They are considered a burden and mostly rejected by the host community thus facing isolation and marginalization. This vicious cycle of poverty, cultural adaptation, and legal status not only magnifies the existing social trauma but also constitutes a barrier to service provision.

Another category of those experiencing trauma are victims of political torture, which is one of the most traumatic threats to psychic integrity that any human being can undergo. Political suppression is another characteristic of LRS (Cunningham & Silove, 1993). El-Bashir's 1989 military coup in Sudan has created restrictions on daily life and political activity to maintain control. The National Security Service was used as a repression tool. They had judicial authority and financial abilities to abduct, detain, and torture opposition in what was locally known as "ghost houses" where torture and abuse were common. Torture in dictatorships aims to destroy the individual's sense of identity and create feelings of "hopelessness, dependency, and fear." Torture effects transcend beyond the individual's traumatic reaction to the community by creating a sense of despair, anger-fueling, potential act of revenge, and violence. Furthermore, torture sends a massage to prevent further political opposition to the ruling regime and creates a social legacy of brutality leading to social traumatization (Dolan, 2009; Ugalde & Ziwi, 1989).

Hence, the combination of poverty, political oppression in LRS expose individuals to several life stressors and increase their vulnerability to marginalization and exploitation factors that lead to systematic social trauma. On the other hand, the political context that is conducive to violence and human rights violations makes accessibility to mental health or protection services challenging.

25.3.3 The Social Trauma Response Spectrum

Individual reactions to traumatic events vary according to different factors including demographic characteristics, social support, and the magnitude of harm and humiliation. According to Papadopoulos (2007), responses to adversity and traumatic events are not linear in the sense that not every individual exposed to a traumatic event will develop a mental disorder; rather, individuals' reaction is understood in a multilayer grid of reactions that include ordinary human suffering response, distressful responses, and psychiatric disorders; these responses constitute the negative reactions to social trauma.

The trauma grid further postulates that trauma has a positive side in which individuals are not only resilient and preserve their personal qualities, but they also evolve to adversity acquired development (AAD) in which individuals acquire new skills and traits. Thus, people and communities not only endure the traumatic event and survive, but also in some cases, they become stronger. The case of Syrian refugees in Sudan reflects this assumption, despite the harsh reality of escaping the Syrian war, only to arrive in Sudan with its minimal resources and inability to provide assistance or support. However, Syrian refugees have preserved their cultural cohesiveness and support and evolved into new careers. In an interview with a Syrian middle-aged woman who lost her family in the Syrian war, she said, "coming to Sudan and not Europe was catastrophic, I could not bear the heat and the persistence of my poverty. However, after six months, I started socializing with local women and gained more mobility and strength that I did not have before, I am no longer the submissive dependent housewife, I became an entrepreneur selling homemade food and am more resilient than before." In another example, political torture survivors once indicated that "the solitary confinement. Although it was harsh, it has allowed me to think, to evaluate and replan. I felt like Mandela."

The gained new qualities (adversity acquired development) are usually missed in the clinical assessment and community intervention of social trauma. Furthermore, the implication of perceiving trauma reaction in a spectrum of negative to positive is important for service providers, as clinicians are usually trained to assess and identify symptoms clustering them into measurable diagnosable disorder. This may have led to several missed opportunities, in the sense that trauma victims were not perceived as survivors with growth potential but rather as victims in need of treatment. The assessment process rarely elaborates on the positive side of social trauma.

The above section explored the amalgamation of factors that contribute to social trauma and obscure the process of service provision in low-recourse settings, including several factors at the border context (social, cultural, economic, and political) and one factor related to the traumatic event and the individual response. The following section will illustrate attempts to surpass the aforementioned factors in trauma service provision in LRS.

25.4 Practical Implications in the Field of Social Trauma

Several attempts have been made by governmental and nongovernmental agencies in LRS to overcome the barriers in trauma service provision. The following example illustrates how a university-based center in Sudan attempts to bridge this gap.

The Ahfad University is a nongovernmental women's university in the capital city Khartoum, which, in 2012, initiated a specialized trauma center. The Ahfad Trauma Center (ATC) sets its mission on offering high-quality community-based mental health services for trauma survivors.

To overcome financial barriers, the ATC provided free mental health service to survivors. This was made possible by mobilizing the university's social responsibility strategy, upon which designated offices were allocated to the center within the university premises. Also, faculty members from the school of psychology were assigned 1 day in the trauma center, which enabled the center to acquire trained staff and free space. Furthermore, university settings are considered a safe neutral space by the local community.

The Ahfad Trauma Center (ATC) introduced its psychosocial support and treatment approaches through a process of cultural adaption that encompasses Afro-Arab cultures in addition to gender- and politically sensitive approach. The treatment models observed the totality of trauma responses and promoted individual resilience and recovery (Eltayeb, Sliep, & Muneghina, 2017). The trauma center addressed issues of social stigma and cultural barriers by mobilizing the existing cultural norms of trust, social support, reciprocity, and by abiding by strict ethical guidelines of privacy and confidentiality. The barrier of accessibility was mitigated by establishing a referral network with legal, medical, and social service providers and raising the survivor's awareness of the new referral network through community mentored awareness activities.

The setup of ATC in LRS paves the way for different modalities in trauma service provision outside the conventional health model. Efforts to address social trauma in low-resource settings needs a broader scope in addressing the barriers and innovative interventions to assist social trauma survivors.

Individuals have a great potential to adapt in the face of adversity; however, this adaptation requires the functioning of several interacting systems within and around the individual. Thus, effective interventions need to focus on a wide range of factors, incorporating the totality of the individual and the complexity of social trauma in low-resource settings.

25.5 Suggested Readings and Further Information

Bubenzer, F. & Tankink, M. (2015). *Conference Report: Healing communities, transforming society. Exploring the interconnectedness between psychosocial needs, practice and peacebuilding.* Retrieved from http://www.ijr.org.za/home/wp-content/uploads/2016/11/IJR-Healing-communities-conference-WEB.pdf, June eighth, 2019.

Manitoba Trauma Information and Education Centre (MTIEC). https://trauma-recovery.ca/introduction/definition-of-trauma/

Papadopoulos, R. K. (n.d.). *A psychosocial framework for with refugees*. Retrieved June 8, 2019, from http://southeastsafenet.eu/sites/default/files/3.pdf

UNHCR Reporting. (n.d.). *South Sudan situation*. Retrieved June 8, 2019, from http://reporting.unhcr.org/southsudansituation

References

Acharya, B., Maru, D., Schwarz, R., Citrin, D., Tenpa, J., Hirachan, S., … Ekstrand, M. (2017). Partnerships in mental healthcare service delivery in low-resource settings: Developing an innovative network in rural Nepal. *Globalization and Health, 13*(1), 2. https://doi.org/10.1186/s12992-016-0226-0

Asgary, R., & Segar, N. (2011). Barriers to health care access among refugee asylum seekers. *Journal of Health Care for the Poor and Underserved, 22*(2), 506–522.

Ayalew Mengiste, T. (2018). Refugee protections from below: Smuggling in the Eritrea-Ethiopia context. *The Annals of the American Academy of Political and Social Science, 676*(1), 57–76.

Brave Heart, M. (2003). The historical trauma response among natives and its relationship with substance abuse: A Lakota illustration. *Journal of Psychoactive Drugs, 35*(1), 7–13.

Caspi, Y. (2009). Shame: A Missing link to the unraveling of complex trauma reactions in non-western communities. Paper presented at the 2009 Annual conference of the international society for traumatic stress studies, November 5–7, Atlanta, GA.

Caspi, Y., Ghafoori, B., Smith, S. F., & Contractor, A. (2013). *On the importance of considering culture when defining trauma.* International Society for Traumatic Stress Studies. Retrieved from http://www.istss.org/education-research/traumatic-stresspoints/2013-october/on-the-importance-of-considering-culture-when-defi.aspx

Cohen, S. (2004). Social relationships and health. *American Psychologist, 59*(8), 676.

Cunningham, M., & Silove, D. (1993). Principles of treatment and service development for torture and trauma survivors. In J. P. Wilson & B. Raphael (Eds.), *International handbook of traumatic stress syndromes* (pp. 751–762). Boston, MA: Springer.

Dolan, C. (2009). *Social torture: The case of northern Uganda, 1986–2006* (Vol. 4). New York: Berghahn Books.

Eltayeb, S., Sliep, Y., & Muneghina, O. (2017). Bridging the gap in mental health and psychosocial services in low resource settings: A case study in Sudan. *Intervention, 15*(2), 151–165.

Gavey, N., & Schmidt, J. (2011). "Trauma of rape" discourse: A double-edged template for everyday understandings of the impact of rape? *Violence Against Women, 17*(4), 433–456.

Golin, C. E., Haley, D. F., Wang, J., Hughes, J. P., Kuo, I., Justman, J., … Hodder, S. (2016). Post-traumatic stress disorder symptoms and mental health over time among low-income women at increased risk of HIV in the US. *Journal of Health Care for the Poor and Underserved, 27*(2), 891.

Hoshmand, L. T. (2007). Cultural–ecological perspectives on the understanding and assessment of trauma. In J. P. Wilson & C. C. So Kum Tang (Eds.), *Cross-cultural assessment of psychological trauma and PTSD* (pp. 31–50). New York: Springer Science & Business Media.

Hustache, S., Moro, M. R., Roptin, J., Souza, R., Gansou, G. M., Mbemba, A., … Baubet, T. (2009). Evaluation of psychological support for victims of sexual violence in a conflict setting: Results from Brazzaville, Congo. *International Journal of Mental Health Systems, 3*(1), 7.

Jennings, K. S., Cheung, J. H., Britt, T. W., Goguen, K. N., Jeffirs, S. M., Peasley, A. L., & Lee, A. C. (2015). How are perceived stigma, self-stigma, and self-reliance related to treatment-seeking? A three-path model. *Psychiatric Rehabilitation Journal, 38*(2), 109.

Krieger, N. (2001). Theories for social epidemiology in the 21st century: An Ecosocial perspective. *International Journal of Epidemiology, 30*, 668–677.

Levy, L. B., & O'Hara, M. W. (2010). Psychotherapeutic interventions for depressed, low-income women: A review of the literature. *Clinical Psychology Review, 30*(8), 934–950.

Papadopoulos, R. K. (2007). Refugees, trauma and adversity-activated development. *European Journal of Psychotherapy and Counselling, 9*(3), 301–312.

Saraceno, B., van Ommeren, M., Batniji, R., Cohen, A., Gureje, O., Mahoney, J., … Underhill, C. (2007). Barriers to improvement of mental health services in low-income and middle-income countries. *The Lancet, 370*(9593), 1164–1174.

Satti, A., Elmusharaf, S., Bedri, H., Idris, T., Hashim, M. S. K., Suliman, G. I., & Almroth, L. (2006). Prevalence and determinants of the practice of genital mutilation of girls in Khartoum, Sudan. *Annals of Tropical Paediatrics, 26*(4), 303–310.
Schneider, A., Conrad, D., Pfeiffer, A., Elbert, T., Kolassa, I. T., & Wilker, S. (2018). Stigmatization is associated with increased PTSD risk after traumatic stress and diminished likelihood of spontaneous remission-a study with east-African conflict survivors. *Frontiers in Psychiatry, 9*, 423. https://doi.org/10.3389/fpsyt.2018.00423
Straus, S. (2005). Darfur and the genocide debate. *Foreign Affairs, 84*, 123.
Tubert, R. H. D. (2006). Social trauma: The pathogenic effects of untoward social conditions. *International Forum of Psychoanalysis, 15*(3), 151–156.
Ugalde, A., & Ziwi, A. (1989). Towards an epidemiology of political violence in the third world. *Journal of Social Science and Medicine, 28*, 633–642.
Wilson, J. P., & Drožđek, B. (2007). Are we lost in translations?: Unanswered questions on trauma, culture and posttraumatic syndromes and recommendations for future research. In B. Drožđek & J. P. Wilson (Eds.), *Voices of trauma* (pp. 367–386). New York: Springer.

Chapter 26
Social Identity Transformations and Social Trauma Nexus

Selma Porobić

This chapter aims to discuss the state-of-the-art research concerning the process of transformations taking place at the level of social identity and intergroup relations in the wake of social trauma, inflicted by sequences of collective violence and gross human rights violations.

26.1 Introduction: Background and Main Theoretical Concepts

To begin to understand the scope of a social trauma, that is the consequence of traumatogenic events or situations, involving a community or one's definable social group (family, peer groups, etc.), we need to look at the underlying and interlinked processes of collective identity formation, constructions of traumatic narratives and social practices of remembrance.

In the aftermath of collective violence, inherent to massive-scale human rights violations, the basic fabric of society is severely shattered and social representations of the traumatic event(s) become a crucial facet of the social identity (re)constructions. Collective traumas often lead to collective memory with a system of meaning(s) that affected groups generate to (re)define their identity and future orientations. For victims, this process may be adaptive and prompt the construction of a trans-generational collective self. For perpetrators, it may involve dealing with the threat to collective identity by denying/revising of history, reducing the blame or projecting it onto other groups, but also accepting responsibility and consequences thereof to keep a positive image of the group (see Hirscheberger, 2018).

S. Porobić (✉)
Palacky University, Olomouc, Czech Republic
Honorary Research Fellow, University College, London, UK

© Springer Nature Switzerland AG 2021

A. Hamburger et al. (eds.), *Social Trauma – An Interdisciplinary Textbook*,
https://doi.org/10.1007/978-3-030-47817-9_26

Observing these developments is crucial to the understanding of the social trauma complexities and dealing with its long-lasting, trans-generational effects.

In this chapter, I will first introduce the social identity theory to explain the *social identities formation processes*. Then, I will describe how perceived social identity threat can lead to conflict, explaining the role of collective memory and binary positioning of the groups involved in the *social trauma responses*. Following this, I will focus on the *post-traumatic outlook* by using case study examples from several post-conflict societies, in a historic and current perspective. Lastly, I will discuss *practical implications* in the field of social trauma studies by referring to 'education for peace' practices.

26.1.1 Social Identity, Intergroup Dynamics and Conflicts

Identity entails both a relationship to ourselves and others. Through the connection with others, an individual creates a social self by engaging in sharing of the group norms, values and principles. This group membership is driven by social dynamics that favour one's group members over the others (Tajfel & Turner, 1979). We affix boundaries and create divisions when we decide that the people who are part of our circle/in-group have more in common with us than the people who are not part of our circle/out-group. Through this favourable comparison, the in-group members are positively perceived, while the out-group members are stereotyped and discriminated against (Jenkins, 2000). Such a process of social categorisation by use of stereotypes, prejudices, discrimination and/or biases towards other groups and their members reinforces the group dynamics and shapes the binary group behaviour of 'us' against 'them' positions (Korostelina, 2007). Thus, we have moulded a world to reinforce our sense of security from people who are not and should not be seen as part of our group.

Moreover, the choice to belong to a group lies at the intersection of our social and political positioning in a society and is often determined by a mix of ascribed and acquired statuses of a person—the first relating to rankings dependent upon a person's kith and kin, his/her gender, race, caste, ethnicity and economic status of his/her birth family, family, race, ethnicity, etc., while the second on personal achievements, merit and the fulfilment of goals.

This collective axiology system based on a notion of value commitments that offers moral guidance to maintain relations with those inside and outside a group also decides upon the group dynamics and actions considered in particular circumstances (Korostelina, 2007, pp. 73–74). Especially, when groups are competing over resources such as land, power, information and legitimacy, the specific identities will be triggered to keep in-group stability by promoting the primacy and the supremacy of in-group values and goals over the individual ones. Social identity then becomes increasingly important, polarising the community that then creates a narrative of the 'virtuous us' and 'demonic them'. Finally, when the society is divided along normative lines—bad/god, protagonist/antagonist, right/wrong—

social identities become a cause of confrontation among groups competing not just for material advantages, but also for defence of their security, beliefs, values and worldview that serve as the basis for in-group identity (see Rothbart et al., 2007).

26.1.2 Collective Trauma Narratives and Their Transmittance

Communities that have experienced mass atrocities often embody the binary understanding of the victim–perpetrator identities formed through the above-described social categorisation but also *transmitted trauma* and formation of *single-sided historical narratives*.

Social representation theory (Moscovici, 1988) suggests that people construe and explain historical events to be able to relate to the present and place expectations on the future. In a society affected by a socially traumatic event, several generations can be subjected to the legacy of the past and pulled apart by stigma and recreational processes of traumatic contents, breeding exclusion and dehumanisation, and quite often leading to future aspirations for revengeful violence maintained by the memory and self-validating identity stories.

This kind of behaviour, observed by Vamik Volkan, is referred to as the 'chosen trauma' (Volkan, 1997, p. 48), and suggests that tragedy is represented in the group memory and transmitted through generations beyond the lives of direct survivors, often by group members temporally and spatially far removed from the actual event. The transmission of the group's 'injured selves' allows for the creation of common history based on ancestral trauma and in-group and out-group dynamics, eventually establishing the connection between trauma, memory and ontological safety (Volkan, 1997, p. 48).

The collective trauma can thus become the epicentre of group identity and a lens through which group members understand their social environment and act upon perceived existential threats. For example, much of the research on post-traumatic responses to the Holocaust, considered the prototypical genocide of the twentieth century, points to the development of the social cohesion and the enhanced adaptive functions of the Jewish population (Bar-Tal, Chernyak-Hai, Schori, & Gundar, 2009). Similarly, other research also points to the fact that collectively traumatic experiences can act as motivation for self-continuation and symbolic immortality of a group (see Castano, Yzerbyt, Paladino, & Sacchi, 2002) if integrated into coherent self-narratives of the survivors (László, 2013; Porobić, 2012, 2018).

On the other hand, this seemingly adaptive caution response can also develop into a paranoid post-traumatic worldview, involving compulsive and an aggressive stance towards any kind of external treat that the exposed group faces (see, e.g. Bruner & Amrami-Plotkin, 2015; Oakes & Turner, 1980).

26.2 Learning Outcomes: Responses and Societal Dealing with Social Trauma

To discontinue its troubling traumatogenic effects in the present, societies affected by social trauma go through significant transformations drawing from the intra-group responses and inter-group dynamics.

Post-Holocaust Germany and post-apartheid South Africa are examples of collective healing progression from a long-term perspective. In Germany, the second generation considered it controversial and engaged in revisionist tendencies when attempts to openly talk about the atrocities committed by the Nazis were 'prematurely' brought to the table (Crownshaw, 2010). It was only the third generation that was able to vocalise the guilt of Nazi crimes committed during World War II.

In South Africa, during the post-apartheid period when the government initiated Truth and Reconciliation Commissions, the process of defining the perpetrator illustrated the gaps between the remembered experience of the victim and that of the perpetrator. In fact, the victim–perpetrator dichotomy limited the truth-telling of the complex narrative and reinforced the idea of simplification by drawing on the belief that people could not have been indoctrinated and forced into unthinkable crimes by social pressure and structures of everyday life (Kraft, 2014, p. 100).

26.3 Preferred Model of Explanation

Reinvestigation into the identifications, such as the victim and the perpetrator, continues to be significant to the understanding of the social trauma response(s) in the post-conflict contexts. Recent research has suggested that the label of a victim, in particular, is changing and becoming more complex to grasp. The normative narrative that the victim is innocent while perpetrator is a self-driven inflictor of criminal acts has been challenged by a number of scholars (Browning, 1992; Drumble, 2007).

In a ground-breaking manner, UN commissioned Report of Graça Machel in 1996, highlighted the disproportionate impact of war on children and identified them as the primary victims of armed conflict. It brought to attention the full spectrum of actors and webs of relations involved in complex temporal and spatial dynamics of victimhood and perpetration positions. Just like her contemporary American feminists of the 1990s' literature studies, Machel stressed the role of *victimhood in perpetration* and critiqued the long-persistent and one-sided dehumanisation of perpetrators.

A case study of Dominic Ongwen, an indicted war criminal and former child soldier in Lord's Resistance Army (LRA) in Uganda, one of the world's most brutal rebel organisations, demonstrates this complexity. In total, as a commander and soldier of LRA, Ongwen was charged with being criminally responsible for 70 counts of war crimes and crimes against humanity committed between 2002 and 2005 in Northern Uganda. Charges include murder, enslavement, inhumane acts of inflicting serious bodily injury and suffering, sexual and gender-based crimes, forced marriage and sexual slavery, torture and more. As a child soldier, typically abducted and forcedly militarised, Ongwen is an illustrative case of both victim and perpetrator at once.

In her article, Erin Baines (2009) uses his case to introduce the concept of *complex political perpetrators* and describe youth who occupy extremely marginal spaces in settings of chronic crisis, and who use violence as an expression of political agency. Ongwen represents young rebels who were 'bred' in the shadows of illiberal war economies, excluded from the polity, or rather never having been socialised within it. She argues that such complex political perpetrators should be adequately recognised in the debate on transitional justice after mass atrocity.

When we look at effects of collective violence and work with social trauma, we need to be aware of the influencing factors relating to the social system and global structures of political, ideological and institutional contexts which promote and legitimise violence. Grasping on complex social trauma positioning does not minimise horrific actions committed by those identified as perpetrators. It rather helps to understand how some individuals enact criminal acts and the societal context that permitted the enactment of such atrocities (Staub, 2006). Ignoring these contexts will inevitably set us up for a failure of exclusion, dehumanisation and possibly new future violence and social traumas.

26.4 Practical Implications in the Field of Social Trauma: Education for Peace

Social traumas directly affect the basic tissue of social life, impairing the bonds between people and a sense of cohesion in a society. Since the central role of intergroup relations' research is to promote conflict resolution and reconciliation, the long-term social trauma effects are considered a hindrance to peace-making, especially when the focus is on the historical victimisations and one-sided narratives.

The literature on in-group responsibility for historical events with traumatising social impact reveals a complex spectrum of motivations to both defend in-group positions and repair relationships with out-group (Gausel, Leach, Vignoles, & Brown, 2012). According to some research, acknowledging the crimes of their group has a positive effect on the attitudes of perpetrator groups towards victims, as well as an increased skill to establish a contact (Čehajić-Clancy, Effron, Halperin, Liberman, & Ross, 2011). Although the acknowledgement of past crimes and responsibility-taking inhibits the in-group identification, such group developments are evident. Part of this process is about understanding the conditions that prompted the interconnection of systems of violence—structural, overt, interpersonal and personal, intimate. It is about uncovering the social dynamics that relegate certain groups to less human and fuel binary group relations, such as victim–perpetrator. Safe environments that encourage reflection support this development. They offer *healing narratives* to protect from political exploitation of trauma and support transformation of antagonistic positions.

A powerful tool in this process is 'pedagogy of remembrance' which arises from the basic need to understand the horrible consequences of wars and genocide and to develop a certain moral framework for 'never again' action-taking. In Germany, the churches have led the process of reconciliation by developing a post-war theology of repentance, while the Holocaust is an integrated part of the school curricula from elementary schools onwards. Also, orientation towards multiculturalism serves a new cultural identity thus creating a positive image in which solidarity and welcome culture towards, for example, Syrian refugees have been central in recent years.

At the same time, in the contemporary Bosnia and Herzegovina (BiH), struggles for a genuine public dialogue on the recent war-past supporting peacebuilding and reconciliation continue two decades after the traumatic events. In her recent empiric research on war memories connected to four highly traumatogenic events that occurred during the 1992–1995 siege of Sarajevo, Alma Jeftić (2019) found that post-war generation does not receive a coherent (or any) war narrative from their parents and are in many ways deprived of forming their own.

In the economically strained everyday reality, traumatising war memories in today's BiH are pushed aside, while communication among diverse social groups (especially ethnic) continues to be fuelled by fear and distrust due to the Dayton Peace Agreement, which in many ways institutionalised the war antagonisms. Likewise, the mono-ethnic school curricula directly hinder the opportunities of the new generation to meet and exchange positions. At the same time, the intruding presence of conflictual war narratives in the highly politicised media continues.

Chaitin and Steinberg (2014) argue that they do not find traumatogenic event memories to be purely transgenerationally transmitted by parents but rather an interpretation of a second generation's attempts to understand what happened. *Psychosocial research has further demonstrated that sharing of personal narratives has a potential to move binary positions closer to reconciliation when these narratives take place in 'safe spaces' that encourage active listening and open dialogue with reflection* (e.g. Albeck, Adwan, & Bar-On, 2002; Chaitin & Steinberg, 2014). The main aspect of such safe environments lies in the development of perspective-taking skills and empathy—both crucial for our ability to listen to the narratives of others and try understanding without judging and arguing.

Museums, connecting past with the present, oftentimes are safe environments. An example of the kind in BiH is the War Childhood Museum (WCM) in Sarajevo with collections of stories, objects and personal belongings of people whose childhood years were marked by 1990s' war, but also child realities from other war-torn countries, like Ukraine and Syria. Encounters in a safe space such as that of the WCM have proven to be positive in enabling the post-war generations both to meet with the narratives they never heard of before and expose themselves to different perspectives and opinions.

These encounters are crucial to systemic efforts in repairing broken intergroup relations and developing peacebuilding programmes ('remembrance for peace' being one of them). In this way, peace education has a potentila to support both educators and students to leave their *memory prisons* behind and become capable of perspective-taking and empathy through experiential learning beyond the classroom. Its role can be critical to societal undertakings towards transgenerational recovery from war-related social traumas.

26.5 Suggested Readings and Further Information

Branscombe, N. R., & Doosje, B. (Eds). (2004) *Collective guilt: International perspectives*. Cambridge: Cambridge University Press.

Browning, C. R. (1992). *Ordinary men: Reserve Police Battalion 101 and the final solution in Poland* (Vol. 1998). New York, NY: HarperCollins.

Halbwachs, M. (1980). *Collective memory.* New York, NY: Harper & Row.

Hamburger, A., Tutnjevic, S., Hancheva, C., Ozcurumez, S., Stankovic B. & Scher, C. (Eds.). (2018). *Migration and social trauma: Interdisciplinary perspectives.* London: Routledge.

Korostelina, K. V. (2007). *Social identity and conflict: Structures, dynamics and implications*. New York: Palgrave Macmillan.

László, J. (2013). *Historical tales and national identity: An introduction to narrative social psychology.* New York, NY: Routledge.

Tropp, L. (2012) (Ed.). *Oxford handbook of intergroup conflict*. New York, NY: Oxford University Press.

Volkan, V. (Ed.). (1997). *Bloodlines: From ethnic pride to ethnic terrorism.* New York, NY: Farrar, Strauss& Giroux.

References

Albeck, J. H., Adwan, S., & Bar-On, D. (2002). Dialogue groups: TRT's guidelines for working through intractable conflicts by personal storytelling in encounter groups. *Peace and Conflict Journal of Peace Psychology, 8*, 301–322.

Baines, E. (2009). Complex political perpetrators: Reflections on Dominic Ongwen. *The Journal of Modern African Studies, 47*(2), 163–191.

Bar-Tal, D., Chernyak-Hai, L., Schori, N., & Gundar, A. (2009). A sense of self-perceived collective victimhood in intractable conflicts. *International Review of Red Cross, 91*, 229–258.

Browning, C. R. (1992). *Ordinary men: reserve police Battalion 101 and the final solution in Poland* (Vol. 1998). New York: HarperCollins.

Bruner, J., & Amrami-Plotkin, G. (2015). Making up 'national trauma' in Israel: From collective identity to collective vulnerability. *Social Studies of Science, 45*(4), 525–545.

Castano, E., Yzerbyt, V., Paladino, M. P., & Sacchi, S. (2002). I belong, therefore, I exist ingroup identification, ingroup entitativity, and ingroup bias. *Personality and Social Psychology Bulletin, 28*, 135–143.

Čehajić-Clancy, S., Effron, D. A., Halperin, E., Liberman, V., & Ross, L. D. (2011). Affirmation, acknowledgement of in-group responsibility, group-based guilt, and support for reparative measures. *Journal of Personality and Social Psychology, 101*, 256–270.

Chaitin, J., & Steinberg, S. (2014). I can almost remember it now: Between personal and collective memories of massive social trauma. *Journal of Adult Development, 21*, 30–42.

Crownshaw, R. (2010). Reading the perpetrator: *Bernhard Schlink's* Der Vorleser (The Reader) *and* Die Heimkehr (Homecoming). In *The afterlife of holocaust memory in contemporary literature and culture* (pp. 145–181). London: Palgrave Macmillan.

Drumble, M. (2007). *Atrocity, punishment and international law*. Cambridge: Cambridge University Press.

Gausel, N., Leach, C. W., Vignoles, V. L., & Brown, R. (2012). Defend or repair? Explaining responses to in-group moral failure by disentangling feelings of shame, rejection, and inferiority. *Journal of Personality and Social Psychology, 102*, 941–960.

Hirscheberger, G. (2018). Collective trauma and the social construction of meaning. *Frontiers in Psychology, 9*, 1441.

Jeftić, A. (2019). *Social aspects of memory: Stories of victims and perpetrators from Bosnia-Herzegovina*. London: Routledge.

Jenkins, R. (2000). Categorisation: Identity, social process and epistemology. *Current Sociology, 48*(3), 7–25.

Korostelina, K. V. (2007). *Social identity and conflict: Structures, dynamics and implications*. New York: Palgrave Macmillan.

Kraft, R. N. (2014). *Uncovering the truth: Confronting perpetrators and victims in violent accounts: Understanding the psychology through South Africa's truth and reconciliation commission*. New York: New York University Press.

László, J. (2013). *Historical Tales and National Identity: An introduction to narrative social psychology*. New York, NY: Routledge.

Moscovici, S. (1988). Notes towards a description of social representations. *European Journal of Social Psychology, 18*, 211–250.

Oakes, P. J., & Turner, J. C. (1980). Social categorisation and intergroup behaviour: Does minimal intergroup discrimination make social identity more positive. *European Journal of Social Psychology, 10*, 295–301.

Porobić, S. (2012). *Resilience and religion in a forced migration context: A narrative study of religiousness as a resilience factor in dealing with refugee experiences from a post-migration perspective of Bosnian refugees in Sweden*. Lund University (Media-Tryck).

Porobić, S. (2018). How can refugees heal? Reflections on healing practices across the refugee process—From displacement to integration, return and beyond. In A. Hamburger, S. Tutnjević, C. Hancheva, S. Ozcurumez, B. Stanković, & C. Scher (Eds.), *Migration and social trauma: Interdisciplinary perspectives* (pp. 105–115). London: Routledge.

Rothbart, D., Korostelina, V., & K. (2007). *Identity, morality and threat*. New York: Lexington Books.

Staub, E. (2006). Reconciliation after the genocide, mass killing, or intractable conflict: Understanding the roots of violence, psychological recovery, and steps toward a general theory. *Political Psychology, 27*, 867–894.

Tajfel, H., & Turner, J. C. (1979). An integrative theory of intergroup conflict. In W. G. Austin & S. Worchel (Eds.), *The social psychology of intergroup relations* (pp. 33–47). Monterey, CA: Brooks/Cole.

Volkan, V. (1997). Chosen trauma: Unresolved mourning. In Blood Lines *From ethnic pride to ethnic terrorism* (pp. 36–49). New York, NY: Farrar, Strauss & Giroux.

Chapter 27
Secondary Traumatization

Marko Živanović and Maša Vukčević Marković

27.1 Introduction

Circumstances involving post-war and forced migration context put helping professionals at increased risk for secondary traumatization. There are several theoretical constructs trying to explain complex effects which can happen to persons working with traumatized individuals (Vukčević Marković & Živanović, 2019). One of the most frequently used, secondary traumatization (ST), refers to a condition that can result from being engaged in work that includes direct exposure to those suffering from Posttraumatic Stress Disorder (PTSD) and their traumatic experiences (Figley, 1995). Therefore, ST has been mainly explored among social workers, trauma counselors, psychologists, health workers, etc., that is, those being directly exposed to the traumatic content/s of others. ST is a condition that mimics PTSD-related difficulties whose effects are shown to be deleterious for the physical and mental health and well-being of service providers, directly or indirectly affecting their personal and professional life. Namely, accumulation of secondary exposure to traumatic content/s and its inadequate processing can leave a wider psychological impact leading to increasing of general depression- and anxiety-related symptomatology (Živanović & Vukčević Marković, submitted), and lower overall quality of life (Vukčević Marković & Živanović, 2019).

Due to conceptual similarities between ST and PTSD, predominant model of ST relies on DSM-based PTSD criteria and includes components of exposure to traumatic content as well as its symptomatology (Elwood, Mott, Lohr, & Galovski, 2011; Živanović & Vukčević Marković, 2009). The fifth edition of DSM (APA, 2013) included "experiencing repeated or extreme exposure to aversive details of

M. Živanović (✉) · M. V. Marković
Department of Psychology, University of Belgrade, Belgrade, Serbia

Psychosocial Innovation Network, University of Belgrade, Belgrade, Serbia
e-mail: marko.zivanovic@f.bg.ac.rs; masa.vukcevic@f.bg.ac.rs

© Springer Nature Switzerland AG 2021

A. Hamburger et al. (eds.), *Social Trauma – An Interdisciplinary Textbook*,
https://doi.org/10.1007/978-3-030-47817-9_27

the traumatic event(s) (e.g., first responders collecting human remains: police officers repeatedly exposed to details of child abuse)" in Criterion A stressors, thus qualifying secondary exposure to traumatic content as a traumatic event per se (APA, 2013; Živanović & Vukčević Marković, 2009). Secondary exposure to trauma represents sine qua non for ST; similarly, direct exposure to one or more traumatic events represents an essential diagnostic feature for PTSD (Criterion A). Symptoms of ST are to a great extent parallel to those found in PTSD but are far less pronounced.

The first important feature of ST is that traumatic events to which service providers were secondarily exposed to are re-experienced in various ways. These recollections can be present in the form of recurrent intrusive and involuntary memories, or unwilling realistic imaginary of the events that were communicated to service providers during their work with clients (e.g., "Sometimes I remember how one of my clients was attacked and almost beaten to death. Even though I was not present at that moment, it's like I can see the images of those guys beating him hard, and it usually takes a while before these thoughts and images disappear") or distressing dreams related to client's traumatic experiences ("I often have disturbing dreams with the fragments of terrifying stories I heard about from my clients"). In addition, these intrusions could be followed by dissociative states ("Sometimes, I get a feeling as if horrible things I learned from my clients are happening in the present just before my eyes, and I completely lose idea on where I am at the moment"), intense psychological distress ("When I remember some of the stories I heard about from my clients I feel overwhelmed with sadness and hopelessness"), or physiological reactivity ("When I remember some of the stories that I heard about my palms start to sweat and my heart starts to beat really fast") which is usually triggered by cues associated with the traumatic content.

The second cluster of symptoms summarizes intentional efforts to avoid stimuli associated with the particular traumatic event. Therefore, a person suffering from ST will tend to avoid memories, thoughts, and feelings associated with clients' traumatic experiences ("I was at some housewarming party and they decided to play a war movie. I just couldn't stand it, so I left the party and went home"), and try to avoid cues (e.g., people, situations, objects) which could facilitate recollection of distressful memories ("I skipped that meeting. I knew we are going to discuss what happened to one of my clients, and I just couldn't stand listening about it once again").

The third cluster of symptoms parallels with DSM-5 Criterion C for PTSD, namely negative alterations in cognitions or mood associated with exposure to the client's traumatic experience. The emergence of these disturbances coincides with the exposure to the traumatic content and they tend to worsen after that exposure. Negative alterations in cognitions could include inability to remember important aspects of traumatizing content ("Sometimes after the session I am not able to remember some of the details of tragic experiences my client spoke about. Like I am trying to forget it"), pervasive distorted views of oneself, others, or the world or pessimistic, depressive-like fatalistic views of the future ("This job just gave me a clear insight into how much this world is mean and unfair and how no one is safe"). Some individuals can consider themselves or their clients responsible for the cause or consequences of the traumatic experiences ("If we all tried better, all this human suffering could have been prevented"). Important aspect of ST is pervasive negative mood resembling prolonged depression-like emotional states which began after the exposure to the traumatizing content ("After seeing so many tragedies on a regular basis, I really feel that my job is meaningless and all my efforts are completely worthless"), usually followed by diminished interest in activities in which a person previously enjoyed in ("I've stopped doing things that used to make me happy, like playing basketball on weekends or organizing board games with my friends. Even the idea of it makes me uncomfortable. I would rather stay at home doing nothing"), feelings of detachment from other people ("I deeply feel that no one can really understand me anymore"), and deficits in capacities to experience positive emotions in comparison to the time before exposure to traumatic content/s ("I can see that my friends are trying to cheer me up, but I just stopped feeling anything, as if I am completely numb").

Finally, people being affected by ST may suffer from generalized alterations in arousal and reactivity, that is, hyperarousal-related disturbances such as impulsive or even aggressive acts, expressing angry outbursts ("A few days ago I almost hit a guy in public transport for standing too close to me"), reckless or self-destructive behavior ("I've been drinking a lot lately. It helps me get away from the horrors I hear about at my workplace. Friends keep telling me to ease it a bit, but I just can't help myself"). These alterations in reactivity are characterized by hypervigilance, that is, elevated sensitivity to potential threats, usually but not exclusively, associated with specific traumatic content ("Despite being a female I was never afraid to walk home late at night, but lately I started carrying pepper spray. I live in a good neighborhood and all, but I am just not feeling safe anymore"). In addition, individuals suffering from ST can be over-reactive to unexpected stimuli, demonstrating exaggerated startle response or pronounced jumpiness ("I feel so tense. A few days ago, my boyfriend tried to hug me unexpectedly from behind. In that split second, I got so scared that I started to scream. He was terrified and so was I"), and can have trouble focusing their attention for a prolonged period of time ("I can't listen to anyone speaking longer than a few minutes anymore, I just can't focus"). Finally, due to generally elevated arousal, sleep difficulties such as troubles in falling or staying asleep may occur, as well as disturbing dreams related to the traumatic content which was communicated to them ("I feel as if I am on some kind of guard all the time, so I never really have a deep sleep or sleep well at all").

Different empirically based concurrent theoretical models of ST were proposed in the last few years. These models differ in terms of the number and content of latent dimensions underlying the concept of ST and heavily rely on the most prominent conceptualizations of PTSD.

The model of ST which primarily relied on DSM-4 (APA, 2000) nomenclature suggested that ST is comprised of three interrelated dimensions: Intrusions, Avoidance, and Hyperarousal. However, changes introduced in DSM-5 suggested that the four-factor model could potentially be a more suitable conceptualization of both PTSD as well as ST (APA, 2013). This model besides the aforementioned dimensions included additional symptom cluster—Negative alterations in cognitions and mood (NACM) which was derived from distinctions between some of the Avoidance indicators. Another four-factor model of ST (so-called Dysphoria model), besides Avoidance, Intrusions, and Hyperarousal suggested the dimension of Dysphoria comprising of general psychological distress which underlies NACM-related symptoms as well as some aspects of Hyperarousal (Simms, Watson, & Doebbeling, 2002).

Dysphoric Arousal model (Elhai et al., 2011) provided even more complex conceptualization of ST including five dimensions underlying symptomatology of ST – Intrusion, Avoidance, and NACM, separating the DSM-4's Arousal cluster into two factors – Anxious Arousal and Dysphoric Arousal. On the other hand, a six-factor Anhedonia model (Armour et al., 2015) suggested differentiation within NACM factor into Negative affect and Anhedonia, while within a six-factor model of Externalizing Behaviors (Tsai et al., 2015), reconceptualization of Dysphoric arousal symptoms was suggested, adding aggressive and self-destructive behaviors into a separate factor. Finally, the most complex model of both PTSD and ST found in the literature is a seven-factor model which includes all aforementioned symptom clusters, namely Intrusions, Avoidance, Anxious arousal, Dysphoric arousal, Negative affect, Anhedonia, and Externalizing behaviors (Armour et al., 2015).

However, some studies (Živanović & Vukčević Marković, 2009) have not found empirical justifications for the separation within Hyperarousal and NACM factors, providing no support for more complex models of ST. Furthermore, some empirical evidence pointed to the very high correlation between NACM/Dysphoria and Hyperarousal factors indicating that these two dimensions, in contrast to PTSD models, could potentially be empirically inseparable, making a single dimension underlying very broad manifestations of both negative alterations in cognitions and mood as well as those in reactivity and arousal (Živanović & Vukčević Marković, 2009).

Bearing in mind that empirical findings published to date provided no support for the unidimensional nature of ST, the fact that each study identified at least three dimensions of this syndrome, and the potential lack of differentiation between some of its factors, it seems probable that the finite number of latent dimensions of ST is limited to three or four interrelated groups of symptoms, which, beyond any doubt, include manifestations of Intrusions, Avoidance, and NACM/Dysphoria, while Hyperarousal symptoms comparable to those found in PTSD and separable from other ST-related disturbances, have yet to be demonstrated.

27.2 Learning Outcome for Social Trauma

When discussing ST in the wider context, especially in the post-war and forced migration circumstances, it should not be overseen that its causes are deeply rooted in social trauma, as well as complex and two-way relations between social trauma and ST. Namely, social trauma is often the main reason for forced migration

(Hamburger et al., 2019). People forcibly leaving their homes are exposed to numerous human rights violations and traumatic experiences including torture, violent death of loved ones, beatings, etc. in their countries of origin (Vukčević, Momirović, & Purić, 2016) and during transit (Purić & Vukčević Marković, 2019), out of which vast majority was made by humans, additionally putting social trauma in the core of their experiences.

Painful and terrifying experiences involving the suffering of individuals and communities create and influence not only narratives of perpetrators and victims who were involved in these traumatic experiences (Hamburger, 2017), but also narratives shared between helpers and the ones in need for help. This is how social trauma is being transmitted to a whole new layer within the social matrix, including not only victims and perpetrators, but also helpers as indirect witnesses. Thus, multiplying effects social trauma can have on individual and community level can go far beyond what could be expected at first. The role of social trauma should, therefore, be carefully considered when trying to understand and address ST, especially in the post-war and forced migration circumstances.

27.3 Preferred Model of Explanation: Social Trauma in the Context of Secondary Traumatization

It has been shown that ST is influenced by both individual and societal factors. Namely, since ST refers to a disorder experienced by a person who is trying to help vulnerable others (Figley, 1995), certain personality traits which could be expected to predispose and shape someone's readiness to get involved in the helping professions such as those related to altruism have shown to be related to more severe ST symptomatology and compassion fatigue (Mahony et al., 2018). Additionally, individual risk factors that are shown to be related to ST include age (Nelson-Gardell & Harris, 2003), female gender (Sprang, Clark, & Whitt-Woosley, 2007), and maladaptive avoidant coping strategies such as denial, substance use, and mental, and behavioral disengagement (Vukčević Marković & Živanović, 2019).

Moreover, susceptibility toward ST is related to specific features of individual and social trauma, including one's own personal history of trauma (Hensel, Ruiz, Finney, & Dewa, 2015), and type and amount of trauma one was were secondarily exposed to (Hensel et al., 2015). In addition, some authors raised the question to which extent one's desire to help is rooted in traumas related to historical experiences (Hamburger et al., 2019). It is suggested that experiences related to social trauma and how well its potential effects were understood and addressed will have an important role in both triggering optimistic compassion as well as fearful avoidance when facing vulnerable others (Hamburger et al., 2019), which later on can have an impact on one's susceptibility toward ST-related difficulties.

27.4 Practical Implications in the Field of Social Trauma

Therefore, it is important to consider ST in the wider context and try to understand numerous links and interrelation between social trauma and ST. In addition to enabling a better understanding of ST, exploration of its interrelation with social trauma should be part of interventions focused on preventing and addressing ST among helping professionals. Only by acknowledging how strongly causes and consequences of ST are related to social trauma, in particular in post-war and forced migration circumstances, it is possible to understand complex and multilayer effects ST can have on the personal and professional life of service providers. Therefore, in order to understand, prevent, and reduce ST among people working with traumatized individuals, it is required to raise a question on individual and societal vulnerabilities, and address various forms of individual and social trauma experienced by both traumatized individuals and the ones trying to help.

27.5 Suggested Reading and Further Information

Vukčević Marković, M., & Živanović, M. (2019). Secondary traumatization in service providers working with refugees. In A. Hamburger, C. Hancheva, S. Ozcurumez, C. Scher, B. Stanković, & S. Tutnjević (Eds.), *Forced migration and social trauma* (pp. 237–248). London: Routledge.

Živanović, M., & Vukčević Marković, M. (2009). Latent structure of secondary traumatic stress, its precursors, and effects on people working with refugees. *Journal of Traumatic Stress* 22(2):153–157.

References

American Psychiatric Association. (2000). *Diagnostic and statistical manual of mental disorders* (4th ed.). Washington, DC: American Psychiatric Association.

American Psychiatric Association. (2013). *Diagnostic and statistical manual of mental disorders* (5th ed.). Arlington, VA: American Psychiatric Association.

Armour, C., Tsai, J., Durham, T. A., Charak, R., Biehn, T. L., Elhai, J. D., & Pietrzak, R. H. (2015). Dimensional structure of DSM-5 posttraumatic stress symptoms: Support for a hybrid anhedonia and externalizing behaviors model. *Journal of Psychiatric Research, 61*, 106–113. https://doi.org/10.1016/j.jpsychires.2014.10.012

Elhai, J. D., Biehn, T. L., Armour, C., Klopper, J. J., Frueh, B. C., & Palmieri, P. A. (2011). Evidence for a unique PTSD construct represented by PTSD's D1–D3 symptoms. *Journal of Anxiety Disorders, 25*(3), 340–345. https://doi.org/10.1016/j.janxdis.2010.10.007

Elwood, L. S., Mott, J., Lohr, J. M., & Galovski, T. E. (2011). Secondary trauma symptoms in clinicians: A critical review of the construct, specificity, and implications for trauma-focused treatment. *Clinical Psychology Review, 31*(1), 25–36. https://doi.org/10.1016/j.cpr.2010.09.004

Figley, C. R. (1995). *Compassion fatigue: Coping with secondary traumatic stress disorder in those who treat the traumatized.* New York, NY: Routledge.

Hamburger, A. (2017). Genocidal trauma. Individual and social consequences of the assault on the mental and physical life of a group. In D. Laub & A. Hamburger (Eds.), *Psychoanalysis and holocaust testimony: Unwanted memories of social trauma* (pp. 66–91). London: Routledge.

Hamburger, A., Hancheva, C., Ozcurumez, S., Scher, C., Stanković, B., & Tutnjević, S. (2019). Dreams to nightmares—Welcoming culture, xenophobia and social trauma along the Balkan route. In A. Hamburger, C. Hancheva, S. Ozcurumez, C. Scher, B. Stanković, & S. Tutnjević (Eds.), *Forced migration and social trauma* (pp. 1–3). London: Routledge.

Hensel, J. M., Ruiz, C., Finney, C., & Dewa, C. S. (2015). Meta-analysis of risk factors for secondary traumatic stress in therapeutic work with trauma victims. *Journal of Traumatic Stress, 28*, 83–91. https://doi.org/10.1002/jts.21998

Mahony, S. O., Ziadni, M., Hoerger, M., Levine, S., Baron, A., & Gerhart, J. (2018). Compassion fatigue among palliative care clinicians: Findings on personality factors and years of service. *Am J Hosp Palliat Care, 35*(2), 343–347. https://doi.org/10.1177/1049909117701695

Nelson-Gardell, D., & Harris, D. (2003). Childhood abuse history, secondary traumatic stress, and child welfare workers. *Child Welfare, 82*(1), 5–26.

Purić, D., & Vukčević Marković, M. (2019). Development and validation of the stressful experiences in transit questionnaire (SET-Q) and its short form (SET-SF). *European Journal of Psychotraumatology, 10*(1), 1–11. https://doi.org/10.1080/20008198.2019.1611091

Simms, L. J., Watson, D., & Doebbeling, B. N. (2002). Confirmatory factor analyses of posttraumatic stress symptoms in deployed and nondeployed veterans of the Gulf war. *Journal of Abnormal Psychology, 111*, 637–647. https://doi.org/10.1037//0021-843x.111.4.637

Sprang, G., Clark, J. J., & Whitt-Woosley, A. (2007). Compassion fatigue, compassion satisfaction, and burnout: Factors impacting a professional's quality of life. *Journal of Loss and Trauma, 12*(3), 259–280. https://doi.org/10.1080/15325020701238093

Tsai, J., Harpaz-Rotem, I., Armour, C., Southwick, S. M., Krystal, J. H., & Pietrzak, R. H. (2015). Dimensional structure of DSM-5 posttraumatic stress symptoms: Results from the National Health and resilience in veterans study. *Journal of Clinical Psychiatry, 76*(5), 546–553. https://doi.org/10.4088/JCP.14m09091

Vukčević, M., Momirović, J., & Purić, D. (2016). Adaptation of Harvard trauma questionnaire for working with refugees and asylum seekers in Serbia. *Psihologija, 49*(3), 277–299. https://doi.org/10.2298/PSI1603277V

Vukčević Marković, M., & Živanović, M. (2019). Secondary traumatization in service providers working with refugees. In A. Hamburger, C. Hancheva, S. Ozcurumez, C. Scher, B. Stanković, & S. Tutnjević (Eds.), *Forced migration and social trauma* (pp. 237–248). London: Routledge.

Živanović, M., & Vukčević Marković, M. (2009). Latent structure of secondary traumatic stress, its precursors, and effects on people working with refugees. *Journal of Traumatic Stress, 22*(2), 153–157.

Part VI
Legal and Ethical Aspects

Chapter 28
Legal and Ethical Aspects of Social Trauma

Saime Ozcurumez

28.1 Introduction

The salience of understanding the impact of social trauma in public life is ever clearer with increasing protracted conflicts, poverty, inequality, and violence around the world. Accordingly, social trauma is an agenda item and a subject for policy-makers in the last few decades. However, designing, adopting, implementing, and assessing the impact of policies for prevention of social trauma and protection of survivors require concerted action among many public policy actors. In order to facilitate coordination for interventions and preventive strategies, policy-makers initiate the policy cycle by defining a challenge that requires immediate attention. The conceptualization of social trauma as a policy challenge constitutes the first step for involving trauma in the policy process. Social trauma, however, is a complex concept which needs to be broken down to its constituent parts to be part of policy implementation. An accessible definition of social trauma focuses on the issue as a process which "occurs as a result of violence, abuse, neglect, loss, disaster, war and other emotionally harmful experiences" (Substance Abuse and Mental Health Services Administration (SAMSHA), 2014, p. 2) and is embedded in the consequences of traumatic events in a community or a social group that an individual identifies with. Moreover, trauma constitutes the "experiences that produce intense emotional pain, fear, or distress, often resulting in long-term physiological and psychosocial consequences" (Bowen & Murshid, 2016, p. 223), and *needs to be contextualized in social and cross-cultural settings* (Good & Hinton, 2016). The Diagnostic and Statistical Manual of Mental Disorders (DSM-5) classifies traumatic events (TE) as "exposure to threatened death, serious injury or sexual violence" (Benjet et al., 2016). Individuals and/or groups may be exposed to TE directly or indirectly (APA, 2013). Accordingly, social trauma as a policy challenge involves

S. Ozcurumez (✉)
Department of Political Science and Public Administration, Bilkent University,
Ankara, Turkey

© Springer Nature Switzerland AG 2021

A. Hamburger et al. (eds.), *Social Trauma – An Interdisciplinary Textbook*,
https://doi.org/10.1007/978-3-030-47817-9_28

psychological, emotional, physiological, and sociological dimensions. As the consequences of social trauma transmit across generations of a social group, the transgenerational dimension also becomes an issue requiring healing interventions across time. In the public policy realm, the multifaceted nature of social trauma comes with the challenge of how to begin addressing the diverse consequences of social trauma, for whom, with which policy tools, and by mobilizing which institutional, financial, and human resources. Second, the multitude of policy actors, constituting policy-makers, decision-makers, and implementors, need to cooperate in the design, adoption, and implementation stages across global, national, and local levels. Coordination for any policy including those addressing social trauma-related challenges among different actors and levels is embedded in legal regulations. This chapter presents how and why social trauma becomes part of public policy through legal and ethical aspects of social trauma by examining the case of forced migration.

28.1.1 Public Policy and Social Trauma Nexus in Forced Migration

The United Nations High Commissioner for Refugees (UNHCR) reports that there are 70.8 million forcibly displaced people in the world (UNHCR, 2019a). While 31% of these forcibly displaced people had experienced violence or/torture (UNHCR, 2019b), the question of how to develop and implement a social trauma-informed public policy in forced migration, especially in the form of mass influx, remains unanswered.

The first challenge is how to respond to whom in the context of international protection by addressing the needs arising from social trauma. Countries address the needs of asylum seekers, refugees, and those who arrive in mass forced migration in varying ways. Asylum seekers are persons who apply for recognition as a refugee under the 1951 Refugee Convention. Asylum seekers mostly live in poverty and isolation while waiting for their applications to be processed with mostly no rights to work (Walsh, 2019). Refugees, however, are able to access the health-care system and social protection schemes almost on equal terms to citizens of the country. Forcibly displaced persons who arrive as part of a mass influx seeking refuge usually remain in temporary protection and in temporary accommodation centers for indefinite periods of time. In most cases, countries address the basic needs of the forcibly displaced who arrive *en masse* with protection programs, humanitarian assistance, and emergency management policies. Consequently, the responsibilities of public policy-makers differ while they attempt to provide social trauma-informed care to the forcibly displaced.

The second challenge for legal and ethical aspects of social trauma is how to proceed with the design of policies that combine refugee protection, protracted displacement path, and (re)settlement/integration/cohesion. The prominent humanitarian protection principles constitute avoiding inflicting more physical and psychological harm to people than they already had experienced. In order to accomplish this task, they aim to ensure access to humanitarian assistance, to assist with rights claims, and to have access to remedies (https://spherestandards.org/humanitarian-standards/). In the protracted displacement path in which the forced displacement may take years, the public policy objective shifts from the initial emergency and disaster management phase toward identifying "durable solutions." When it comes to the (re)settlement/integration/cohesion phase, the policy objective is to assist refugees to be able to become self-reliant and participate in the social, economic, and civic life of the receiving countries.

The third challenge concerns the implementation of policies by accounting for legal and ethical aspects of social trauma. The priorities in this area include facilitating conditions for community mobilization, ownership of policies by the local communities as well, control of emergency response in all sectors; community self-help and social support; conditions for appropriate communal cultural, spiritual, and religious healing practices; and support for young children (0–8 years) and their caregivers (UNHCR, 2013, p. 26). Moreover, international organizations highlight the significance of assessing relevant contextual information, the experience of people within the emergency, and their Mental Health & Psychosocial Support (MHPSS) needs while designing and implementing policies that target these populations. Including contextual information to provide trauma-informed care requires awareness of culture-specific beliefs and practices, practices around death and mourning, attitudes toward severe mental disorders, and specific needs of at-risk groups. As such, policy-makers, health-care practitioners, and all service providers working in social trauma need to advance their knowledge of culture-specific expressions of distress, priority mental health-related problems, and the consequences of social trauma for the impairment of daily activities. The existing sources of psychosocial wellbeing and mental health are designed through the implementation of methods for developing coping mechanisms and developing community sources of support and resources (IASC, 2010).

28.2 Learning Outcome Related to Social Trauma

In this chapter, the learning outcome related to social trauma is that the students will acquire knowledge about how policy design and legal framework in different countries work through incorporating the variety of effects of social trauma as well as its consequences.

28.3 Preferred Model of Explanation

As the American Psychiatric Association notes, "an experience could be defined as traumatic if it involves a threat to one's physical or emotional well-being, if it leaves people feeling overwhelmed or helpless, and if it changes the way people understand themselves, the World and the others" (Clervil, Guarino, DeCandia, & Beach, 2013, p. 11). Traumatic experiences in migration contexts are divided into three phases as premigration, during migration, and postmigration trauma experience. A person may experience trauma before migrating from her/his country as a result of war, political instability, or being confronted with violence. A person would experience trauma during the migration process in which s/he would feel that s/he lost her/his home, family, and friends. The uncertainty about what awaits the person in the future may also constitute a reason for experiencing trauma. As the person aims to become part of the society s/he arrives in, another traumatic experience may present itself. Several different types and layers of exclusion which may emanate from language barriers, difficulties in finding employment, or integrating into the education ecosystem may constitute complex sources of social trauma.

Service providers in the receiving communities play a critical role in helping people with traumatic experiences to heal and gradually become part of the receiving societies, and "trauma informed care" is viewed as one approach to overcome the complex legal and ethical challenges while providing services to persons with traumatic experiences. As Bowen and Murshid (2016) define "a trauma-informed care approach recognizes the intersection of trauma with many health and social problems for which people seek services and treatment, aiming to sensitively address trauma along with an individual's issues" (p. 223). The "Trauma informed care" approach also aims to account for the "physical, psychological, and emotional safety for both providers and survivors" while emphasizing programs that will help "survivors to rebuild a sense of control and empowerment" (Clervil et al., 2013, p. 18).

Principles of "trauma informed care" constitute "safety, trustworthiness and transparency, collaboration, empowerment, choices and options, and intersectionality" (US Substance Abuse and Mental Health Service Administration). The key principle is to construct a safe environment to prevent retraumatization. The policies are expected to ensure transparency in policies as well as procedures among service providers, the beneficiaries, and the community members to contribute to collaborative efforts anchored in trust and sustainability. Service providers implement programs that view persons with traumatic experiences as active participants in identifying their own challenges, contributing to their own healing paths and their own empowerment. Through such practices, service providers aim to identify better treatment outcomes while also incorporating specific needs emanating from different identity characteristics of beneficiaries including race, gender, and sexual orientation, as well as impacts of multiple sources of socioeconomic vulnerabilities on these individuals.

This section reviewed "trauma informed care" as a model that may inform design and implementation of social policies and health-care systems. Trauma-informed responses are expected to facilitate "participatory, transparent and collaborative" policy processes, and also alleviate overall health and well-being challenges by contributing to "the safety and empowerment of target groups" (Bowen & Murshid, 2016, p. 228). Recognition of trauma experience as part of the migration processes advances understanding of the sources of difficulties in social integration experienced by forcibly displaced people and the complex contexts within which social policy implementation takes place. Accordingly, trauma-informed interventions provided for all vulnerable populations including forcibly displaced people would facilitate social cohesion processes by promoting integrated and comprehensive approaches to social cohesion.

28.4 Practical Implications in the Field of Social Trauma

This section will present three areas to present the implementation of legal and ethical aspects of social trauma with a "trauma informed care" approach: forced migration, health-care systems, and education. Forcibly displaced people suffer from traumatic experiences as they flee conflict and war in their countries of origin and remain at risk during their journey as well as during settlement. Trauma Systems Therapy for Refugees (TST-R) is one example of practices aiming to incorporate a "trauma informed care" system for refugee youth. The TST-R aims to promote "community and parent engagement," include preventative interventions such as "increasing self-regulation skills, decreasing acculturative stress and increasing social support" and receive "community-based, linguistically and culturally sensitive care" (NCTSN, 2016), which aim to address the mental health needs of refugee youth in a comprehensive manner and over time.

The health-care ecosystem also is a field for which the legal and ethical aspects of social trauma have significant implications. Having a trauma-informed lens in health-care policies is likely to have long-term consequences on who would be part of the health policy goals and how so (Hankivsky et al., 2014). In the Constitution of the World Health Organization (WHO), health is defined as "a state of complete physical, mental, and social well-being and not merely the absence of disease or infirmity." Moreover, for WHO, "the enjoyment of the highest attainable standard of health is one of the fundamental rights of every human being without distinction of race, religion, political belief, economic or social condition" (WHO, 2017, Constitution section). In the context of Canada, "trauma and violence informed care" (TVIC) has become a major part of the public health agenda. There are increasing efforts to integrate this approach into policy practices across all provinces with formal initiatives such as developing tool kits for "addressing and preventing community trauma" and resources to inform service providers of different practices for a variety of fields in mental health services and homelessness among others. All the different practices aim to design and implement interventions to account for individual and community level causes (poverty, substance use and addiction, and mental health) as well as consequences (physical, psychological, emotional, and economic) of social trauma. Innovative approaches to expand knowledge on "trauma informed care" have also been noted as the use of digital technologies to address the negative effects of trauma on different groups such as those who have been subject to sexual assault and domestic family violence (https://www.1800respect.org.au/) and on-line training sessions on "trauma informed interviewing techniques" for professionals (https://digitalmedic.stanford.edu/our-work/trauma/).

Constructing and maintaining a "trauma-sensitive school environment" (Cole et al., 2005) has significant implications for overcoming the educational impacts of social trauma. In order to advance learning and promote physical and emotional health and well-being of traumatized children, many initiatives are promoted such as the "Trauma and Learning Policy Initiative" and training packages for understanding the context as well as the impact of trauma, which focus on engaging teachers, parents, and school administrators in fostering. Understanding of the complexity of determinants of an individual's well-being keeps expanding. Accordingly, prevention of and responding to social trauma with comprehensive policies have been identified as central in promoting the health and well-being of all societies.

This chapter highlighted how the legal and ethical aspects of social trauma manifest themselves in different policy areas and why. In the coming years, "trauma sensitive care" and "trauma sensitive policies" shall characterize the discussions on legal and ethical aspects of social trauma globally, nationally, and locally.

28.5 Suggested Reading and Further Information

Ardino, V. (2014). Trauma-informed care: Is cultural competence a viable solution for efficient policy strategies? *Clinical Neuropsychiatry, 11*(1), 45–51.

Butler, L. D., Critelli, F. M., & Rinfrette, E. S. (2011). Trauma-informed care and mental health. *Directions in Psychiatry, 31*, 197–210.

Fallot, R. D., & Harris, M. (2009). Creating Cultures of Trauma-Informed Care (CCTIC): A self-assessment and planning protocol. Peoria, IL: Community Connections.

Schulman, M., & Menschner, C. (2018). *Laying the groundwork for trauma-informed care*. Retrieved from https://www.chcs.org/media/Laying-the-Groundwork-for-TIC_012418.pdf

Wylie, L., Van Meyel, R., Harder, H., Sukhera, J., Luc, C., Ganjavi, H., … Wardrop, N. (2018). Assessing trauma in a transcultural context: Challenges in mental health care with immigrants and refugees. *Public Health Review, 39*, 22.

https://mentalhealthactionplan.ca/

http://invitingresillience.ca

https://www.canada.ca/en/public-health/services/publications/health-risks-safety/trauma-violence-informed-approaches-policy-practice.html

https://spherestandards.org/humanitarian-standards/.

https://www.justice.gc.ca/eng/rp-pr/cj-jp/victim/rd9-rr9/p2.html

safesupportivelearning.ed.gov
http://traumasensitiveschools.org
https://www.nctsn.org/resources/culture-the-migration-journey-trauma-and-assessment
https://www.nctsn.org/resources/exploring-policy-challenges-solutions-and-resources-addressing-trauma-among-refugee-youth

References

American Psychiatric Association (APA). (2013). *Diagnostic and statistical manual of mental disorders: DSM-5™* (5th ed.). Arlington, VA: American Psychiatric Publishing.

Benjet, C., Bromet, E., Karam, E. G., Kessler, R. C., Mclaughlin, K. A., Ruscio, A. M., ... Koenen, K. C. (2016). The epidemiology of traumatic event exposure worldwide: Results from the world Mental Health survey consortium. *Psychological Medicine, 46*(2), 327–343.

Bowen, E. A., & Murshid, N. S. (2016). Trauma-informed social policy: A conceptual framework for policy analysis and advocacy. *AJPH Perspectives, 106*(2), 223–229.

Clervil, R., Guarino, K., DeCandia, C. J., & Beach, C. A. (2013). *Trauma-informed care for displaced populations: A guide for community-based service providers*. Waltham, MA: The National Center on Family Homelessness, a practice area of American Institutes for Research Health and Social Development Program.

Cole, S. F., O'Brien, J. G., Gadd, M. G., Ristuccia, J., Wallace, D. L., & Gregory, M. (2005). *Helping traumatized children learn: Supportive school environments for children traumatized by family violence*. Massachusetts: Massachusetts Advocates for Children.

Good, B., & Hinton, D. E. (2016). Introduction. Culture, trauma, and PTSD. In D. E. Hinton & B. Good (Eds.), *Culture and PTSD: Trauma in global and historical perspective* (pp. 3–49). Philadelphia: University of Pennsylvania Press.

Hankivsky, O., Grace, D., Hunting, G., Giesbrecht, M., Fridkin, A., Rudrum, S., ... Clark, N. (2014). An Intersectionality-based policy analysis framework: Critical reflections on a methodology for advancing equity. *International Journal for Equity in Health, 13*, 119–135.

IASC Reference Group for Mental Health and Psychosocial Support in Emergency Settings. (2010). *Mental Health and psychosocial support in humanitarian emergencies: What should humanitarian Health actors know?* Geneva, Switzerland: IASC.

Substance Abuse and Mental Health Services Administration (SAMSHA). (2014). *SAMHSA's concept of trauma and guidance for a trauma-informed approach*. HHS Publication No. (SMA) 14–4884. Rockville, MD: Substance Abuse and Mental Health Services Administration.

The National Child Traumatic Stress Network (NCTSN). (2016). *TST-R: Trauma systems therapy for refugees*. Retrieved from https://www.nctsn.org/sites/default/files/interventions/tstr_fact_sheet.pdf

UN High Commissioner for Refugees (UNHCR). (June, 2013). *UNHCR's mental health and psychosocial support: For persons of concern*. Retrieved from https://www.unhcr.org/research/evalreports/51bec3359/unhcrs-mental-health-psychosocial-support-persons-concern.html

UN High Commissioner for Refugees (UNHCR). (2019a). *Figures at a glance*. Retrieved November 7, 2019, from http://www.unhcr.org/figures-at-a-glance.html

UN High Commissioner for Refugees (UNHCR). (2019b). *Resettlement data*. Retrieved November 7, 2019, from http://www.unhcr.org/resettlement-data.html

Walsh, P. W. (2019). *Migration to the UK: Asylum and resettled refugees*. Oxford, UK: The Migration Observatory of the University of Oxford. Retrieved from https://migrationobservatory.ox.ac.uk/wp-content/uploads/2019/11/Briefing-Migration-to-the-UK-Asylum-and-Resettled-Refugees.pdf

World Health Organization (WHO). (2017). *Health is a fundamental human right*. Retrieved from https://www.who.int/mediacentre/news/statements/fundamental-human-right/en/

Chapter 29
Sexual and Gender-Based Violence and Social Trauma

Saime Ozcurumez

29.1 Introduction

Gender-based violence (GBV) intersects with multiple vulnerabilities including gender inequality and poverty, and is closely linked with social trauma. The risk of GBV and sexual gender-based violence (SGBV) increases in armed conflict, humanitarian crisis, and displacement. Combatting against GBV including sexual violence has been identified as a global challenge with international agencies alerting to the gravity of the situation noting "more than one third of women and girls globally will experience some form of violence in their lifetime" and that this experience has adverse overall health, education, and livelihood effects on the survivors (United Nations Office for Coordination of Humanitarian Affairs [UNOCHA], 2020, p. 15). Men and boys are also targeted by this brutality. The Rome Statute of International Criminal Court identifies SGBV among the "crimes against humanity" (Article 7 (g)) and refers to GBV as a specific theme for the processes of investigation, prosecution, as well as the protection of victims and witnesses (International Criminal Court, 2011).

In the 1993 Declaration, violence against women is defined as:

> any act of gender-based violence that results in, or is likely to result in, physical, sexual or psychological harm or suffering to women, including threats of such acts, coercion or arbitrary deprivation of liberty, whether occurring in public or in private life (UN, 1993).

In 2011, the Istanbul Convention highlights "violence against women" as:

> …a violation of human rights and a form of discrimination against women and shall mean all acts of gender-based violence that result in, or are likely to result in, physical, sexual, psychological or economic harm or suffering to women, including threats of such acts, coercion or arbitrary deprivation of liberty, whether occurring in public or in private life;…

S. Ozcurumez (✉)
Department of Political Science and Public Administration, Bilkent University, Ankara, Turkey

© Springer Nature Switzerland AG 2021

A. Hamburger et al. (eds.), *Social Trauma – An Interdisciplinary Textbook*,
https://doi.org/10.1007/978-3-030-47817-9_29

> "gender" shall mean the socially constructed roles, behaviours, activities and attributes that a given society considers appropriate for women and men;... gender-based violence against women" shall mean violence that is directed against a woman because she is a woman or that affects women disproportionately... (Article 3, a, c, d). (Council of Europe, 2011)

Gendered dimensions of violence also cover violence toward men, boys, as well as the LGBTI people (Inter-Agency Standing Committee, 2015).

GBV emphasizes gendered components of violence including but not limited to domestic violence, economic violence, human trafficking, forced marriages, genital mutilation, and sexual violence (Simon-Butler & McSherry, 2019). Studies document the prevalence of GBV in armed conflict across many contexts (Mootz, Stabb & Mollen, 2017; Wirtz et al., 2014). In settings of conflict and displacement, GBV constitutes a range of violent acts such as threats of harm to family members, rape, trafficking, abduction, and reproductive control perpetrated by "unknown individuals" alongside family members and intimate partners (Wirtz et al., 2014). Sexual violence is documented as a seriously humiliating part of armed conflicts, gaining more visibility with the conflicts of Rwanda and the former Yugoslavia, and is identified as a war crime. The GBV experience is the cause of posttraumatic stress (Gupta et al., 2014) causing mental and physical ailments such as recurrent nightmares, concentration difficulties, anger, physical pain, suicidal thoughts (Emusu et al., 2009; Liebling & Kiziri-Mayengo, 2002), and acute and chronic health problems ranging from sexually transmitted infections to gastrointestinal problems (World Health Organization, 2013). The mental, physical, and social consequences of the SGBV experience result in life-long suffering for the survivors and adverse mental and physical consequences for their children (Kerker et al., 2015; Robertson et al., 2006).

In an armed conflict and displacement, sexual violence is identified as requiring recognition for specific measures to be implemented for prevention and response. The United Nations puts further emphasis on sexual violence by defining sexual exploitation as "any actual or attempted abuse of a position of vulnerability, differential power, or trust, for sexual purposes, including, but not limited to, profiting, monetarily, socially or politically from the sexual exploitation of another" (UN Secretary General, 2003) and sexual abuse as "the actual or threatened physical intrusion of a sexual nature, whether by force or under unequal or coercive conditions." Moreover, "gender" is defined through both biological and social aspects of the construction of gender identity, and SGBV covers "an act that is perpetrated against a person's will and is based on gender norms and unequal power relationships; and also a violation of human rights since it denies the human dignity and hurts human development" (UNHCR, 2003). In contexts of forced migration, scholars refer to the need to adopt a gendered lens for both studying and responding to SGBV to include complex individual and collective experiences of different groups across the journey from displacement to settlement (Ozcurumez, Akyuz, & Bradby, 2020).

29.2 Learning Outcome Related to Social Trauma

In this chapter, the learning outcome related to social trauma is that the students will expand their understanding of GBV in armed conflict and displacement contexts and how the challenges posed by GBV in forced migration are addressed by different local, national, and international actors. The broader conceptualization of GBV since the late 1990s has had a major consequence for studying the nexus of GBV and social trauma: Scholars, policy-makers, and service providers approach SGBV by aiming to understand its multiple causes and design responses that target the multiplicity of vulnerabilities and inequalities that cause SGBV. Accordingly, first, scholars began to study SGBV within the debates on power relations, socio-economic inequalities, cultural attitudes, and discrimination. Second, scholars and policy-makers aim to address physical and psychosocial impact of SGBV in a comprehensive manner. Third, policy-makers recognize the value of expanding the scope of efforts for responding to, prevention of, and protection from SGBV alongside social trauma in settings of conflict, displacement, and beyond.

29.3 Preferred Model of Explanation

The socio-ecological approach (Heise, 1998) explains SGBV in armed conflict and displacement, and provides links to social trauma by bringing together structural, individual, family, and community-related processes (Bronfenbrenner, 1977). Different factors from individual, family, and community levels contribute to increased SGBV: silence of women and alcohol consumption of intimate partners (Keygnaert, Vettenburg, & Temmerman, 2012), lack of social support and male unemployment (Laisser, Nystrom, Lugina, & Emmelin, 2011), and stigmatization by the community. Studies also note that structural factors such as lack of effective policies on gender equality, poverty, and patriarchal societies lead to SGBV (Heise & Kotsadam, 2015). The social constructivist approach supported by the feminist discourse highlights the role of expression of masculinities through aggression and militarization in armed conflict settings (Patton, 2014). The socio-ecological approach also points out the diversity of forms that violence may take in a variety of settings (Grych & Swan, 2012).

The socio-ecological model can be used to explain the evolution of refugee status and recognition of SGBV in the international protection context. In the earlier implementation of the 1951 Convention, women were regarded as spouses of men refugees (Simon-Butler & McSherry, 2019) while recently more sensitive assessment of GBV is becoming a part of the asylum claim guidelines for different countries. For example, the UK government initiated The Violence Against Women and Girls Strategy, and included relevant details on different countries' gender-based violence in Country Policy and Information Notes. The UNHCR (2002) and the European Union (2013) issued a legislation to account for gender-related violence in processing asylum claims. *Guidelines on the Protection of Refugee Women* (1991) highlights the special needs for refugee women to be protected from "manipulation, sexual and physical abuse and exploitation, and protection against sexual discrimination in the delivery of goods and services," and later identified sexual violence to refer to "all forms of sexual threat, assault, interference, and exploitation, including 'statutory rape' and molestation without physical harm or penetration."

SGBV comprises cultural, economic, social, and sexual dimensions, and war zones constitute places of "militaristic masculinity" (Skjelsbaek, 2001). The complex and contingent nature of SGBV becomes more prevalent in forced migration contexts due to mainly under-reporting resulting in reproduction of gender-related vulnerabilities and insecurities (Ozcurumez, Akyuz & Bradby, forthcoming). The critical issue that seems to prevail through all contexts where SGBV takes place is the multiple faces of forms of victimization (Keygnaert et al., 2012).

29.4 Practical Implications in the Field of Social Trauma

Studies note that GBV is among the main causes of PTSD (Silove, Tay, Kareth, & Rees, 2017) and the likelihood of women developing PTSD as a consequence of GBV is higher in all contexts. Many studies highlight that fear of verbal and physical harassment keep girls from going to school and also engaging in public life, especially in contexts of humanitarian crisis. There are several initiatives that address the social trauma consequences of SGBV such as guidelines that aim to support victims to end abusive relationships, to raise awareness of consequences and signs of SGBV, and to provide safety plans as well as resources for medical care and psychosocial support. Many international agencies have developed guidelines to highlight that supporting SGBV survivors needs to involve a comprehensive approach involving essential health services, justice and policing, social services, and also focusing on coordination among different actors at various governance levels.

SGBV occurs severely in contexts of armed conflict, poverty, and patriarchy embedded in family- and community-related sources of violence. A major problem that stands in the way of ending SGBV is that survivors/victims/those at risk of GBV prefer not to speak of their experience and the risks they have been living through. Supporting all actors to engage in mobilization of resources to facilitate the sharing of traumatic experience is a priority in social trauma implications of SGBV. Addressing the trauma impact of SGBV effectively begins with facilitating accessibility of mental health and psychosocial services for all survivors, and designing and implementing policies to eliminate the root causes of SGBV across all contexts.

29.5 Suggested Reading

Barstow, A. L. (2001). *War's dirty secret: Rape, prostitution, and other crimes against women*. Cleveland: The Pilgrim Pr.

Fiddian-Qasmiyeh, E. (2014). Gender and forced migration. In E. Fiddian-Qasmiyeh, G. Loescher, K. Long, & N. Sigona (Eds.), *The Oxford handbook of refugee and forced migrations studies* (pp. 395–408). Oxford: Oxford University Press.

Freedman, J., Kıvılcım, Z., & Baklacıoglu, N. O. (2017). *A gendered approach to the Syrian refugee crisis*. London: Routledge.

Giles, W., & Hyndham, J. (2004). *Sites of violence: Gender and conflict zones*. Berkeley: University of California Press.

Hough, C. (2013). Understanding refugees' concepts of sexual and gender-based violence. *Forced Migration Review, 43*, 81–83.

Štirn, M., Minič M., Miklič, N., Tomažič R. B., Zemljič, I., Chaudary, S., … Peykova, R. (2017). *Psychosocial support for victims of domestic and gender based violence handbook, FIRST action against violence*. Slovenia: The Aire Centre. Retrieved from http://www.firstaction.eu/wp-content/uploads/2017/03/Handbook-FIRST.pdf

United Kingdom. (2016). *Ending violence against women and girls: Strategy 2016–2020*. Retrieved from https://assets.publishing.service.gov.uk/government/uploads/system/uploads/attachment_data/file/783596/VAWG_Strategy_Refresh_Web_Accessible.pdf

UNHCR. (2012). *Working with men and boy survivors of sexual and gender-based violence in forced displacement*. Retrieved from https://www.refworld.org/docid/5006aa262.html

UNHCR. (2015). *Sexual and gender-based violence prevention and response in refugee situations in the Middle East and North Africa*. Retrieved from https://www.refworld.org/docid/568f9a014.html

https://www.birmingham.ac.uk/research/superdiversity-institute/sereda/index.aspx

References

Bronfenbrenner, U. (1977). Toward an experimental ecology of human development. *American Psychologist, 32*(7), 513–531. https://doi.org/10.1037/0003.066X.32.7513

Council of Europe. (2011). *Council of Europe convention on preventing and combating violence against women and domestic violence*. Retrieved from https://www.coe.int/fr/web/conventions/full-list/-/conventions/rms/090000168008482e

Emusu, D., Ivankova, N., Jolly, P., Kirby, R., Foushee, H., Wabwire-Mangen, F., … Ehiri, J. (2009). Experience of sexual violence among women in HIV discordant unions after voluntary HIV counselling and testing: A qualitative critical incident study in Uganda. *AIDS Care, 21*(11), 1363–1370.

European Union. (2013). *Directive 2013/33/EU of the European Parliament and of the Council of 26 June 2013 laying down standards for the reception of applicants for international protection*. Retrieved from https://easo.europa.eu/sites/default/files/public/Dve-2013-33-Reception-conditions.pdf

Grych, J., & Swan, S. (2012). Toward a more comprehensive understanding of interpersonal violence: Introduction to the special issue on interconnections among different types of violence. *Psychology of Violence, 2*, 105–110. https://doi.org/10.1037/a0027616

Gupta, J., Falb, K. L., Carliner, H., Hossain, M., Koebo, D., & Annan, J. (2014). Associations between exposure to intimate partner violence, armed conflict and probable PTSD among women in rural cote d'Ivoire. *PLoS One, 9*(5), e96300. https://doi.org/10.1371/journal.pone.0096300

Heise, L. (1998). Violence against women: An integrated, ecological framework. *Violence Against Women, 4*, 262–290. https://doi.org/10.1177/1077801298004003002

Heise, L. L., & Kotsadam, A. (2015). Cross-national and multilevel correlates of partner violence: An analysis of data from population-based surveys. *The Lancet Global Health, 3*, e332–e340. https://doi.org/10.1016/s2214-109x(15)00013-3

Inter-Agency Standing Committee (IASC). (2015). *Guidelines for integrating gender-based violence interventions in humanitarian action: Reducing risk, promoting resilience and aiding recovery*. Retrieved from https://gbvguidelines.org/wp/wp-content/uploads/2015/09/2015-IASC-Gender-based-Violence-Guidelines_lo-res.pdf

International Criminal Court. (2011). *Rome statue of the International Criminal Court*. Retrieved from https://www.icc-cpi.int/resource-library/documents/rs-eng.pdf

Kerker, B. D., Zhang, J., Nadeem, E., Stein, R. E., Hurlburt, M. S., Heneghan, A., … McCue Horwitz, S. (2015). Adverse childhood experiences and mental health, chronic medical conditions, and development in young children. *Academic Pediatrics, 15*(5), 510–517.

Keygnaert, I., Vettenburg, N., & Temmerman, M. (2012). Hidden violence is silent rape: Sexual and gender-based violence in refugees, asylum seekers and undocumented migrants in Belgium and the Netherlands. *Culture Health and Sexuality, 14*, 505–520. https://doi.org/10.1080/13691058.2012.671961

Laisser, R. M., Nystrom, L., Lugina, H. I., & Emmelin, M. (2011). Community perceptions of intimate partner violence—A qualitative study from urban Tanzania. *BMC Women's Health, 11*(13), 1–12. https://doi.org/10.1186/1472-6874-11-13

Liebling, H., & Kiziri-Mayengo, R. (2002). The psychological effects of gender-based violence following armed conflict in Lowero District, Uganda. *Feminism and Psychology, 12*(4), 553–560.

Mootz, J. J., Stabb, S. D., & Mollen, D. (2017). Gender-based violence and armed conflict: A community-informed Socioecological conceptual model from northeastern Uganda. *Psychology Women Quarterly, 41*(3), 368–388.

Ozcurumez, S., Akyuz, S., & Bradby, H. (2020). The conceptualisation problem in research and responses to sexual and gender-based violence in forced migration. *Journal of Gender Studies*, 1. https://doi.org/10.1080/09589236.2020.1730163

Patton, M. Q. (2014). *Qualitative research & evaluation methods: Integrating theory and practice* (4th ed.). Thousand Oaks, CA: Sage Publications.

Robertson, C. L., Halcon, L., Savik, K., Johnson, D., Spring, M., Butcher, J., … Jaranson, J. (2006). Somali and Oromo refugee women: Trauma and associated factors. *Journal of Advanced Nursing, 56*(6), 577–587.

Silove, D., Tay, A. K., Kareth, M., & Rees, S. (2017). The relationship of complex post-traumatic stress disorder and post-traumatic stress disorder in a culturally distinct, conflict-affected population: A study among west Papuan refugees displaced to Papua New Guinea. *Frontiers in Psychiatry, 8*, 73. https://doi.org/10.3389/fpsyt.2017.00073

Simon-Butler, A., & McSherry, B. (2019). *Defining sexual and gender-based violence in the refugee context*. IRiS working paper series, 28. Birmingham: Institute for Research into Superdiversity.

Skjelsbaek, I. (2001). Sexual violence and war: Mapping out a complex relationship. *European Journal of International Relations, 7*(2), 211–237.

UNHCR. (1991). *Guidelines on the protection of refugee women*. Retrieved from https://www.unhcr.org/publications/legal/3d4f915e4/guidelines-protection-refugee-women.html

UNHCR. (2002). *Guidelines on international protection: Gender-related persecution within the context of Article 1(A)2 of the 1951 convention and/or its 1967 protocol relating to the status of refugees*. Retrieved from https://www.unhcr.org/publications/legal/3d58ddef4/guidelines-international-protection-1-gender-related-persecution-context.html

UNHCR. (2003). *Sexual and gender-based violence against refugees, returnees and internally displaced persons: Guidelines for prevention and response*. Retrieved from https://www.unhcr.org/protection/women/3f696bcc4/sexual-gender-based-violence-against-refugees-returnees-internally-displaced.html

United Nations. (1993). *Declaration on the elimination of violence against women*. Retrieved from https://www.ohchr.org/Documents/ProfessionalInterest/eliminationvaw.pdf

United Nations Secretary-General. (2003). *Secretary's bulletin: Special measures for protection from sexual exploitation and sexual abuse*. Retrieved from https://www.unhcr.org/protection/operations/405ac6614/secretary-generals-bulletin-special-measures-protection-sexual-exploitation.html

UNOCHA. (2020). *Global humanitarian overview 2020*. Retrieved from https://www.unocha.org/sites/unocha/files/GHO-2020_v9.1.pdf

Wirtz, A. L., Pham, K., Glass, N., Loochkartt, S., Kidane, T., Cuspoca, D., … Vu, A. (2014). Gender-based violence in conflict and displacement: Qualitative findings from displaced women in Colombia. *Conflict and Health, 11*(8), 10. https://doi.org/10.1186/1752-1505-8-10

World Health Organization. (2013). *Global and regional estimates of violence against women: Prevalence and health effects of intimate partner violence and non-partner sexual violence*. Retrieved from http://apps.who.int/iris/bitstream/10665/85239/1/9789241564625_eng.pdf

Chapter 30
Environmental Violence and Social Trauma in a Post-War Context: A Psychoanalytic Approach

Damir Arsenijević

30.1 Introduction: Background and Main Theoretical Concepts/Discussions

In this chapter, I propose to examine social trauma from the unexplored perspective of environmental violence. Why is environmental violence a useful lens through which to approach social trauma? This chapter argues and develops new insights into how environmental violence sheds light on the continuation of the logic of war-time long after the military conflict has ended. This is evidenced in the phenomenon of deaths that are caused by lingering conditions that kill slowly, over an extended period of time—meaning that they are usually not recognised as connected to, or caused by, the environmental violence of conflict. These deaths thus remain officially unregistered in political discourse and in popular memory. Working with the concept of "slow violence," I analyse the pervasiveness of disavowal by communities in relation to such violence, which testifies to their overwhelming anxiety. Particularly, this is relevant for post-socialist contexts, like in former Yugoslavia, in which current authoritarian regimes continue to maintain ethnic hostility in order to disguise the continuation of sacrificing and disposing of people in the name of profit. Such authoritarian regimes have managed to enforce internal compliance by populations, threatening the part of self, in individuals and groups, that seeks reality with violence and exclusion. The "myth of apathy" of communities, promoted within and without Bosnia and Herzegovina, further entrenches the victimised position and thus enables the extractivist and exploitative logic to persist. In efforts to analyse slow environmental violence, psychoanalysis has much to offer towards understanding the unconscious mechanisms at play by insisting on the subject of the unconscious—non-rational and split subject—which underpins any emancipatory thought and action.

D. Arsenijević (✉)
School of Humanities and Social Sciences, University of Tuzla,
Tuzla, Bosnia and Herzegovina
e-mail: damir.arsenijevic@untz.ba

© Springer Nature Switzerland AG 2021

A. Hamburger et al. (eds.), *Social Trauma – An Interdisciplinary Textbook*,
https://doi.org/10.1007/978-3-030-47817-9_30

Violence is polyvalent. It ranges from strikingly large and obvious—such as the war-time violence of executions and mass graves, or the violence of the asset-stripping of companies during their privatisation or in ecological catastrophes—to a less obvious and less visible type of violence, such as the destructive work of toxic waste and toxic narratives on our bodies.

In relation to the environment, it is maintained either through the direct exploitation and destruction of natural resources or through so-called "waste colonialism," which predominantly refers to the removal of toxic waste from privileged and affluent countries to those countries that are kept in poverty. The term "waste colonialism" was first recorded at the United Nations Environmental Programme Basel Convention working group, during which African countries voiced anxieties about rich countries from Europe and North America accessing and using African land for the disposal of toxic waste (Porter, Welsh Brown, & Chasek, 2000, p. 105). However, we ought also to widen the meaning of this term: we must include in it those deindustrialising practices of finance capital that exploit factories by stripping them of their assets, removing capital from communities where these factories are located, and then by leaving toxic substances, unemployment, and toxic narratives to circulate in these communities. From the psychoanalytic perspective, greed for such exploitation can be explored in terms of the arrogance of narcissistic entitlement, which aims at exploiting others on the grounds of a felt superiority or entitlement in relation to those "others." As Weintrobe (2013b, p. 38) argues, "with arrogance, a destructively narcissistic part of the psyche has gained the upper hand in a power struggle with the part that feels wedded to reality. A sense of narcissistic entitlement to be immune to emotional difficulties has triumphed over a lively entitlement to a relationship with reality." Some authors have even analysed the greed of neoliberal capitalism as an aspect of a much larger and organised phenomenon, which is referred to as the perverse structure (Long, 2008). In such a structure, bearing in mind that Freud discusses perverse responses as "artful" (Freud, 1927), neoliberal capitalism relies and thrives on "ambiguity, illusion, evasiveness, trickery, collusion and guile" and leads to pseudo-political responses "or 'as if' politics in which enormous energy is put into the specification of objectives, targets and indicators and the corresponding demonstration that one's performance is moving towards such targets" (Hoggett, 2013, pp. 60 and 68).

There is also the form of violence that is difficult to perceive and is slow to be noticed; the so-called "slow violence," which takes place "gradually and is out of sight, a violence of delayed destruction that is dispersed across time and space, an attritional violence that is typically not viewed as violence at all" (Nixon, 2011, p. 2). This is the violence of landmines and toxic waste that are the daily reality of post-war Bosnia and Herzegovina, or in countries that were former colonies of the industrialised West, that speaks of the disposability of its population, and, as such, is a continuation of the war-time logic. Such violence "sediments" gradually and is felt on a different temporal scale. This scale also provides testimony to the continuing but invisible deaths. These deaths are a prolongation of war-time injury, despite them not being present in our daily memory, because there exists no holding form which could acknowledge and register these deaths as such. At this level of the normalisation of the disposability of people, a question may arise: how is it possible for politicians to be oblivious to this, and how come people do not oppose this? In order to begin answering this question, at the societal level, we should consider it as an organised disavowal. This type of disavowal is characteristic of a cynical position, with the formula: "I know very well this is happening but…," which also sits comfortably with the perverse structure of neoliberal capitalism. Disavowal, unlike straightforward negation, speaks of dealing with the anxiety of loss as a systematic and organised avoidance. As Weintrobe (2013a, p. 7) points out, "the more reality is systematically avoided through making it insignificant or through distortion, the more anxiety builds up unconsciously, and the greater is the need to defend with further disavowal. In the long run, disavowal can lead to a spiral of minimizing reality with an underlying build-up of anxiety and this makes it dangerous." In the context of the perversion that is waste colonialism, one can also track the argument that, in the context of too much anxiety caused by the build-up of disavowal, our self is also colonised (Weintrobe, 2013c, p. 207), and perceived as either powerless and paralysed, or omnipotent and greedy. In addition, in our discussions of the environment, therein lies the power of the unconscious; not as the unconscious mechanisms of our behaviour in relation to environment, i.e. not a reduction of environmental concerns to mere psychologisation, but as a properly structural element—that accounts for the subject of the unconscious, the split subject in the field of environmental concerns. This may be a way of decolonising the self by acknowledging how we harbour within us contradictory and contesting narratives, some of which we may not even be aware, and from the position of the split and non-rational self, imagine ways of overcoming the predominant disavowal. A starting position may be, as Steiner (2013, p. 82) argues, "that the best we can do is to become alert to the likelihood that we are under the sway of a perverse argument and to be aware of our own propensity to join in the collusions."

30.2 Learning Outcome Related to Social Trauma

With regard to social trauma, there are four major learning outcomes. These outcomes also indicate the potential further development of this topic in terms of research and teaching:

The interpretation of the concept of violence in all its valences and complexities is extrapolated through research. This nuanced understanding is used to inform political and environmental policy development in post-conflict societies where peace exists only as an absence of military conflict.

In order to counteract the impact of the social trauma of victimisation on a traumatised country's development, the persistence of the logic of war or colonialism must be analysed. The production and maintenance of this victimhood are rooted in the original scene of the social trauma, namely, the normalisation of the disposability and expendability of people for profit.

The extractivist and exploitative practices employed by a network of international and local elites are examined and evaluated to demonstrate, with evidence, how these elites ensure internal compliance by populations and how this specifically plays out in relation to environmental violence. Pathologising populations, through the narratives of their "apathy" or "passivity" in post-war or post-colonial contexts, precludes the possibility of mourning the losses by these populations through preventing any relationality amongst these losses to be created.

New intergenerational connections are established, between those who remember the war and those who were born after it, through designing insights and settings that counter environmental violence. Creating these conditions for productive intergenerational connections to be made can open and explore creative avenues to signify and give meaning to the effects of such violence.

30.3 Preferred Model of Explanation

A vignette: in Tuzla today, the former Chlorine Alkaline Power House (known locally by its Bosnian acronym, HAK) is a disintegrating and abandoned post-industrial skeleton. This used to be one of the largest socialist Yugoslav mining and chemical industrial complexes, but currently, it sits as an unexploded bomb—encasing huge volumes of toxic waste that lies unsupervised in its over-ground spheres and its underground pipes in unmarked locations around the former factory. It is a dystopic site that speaks about the connection between environmental instability, finance capital, violence, and power.

In the early 1990s, predatory capital first targeted the working class in socialist Bosnia and Herzegovina. Its mercenaries, the ethno-nationalist elites who were in charge of bringing capitalism to Yugoslavia, targeted and executed the working class in the war and the genocide that ensued and buried it in hidden mass graves, scattered throughout this country. In this, they were helped by the international right-wing forces and paramilitaries, including members of Golden Dawn. This was called *transition into capitalism*. Then, it came for the factories, leaving tens of thousands unemployed, stripping factories of assets, and creating post-industrial wastelands. This was called *privatisation*. Now, it is coming for the country's natural resources—its water and air, forests, and land—changing entire ecosystems in order to build hydro-electric plants (Neslen, 2015) and despoiling its territory into one gigantic waste dump for hazardous materials. This is called *growth*. This logic of growth creates conditions for an explosion of popular revolt in Bosnia and Herzegovina today.

The rusting pipes of the asset-stripped skeleton of HAK still hold more than 47 tons of stagnant, highly flammable propylene oxide. These pipes are surrounded by a stack of 120 abandoned and corroding barrels, from which, slowly, over a quarter of a century, mercury, cadmium, and arsenic have been leaking into the ground. Around HAK, protruding from the ground, the black sheen of cakes of carcinogenic toluene diisocyanate (TDI) waste can be seen, shaping the outline of the many landfill sites scattered across the no man's land between the two spheres. The accurate size and exact locations of these landfills are undocumented by the government or any other official body. The only people who go anywhere near the lethal skeleton of HAK are the impoverished and unemployed former industrial workers, who disassemble and pick through the site for scrap metal to sell. As a result of this "work," they are regularly exposed to toxic waste, which, as a result of their exposure to it, leads to statistically high levels of untimely deaths, either as a result of accidents, and via more prolonged "slow" deaths from the chronic conditions they develop (CIN, 2018).

> Aldin Bejhanović is a metal picker who suffered from a pulmonary embolism, caused by poisons at HAK. He says: "We took off gunmetal valves from the pipes below the manhole covers. There was work. But after some time the barrels appeared. It was stinking...It stank so strongly that it hurt my eyes. I could not take it... I stopped for a while, but later I, father and a neighbor arrived to cut out pipes. And we found it there. We did not know that it was a poison. The place was not even marked." He describes being poisoned thus: "I was feeling out of air when I would bend down to pick something, and I had put up with this for around 14 days. I thought it was cigarettes." "When it grabbed me and threw me down and when blackness fell over my eyes, I could not reach my car" (ibid.). Bejhanović's uncle was not so lucky; his lungs were burnt after he had inhaled poisonous gas from the pipes that he had cut.

Any psychoanalytically oriented approach must start by listening to and enabling settings for the autobiographies of all those whose lungs are burnt as a result of being forced to pick scrap metal in order to survive or those who have developed cancer or asthma as a result of exposure to unsupervised and hidden toxic waste. These personal narratives "profoundly biological as bodies and selves are constructed from the very stuff of the toxic places they have inhabited. As various toxins take up residence within the body, the supposedly inert 'background' of place becomes the active substance of self" (Alaimo, 2010, p. 102). To be aware of how such surroundings are integral to and inseparable parts of our bodies is the start of a different kind of listening in and to our communities—communities that are suffering from environmental violence.

30.4 Practical Implications in the Field of Social Trauma

One of the ways to alert ourselves to how our unconscious joins in the perverse collusions of neoliberal capitalism is to keep reminding ourselves of the unspectacular time of slow violence. The lesson of psychoanalysis is that time is fragmented, nonlinear, and subjective, as evidenced from retroactivity to the timelessness of the unconscious, whose traces are simultaneously represented in the past, present, and the future. Remaining constantly alert to the unspectacular time of slow violence is to acknowledge the existence of hitherto unspoken words that testify to the effects of such violence in settings in which they can be heard. As Rob Nixon (2011, p. 6) argues, "chemical and radiological violence, for example, is driven inward, somatised into cellular dramas of mutation that—particularly in the bodies of the poor—remain largely unobserved, undiagnosed, and untreated. From a narrative perspective, such invisible, mutagenic theater is slow-paced and open-ended, eluding the tidy closure, the containment, imposed by the visual orthodoxies of victory and defeat."

And, indeed, in the post-conflict setting, such as Bosnia and Herzegovina, where the boundary between victory and defeat is blurred, time is mostly perceived as frozen time, in which lives have been placed on hold. Almost a quarter of a century after the end of the war in Bosnia and Herzegovina, outside observers deem the peace to be fragile. The people of Bosnia and Herzegovina are suspended between the war that has not quite ended and a future that has not yet commenced. However, the time of the future has been hijacked and pawned by the victors of the war—those elites who profited from the war and who impoverished the citizens of Bosnia and Herzegovina—by planting landmines, creating hidden mass graves, and leaving toxic waste. These landmines, hidden mass graves, and toxic waste labour slowly; they follow their own temporal logic all the while constantly producing a threat. The peace agreement installed, what Steff Jansen (2014, p. 90) calls, "meantime," as a liminal temporality of "endless loop" of depoliticisation, which puts people in an endless "transition" to capitalism. In such a transition, what is produced is a "victim," as a privileged identitarian position in the ethno-capitalist order, forever grieving for the lost object that is hidden and withheld. The message that the ethno-capitalist elites send to the citizens of Bosnia and Herzegovina is that citizens are worthless and expendable. In acting this way, these elites can be said to enact gang-type phantasies and thus impact on the mental functioning of individuals and whole societies, arresting and overpowering the libidinal self—that cannot oppose the destructive process—thus maintaining the status quo (Rosenfeld, 1988, p. 243).

The prognosis as to how the reality of slow violence in Bosnia and Herzegovina is impacting on the country is gloomy: Bosnia and Herzegovina is ranked as the second deadliest country in the world by the UN Environment Programme when it comes to the number of deaths per head of population caused by air pollution (UN Environment Programme, 2018), while in some areas around Tuzla, polluted by coal-fuelled power plants, there are record numbers of cancers. To return to the question: why don't people oppose this and try to change the status quo? First, the role of such a relationship to the subservience to the status quo should be examined and understood in terms of the overpowering anxiety that is present in Bosnian society. We can talk about there being a surplus of anxiety, as Weintrobe (2013b, p. 40) argues, in which "the sane self suffers survival anxiety if it speaks out, and survival anxiety if it remains silent. But the sane self can also feel puny in the face of a needed social group that threatens it with rejection, social exclusion, or worse."

Further, there has been a tendency, both within Bosnia and Herzegovina and beyond its borders, to conceptualise as apathy the perceived inaction and paralysis of the population in Bosnia and Herzegovina in relation to the status quo. Apathy, however, is a toxic narrative itself, that only endorses and strengthens exploitative attitudes. As Lertzman (2015, pp. 9 and 19) argues, this "myth of apathy" pathologises and patronises populations as disinterested, selfish, limited, or as being in denial, and privileges the notion of a rational subject, all of which obscures complex social and cultural processes as well as our understanding of psychic defences. As such, the discourse of apathy plays a significant ideological role in maintaining the grip of the victimised position in a post-war society such as Bosnia and Herzegovina. This then precludes the possibility for its people to begin to mourn the multiple losses that have been sustained by them. In order for us to go beyond the obscurantism which the discourse of apathy promotes, Lertzman (2015, p. 150) proposes approaching denial and apathy as "informed with insights derived from psychodynamic practices, such as the creation of a 'safe space' and containment via group conversations. This can and should inform how we design messaging, branding and outreach platforms."

In view of this, as I have argued elsewhere, we ought to follow extant literary and artistic practices in Bosnia and Herzegovina that are already enabling a "public language of grief" and, indeed, assist in generating such creative ways of engaging with loss and mourning, (Arsenijević, 2011). It is in such practices that loss from those political projects that permit harm in the name of profit is spoken, not only as personal and familial, but as properly social and political.

30.5 Suggested Reading and Further Information

Carbon Conversations: http://www.carbonconversations.co.uk/p/about.html

International Psychoanalytical Association: https://www.ipa.world/ipa/en/comment/climate_change.aspx

Sally Weintrobe's Lecture: https://vimeo.com/78805269

Undisciplined Humanities Collective: https://undisciplinedenvironments.org/2017/11/03/toxic-bios-a-guerrilla-narrative-project-mapping-contamination-illness-and-resistance/

References

Alaimo, S. (2010). *Bodily natures: Science, Environment, and the material self.* Bloomington: Indiana University Press.

Arsenijević, D. (2011). Mobilising unbribable life: The politics of contemporary poetry in Bosnia and Herzegovina. In A. Mousely (Ed.), *Towards a new literary humanism* (pp. 166–180). London: Palgrave Macmillan.

CIN. (2018, 22 June). *Hazardous waste under the feet of Tuzla residents.* Retrieved from https://www.cin.ba/en/otrovni-otpad-pod-nogama-tuzlaka/

Freud, S. (1927). Fetishism. In J. Strachey (Ed.), *The standard edition of the complete psychological works of Sigmund Freud* (Vol. XXI, pp. 149–157). London: Hogarth Press.

Hoggett, P. (2013). Climate change in a perverse culture. In S. Weintrobe (Ed.), *Engaging with climate change: Psychoanalytic and interdisciplinary perspectives* (pp. 56–71). New York, NY: Routledge.

Jansen, S. (2014). Rebooting politics? Or, towards a <ctrl-alt-Del> for the Dayton meantime. In D. Arsenijević (Ed.), *Unbribable Bosnia and Herzegovina: The fight for the commons* (pp. 89–96). Baden-Baden: Nomos.

Lertzman, R. (2015). *Environmental melancholia: Psychoanalytic dimensions of engagement*. New York, NY: Routledge.

Long, S. (2008). *The perverse organization and the seven deadly sins*. London: Karnac.

Neslen, A. (2015, 11 December). Major banks put up nearly €1bn for controversial Balkan dams, says report. *The Guardian*. Retrieved from https://www.theguardian.com/environment/2015/dec/11/major-banks-put-up-nearly-1bn-for-controversial-balkan-dams-says-report

Nixon, R. (2011). *Slow violence and the environmentalism of the poor*. Cambridge, MA: Harvard University Press.

Porter, G., Welsh Brown, J., & Chasek, P. (2000). *Global environmental politics* (3rd ed.). Boulder, CO: Westview.

Rosenfeld, H. (1988). A clinical approach to the psychoanalytic theory of the life and death instincts: An investigation into the aggressive aspects of narcissism. In E. Bott Spillius (Ed.), *Melanie Klein today: Developments in theory and practice* (pp. 233–250). London: Routledge. (Original work published 1971).

Steiner, J. (2013). Climate change in a perverse culture. In S. Weintrobe (Ed.), *Engaging with climate change: Psychoanalytic and interdisciplinary perspectives* (pp. 80–83). New York, NY: Routledge.

UN Environment Programme. (2018, January). *Coming up for clean air in Bosnia and Herzegovina*. Retrieved from https://www.unenvironment.org/news-and-stories/story/coming-clean-air-bosnia-and-herzegovina

Weintrobe, S. (2013a). Introduction. In S. Weintrobe (Ed.), *Engaging with climate change: Psychoanalytic and interdisciplinary perspectives* (pp. 1–15). New York, NY: Routledge.

Weintrobe, S. (2013b). The difficult problem of anxiety in thinking about climate change. In S. Weintrobe (Ed.), *Engaging with climate change: Psychoanalytic and interdisciplinary perspectives* (pp. 33–47). New York, NY: Routledge.

Weintrobe, S. (2013c). On the love of nature and on human nature: Restoring split internal landscapes. In S. Weintrobe (Ed.), *Engaging with climate change: Psychoanalytic and interdisciplinary perspectives* (pp. 199–213). New York, NY: Routledge.

Chapter 31
Ethical Aspects of Social Trauma Research

Nikola M. Petrović

31.1 Introduction

In the field of social trauma research, ethical questions are of great importance, because whenever researchers choose traumatized people as respondents, there is a possibility to cause them further harm by exploring their trauma. In this chapter, we talk about applied ethics, that is, practical application of moral considerations in research.

If research of this kind is dangerous, is it worth doing? If we remind the people about the adverse events they experienced, are we retraumatizing them, especially those with PTSD? First of all, it is very different to directly experience a traumatic event and to ask someone about it in a safe environment (Newman, Risch, & Kassam-Adams, 2006). Of course, examining these topics can cause unwanted and unpleasant thoughts and emotions, but research has shown that only a portion of participants experience distress during trauma-related research (Newman & Kaloupek, 2005). The likelihood of significant emotional harm in trauma-focused studies is low, and while some participants are distressed and regret being part of the research, most find the experience tolerable and report positive outcomes even in the acute aftermath of trauma (Newman et al., 2006).

On the other hand, disclosure of trauma, even just in writing, was shown to be therapeutic for the survivors (Pennebaker & Susman, 1988). Both trauma-related interviews, as well as survey research on this topic, have a favorable cost–benefit ratio for the participants (Carlson et al., 2003; Cromer, Freyd, Binder, DePrince, & Becker-Blease, 2006). This is also true for children (Chu, DePrince, & Weinzierl, 2008). What can be beneficial for respondents? They can share their story (experience catharsis or get closure, which could lead to posttraumatic growth), gain insights about their experiences, feel valued and listened to, help others through

N. M. Petrović (✉)
Department of Psychology, Faculty of Philosophy, University of Belgrade, Belgrade, Serbia

© Springer Nature Switzerland AG 2021
A. Hamburger et al. (eds.), *Social Trauma – An Interdisciplinary Textbook*,
https://doi.org/10.1007/978-3-030-47817-9_31

increasing scientific knowledge, get referrals for treatment and talk freely without being subject to unwanted advice (Newman et al., 2006). To conclude, there are great societal costs for not asking about trauma because we have to know about the impact of trauma in order to help people (Becker-Blease & Freyd, 2006). However, we should keep in mind that there are other risks which are usually preventable, such as overburdening of the respondents (participation in multiple studies), stigmatization, and even retribution of the community for associating with the researchers (Beyrer & Kass, 2002).

31.2 Learning Outcome Related to Social Trauma

The purpose of this chapter is foremost prevention of unethical behavior resulting from gaps in knowledge about ethical standards in research. Readers will be able to identify and avoid ethical pitfalls in doing research in this field.

31.3 Preferred Model of Explanation

If we do not research social trauma, we are not giving survivors of trauma a voice and, therefore, we are participating in the conspiracy of silence. In order to do it properly, however, there are some prerequisites as well as standards that need to be followed.

31.3.1 Competence

In order to prevent ethical violations, researchers first have to be ethically sensitive and to recognize potential ethical dilemmas. They also need to know what to do if there are complications. This means researchers need to be competent to carry on the research project and not only in the methodological and technical sense (Mooney-Sommers & Olsen, 2017). They need to know the laws of the country where they are conducting the research, as well as to be emotionally stable and be able to show empathy when working with survivors of trauma. Vicarious traumatization, insufficient experience, insufficient knowledge of the sociopolitical context, and culture of the respondents can all be considerable limiting factors of the researcher's competence. Research supervisors need to assure that the study is conducted competently and that the risk is reduced to a minimum (Urquiza, Wyatt, & Goodlin-Jones, 1997). Supervisors can also organize 'emotional check-ins', where emotional reactions of the research team can be validated, normalized, and discussed.

31.3.2 Informed Consent

Sometimes the capacity of traumatized people to give a valid consent to participate in research is questioned, but we should not be paternalistic in assuming that all trauma victims are so vulnerable that they cannot do it (Newman & Kaloupek, 2009). Research suggests that decision-making capacity is not compromised for most trauma survivors (Collogan, Tuma, Dolan-Sewell, Borja, & Fleischman, 2004). They should, however, be given sufficient time to consider participation, to ask questions and receive answers, particularly about the risks involved and the limits of confidentiality (mandated reporting). The form should use simple nontechnical language, but we should keep in mind that even then there could be problems such as participants signing it without reading it, literacy and translation issues, fear of giving signature, etc. If people live in an oppressive environment, they could fear repercussions for declining participation (Pittaway, Bartolomei, & Hugman, 2010) and therefore give socially acceptable but inaccurate responses (Beyrer & Kass, 2002). Some participants might join the research out of unrealistic expectations of assistance in getting asylum for example (Vukčević Marković & Bjekić, 2018).

31.3.3 Confidentiality

As we mentioned laws, sometimes researchers are put in a scientist–citizen dilemma, since some countries have rules about mandated reporting of violence. This is especially important to have in mind when researching perpetrators as they could face legal consequences if they say something that could incriminate them. We should keep data confidential forever (or destroy them after a period of time), even if participants or researchers die (this issue could be solved with a professional will).

But can the responses really be completely anonymous in qualitative research? Since sample sizes are often small and reports usually include interview excerpts, respondents can still be identifiable despite deidentification and data alteration (Baker et al., 2016).

In longitudinal research, codes are usually made for the participants in order to identify them. Researchers should be careful not to use elements of personal information found on an ID card to make the code because these elements could be identifiable. Even innocuous data might inadvertently lead to harm for participants (Beyrer & Kass, 2002).

At last, we have to think about the working conditions. In some countries, there is a probability of state surveillance that could endanger the privacy of interviews. Similarly, working conditions in refugee camps, for example, are not very good for keeping data confidential, which could lead to participants refraining to discuss sensitive topics, therefore ruining the validity of the data (Vukčević Marković & Bjekić, 2018).

31.3.4 Recruitment of Participants

When working in a culture that is different from our own, we should seek help from local institutions and NGOs to recruit participants in a culturally appropriate manner. Sometimes recruitment needs to be done through a "liaison" who is trusted by the prospective participants. If researchers offer encouragement for participation they should make reasonable effort to avoid offering excessive or inappropriate financial or other inducements which are likely to coerce participation (Leaning, 2001), particularly in poor postconflict societies.

31.3.5 Relations and Boundaries

When you build a rapport, you become close to the participants, especially if you spend a lot of time in their small community. If we also share our personal narratives to influence the participants to share more with us, they might start considering us as friends and vice versa and this can influence our objectivity. An interview may be longer than a therapy session and may elicit more recollections of traumatic events (Bass-Wichelhaus, 1994). Therefore, relations with participants are sometimes viewed as quasitherapeutic or as "faked friendship." Participants may become dependent, ask for help or favors in return for participation, give us gifts, etc. This and their vulnerability could lead to their exploitation or harm. Even a touch, like a pat on the back, can sometimes be problematic with traumatized people. However, not all power differentials are de facto exploitative (Cromer & Newman, 2011), but we have to be careful and keep the best interests of the participants in our mind at all times as well as respect them as equals.

31.3.6 Representation

What if research participants are dissatisfied or even angry when they learn how they are characterized in the published paper? For example, some people who experienced trauma prefer to be labeled with the term "survivor" rather than "victim." Sometimes, victims express some chauvinistic or hateful attitudes, and presenting them even slightly in a bad light could be viewed as politically incorrect. This is an especially important topic for qualitative research. While some researchers reserve the right to have explicit ownership of interpretive authority others sometimes ask participants to edit or approve interpretations that are related to them (Preissle & Han, 2012). Disputed parts can be omitted or the researcher can state that there were disagreements over representation. Research reports may be composed in a way to include multiple voices (Blakeslee, Cole, & Conefrey, 1996). We should always keep in mind that the participants usually think about data as a faithful representation of reality and researchers see data as a product of the interaction between them and the researched (Carusi, 2008). Researchers need to explain to participants how they will present the data in the publication (e.g., that they will see themselves in fragments, not as whole persons).

31.3.7 Neutrality, Advocacy, and Politics

Can we control our prejudices, emotions, and values from interfering in the research process? It is very difficult to prevent displays of emotion during the interviews if the participant talks about something very sad. More inexperienced researchers usually neglect the impact that research on sensitive topics may have on them (Hubbard, Backett-Milburn, & Kemmer, 2001). After all, we are only human and cannot be completely objective, and, therefore, there is no real neutral position for a researcher, especially in qualitative research. This does not mean that we cannot trust the researchers if they are honest about how they collected the data and transparent regarding the interpretation process and their relations to the participants. Also, there are situations where we should not be neutral like ongoing human rights abuses and violence (Pittaway et al., 2010). Some approaches, like action research, are intentionally biased. When researchers are advocating an agenda, they can be under pressure from sponsors or other stakeholders. They should not make definite statements or exaggerate the weight of a single research (Vukčević Marković & Bjekić, 2018), nor should they alter or hide results not in line with the advocacy agenda. There is also the question of how to interpret the results when there are "different truths." The influence of political propaganda in postconflict societies can make researchers feel that they have divided loyalties to their ethnic group and to science. If they report the truth or present the story of the "other side," they could be seen as traitors or can be pressured. This could especially create problems in multiethnic research teams composed of researchers from "opposite" sides of the conflict (Chaitin, 2003). Research can be a tool for political interventions, but can also be misused, particularly in today's political climate and the era of fake news. We should also keep in mind the social impact of the research that could potentially lead to stigma and further divisions between people, as it can influence the public image of a group of respondents, such as refugees (Vukčević Marković & Bjekić, 2018).

31.3.8 Postresearch Obligations

Sometimes participants experience negative feelings if the research ended sooner than they expected. These feelings need to be addressed and discussed. Researchers can organize follow-ups and stay in touch with them (i.e., send them holiday greeting cards). They could also give participants a small gift in order to show their gratitude (Stein et al., 2000). Some also organize a farewell gathering or a celebratory meal as a closing ritual.

If researchers notice that participants are experiencing mental health problems, they should give them referrals in order to get the professional treatment they need (Stein et al., 2000). Likewise, if researchers think that participation in the research puts the participants in some sort of danger, they should warn them and refer them to the police. Similarly, if researchers notice that research has somehow harmed a participant, they have to minimize the harm with debriefing and other measures. It is important for researchers to have an "exit strategy" when they are working with vulnerable people and to enter into a dialogue of closure with participants in order to prevent them from feeling used and prepare them for the transition (Morrison, Gregory, & Thibodeau, 2012).

31.4 Practical Implications in the Field of Social Trauma

Based on what was mentioned above, some concrete implications can be drawn. These are some recommendations for researchers who want to conduct research on this topic:

- Create a research project that could result in something beneficial for the participants.
- When you send your application to an IRB, you should probably cite research that shows low probability of your questions distressing respondents.
- Conduct the research in an environment where the participants would feel safe.
- Use the participatory research design to reduce the power differential. Involve the local community in all parts of the research.
- Draw on multiple sources of data and use culturally adequate instruments.
- Avoid helicopter research (when a researcher disappears after collecting data), as the respondents may feel used.
- If you use translators, keep in mind that there are confidentiality issues, risks of secondary victimization for them, as well as the influence of multiple relations they could form with the participants.
- Ask questions in a sensitive manner and provide the opportunity for participants to skip questions.
- Measure the participant reaction to your study to see if they were distressed.
- Be reflexive, critically examine your own a priori assumptions, and try to anticipate problems.
- If things go wrong, use debriefing to help subjects cope with their feelings (emotional restoration) and check for any confusion they might have.
- Researchers are also at risk. They can become too emotionally overwhelmed or frightened because they work in dangerous conditions; they might try to minimize and forget what they heard, could experience "researcher guilt" because they cannot help the participants or suffer vicarious traumatization. Provision of

continuous emotional support and a plan for self-care for researchers must be a part of the research protocol.

31.5 Suggested Reading and Further Information

European Commission. (2010). *European textbook on ethics in research*. Luxembourg: Publications Office of the European Union.

References

Baker, L., Phelan, S., Snelgrove, R., Varpio, L., Maggi, J., & Ng, S. (2016). Recognizing and responding to ethically important moments in qualitative research. *Journal of Graduate Medical Education, 8*, 607–608.

Bass-Wichelhaus, H. (1994). The interviewer as witness: Countertransference, reactions, and techniques. In J. S. Kestenberg & E. Fogelman (Eds.), *Children under the Nazi reign: Psychological perspective on the interview process* (pp. 175–188). Westport, CT: Praeger.

Becker-Blease, K. A., & Freyd, J. J. (2006). Research participants telling the truth about their lives: The ethics of asking and not asking about abuse. *American Psychologist, 61*, 218–226.

Beyrer, C., & Kass, N. E. (2002). Human rights, politics, and reviews of research ethics. *The Lancet, 360*, 246–251.

Blakeslee, A. M., Cole, C. M., & Conefrey, T. (1996). Constructing voices in writing research: Developing participatory approaches to situated inquiry. In G. Kirsch & P. Mortensen (Eds.), *Ethics and representation in qualitative studies of literacy* (pp. 134–154). Urbana, IL: NCTE.

Carlson, E. B., Newman, E., Daniels, J. W., Armstrong, J., Roth, D., & Loewenstein, R. (2003). Distress in response to and perceived usefulness of trauma research interviews. *Journal of Trauma & Dissociation, 4*, 131–142.

Carusi, A. (2008). Data as representation: Beyond anonymity in e-research ethics. *International Journal of Internet Research Ethics, 1*, 37–65.

Chaitin, J. (2003). "I wish he Hadn't told me that": Methodological and ethical issues in social trauma and conflict research. *Qualitative Health Research, 13*, 1145–1154.

Chu, A. T., Deprince, A. P., & Weinzierl, K. M. (2008). Children's perception of research participation: Examining trauma exposure and distress. *Journal of Empirical Research on Human Research Ethics, 3*, 49–58.

Collogan, L. K., Tuma, F., Dolan-Sewell, R., Borja, S., & Fleischman, A. R. (2004). Ethical issues pertaining to research in the aftermath of disaster. *Journal of Traumatic Stress, 17*, 363–372.

Cromer, L. D., Freyd, J. J., Binder, A. K., DePrince, A. P., & Becker-Blease, K. (2006). What's the risk in asking? Participant reaction to trauma history questions compared with reaction to other personal questions. *Ethics & Behavior, 16*, 347–362.

Cromer, L. D., & Newman, E. (2011). Research ethics in victimization studies: Widening the lens. *Violence Against Women, 17*, 1536–1548.

Hubbard, G., Backett-Milburn, K., & Kemmer, D. (2001). Working with emotion: Issues for the researcher in fieldwork and teamwork. *International Journal of Social Research Methodology, 4*, 119–137.

Leaning, J. (2001). Ethics of research in refugee populations. *The Lancet, 357*, 1432–1433.

Mooney-Sommers, J., & Olsen, A. (2017). Ethical review and qualitative research competence: Guidance for reviewers and applicants. *Research Ethics, 13*, 128–138.

Morrison, Z. J., Gregory, D., & Thibodeau, S. (2012). "Thanks for using me": An exploration of exit strategy in qualitative research. *International Journal of Qualitative Methods, 11*, 416–427.

Newman, E., & Kaloupek, D. (2009). Overview of research addressing ethical dimensions of participation in traumatic stress studies: Autonomy and beneficence. *Journal of Traumatic Stress, 22*, 595–602.

Newman, E., & Kaloupek, D. G. (2005). The risks and benefits of participating in trauma-focused research studies. *Journal of Traumatic Stress, 17*, 383–394.

Newman, E., Risch, E., & Kassam-Adams, N. (2006). Ethical issues in trauma-related research: A review. *Journal of Empirical Research on Human Research Ethics, 1*, 29–46.

Pennebaker, J. W., & Susman, J. R. (1988). Disclosure of traumas and psychosomatic processes. *Social Science & Medicine, 26*, 327–332.

Pittaway, E., Bartolomei, L., & Hugman, R. (2010). 'Stop stealing our stories': The ethics of research with vulnerable groups. *Journal of Human Rights Practice, 2*, 229–251.

Preissle, J., & Han, Y. (2012). Feminist research ethics. In S. N. Hesse-Biber (Ed.), *Handbook of feminist research: Theory and praxis* (2nd ed., pp. 583–605). Thousand Oaks, CA: Sage.

Stein, D. J., Herman, A., Kaminer, D., Rataemane, S., Seedat, S., Kessler, R., & Williams, D. (2000). Ethical aspects of research on psychological trauma. *Dialogues in Clinical Neuroscience, 2*, 31–36.

Urquiza, A. J., Wyatt, G. E., & Goodlin-Jones, B. L. (1997). Clinical interviewing with trauma victims: Managing interviewer risk. *Journal of Interpersonal Violence, 12*, 759–772.

Vukčević Marković, M., & Bjekić, J. (2018). Methods and ethics in refugee research. In A. Hamburger, C. Hancheva, S. Özcürümez, C. Scher, B. Stanković, & S. Tutnjević (Eds.), *Forced migration and social trauma. Interdisciplinary perspectives from psychoanalysis, psychology, sociology and politics* (pp. 126–135). London: Routledge.

Chapter 32
Social Trauma Between Psycho-Criminology and Psycho-Victimology

Astrid Hirschelmann and Abdul Rahman Rasho

32.1 Introduction: The History of Humanity Is Based on Violence—But Why Violence?

Society as a victim of a crime, but also, to a certain extent, responsible for the crime, is the subject of much research which is evolving in the same way as law, medicine, or psychoanalysis. The beginnings of the sociological trend were marked by a rejection of endogenous etiology, which assumed a relationship between the criminal act and the organic constitution of the individual. Favoring the approach of delinquent behavior through a study of the exogenous context, the first sociological research only shifted the problem of internal, psychological, or organic determinism.

Emile Durkheim (1858–1917) studied crime as an instrument of social regulation (1938, 2013) in a nuanced manner. Posing crime as inherent to the very structure of the culture to which it belongs, he explains the delinquent conduct by the anomie that corresponds to a state of disorganization, destruction, of a group or society, due to the partial or total disappearance of the norms and values common to its members. Robert K. Merton (1968) later adopted this idea adding that social cohesion is endangered when there is too great a tension between the goals proposed and the legitimately accessible means.

Sociologist and jurist Enrico Ferri (1856–1929) proposed a multifactorial approach juxtaposing various endogenous (referring to the characteristics of Lombroso criminal type) and exogenous determinisms (grouping together the factors of the physical environment, such as climate, the nature of the soil, the constitution

A. Hirschelmann (✉)
Laboratoire de Psychologie de Caen Normandie (LPCN), Université de Caen Normandie, Caen, France
e-mail: astrid.hirschelmann@unicaen.fr

A. R. Rasho
University of Rennes 2, Rennes, France
e-mail: abdul-rahman.rasho@univ-rennes2.fr

© Springer Nature Switzerland AG 2021

A. Hamburger et al. (eds.), *Social Trauma – An Interdisciplinary Textbook*,
https://doi.org/10.1007/978-3-030-47817-9_32

of the family, and economic and political organization). Advocating that there is no such thing as free will and that crime is the result of an addition of multiple factors facilitating delinquency, he offers a valuable model for his effort to encompass both endogenous and exogenous aspects thereby reconciling medical and sociological approaches. This initial research then gives way to etiological research on the social environment, which remains unsatisfactory because it is reductive and often invalidated by the reality of things. From a sociological point of view, the question arises, why not everyone commits a crime and responds by committing to the criminal law (Becker, 1968) or the strength of the social bond (Hirschi, 1969). The more deeply rooted the subject in his or her family, the less temptation he or she will have to commit crimes. Marvin Wolfgang and Franco Ferracuti (1964) begin to reconcile sociological and clinical approaches by considering that violence becomes an integral part of the society through learning or identification that distorts people values judgments. Walter C. Reckless (2010) develops the theory of containment and contrasts internal and external barriers. While the former corresponds to a kind of ego force that controls and limits the subject's impulses, the latter refers to the social structure and teaches the subject to respect others.

Sociological approaches emphasize the influence of certain social phenomena on crime and the criminal, the impact of crime on the society, and the need for social rehabilitation of the criminal. Since the society or the environments represent both a place of exchange and a limit that the subject encounters, the notion of the victim arises. The approaches discussed above lead to a double notion of the victim: the victim of a crime and the criminal subject as the victim of the society. Representing the relational mode that links the subject to others, these aspects refer to a phenomenon of a constant interaction between the environment and the individual. The subject is modified by the action of the environment as much as it exerts influence on him or her. In that sense, violence describes the way of being in the world. The passage to criminal acts cannot be thought of in the subjective network of motivations without the context that gives it meaning. The act arises and makes sense, not only for the subject, but also in the world, from a situation in the world.

32.2 Learning Outcome for Social Trauma: The Psychological Work Between Crime, Social Trauma, and Individual Trauma

The evolution of scientific discourse in general means that knowledge and prevention are necessary. Thus, the duty of psychopathology is to make the act or symptom no longer recognized as foreign to the subject, but, being of its own making, to allow from there the possibility of therapy or re-education by helping the individual to become the subject of his history, that is to say, of his past when it takes on meaning, or to allow the sentence to become evolutionary (Pouget, 1987, pp. 31–34).

In this way, psychopathology has to confront both the care for the subject and the society expectations, and must respond to a twofold need, in the face of which it must define its position.

As a human fact, violence refers to the individual or collective personality of its perpetrators in a given situation, and is distinguished by nature, which is objective and which, alone, exists outside of consciousness.

The event does not leave the individual indifferent. In some cases, a trauma is established in survivors, participants, and witnesses. The occurrence of a potentially traumatic event, regardless of the level of violence, can lead to reactions and psychological repercussions that are more or less pronounced and specific to each individual. Indeed, the impact and the level of trauma in individuals vary according to several factors: the intensity of the event, the level of involvement (direct or indirect), sociocultural characteristics (age, gender, ethnicity, etc.), previous victimization, psychological vulnerability, social reactions, etc. (Crocq, 2012; Wemmers, 2017).

Psychological trauma is defined as a strong, sudden, and unexpected intrusion into the individual psyche. Following Laplanche and Pontalis, psychical trauma is an event in the subject's life defined by its intensity, by the subject's incapacity to respond adequately to it, and by the upheaval and long-lasting effects that it brings about in the psychical organization. In economic terms, the trauma is characterized by an influx of excitations that is excessive by the standard of the subject's tolerance and capacity to master such excitations and work them out psychically (Laplanche & Pontalis, 1973/1967, p. 466).

Trauma has often been discussed in its individual dimension, but what about its social dimension?

Psycho-criminology with its analysis of criminogenic processes on the one hand and the psychological and social rehabilitation through criminal punishment on the other paves the way to psycho-victimology, which essentially places the victim into a relationship with the perpetrator and the perpetrated or suffered act(s) of violence.

More precisely, psycho-victimology sees the event as a test of reality requiring a singular psychological work with the victim. This work consists of psychologically elaborating the event as well as the psychopathological repercussions caused by the impact it may have had on the psyche. Pascal Pignol and Guillaume Galinand (2016) observe that the social dimension is sometimes added to the statement that certain psychological traumas are treated more with the intention of a social adaptation than with the aim of a psychological reconstruction of the "subject."

Psycho-victimology does not deny the always current bases of psychotherapy for traumatized subjects, so that the event reaches consciousness, to assist in elaborating it, to provoke purging of the emotions that remained attached to the event, to lead to the integration of the event into consciousness through the "act of memory," which then gives it the value of a memory. But, in addition, the analysis of spontaneous statements of victimized subjects reveals a clinic that we could describe as the "clinic of the *why?*" since a set of often dead-end questions is omnipresent, the content of which refers to the same issues of guilt and responsibility that any judicial process attempts to answer. The challenge will then be to devise a framework for development and intervention that incorporates the characteristics of this socio-legal condition in order to bring out the dimensions of the singular psychological work it requires.

According to Carole Damiani (2008), the judicial process would have the essential function of restoring the bond of belonging to the community that the trauma has more or less seriously destroyed by breaking into the "group envelopes," causing what Claude Barrois (2010) refers to this as the "*community breakdown.*" The experience of abandonment and the questioning of collective values justify a double work. On the one hand, the search for personal meaning in the event and, on the other, the restoration of a sense of belonging to the community. It will be justified in that what is at issue is the psychological damage, whether or not the facts have been brought to court. The term "victim" cannot be used, as can the term "perpetrator," unless a judicial process has been initiated. The result in practice is that there are many initiatives (particularly in associations) offering innovative support practices such as psycho-judicial support and group practices.

What is at stake is the creation of a history, a history that is not only a knowledge of the past but also a recognition without which no true reconstruction seems possible. Janine Altounian's writings (1999, 2000) on the Armenian genocide offer a remarkable example of this.

Yet Sandrine Lefranc and Lilian Mathieu, (2009), in a work devoted to victim groups advocacy movements, show how difficult it has been and continues to be for victims to assert rights that often had been completely ignored before they denounced the problems resulting from this denial. Victims' associations must therefore work to create the law that will enable them to assert their prejudices, in a double work of claiming.

In summary and formulated as a learning outcome of this contribution: In psycho-victimology, the challenge will be to devise a framework for elaboration and intervention that incorporates the characteristics of the socio-legal condition in order to bring out dimensions of the psychological work that it requires: the psychological work of the victim.

32.3 Preferred Model of Explanation: The Specific Example of the Social Trauma of Yezidi Women

The Yezidi, who live in northern Iraq in the Sinjar region, are a Kurdish minority group distinguished by their religion rather than by ethnic or linguistic differences. In August 2014, this minority was under attack by the Islamic State (ISIS) because of their religious beliefs. Men were killed, women and children were taken as hostages, and only a few people were able to flee to Mount Sinjar. The children must now feed the terrorist ideology and serve as future suicide bombers. Women are being used as sex slaves. Today, most of the survivors are settled in refugee camps in Iraqi Kurdistan, in precarious life conditions. The majority of these women testify that they saw themselves die during their escape in August 2014: they had to walk for a long time under gunfire or threats, they were forced to abandon a sick child or an elderly relative, they came across many corpses on their way to escape and tried to survive in the open air and without means or food for several days. On the other hand, the captured women have testified about their complete powerlessness in situations where they were sold and bought on the market, raped almost every day, and physically and psychologically abused. In addition, most of these women were direct or indirect witnesses (via social networks, ISIS propaganda videos, etc.) of the death of their spouses, sons, fathers, and brothers.

In order to better understand this trauma, we administered the Damiani & da Costa's "Traumaq" questionnaire (Damiani and da Costa, 2006) to 52 surviving Yezidi women, widows, aged between 28 and 52 years old, living in refugee camps in Iraqi Kurdistan, who voluntarily agreed to fill it out. The 'Traumaq' questionnaire, addressed to the target population, contains socio-cultural characteristics, the nature of the event, the medical and psychological history of the individual before and after the event.

The Yezidi women completed the questionnaire 5 years after the event that the Yezidi community calls genocide.

Results pointed to extremely high scores of complex trauma. These results were confirmed in clinical interviews. These results are consistent with those of many similar studies (Denkinger et al., 2018; Kizilhan, 2018; Gerdau et al., 2017; Kizilhan and Noll-Hussong, 2017).

This type of psychological trauma can be explained by the intensity of violence these women were exposed to, their personal history, and it is further heightened by a traumatic collective memory. According to the psycho-victimological approach, the trauma of the subjective position merges with the history of victimhood shared by the community. Indeed, psychological trauma has taken a very special place in the collective mind. "*Trauma now refers to both individual and collective injury that does not refer to a singular history but to an extraordinary event. My injury becomes the testimony of what happened to the whole community*" (Sarthou-Lajus & Rechtman, 2011, p. 175). The similarity in the severity of trauma in these Yezidi women, regardless of the level of personal involvement, can be explained by a collective reaction linked to the past of this religious minority. In fact, it is estimated that 74 genocides have been committed against Yezidis over the past 800 years (Kizilhan, 2016). When the object of violence concerns the principles and values of the group, in this case, the "genocidal" attack, a kind of collective identification occurs in the form of social trauma in which each individual shares the same feelings and affects regardless of his or her level of involvement in the traumatic event.

32.4 Practical Implications of Psycho-Victimology in the Context of Social Trauma

Any victimization, whether or not it has had more or less serious psychological repercussions, not only tests the victimized subjects in their ability to deal with the common legal and more generally social norms and values, but also solicits, if not puts to the test, their personal norms and values around the same issues, in the framework of a real internal process in which they can hold all the places simultaneously or successively. The integration of judicial responses by the victimized subject and his or her internal elaborations turn out to be two sides of the same process, the issue at stake being the after-the-fact test of his or her presence at the event and its repercussions.

According to Gérard Lopez (2010), the main points of intervention consist of the following:

- Ask questions about the traumatic past clearly and simply, from the first interview.
- Be prepared to receive and manage the answers by familiarizing with the medical–social–judicial care network; clearly take the victim's side so as not to become the (involuntary) accomplice of the (involuntary) denial, characteristic of the "aggressor system" that maintains the confusion.
- Establish a relationship of trust with these subjects, who have always been betrayed by the people that were responsible for protecting them, but who are indispensable for good therapeutic compliance.
- Refer constantly to the law, but not to impose the filing of a complaint as an indispensable prerequisite for therapeutic work.
- Define the therapeutic framework democratically with a subject who has always lived in a system of imposed domination (the law of the strongest) and reframe each attempt to transgress the framework.
- Show empathy by trying to identify the emotions felt by the patient, while keeping the distance that keeps the therapeutic framework within the previously defined limits (this is not sympathy, which would consist in identifying oneself completely with the suffering person).
- Control the traumatic counter-transference and the projective identification mechanisms so as not to risk unconsciously putting oneself in the position of the aggressor; prohibit any passage to the act, sexual in particular, which would be the literal repetition of traumatic events (the therapist must ask himself/herself whether he has a tendency to behave in an aggressive way).

We can see the risks of aberrations to which social trauma exposes a professional who is dislodged from his/her traditional position of neutrality; when listening to 'subjectivity', he/she is confronted with a subject who is the victim of such violations of his/her rights that he can no longer assert or defend them. It is the citizen within him who is also mobilized. Is there still a place for a psychologist's position that respects both a "duty to abstain," which is the foundation of his or her professional singularity, and a commitment without which the victimized subject risks experiencing psychological "help" as a new disavowal?

It is then perhaps his deontology rather than his ethics that becomes the major issue of this meeting: a psychologist or psychiatrist at the risk of his/her professional obligations. From this point of view, the psychological approach to victims appears as a new challenge, an invitation, if not an intimation, to think about the strictly ethical dimension of the framework of practice. The characteristic of any psychological practice is its ability to use institutional practices. It serves as a pretext for the development of a clinical space driven by the search for psychological change. Thus, keeping as close as possible to the changes in our society, psychologists are constantly solicited by new fields, new questions, new problems, forcing them to make methodological, technical, and notional inventions that incorporate these new conditions of practice and the characteristics of the new populations in charge.

We have highlighted what constitutes the generic principle, that is, contextualization, or, more precisely, a systematic search for an event and/or a current or past context likely to account for the occurrence of the disorders presented by the subject. This search for the context will involve a systematic questioning of the existential situation encountered and the search for possible moments of rupture. We have also seen that the contextualization-related activities cannot be limited to the sole impact of an event or a context, but must also involve the reactions of the victim's entourage (including social, medical, judicial, etc.), in a search for possible "secondary trauma" factors, as well as the aggressor's *modus operandi* and possible decriminalization strategies, when there has been an aggressor.

32.5 Recommended Further Reading and Information

European Society for Traumatic Stress Studies (http://www.estss.org).

International Journal of Victimology (http://www.jidv.com).

L'institut de victimologie (http://www.institutdevictimologie.fr/).

The Association of Training and Research of Medical-Psychological Emergency Cells - French Society of Psychotraumatology (http://www.aforcump-sfp.org/index.html).

The European Network for Traumatic Stress (http://www.tentsproject.eu).

The French Language Association for the Study of Stress and Trauma (http://www.alfest-trauma.com/).

The International Review of Victimology (https://journals.sagepub.com/home/irv).

References

Altounian, J. (2000). *La survivance [Survival]*. Paris: Dunod.

Altounian, J. (1999). Putting into words, putting to rest and putting aside the ancestors. *The International Journal of Psychoanalysis, 80*(3), 439–448.

Barrois, C. (2010). Le trauma, un symptôme de la culture de notre époque? [Trauma, a symptom of today's culture?]. *Revue francophone du stress et du trauma, 10*(4), 199–205.

Becker, G. S. (1968). Crime and punishment: An economic approach. *Journal of Political Economy, 76*, 169–217.

Crocq, L. (2012). *16 leçons sur le trauma [16 lessons on trauma]*. Paris: Odile Jacob.

Damiani, C., & da Costa, M. P. (2006). *Traumaq: questionnaire d'évaluation du traumatisme [Traumaq: trauma assessment questionnaire]*. Paris: ECPA, Les Editions du Centre de Psychologie Appliquée.

Damiani, C. (2008). L'accompagnement psychologique durant le parcours judiciaire [Psychological support during the judicial process]. *Psycho Média, 16*, 71–77.

Denkinger, J. K., Windthorst, P., Rometsch-Ogioun El Sount, C., Blume, M., Sedik, H., Kizilhan, J. I., & Nikendei, C. (2018). Secondary traumatization in caregivers working with women and children who suffered extreme violence by the "Islamic state". *Frontiers in Psychiatry, 9*, 234.

Durkheim, E., & Lukes, S. (2013). Durkheim: *The division of labour in society*. Basingstoke (Hampshire) : Palgrave Macmillan.

Durkheim, E., Catlin, G. E. G., Mueller, J. H., & Solovay, S. A. (1938). *The rules of sociological method* (Vol. 8). New York: Free Press.

Gerdau, I., Kizilhan, J. I., & Noll-Hussong, M. (2017). Posttraumatic stress disorder and related disorders among female Yazidi refugees following Islamic state of Iraq and Syria attacks—A case series and mini-review. *Frontiers in Psychiatry, 8*, 282.

Ferracutti, F., & Wolfgang, M. E. (1964). Violent aggressive behavior as a socio-psychological phenomenon. *Revista Jurudica de la Universidad Puerto Rico, 33*(2), 251–262.

Hirschi, T. (1969). *Causes of delinquency*. Berkeley: University of California Press.

Kizilhan, J. I. (2018). PTSD of rape after IS ("Islamic state") captivity. *Archives of Women's Mental Health, 21*(5), 517–524.

Kizilhan, J. I., & Noll-Hussong, M. (2017). Individual, collective, and transgenerational traumatization in the Yazidi. *BMC Medicine, 15*(1), 198.

Kizilhan, J. I. (2016). *Die Psychologie des IS: Die Logik der Massenmörder*. Europa Verlag GmbH & Company KG.

Laplanche, J., & Pontalis, J. B. (1967). *Vocabulaire de la psychanalyse*. Paris: PUF.

Lefranc S., & Mathieu L. (2009). *Mobilisation de victimes*. Rennes: Presses Universitaires de Rennes.

Lopez, P. (2010). *La victimologie*. Paris: Dalloz.

Merton, R. K. (1968). *Social theory and social structure*. New York: Free Press.

Pignol, P., & Galinand, G. (2016). Quinze ans d'expérience d'une consultation spécialisée en victimologie au CH Guillaume Régnier de Rennes. *L'information psychiatrique, 92*(2), 151–162. https://doi.org/10.1684/ipe.2016.1453.

Pouget, R. (1987). Ethique et expertise psychiatrique. *Actualités Psychiatriques, 3*, 31–34.

Reckless, W. C. (2010). Containment theory. In F. T. Cullen & P. Wilcox (Eds.), *Encyclopedia of criminological theory* (pp. 777–782). Thousand Oaks: Sage Publication. https://doi.org/10.4135/9781412959193.n213

Sarthou-Lajus, N., & Rechtman, R. (2011). Enquête sur la condition de victime. *Etudes, 414*(2), 175–186.

Wemmers, J. A. M. (2017). *Victimology: A Canadian perspective*. University of Toronto Press.

Part VII
Specific Methodology and Practice in Social Trauma Research

Chapter 33
Social Trauma Research

Vladimir Hedrih

33.1 Introduction

When considering the relationship between social trauma and scientific research, one should have in mind two categories of issues:

- Situations in which scientific research or the results of scientific research are the cause or are used as justification for social traumatic events.
- Specific methodological issues in researching social trauma.

33.1.1 Scientific Research as Cause/Justification of Social Traumatic Events

While modern scientific research is typically very strictly regulated in the area of ethics and the preservation of well-being of research participants is of prime importance, this was not always the case. History of science records such famous cases like the "experiment" allegedly carried out by orders of Emperor Frederick II of the Holy Roman Empire where an attempt was made to raise children without human interaction to test if they would start speaking a language by themselves and which language it would be. According to the legend about this experiment, the babies died. Much better documented is the Tuskegee syphilis study (Brandt, 1978), that lasted for 40 years, between 1932 and 1972. In this case, researchers aiming to study the natural progression of syphilis without treatment, caused or contributed to the deaths of a hundred study participants and caused significant health problems to other participants. They did this by deceiving infected research participants that

V. Hedrih (✉)
Faculty of Philosophy, University of Niš, Niš, Serbia
e-mail: vladimir.hedrih@filfak.ni.ac.rs

© Springer Nature Switzerland AG 2021

A. Hamburger et al. (eds.), *Social Trauma – An Interdisciplinary Textbook*,
https://doi.org/10.1007/978-3-030-47817-9_33

they were receiving effective cure for syphilis, while actively preventing them from receiving the already available cure. A very important aspect of this study is the fact that researchers performing it believed their treatment of participants was justified by the fact that the skin of the participants was dark, that is, that participants belonged to the "Negro race" as it was referred to by scientists of the time. The "race theory" that dominated the social science of the time claimed that there are "races" of humans that differ in their properties. The "Negro race" was considered to have particularly bad characteristics – that it is prone to disease, vice, and crime, and in a degenerative evolution process (Brandt, 1978). This attitude also included the perception of these people as being of lower value; hence, the mistreatment toward them was justified.

The history of psychological science is also riddled with studies in which researchers ended up causing harm or showing extreme disregard for the well-being of study participants. The famous case of "Little Albert" (Griggs, 2015) who was used as a subject in a study exploring emotional conditioning (i.e., a study applying classical conditions on an emotionally typical-development infant with the goal of causing a phobia) and that sparked a debate about the preservation of well-being of research participants that lasts to this day is an example of this. The same can be said for the famous Stanford prison experiment or the famous Milgram's experiment (Haslam & Reicher, 2012).

While all the listed studies ended up at least temporarily compromising the well-being of study participants, from the aspect of the topic of social trauma, the Tuskegee syphilis study stands out. Unlike the other listed examples, in this study, beliefs about the group the study participants belonged to made researchers see their mistreatment as justified. It should be noted that this happened in a climate where social scientists, or at least a substantial proportion of them was actively "warning" the public about the adverse effects of mixing with "races" they considered lower (e.g., Grant, 1916) or even of the very existence of such "races" (Brigham, 1923).

Another important phenomenon to consider are studies that, while not causing harm to their direct participants, provided a "scientific" justification or even inspired the infliction of traumatic events on people based on their group membership. An example of this are scientific publications and inferences made from the early applications of intelligence tests in testing immigrants to the United States and recruits for the US Army in the first decades of the twentieth century. Based on the firm (but wrong) assumption that nonverbal intelligence tests are free of cultural influences, researchers reported pronounced differences between ethnic groups in their intelligence levels making alarming (but wrong) conclusions that intelligence of Americans will decline in the future until it falls so low that it will destroy the structure of the society if action is not taken (e.g., Brigham, 1923). Reporting and summarizing the results of these studies, Carl Brigham, a prominent US psychologist of the first decades of the twentieth century, for example, calls for steps to be taken "toward the prevention of the continued propagation of defective strains in the current population" (Brigham, 1923, p. 210). Recommendations such as these were applied only a few decades later by Nazi Germany and its allies in the form of policies of extermination of "unwanted" and

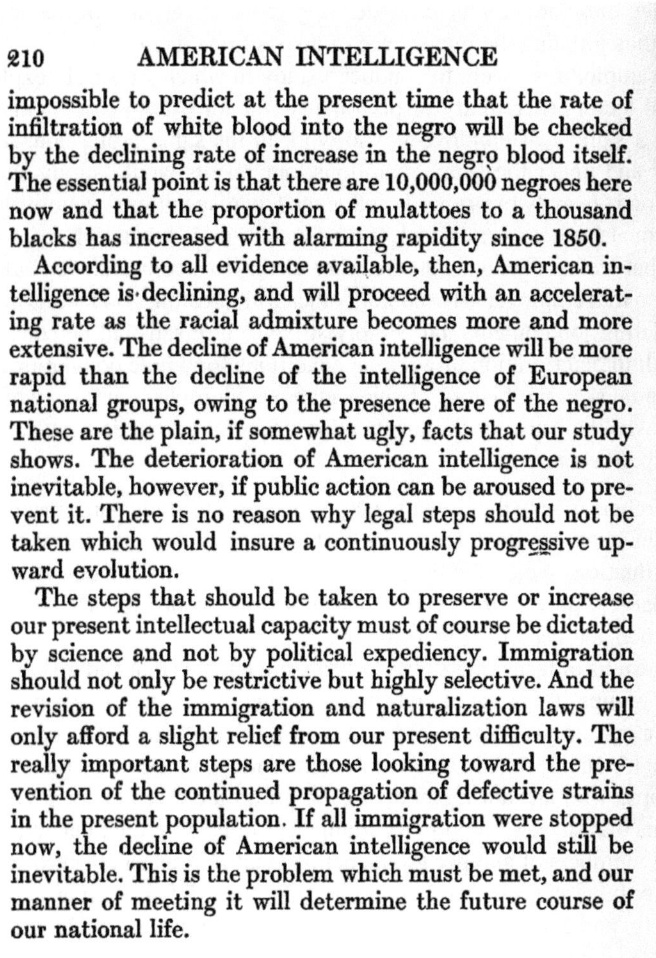

210 AMERICAN INTELLIGENCE

impossible to predict at the present time that the rate of infiltration of white blood into the negro will be checked by the declining rate of increase in the negro blood itself. The essential point is that there are 10,000,000 negroes here now and that the proportion of mulattoes to a thousand blacks has increased with alarming rapidity since 1850.

According to all evidence available, then, American intelligence is declining, and will proceed with an accelerating rate as the racial admixture becomes more and more extensive. The decline of American intelligence will be more rapid than the decline of the intelligence of European national groups, owing to the presence here of the negro. These are the plain, if somewhat ugly, facts that our study shows. The deterioration of American intelligence is not inevitable, however, if public action can be aroused to prevent it. There is no reason why legal steps should not be taken which would insure a continuously progressive upward evolution.

The steps that should be taken to preserve or increase our present intellectual capacity must of course be dictated by science and not by political expediency. Immigration should not only be restrictive but highly selective. And the revision of the immigration and naturalization laws will only afford a slight relief from our present difficulty. The really important steps are those looking toward the prevention of the continued propagation of defective strains in the present population. If all immigration were stopped now, the decline of American intelligence would still be inevitable. This is the problem which must be met, and our manner of meeting it will determine the future course of our national life.

Fig. 33.1 The conclusion of the 1923 book *A Study of American Intelligence* by Carl Brigham, Chief of Psychology Division, Office of the Surgeon General of the US Army at the time

"lower" races. In this way, this can be considered to represent a case in which (flawed) scientific conclusions were used as a direct justification for social traumatic events (Fig. 33.1).

Another type of research studies in psychology where one should consider their potential to inspire harmful social consequences are those focusing exclusively on dispositional or inborn factors of certain behavior of interest while neglecting the non-dispositional and environmental factors. It often happens that researchers studying certain behavior focus exclusively on dispositional psychological factors, as these can easily be assessed using psychological tests, even when these explain only a minuscule part of the variance of the studied behavior, while neglecting the non-dispositional factors that are not as easy to assess. It might also happen that studies like these are conducted under very reduced variance of the environmental variable thus inflating the importance of dispositional factors.

For example, if we were to conduct a study in which we would explore the dispositional factors (hereditary or personality) of, for example, job satisfaction, but did it on a sample of employees who work in the same profession, for the same company and under the same conditions, our results would surely show that job satisfaction is heavily or primarily influenced by dispositional factors, while effects of situational factors are minimal. If we failed to notice that such results are due to the fact that we have reduced all the other factors to a constant, we could come to a conclusion that employers should not bother with creating good working conditions or stimulating job contents, but simply strive to hire satisfied persons. This could then result in deterioration of working conditions for whole population groups.

To summarize, the history of science shows multiple examples when scientific research was the cause or the justification of social traumatic events. These situations happen when:

- Researchers, due to their own views, cause harm to study participants while finding that harm justified for reasons of participants' group membership. While such situations seemed to have been abundant in the past, modern ethical regulations largely prevent this type of behavior from occurring, or at least from being published and becoming mainstream.
- Conclusions of researchers lead to or inspire policies that end up harming certain social groups. This case often happens in situations when researchers, striving to solve a certain problem in order to help a certain group, end up causing harm (through policies based on research conclusion) to members of another group or to people who are not members of the group the researchers strive to protect. Actions that strive to support a certain discriminated group, but end up discriminating members of another group, actions that start as an effort to create greater equality but end up in mass violations of human rights (such as was the case of Marxism and communist states) (Acemoglu & Robinson, 2013) and all the other possible situations where researchers proposing measures to improve the situation of a certain group neglect the consequences of these measures on other groups or neglect to take into account the practicalities needed to apply such measures are all examples of this.
- Scientific research focuses on easy-to-measure or accessible variables, convenient ranges of values of these variables, or conveniently available groups of participants, but generalize their findings to all variables, full range of variable values and entire populations. Such results may then lead to actions that are inadequate for large groups of people and situations (those not represented in the studies) thus failing to provide them with the needed support or outright causing harm.

33.1.2 *Specific Methodological Issues in Researching Social Trauma*

To avoid this, it is very important that, when reflecting on their research results and particularly when formulating recommendations for action:

- Researchers take into account all the stakeholders, groups, and individuals affected by proposed actions, not just those that are the focus of the effort the study is a part of and reflect on how the recommended actions would affect each of them.
- Researchers be aware of the limitations of their studies, especially the limitations of the study sample, the study variables, and their operationalizations and restrict any generalizations only to populations, variables, and ranges of variable values that were adequately represented in the study.
- Researchers reflect on and maintain awareness of parts of the population of interest that were not represented in the study, variables that were not included in the study, and kinds of values of study variables that were not included in the study, and provide reasons for that.
- Researchers should also be aware of the effect sizes obtained between the study variables as often detected effects can be negligible, although shown as statistically significant.

33.2 Learning Outcome Related to Social Trauma

Planning a research on social trauma requires taking into account specific methodological issues appearing in the field. For this reason, we will first make an overview of the (desired) properties of scientific knowledge and discuss issues related with achieving these properties in social trauma research. For methodological consideration, it should be noted that key properties of social-trauma-related phenomena are that they include traumatic events, that they involve relations between at least two large social groups, that these events will typically be unrecognized or perceived differently by at least one of the groups involved; there is often a conspiracy of silence around them in the group causing or maintaining the traumatic situation, and they are essential or at least very important for group identity (Hamburger, 2018). How do these properties interact with the desired properties of scientific method and scientific knowledge? Scientific knowledge should be as follows:

- Tentative—meaning that all scientific knowledge is only provisional, scientific theories, explanations, and generalizations accepted only as long as they are supported by available data and readily replaced as soon as a better theory, explanation, or generalization becomes available. When social trauma research is in question, given that narratives about traumatic events often become parts of collective identities of groups, often even fixed in laws, official documents, and memorials, tentativeness can be very hard to achieve, as changes in the scientific narrative about particular traumatic events or their consequences or antecedents could be opposed by parties from the society with a stake in keeping the existing narrative unchanged, leading to pressure against the scientists or possibly even their prosecution.

- Easy to replicate—meaning that results of scientific research should always be presented in such a way that other researchers could repeat the procedures to test whether the same result would be obtained. However, with social trauma research, researchers often study consequences of traumatic events that have already happened without the involvement of the researcher and that cannot be replicated for both practical and ethical reasons (e.g., Gorup, 2011; Volkan, 2001);.
- Based on observation—scientific knowledge should come as a product of observation, and direct observation of phenomena under study at best. But with social trauma, researchers are typically able to study narratives and properties of survivors and only of those survivors that are accessible to the researchers. They might also be sometimes able to study physical traces or consequences of traumatic events if any, but this is usually only possible much after the event has taken place. For example, research on the Holocaust only became possible after the World War Two ended, and this means several years after most of the horrors took place and a large part of it was made possible owing to the preservation of archives documenting the atrocities, which is a rare case (e.g., Blanke & Kristel, 2013). Research on the traumatic consequences of actions of the communist regime in Eastern Europe became possible only after the fall of communism, meaning decades after traumatic events occurred (e.g., Bezo & Maggi, 2015; Gorup, 2011; Volker & Flap, 1997).
- Objective/unbiased—one important classical requirement is that scientific knowledge be "objective," "ideologically neutral," "unbiased," requiring the researcher to be only guided by results of his/her research. However, more novel contributors to the scientific thought correctly noticed that such requirements are not realistic, because a researcher cannot suddenly just suspend his/her own subjective beliefs by deciding to do so, nor does any researcher possess a "god's eye" perspective on the phenomenon he/she is studying, allowing him/her to see every detail and then decide to take them all into account impartially. The reality is that even if we could somehow prevent personal beliefs of the researcher to influence interpretations of research results, personal beliefs of the researcher will surely influence the question he/she is posing and thus also the data he/she is collecting. For this reason, this requirement to be objective has been replaced with the requirement that the researcher reflects on ways in which his/her personal beliefs and opinions influence his/her research in all aspects of that research (Mantzoukas, 2005; Wittgenstein, 1958). This demand is especially important when researching social trauma-related topics as these are typically subject to contested interpretations held by various stakeholders in these events. For example, reading research studies related to traumatic events caused by the Israeli-Palestinian conflict shows quite different views of the context in which these

events happen, depending on the side from which the authors come (e.g., Alhajjar, 2014; Berger, Gelkopf, & Heineberg, 2012). While this conflict is just an example, the same issue happens in studies dealing with topics related to any conflict between large groups, and social trauma topics are always about relations between large groups.

- Transparent—researchers should clearly present all steps they took in designing the study, providing justification for all decisions, and present the logical process that leads from becoming aware of the research problem, through research questions to the conclusions.

33.3 Preferred Model of Explanation

Having these requirements in mind, we should consider the typical problems that plague research in general but that can often be exacerbated in social trauma research if researchers are not aware of them and are not careful enough to prevent them:

- Inaccurate observations happen when observations of researchers are simply not correct or accurate. Inaccurate observations may happen for a number of reasons; social trauma research is particularly vulnerable in that sense. In a research situation, the phenomenon of the "conspiracy of silence" (Hamburger, 2018) may easily create a situation where research participants intentionally withhold important information related to traumatic events abiding by the "conspiracy of silence" within their group. It might also happen that researchers, due to pressures of their own group or their personal loyalties and beliefs, record observations that are inaccurate, that do not accurately represent what they have observed, or omit recording observations that would go against their belief or cause researchers to come under pressure from authorities in their social group.
- Overgeneralization happens when a study is performed on limited or selected samples and the results generalized to the entire population, that is, to a much broader population than the content of the sample merits. In social trauma research, this might happen when research is performed on, for example, refugees, but only those who came to the country of researchers and, of them, only those who are available to researchers, that is, those willing to participate, available in a collective center, or registered with some central authority. It might also happen when only a single social-trauma-related event is studied, but generalizations are made about a whole class of events or phenomena.
- Selective observation happens when a researcher deliberately or by omission fails to observe all important aspects of the phenomena under study, or records only some. It might also happen that authorities in the place of study prepare a "showcase exhibit," allowing them to study, but preventing them access to other places of interest, which might create a completely different picture. Examples of this include accounts of a party participating in a war, improving the living conditions and treatment of detainees or prisoners of war just before an external

inspection, or allowing the inspection of only the "showcase" facilities in which conditions are good. This type of methodological omission is performed also when researchers take into account only the information provided by one source, while not looking for or deliberately omitting to look for others.

- Ex post facto hypothesizing happens when a process is studied only after it had already happened. Researchers then know only the end condition of the phenomenon under study and go on to derive hypothesis and conclusions about the causes of the result they are observing from the result only. While this is an undesirable situation in science and ex post facto hypothesizing is generally considered bad methodology, it is often the only available approach to study with many social-trauma-related phenomena. In general, researchers can study the effects of social traumatic events only after they have happened. They may not cause traumatic events in order to study them nor would it be ethical for them to let a social-trauma-related process take its course in order to study it. Researchers also typically find out about social traumatic events or gain the access needed to study them after they have already taken place.
- Personal interests in the outcome: Social-trauma-related processes are in general emotionally involving and include relations between large groups. Researchers are also members of large groups and even if their group is not directly involved in the traumatic processes studied, they may feel closer to one party, then another. This may result in researchers seeking data that are more likely to provide results that promote the interests of the party they favor, while neglecting data that go against their interests.
- Premature closure of inquiry happens when researchers finish their data collection too early, before the key developments have already happened. They may do this due to a lack of funds or poor understanding of the studied phenomenon, but it might also happen that they are prevented from continuing data collection so that they do not discover what the party controlling the work of researchers (authorities of the place where the research is taking place funders of the research) would not like to be discovered, while still pretending to be open for research. In this way, for example, researchers investigating the negative health effects of some government-supported action might be forced to stop the investigation before the negative health effects they were looking for had time to develop. Researchers investigating the situation of a minority group might be forced to close their inquiry into their status right before aggressive actions toward that minority start, etc. In this way, researchers might report negative results even though continued study of the phenomenon would yield positive results.
- Illogical reasoning happens when researchers draw conclusions that do not logically follow from the available data or are in direct contradiction to it. Drawing causal inferences from correlation data, drawing conclusions for which there is no basis in the data, or interpreting data in only one way when both theory and structure of data would allow for multiple explanations; drawing conclusions that are in opposition to what data shows are all examples of this type of issue. Illogical reasoning may be, and often is, the result of poor methodological training of researchers, but can also be the result of wishful thinking, where the

researcher ignores the data altogether and writes conclusions that he/she likes or favors although they do not stem from the data.

- Pseudoscience is probably the most extreme breach of good scientific conduct. With pseudoscience, a researcher blatantly pushes his/her agenda (political, personal or other) with total disregard for the tenets of science, while all the way pretending that his/her work is scientific, in order to keep the authority and respect science has. In social trauma research, such a researcher would push his/her view and use any means necessary to deceive others that conclusions and views he/she pushes are results of the scientific research. Made up or falsified data, cherry-picking, illogical reasoning, deliberately inaccurate, or selective observations are all tools used to make others believe in the claims of the pseudoscientists. In research of social-trauma-related phenomena, it is not rare to see people pretending to be researchers behaving in the way described above in order to promote views of his/her social group and convince the public in their veracity.

When doing research in the area of social trauma, but also when studying results provided by others, researchers should be aware of all these issues and critically examine both their own work and research they rely on and evaluate if any of these issues or deficiencies are present. They should then either take steps to correct them or take them into account when assessing the value of scientific research done by others.

33.4 Practical Implications

There are at least three major issues to be taken into account when planning research in social trauma—the social trauma research, context, sampling issues, and finding scientific publications in the area of social trauma.

33.4.1 The Social Trauma Research Context

Researchers in the area of social trauma should take into account that social trauma research usually happens in a specific social context that is starkly different from the research context in most other areas of psychology or social science in general.

The first thing to consider is that the context of social trauma research is very emotionally involving and intensive. Psychological trauma is by its very nature something that involves intense emotions, and unprepared researchers might find themselves easily emotionally overwhelmed and experiencing secondary or vicarious trauma. For this reason, good planning requires that researchers be ready to work in such a context, and sources of support be prepared that would help them overcome the resulting emotional strain.

Social trauma research always, in one way or another, deals with relations between two or more large groups. A researcher might personally belong to one of those groups, but even if he/she does not, he/she will have to establish a relationship and form an attitude toward them. These groups might also apply direct or subtle pressure toward the researcher to provide conclusions that favor their standpoint.

Social trauma research generally takes place after a traumatic experience has already taken place and sometimes even after the social context that resulted in trauma has changed. This usually means that the researcher is left only with ex post facto hypothesizing as a way to build theory.

Another important issue when working with people who have experienced social trauma is the danger of revictimization. Apart from the fact that the researcher will ask the study participants to recall terrifying, traumatic experiences for the sake of research, thus making them relive the extreme negative emotions of the event, there are other possible and much more serious forms of revictimization to which the researcher might inadvertently expose research participants. For example, as it was mentioned before, the conspiracy of silence (Hamburger, 2018) is an important property of the social trauma context. It might be possible that by having research participants talk about traumatic events they have experienced to the researcher and thus acknowledging that these events have happened, participants would be breaking the conspiracy of silence, which might result in negative consequences for the participants themselves, especially after the researcher leaves. These consequences might include condemnation by their social group, harassment, prosecution, and, sometimes, involve bodily harm or death (the participant being murdered for talking). Another example is when researchers are studying members of a persecuted group who are living among members of the group persecuting them by hiding their group identity. In such cases, the researcher's interaction with such people creates the risk of revealing the true group identity of participants to the public, thus putting them at risk of further persecution, bodily harm, or even death.

Researchers in the area of social trauma should also be aware that information obtained during their research data collection might have legal implications for the participants. Inquiries into social trauma-related topics might result in obtaining information about atrocities, illegal activities, misuse, harassment, violence toward certain groups, all of this performed either individually or in an organized way. For example, if the researcher is interviewing war veterans, such research might reveal that a war veteran participating in the research has been involved in war crimes or criminal conduct. It might also turn out that a person now listed as a refugee participated in hostilities and was involved in atrocities. Researchers might find out that a participant of the study was a witness or an active party to violent events that brought bodily harm to others or were criminal in another way. Before starting the data collection, researchers should reflect on the possible discoveries of this type and agree on a policy on how to deal with such information if it is acquired.

Political implications of findings are another defining feature of social trauma research. Either by confirming the existence of a traumatic event or confirming that it resulted in trauma or even by denying that a traumatic event important for group identity happened or that it happened in the way it is remembered, research findings will almost always have political implications, either by supporting or denying support to certain policies and stances of the large groups involved in the phenomena studied. Due to this, researchers should expect and be ready to deal with political pressures from interested parties and uphold the scientific standards of work and thoroughness of research in spite of those.

Finally, an important aspect of social trauma research context is the cross-cultural aspect—social trauma research by definition deals with events in which at least two large groups are involved, they may often include people residing in another country, and people speaking a different language and coming from a different culture than the researcher. Such a situation raises the issue of obtaining adequate psychological assessment instruments for participants, instruments adapted for people from their countries, which might not be readily available. Researchers should also be aware that social-trauma events can be very diverse in scope, causes, nature, duration, and many other properties, so the study design should take this into account in all its elements.

33.4.2 Sampling Issues

A good research study needs to be conducted on a sample that is as representative of the population of interest as possible. However, when studying social-trauma-related phenomena, researchers will typically face a number of issues they should take into account, as these issues may not only impact the validity of conclusions the researchers draw, but also define the very questions researchers are able to answer through empirical study:

- Social trauma research can only be conducted on those who have survived the traumatic events (e.g., Morina et al., 2010), and due to the nature of psychological research that favors big samples, this means that traumatic processes and events with higher rates of survival will be studied more. This then results in researchers focusing more on traumatic events with higher survivability, making these events more visible and better documented to the general public, although their consequences are typically milder for those suffering through these events. In other words, except in rare cases, this will result in a refugee crisis being much more visible to both science and public than genocide.
- Not all people show detectable signs of trauma-related disorders after exposure to traumatic events. However, it is typically easier for researchers to include in a study those that do and especially if they need treatment or other forms of social support, so they are registered with the help providers. This might result in researchers overestimating the prevalence of various trauma-related disorders in the exposed population.
- As said earlier, research is conducted only on survivors, but only some of those survivors are accessible to researchers—usually, those who are involved with an institution providing help or support, thereby making it possible for the researcher

to identify and contact them. Also, only some of them are willing to participate in research and talk about their traumatic experiences.
- Of those who are accessible to the researcher and who are willing to participate in the study, only some may speak about traumatic experiences without the fear of consequences. This includes professional soldiers or policemen who risk discharge from the army/police (on the grounds of health fitness for service) if diagnosed with a more serious psychological disorder (such as PTSD for example), over people who risk criminal charges should their involvement in war crimes and atrocities become known to those who risk punishment by their peers or prosecution by the authorities or the powerful group should their group identity become known, or should they break the conspiracy of silence and talk about the traumatic events.

33.4.3 Finding Scientific Literature on the Topic of Social Trauma

Although the amount of scientific literature on the topic of social trauma is growing, it is still a relatively novel term, so searching for it on the internet will still not yield many results. However, social trauma and related phenomena are indeed topics of many studies, but most such studies do not use the name "social trauma" as they come from different theoretical backgrounds. Therefore, when searching for literature on social trauma, depending on the focus of their interest in the area of social trauma, it can be useful to look up papers dealing with:

- Prevalence or epidemiology of trauma manifestations (e.g., Alhajjar, 2014; Priebe et al., 2010).
- Dispositions for trauma.
- Variables related to the likelihood of experiencing traumatic events or of traumatic events occurring (e.g., Goodman, Saxe, & Harvey, 1991).
- Diversity of reactions to traumatic events, manifestations of trauma, dispositions determining reactions to traumatic events (Morina et al., 2010).
- Consequences of trauma, immediate or transgenerational (e.g., Volkan, 2001).
- Treatment of trauma, program evaluation (e.g., Berger et al., 2012).
- Elements of large group dynamics relevant for the occurrence of traumatic events and reactions to traumatic events (e.g., Bakke et al., 2009; Kolesovs, 2019).

It might also be useful to look up studies involving variables such as exposure to traumatic events, ASD, PTSD or complex trauma, stress symptoms (especially lasting or recurring), traumatic memory, well-being, quality of life, resilience, coping, dissociative phenomena, various sociodemographic variables describing populations known to have experienced traumatic events, trust/mistrust. One might also find studies relevant for the topic of social trauma by searching for specific PTSD manifestations as some studies involve only particular variables that are known manifestations of PTSD, but do not mention PTSD as a syndrome.

33.5 Suggested Reading and Further Information

Ellis, B. H., Kia-Keating, M., Yusuf, S. A., Lincoln, A., & Nur, A. (2007). Ethical research in refugee communities and the use of community participatory methods. *Transcultural Psychiatry, 44*(3), 459–481. https://doi.org/10.1177/1363461507081642

Hedrih, V. (2020). *Adapting psychological tests and measurement instruments for cross-cultural research.* Oxon: Routledge. https://doi.org/10.4324/9780429264788

Shaughnessy, J. J., Zechmeister, E. B., & Zechmeister, J. S. (2000). *Research methods in psychology* (5th ed.). McGraw-Hill.

In one of the previous parts of this chapter, cases where authorities have set up specific "showcase exhibits" to convince the public that their policies and conduct are different from what they actually are and thus encourage selective observation have been mentioned. A famous historical example of a situation similar to this is the way Theresienstadt concentration camp was represented by the Nazi German government during WW2 (https://encyclopedia.ushmm.org/content/en/article/theresienstadt).

References

Acemoglu, D., & Robinson, J. (2013). *Why nations fail: The origins, of power, prosperity and poverty*. London: Profile Books.

Alhajjar, B. (2014). Gaza nurses after war: Are they traumatized? *Procedia - Social and Behavioral Sciences, 114*, 802–809. https://doi.org/10.1016/j.sbspro.2013.12.789

Bakke, K. M., Cao, X., O'loughlin Nnn And, J., & Ward, M. D. (2009). *Social distance in bosnia-herzegovina and the north caucasus region of Russia: Inter and intra-ethnic attitudes and identities n. Nations and Nationalism, 15*(2), 227–253.

Berger, R., Gelkopf, M., & Heineberg, Y. (2012). A teacher-delivered intervention for adolescents exposed to ongoing and intense traumatic war-related stress: A quasi-randomized controlled study. *Journal of Adolescent Health, 51*(5), 453–461. https://doi.org/10.1016/j.jadohealth.2012.02.011

Bezo, B., & Maggi, S. (2015). Living in "survival mode:" intergenerational transmission of trauma from the holodomor genocide of 1932–1933 in Ukraine. *Social Science and Medicine, 134*, 87–94. https://doi.org/10.1016/j.socscimed.2015.04.009

Blanke, T., & Kristel, C. (2013). Integrating holocaust research. *International Journal of Humanities and Arts Computing, 7*(1–2), 41–57. https://doi.org/10.3366/ijhac.2013.0080

Brandt, A. M. (1978). Racism and research: The case of the Tuskegee syphilis study. *The Hastings Center Report, 8*(6), 21–29.

Brigham, C. C. (1923). *A study of American intelligence*. Princeton: Princeton University Press.

Goodman, L., Saxe, L., & Harvey, M. (1991). Homelessness as psychological trauma. *American Psychologist, 46*(11), 1219.
Gorup, R. (2011). Representations of trauma in narratives of Goli Otok. *Serbian Studies: Journal of the North American Society for Serbian Studies, 21*(2), 151–160. https://doi.org/10.1353/ser.2011.0025
Grant, M. (1916). The passing of the great race. *Geographical Review, 2*(5), 354–360.
Griggs, R. (2015). Psychology's lost boy: Will the real little Albert please stand up? *Teaching of Psychology, 42*(1), 14–18. https://doi.org/10.1177/0098628314562668
Hamburger, A. (Ed.). (2018). *Trauma, trust, and memory: Social trauma and reconciliation in psychoanalysis, psychotherapy, and cultural memory*. London: Karnac Books Ltd..
Haslam, S. A., & Reicher, S. D. (2012). Contesting the "'nature'" of conformity: What Milgram and Zimbardo's studies really show. *PLoS Biology, 10*(11), 1–4. https://doi.org/10.1371/journal.pbio.1001426
Kolesovs, A. (2019). Sense of belonging to Latvia in Latvian-and Russian-speaking residents of Latvia. *PSIHOLOGIJA, 52*(3), 249. https://doi.org/10.2298/PSI181108002K
Mantzoukas, S. (2005). The inclusion of bias in reflective and reflexive research: A necessary prerequisite for securing validity. *Journal of Research in Nursing, 10*(3), 279–295. https://doi.org/10.1177/174498710501000305
Morina, N., Böhme, H. F., Ajdukovic, D., Bogic, M., Franciskovic, T., Galeazzi, G. M., … Priebe, S. (2010). The structure of post-traumatic stress symptoms in survivors of war: Confirmatory factor analyses of the impact of event scale-revised. *Journal of Anxiety Disorders, 24*(6), 606–611. https://doi.org/10.1016/j.janxdis.2010.04.001
Priebe, S., Bogic, M., Ashcroft, R., Franciskovic, T., Galeazzi, G. M., Kucukalic, A., … Ajdukovic, D. (2010). Experience of human rights violations and subsequent mental disorders - a study following the war in the Balkans. *Social Science and Medicine, 71*(12), 2170–2177. https://doi.org/10.1016/j.socscimed.2010.09.029
Volkan, V. D. (2001). Transgenerational transmissions and chosen traumas: An aspect of large-group identity. *Group Analysis, 34*, 79–97. https://doi.org/10.1177/05333160122077730
Volker, B., & Flap, H. (1997). The comrades' belief: Intended and unintended consequences of communism for Neighbourhood relations in the former GDR. *European Sociological Review, 13*(3), 241–265. https://doi.org/10.1093/oxfordjournals.esr.a018217
Wittgenstein, L. (1958). *Philosophical investigations*. Oxford: Basil Blackwell.

Chapter 34
Quantitative Research in Social Trauma

Sonja Protić

34.1 Introduction

Scientific approach (in the social trauma field) is an organized way of studying questions of interest, which could help us (a) better understand the nature, cause, and correlates of some phenomena, as well as (b) its impact on people and environment, and (c) establish effective preventive and treatment interventions. In conducting scientific research, we rely on both evidence-based theories, which are built on the insights of the well-design studies, which rigorously and repeatedly have tested several alternative hypotheses, as well as on the scientific method. The scientific method is a set of procedures involving: (a) definition of research problem and hypotheses, (b) developing study design, (c) sampling and measurement, (d) data analysis and interpretation, which lead to (e) confirmation or modification of hypotheses.

The aim of this chapter is to introduce specific characteristics of quantitative approach in the social trauma field, to link theoretical with practical learning outcomes through the discussion of an invented study example, as well as to review the implications and assumptions of quantitative method. In the end, the reader can find some useful references for further readings in order to achieve a deeper understanding of the presented concepts.

S. Protić (✉)
Institute of Criminological and Sociological Research, Belgrade, Serbia

International Psychoanalytic University Berlin, Berlin, Germany
e-mail: sonja.milojevic@iksi.ac.rs; sonja.protic@ipu-berlin.de

© Springer Nature Switzerland AG 2021
A. Hamburger et al. (eds.), *Social Trauma – An Interdisciplinary Textbook*,
https://doi.org/10.1007/978-3-030-47817-9_34

34.2 Learning Outcomes Related to Social Trauma

The quantitative approach represents a systematic investigation of phenomena, characterized by a collection of quantifiable data using standardized techniques and application of statistical methods for data analyses. Nevertheless, quantitative strategies are implemented at all stages of the research process.

34.2.1 Research Questions

We can recognize some common research topics in quantitative studies on social trauma. The first group is related to questions on incidence (i.e., the extent to which new cases of a disorder appear over a specified period), prevalence (i.e., all cases (new and existing) observed during a specified period), and co-occurrence of social-trauma-related symptomatology and disorders which are investigated in, so-called, epidemiological studies. As an example, one such study detected that current trauma around three times increases the risk of PTSD after a subsequent trauma only among persons who developed PTSD in a response to the prior trauma, regardless the gender, race, and education (Breslau, Peterson, & Schultz, 2008).

Probably the most frequent group of studies deals with correlates, risk, and protective factors of social trauma. Correlates are variables that are connected without clear evidence that one precedes the other. For example, research indicates that factors, such as a sense of coherence and perceived social support, are associated with secondary traumatic stress and role satisfaction in nonprofessional trauma counselors (Ortlepp & Friedman, 2002). On the other hand, both risk and protective factors precede the target outcome variable, whereas while the former decreases, the latter increases the chance of a positive outcome. For instance, depending on their quality, individual coping skills, attachment relationships, and community attitudes toward mental health and healing may play the roles of risk and protective factors among children who have experienced war trauma (Betancourt & Khan, 2008).

Next group of studies on mediators (i.e., variables that explain the relationship(s) of target variables, by revealing the underlying processes or mechanisms) and moderators (i.e., variables that influence the direction or strength of the relationship of target variables) is not that common probably because it requires a complex study design and sophisticated statistical analyses. For example, feelings of anger and guilt proved to be significant mediators of the relationship between war experience and PTSD in Uganda children (Murphy, Elklit, Dokkedahl, & Shevlin, 2017). On the other hand, the same study has shown that the fact that a child was (not) engaged as a soldier did not moderate the relationship between feelings (anger and guilt) and basic variables, that is, trauma and PTSD.

Last but not the least is a heterogeneous set of studies aiming at establishing evidence-based prevention and treatment for social trauma (see Chaps. 7–16). This group includes both studies of outcome (e.g., PTSD symptomatology) and process (e.g., mediators, such as therapeutic alliance).

34.2.2 Study Design

There are several methodological decisions that should be made, which to a large extent influence the way we will analyze and interpret research results. First, we need to specify *the study type*, that is, if the study is by its nature descriptive, non-experimental, experimental, review, or meta-analytical.

Descriptive research serves to illustrate target phenomena, mainly by providing its incidence/prevalence rate(s). The main distinction between *experimental* and *nonexperimental*, that is, *correlation study* type is in the extent to which a researcher succeeds to manipulate values of the variable(s) of interest while, at the same time, controls or keeps constant other factors that could influence the results. Specifically, by true experiment, we mean that subjects are assigned by chance to the experimental and control group (the process called randomization), whereas participants in the experimental group are exposed to target variable(s) or condition(s). Since many important variables, such as exposure and severity of social trauma, cannot be manipulated directly, correlation studies are more often in the social trauma filed. Nevertheless, they prevent us from interpreting causal relationships between the investigated variables.

Probably the most used version of the correlation study is the natural or quasi-experiment, in which comparisons are made between conditions that already exist (the intact groups), for example, between people who have experienced social trauma and those who have not. Still, experimental design may be found in research on psychotherapy effects on (social) trauma symptomatology. The quality of studies on interventions is evaluated in terms of whether (a) there is/are control group(s), (b) the participants have been tested before and not only after treatment, and (c) randomization has been applied (Kazdin, 1992). When all of the above conditions are met, we are talking about randomized controlled trials (RCT).

Finally, we can do *a systematic review* in order to critically appraise and synthesize the best existing evidence. Moreover, we can conduct a *meta-analysis* by applying powerful statistical procedures for combining data from multiple studies in order to estimate if there is a common effect size and possible source of the inconsistent findings.

The next step is choosing the proper *study design*, that is, deciding on the way of organizing conditions (e.g., research participants, assessment) in order to test hypotheses. For example, by applying *a case study design*, the researcher aims to qualitatively or quantitatively describe the functioning of an individual and to deeper understand the idiosyncratic processes related to social trauma. Therefore, the authors do not intend to generalize their results, although this limitation is often considered a disadvantage in this type of the study (Fonagy, 2015). The quantitative case study involves a systematic repeated assessment of behavior over time and that the subject serves as own control (by being tested before and after treatment).

Between-groups comparison design is based on comparisons between one group of participants assigned to one or more conditions and other groups of participants assigned to one or more different conditions. The assignment is preferably both blind (i.e., participants and assessors do not know which person is assigned to which group) and randomized. However, those options are often not applicable since authors in the social trauma field usually deal with the known or intact group.

Authors can also decide to conduct *correlative design* in which they will examine the relationships between different variables at one or several time points in the cohort sample. The bigger the data set, the more representative results are obtained, but also more focused on average than idiosyncratic cases.

Researchers should also decide regarding the *study strategy*. First, if they will gather data for the same subjects repeatedly over a period of time (i.e., *longitudinal study*) or they will compare different groups of people at a single time point (i.e., *cross-sectional study*). The former gives space for considering causal relationships, but, at the same time, it is far more time and financially consuming, as well as more susceptible to sample attrition.

The other issue is if participants will be asked for information relating to trauma that had happened before some amount of time (i.e., *retrospective type of study*) or if the subject will be recruited at the time when trauma has occurred and asked about current experiences (*prospective type of study*). Clearly, data in retrospective studies are highly susceptible to bias and distortion in recall while prospective studies in social trauma could be more psychologically challenging for the researcher sharing the same trauma, which was discussed in previous chapters.

34.2.3 Sampling Procedures

Commonly, we differ two sampling techniques—*random*, based on the equal chance of all eligible individuals to be selected, and *non-probability sampling* when some individuals have lower or no chances to participate in the study. Different types of random sampling are described in the literature (e.g., simple, systematic and stratified sampling), and, in comparison to nonrandom group (e.g., convenience, quota, and snowball sampling and so on), they lead to more representative and consequently more generalizable data (Ben-Shlomo, Brookes, & Hickman, 2013). Still, *convenience sampling*, in which participants are selected based on availability and willingness to take part in the study, is likely the most frequent strategy in clinical research, due to specific characteristics of target populations, their accessibility, and conditions they experience.

It is important to emphasize that, in addition to the variables that are generally controlled in studies (e.g., gender, age, and education), authors in social trauma field should be aware of specific characteristics of their sample, which may moderate their results (e.g., sample reduced to inpatients or refugee camp inmates, and the existence of comorbid disorders).

34.2.4 Measurements

Common taxonomy of measurements differentiates (1) psychological tests, questionnaires, and interviews; (2) observational methods; (3) psychophysiological methods; (4) electrophysiological measurements; and (5) neuroimaging methods. Assessment tools are one of the core features of quantitative studies and based on their psychometric properties we judge on research quality. By these properties, we mainly, but not exclusively, mean reliability and validity.

Reliability refers to the internal consistency of the instrument, as well as the results repeatability and stability over time and across raters. By validity, we assume several aspects which all describe the extent to which an assessment measures what it is designed to measure. Face and construct validity refers to the degree to which the content of the measurement reflects the theoretical construct, while concurrent and predictive validity reflects how measurement relates to the other constructs' measures.

How can we decide which measure is the most suitable for our study purposes? An online source named COSMIN provides methodology (i.e., guidelines for conducting systematic reviews and selecting outcome measure in a core outcome set) and practical tools for selecting the right measure (e.g., checklists for assessing the quality of a study on instrument validity), as well as a database of systematic reviews on instruments quality. Basic COSMIN search reveals the lack of systematic reviews or meta-analyses on social trauma instruments and only few on psychological trauma. Thus, authors should consider validation study and the number of citations of a particular instrument, as well as colleagues' feedback on its utility.

The Harvard Trauma Questionnaire (HTQ; Mollica et al., 1992) is developed as a cross-cultural instrument for assessing (actual) trauma and torture related to mass violence and PTSD, as well as some culturally specific symptoms; for each refugee group is advised that a new instrument version is adapted (Mollica, MCdonald, Massagli, & Silove, 2004). The original version, made for Indochinese refugee patients, contains four parts measuring: (1) trauma events and torture list, (2) personal description, (3) brain injury, (4) PTSD symptomatology.

Among trauma instruments designed for childhood age, The Trauma Exposure Symptom Inventory-Parent Report (TESI-PR; Ford et al., 2000) has the best psychometric properties (Stover & Berkowitz, 2005). This initial version assesses trauma exposure of children aged 3–18 years, using parents' reports on trauma type(s), which a child has experienced, the child's age(s) when trauma(s) occurred, and whether the child experienced reactions in a response to the stressor, such as becoming extremely frightened, confused or helpless, shocked or horrified, or behaved differently after the event was over. Since the TESI-PR lacks some of the potentially traumatic events of early childhood (e.g., separation from a primary caregiver), it was revised to more specifically address preschool children (The Trauma Exposure Symptom Inventory-Parent Report Revised, TESI-PRR; Ghosh-Ippen et al., 2002)). The TESI-PRR is still to be validated.

34.2.5 Data Analysis

We distinguish different levels of analysis. The basic descriptive statistics provide a summary of the sample and measure features, such as mean or frequency scores, variance, and measurement errors. On the next level, we differ some basic types of analyses: univariate (the analysis of one independent variable), bivariate (exploration of the association between two variables), and multivariate analyses (the analysis of several dependent variables, i.e., outcomes). Finally, contemporary and most promising trend is the use of explicit quantitative models, that is, mathematical and statistical equations (e.g., structural-equation models, item-response models, and other latent-variable models), in order to describe and predict psychological phenomena. Krueger and Markon find these methods to be of great importance for understanding psychopathology, "because they allow empirical comparison of different classification paradigms by comparing the fit of those models to psychological data" (Krueger & Markon, 2006, p. 114).

34.3 Preferred Model of Explanation

Let us try implementing what has been learned so far. Imagine we examine how the experience of social trauma is reflected on dream affect regulation. Our research question "Are there specific characteristics of affect regulation in dreams and their relationship with the PTSD status in people who experienced social trauma in comparison with those who experienced trauma, not caused by humans, and community sample?" would be marked as a *research question regarding correlates of social trauma.* This study would represent a natural experiment, since we would compare three intact groups of people (i.e., survivors of a war trauma, survivors of a natural disaster, and people without significant trauma of this kind). We would deal with *between-groups comparison design.* The study would be *cross-sectional*, since we would assess three groups of participants at the same time point, and we would measure *prospective data* (current affect regulation in dreams and the PTSD status). We could choose *quota sampling strategy* and test 30 people from each group (90 in total), whereas half of them would be women (n = 45, equal number per group). Trauma event types, as well as PTSD severity, would be measured by *PDS-5* (Foa et al., 2016), while affect regulation in dream diaries would be coded using the *ZDPCS* (Moser & von Zeppelin, 1996). Data analysis would consist of *descriptive statistics* and *multivariate analyses*.

34.4 Practical Implications in the Field of Social Trauma

We may summarize that conducting quantitative research represents the way of learning about social trauma through: (a) the investigation of its factors, associations, and its predictive power; (b) hypotheses testing in a large sample, dealing with a large amount of variables; (c) the use of different methodological and statistical techniques, which enables more generalized, reliable, and objective conclusions; (d) the possibility to examine and establish causal effects in highly controlled circumstances. These advantages promote quantitative studies as important and needed tools for establishing evidence-based theories and interventions in the social-trauma field.

When it comes to the weaknesses and limitations of the quantitative approach, the main concerns are related to random and systematic biases and errors (Krishna, Maithreyi, & Surapaneni, 2010). These specific problems, as well as how they relate to social trauma research, are already discussed in Chap. 35.

In the end, how can we minimize bias effects and ensure the respect of ethical principles (see Chap. 33)? In addition to the respect of the above-emphasized standards of good practice (e.g., randomized and blinded group assignment, and valid instrument usage), these are some of the procedures and instances, which serve as forms of external control: (a) all studies in the social trauma field need to be approved by an ethical committee, (b) the majority of funding agencies organize their own evaluation processes, (c) authors are requested to share their research protocols. These steps enable a critical review of clinical research, while protocol sharing also helps in identifying and preventing the selective reporting of outcomes and analyses.

34.5 Suggested Reading

COSMIN: COSMIN. (n.d.). Retrieved December 1, 2019, from http://www.cosmin.nl/

PRISMA; PRISMA. (n.d.) *PRISMA—Transparent reporting of systematic reviews and meta-analyses*. Retrieved December 1, 2019, from http://www.prisma-statement.org/

PROSPERO: Moher, D., Shamseer, L., Clarke, M., Ghersi, D., Liberati, A., Petticrew, M., … Stewart, L. A. (2015). Preferred reporting items for systematic review and meta-analysis protocols (PRISMA-P) 2015 statement. *Systematic Reviews*, *4*(1), 1.

SEPTRE: SEPTRE. (n.d.) *SEPTRE—SPIRIT electronic protocol tool and resource.* Retrieved December 1, 2019, from https://www.spirit-statement.org/implementation-tools/

SPIRIT: Chan, A. W., Tetzlaff, J. M., Altman, D. G., Laupacis, A., Gøtzsche, P. C., Krleža-Jerić, K., … Doré, C. J. (2013). SPIRIT 2013 statement: Defining standard protocol items for clinical trials. *Annals of Internal Medicine*, *158*(3), 200–207.

References

Ben-Shlomo, Y., Brookes, S., & Hickman, M. (2013). *Lecture notes: Epidemiology, evidence-based medicine and public health* (6th ed.). Oxford: Wiley-Blackwell.

Betancourt, T. S., & Khan, K. T. (2008). The mental health of children affected by armed conflict: Protective processes and pathways to resilience. *International Review of Psychiatry, 20*(3), 317–328.

Breslau, N., Peterson, E. L., & Schultz, L. R. (2008). A second look at prior trauma and the post-traumatic stress disorder effects of subsequent trauma: A prospective epidemiological study. *Archives of General Psychiatry, 65*(4), 431–437.

Foa, E. B., McLean, C. P., Zang, Y., Zhong, J., Powers, M. B., Kauffman, B. Y., … Knowles, K. (2016). Psychometric properties of the posttraumatic diagnostic scale for DSM-5 (PDS-5). *Psychological Assessment, 28*(10), 1166.

Fonagy, P. (2015). Methodological considerations in evaluating the outcome of psychoanalzsis. In M. Leuzinger-Bohleber & H. Kächele (Eds.), *An open door review of outcome and process studies in psychoanalysis* (pp. 61–80). London: International Psychoanalytical Association.

Ford, J. D., Racusin, R., Ellis, C. G., Daviss, W. B., Reiser, J., Fleischer, A., & Thomas, J. (2000). Child maltreatment, other trauma exposure, and posttraumatic symptomatology among children with oppositional defiant and attention deficit hyperactivity disorders. *Child Maltreatment, 5*(3), 205–217.

Ghosh-Ippen, C., Ford, J., Racusin, R., Acker, M., Bosquet, K., Rogers, C., & Edwards, J. (2002). Traumatic events screening inventory-parent report revised-long version. *PsycTESTS Dataset*. https://doi.org/10.1037/t30813-000

Kazdin, A. E. (1992). *Research design in clinical psychology* (Vol. 3). Boston: Allyn and Bacon.

Krishna, R., Maithreyi, R., & Surapaneni, K. M. (2010). Research bias: A review for medical students. *Journal of Clinical and Diagnostic Research, 4*(2), 2320–2324.

Krueger, R. F., & Markon, K. E. (2006). Understanding psychopathology: Melding behavior genetics, personality, and quantitative psychology to develop an empirically based model. *Current Directions in Psychological Science, 15*(3), 113–117.

Mollica, R., MCdonald, L., Massagli, M., & Silove, D. (2004). *Measuring trauma, measuring torture: Instructions and guidance on the utilization of the Harvard program in refugee Trauma's versions of the Hopkins symptom Checklist-25 (HSCL-25) and the Harvard trauma questionnaire (HTQ)*. Cambridge, MA: Harvard Program in Refugee Trauma.

Mollica, R. F., Caspi-Yavin, Y., Bollini, P., Truong, T., Tor, S., & Lavelle, J. (1992). The Harvard trauma questionnaire: Validating a cross-cultural instrument for measuring torture, trauma, and posttraumatic stress disorder in Indochinese refugees. *Journal of Nervous and Mental Disease, 180*, 111–116.

Moser, U., & von Zeppelin, I. (1996). *Der geträumte Traum: wie Träume entstehen und sich verändern*. Kohlhammer.

Murphy, S., Elklit, A., Dokkedahl, S., & Shevlin, M. (2017). Anger, guilt and shame as mediators in the relationship between war experiences and PTSD: Testing the moderating role of child soldier status. *Journal of Child & Adolescent Trauma, 10*(4), 323–331.

Ortlepp, K., & Friedman, M. (2002). Prevalence and correlates of secondary traumatic stress in workplace lay trauma counselors. *Journal of Traumatic Stress, 15*(3), 213–222.

Stover, C. S., & Berkowitz, S. (2005). Assessing violence exposure and trauma symptoms in young children: A critical review of measures. *Journal of Traumatic Stress, 18*(6), 707–717.

Chapter 35
Qualitative Approach to Social Trauma Research

Biljana Stanković

35.1 Introduction

Although qualitative methodology already has a relatively long history in social sciences (Brinkmann, Jacobsen, & Kristiansen, 2014), it is still considered far from the mainstream research approach in most areas, and social trauma field is no exception (Keats & Keats-Osborn, 2014). The aim of this chapter is to introduce qualitative methodology as a relevant and trustworthy approach to socio-traumatic phenomena.

The qualitative approach encourages researchers to get involved in the world of their participants and to study the phenomena in their natural setting (Denzin & Lincoln, 2005), which is crucial when dealing with historically and culturally specific phenomena. Besides promoting a natural setting as a source of data, the data itself should be naturalistic—which means that it should not be "coded, summarized, categorized or otherwise 'reduced' at the point of collection" (Willig, 2013, p. 90). This aims at producing rich, deep, nuanced, and contextual data, which proves to be especially relevant when assessing complex and ambiguous phenomena. Qualitative researchers are expected to constantly submit their own activities and their involvement in the research under critical scrutiny in order to recognize and acknowledge how their personal, professional, or political commitments shape different aspects of the research process (Parker, 1994/2002). At the same time, the traditional role of the research participants is also questioned and transformed, so they are seen as experts and active cocreators (Leavy, 2014). This balancing of power relations between researchers and participants (that are markedly unbalanced in traditional and mainstream research in psychology) is of the greatest importance when working with a vulnerable population.

B. Stanković (✉)
Faculty of Philosophy, University of Belgrade, Belgrade, Serbia
e-mail: biljana.stankovic@f.bg.ac.rs

© Springer Nature Switzerland AG 2021

A. Hamburger et al. (eds.), *Social Trauma – An Interdisciplinary Textbook*,
https://doi.org/10.1007/978-3-030-47817-9_35

Even this very brief and selective overview of principal common characteristics of the qualitative approach indicates its relevance for research in the field of social trauma, and, in the following sections, this relevance will be further explored and elaborated.

35.2 Learning Outcome Related to Social Trauma

Potentials of qualitative methodology when dealing with complex and interdisciplinary socio-traumatic phenomena:
Addressing sociocultural forces as complex processes and representations and in a contextualized manner.
Providing the opportunity for both personal and collective trauma narratives to be voiced and articulated.

Although it is hard (if not impossible) to find a psychological phenomenon that is not intertwined with the social and the cultural, there are phenomena for which this is obviously and particularly so. In the case of social trauma, the name itself refers to the fact that "social and individual aspects are inseparably tied together" (Hamburger, 2018, p. 14), which poses both conceptual and methodological challenges to the way research in psychology is usually performed. Similar to most (or even all) psychological phenomena, trauma is recognized as something happening or belonging to the individual that is primarily connected to his or her internal characteristics—that is, trauma has been individualized and essentialized. This process happening on a theoretical or conceptual level of the discipline is fully compatible with the usual methodological approach in psychology—investigating individual subjects by assessing their dispositions. When the importance of sociocultural or environmental factors is recognized, they are treated solely as antecedents or factors and as isolated variables. This kind of treatment of socio-traumatic phenomena therefore typically reduces them to individual psychopathological problems and fails to grasp the societal aspect and qualitative specificity of this complex subject (see also Hamburger, 2020a, this volume).

The qualitative approach could be a valuable resource when tackling reductionistic and simplistic depiction of culture and the way it shapes socio-traumatic phenomena, since it relies on the epistemological stances (e.g., constructivism) and theoretical approaches (e.g., cultural psychology, ethnomethodology) that offer a more complex, dynamic, and contextualized view of both culture and its relationship to individuals and groups. A challenge of properly accounting for cultural aspects involved in the socio-traumatic phenomena becomes especially important when researching a culturally distant group, which is often the case, especially at the intersection of social trauma studies and migration/refugee studies. In those cases, it becomes particularly problematic to simply apply the existing theories and methodologies, since we cannot be sure they would work with diverse, especially non-Western communities (Mattar & Vogel, 2014). Additionally, a straightforward interpretation of quantitative findings becomes contested, so a bottom-up, contextual, and sensitive qualitative approach is much better suited.

Another crucial aspect of socio-traumatic phenomena is related to the importance of articulating and narrating traumatic experiences, regardless of how difficult, painful, and unspeakable they might seem. Giving a voice to traumatic experiences on an individual level, in cases of social trauma, is inextricably connected to opening up a space for voicing/hearing about trauma on the level of community (Hamburger, 2017), since, as Judith Herman rightly suggests "denial, repression, and dissociation operate on a social as well as an individual level" (1992/2015, p. 2). This makes breaking a conspiracy of silence, when dealing with social trauma, especially challenging (see, e.g., Delić & Avdibegović, 2018). One small step in that direction might be choosing more open and sensitive techniques when assessing traumatic experiences of people scientifically, which might prove relevant for the abovementioned issues given that science is a public endeavor and that it contributes to the public discourse. Instead of (or at least in addition to) asking people to fit into the already existing categories and to relate to the already articulated meanings—usually expressed in a simplistic form of questionnaire items, researchers could offer them an opportunity to narrate their experience more freely. The next section will discuss relevant qualitative techniques for data collection and analysis that could enable something like that.

35.3 Preferred Model of Explanation

Qualitative methods of data collection (e.g., semi-structured interviews, oral histories, testimonies) are a way to elicit and facilitate the recollection and retelling of the relevant events and experiences by the participants, and in a personal, detailed, and emotionally involved way.
Qualitative methods of data analysis (e.g., narrative and discursive analysis) are a way to reconstruct and hermeneutically grasp contents, structures, emotional aspects, and psychosocial implications of trauma narratives.

There are different ways to engage with qualitative methods and to incorporate them into the study design. Sometimes, qualitative approach is included in a mixed-methods research design in order to supplement what quantitative methods can offer. One example is relying on focus groups in the process of adaptation of the existing instruments in order to make their content more culturally sensitive and contextually relevant when studying culturally distant groups of, for example, refugees (Vukčević, Momirović, & Purić, 2016). The other is coding qualitative data on social trauma with the categories derived from theory developed in other contexts and then correlating them with quantitative indicators of mental health (e.g., Jaeger, Lindblom, Parker-Guilbert, & Zoellner, 2014). Although such inclusion of qualitative methods is undoubtedly useful and offers relevant contributions to the field, it leaves no room for the specificities of personal meanings and experiences, or the specificities of the cultural context and its involvement in the socio-traumatic phenomena. Therefore, the full potential of qualitative approach is not utilized.

Qualitative methods of both data collection and analysis are especially suited to facilitate *giving voice* to the participants and *making sense* of their personal stories (Larkin, Watts, & Clifton, 2006). Semi-structured interviewing is definitely the most commonly used qualitative method of data collection in the field. Interview is a technique of choice in research dealing with human experience, since open conversation ensures that participants have a possibility to articulate their experience in detail and in a way that is meaningful to them (Smith, 1995). A flexible and sensitive approach to different topics allows for unexpected aspects of phenomena to emerge and personal narratives to be structured relatively freely. It also provides a more balanced relationship between the researcher and the participants. However, semi-structured interviewing requires sensitive and ethical negotiation of rapport, especially considering the ambiguity of roles: formal/informal conversation, personal/public encounter, expert/laypersons (Willig, 2013).

Especially prominent in the field of social trauma are approaches relying on the technique of interviewing, but with a special focus on participants' narration of their lives, important experiences or events they have witnessed or participated in—namely the genres of testimony, oral history, and biographical narrative (for more details see Habermas & Bartoli, 2020, this volume; Hamburger, 2020b, this volume). They are aimed at supporting participants to engage with the recollection and retelling of the relevant events and experiences in a personal, detailed, and emotionally involved way. Among testimonies of the social traumatic events, Holocaust testimonies have a prominent place in the field (e.g. Laub & Hamburger, 2017; Langer, 1991; Greenspan, 1998). However, we should keep in mind that these approaches to data collection, even though they offer a lot of space, time, and freedom to the participants, are nevertheless researcher-driven, often institutionalized, with established protocols and procedures and therefore staged to a greater or lesser extent (Greenspan et al., 2014).

Narrative and discourse analysis can be recognized as the most relevant methods of data analysis in the field, aimed at reconstructing the retelling of traumatic experiences and events on both individual and collective level. Both approaches engage with a narrative or a text (in the broadest sense of the term) without fragmenting it (breaking the text down into codes and themes), but instead moving from parts to the whole and vice versa in a hermeneutical process that is driven by a range of theoretical positions and aimed at answering diverse research questions. Usual outcomes of this interpretative endeavor are concerned not just with the content of the trauma narrative but also its structure, emotional undertone, and psychosocial consequences (Willig, 2013). A specific pattern of trauma narrative is sometimes recognized by the absence of narrative order, since traumatic events are experienced as overwhelming and without discernable causality. As Arthur Frank describes, "those who are truly *living* the chaos cannot tell in words; to turn the chaos into a verbal story is to have some reflective grasp of it" (1997, p. 98). Considering the dynamics and process of narration of (socio)traumatic experiences, characterized by "the conflict between the will to deny horrible events and the will to proclaim them aloud" (Herman, 1992/2015, p. 1), interviewers and researchers are confronted with a challenging and difficult task. They are expected to provide a holding environment to the participants, to be emotionally engaged and sensitive to the layers of meaning and emotional nuances of their stories (Laub, 1992), while, at the same time, they have to deal with their own defensive reactions and vulnerabilities (Langer, 1991).

35.4 Practical Implications in the Field of Social Trauma

By offering a theoretical reconceptualization of the phenomena and encouraging a different engagement in the process of research and working with participants, the qualitative approach to social trauma also leads to some beneficial ethical-political consequences.

The qualitative approach leads not only to new empirical insights in the social trauma field but also encourages a theoretical reconceptualization of the phenomena itself. Both culture and individuals, but also their relationship, are approached in a more complex and contextualized manner and not operationalized through simple and fixed categories and dispositions. The political potential of this reconceptualization is exemplified in the next question: "Will psychologists minimally adapt existing approaches to pay lip service to cultural factors? Or will they re-conceptualize their approaches from the ground-up to build a new psychology which is derived from the acknowledgement that human nature is fundamentally culturally mediated?" (Mattar & Vogel, 2014, p. 366).

A qualitative inquiry is often recognized as "an essentially ethical enterprise" (Traianou, 2014, p. 66), since the preoccupation with ethical issues pervades the whole research process—from the formulation of the research question, through data collection and analysis, to the dissemination of the findings (Brinkmann & Kvale, 2008). A greater sensitivity to ethical challenges is often related to a greater sensitivity to political issues or even a commitment to emancipatory political goals, especially in more critical qualitative approaches (Christians, 2005), which is also particularly relevant when it comes to a politically saturated field of social trauma studies.

It is suggested that the quantitative approach can miss the complexity of traumatic responses and offer only a limited picture of the nature of human suffering (Mattar & Vogel, 2014). However, approaching traumatic experiences in a less reductionistic and more open way, by providing the opportunity to trauma survivors to narrate their experiences, can lead to ethical, and not just epistemological consequences. In one study, only 24% of participants reported a research-related benefit after fulfilling a questionnaire, but 86% of them reported so following an interview (Newman, Walker, & Gefland, 1999). Personal benefits of narrating traumatic memories and experiences are widely recognized in the literature and related to the process of integrating them into a person's life story and thus supporting the coping processes (Bochner & Riggs, 2014).

Since qualitative research facilitates the articulation and dissemination of sociotraumatic experiences, it also participates in the construction of different social representations and public discourses on the collective level, which is particularly relevant for the communities and contexts dominated by the conspiracy of silence. Given that "public voice is deeply connected to the acknowledgment, and thus to the perpetuating, of the trauma itself" (Hamburger, 2018, p. 15), we can recognize the engagement with qualitative research in the social trauma field and the dissemination of its findings as, in a way, a political gesture in itself.

Engaging with qualitative research, of course, is not a guarantee that a complex and elusive topic of social trauma will be adequately grasped, since this approach has its own blind spots and limitations. Most qualitative studies are focused exclusively on verbalized experiences of people, which offers only a partial depiction, especially when it comes to dealing with trauma—since incoherent, pre-reflective, and embodied aspects of experience are being largely neglected. The description of qualitative approach as inherently ethical and as committed to giving a voice to vulnerable or underprivileged groups and individuals has also been questioned and contested (Traianou, 2014). Furthermore, the depiction of culture and its involvement in psychological phenomena in qualitative research (at least in psychology) is very often partial, since there is a preoccupation with meanings, representations, and symbolic aspects of culture—which leads to the neglect of the material aspects of the sociocultural environment, institutional conditions, and the uneven distribution of economic and political power in society.

All this warns us that complex and inherently transdisciplinary phenomena such as social trauma should always be addressed in a multiperspectivist way, by relying on multiple approaches, methods, and theoretical orientations that could enable us to adequately understand the various aspects of the phenomenon and their interrelatedness. It also urges us to always keep a critical self-scrutiny and awareness of the limitations of our perspective, while staying open to the potentially unexpected and contested individual and collective voices.

35.5 Suggested Reading

Frank, A. W. (1997). *The wounded storyteller: Body, illness, and ethics*. Chicago: University of Chicago Press.

Leavy, P. (Ed.). (2014). *The Oxford handbook of qualitative research*. Oxford: Oxford University Press.

Willig, C., & Stainton Rogers, W. (Eds.). (2008). *The Sage handbook of qualitative research in psychology*. London: Sage.

References

Bochner, A. P., & Riggs, A. R. (2014). Practicing narrative inquiry. In P. Leavy (Ed.), *The Oxford handbook of qualitative research* (pp. 195–222). Oxford: Oxford University Press.

Brinkmann, S., Jacobsen, M., & Kristiansen, S. (2014). Historical overview of qualitative research in the social sciences. In P. Leavy (Ed.), *The Oxford handbook of qualitative research* (pp. 17–42). Oxford: Oxford University Press.

Brinkmann, S., & Kvale, S. (2008). Ethics in qualitative research. In C. Willig & W. Stainton Rogers (Eds.), *The sage handbook of qualitative research in psychology* (pp. 263–279). London: Sage.

Christians, C. G. (2005). Ethics and politics in qualitative research. In N. K. Denzin & Y. S. Lincoln (Eds.), *The sage handbook of qualitative research* (3rd ed., pp. 139–164). Thousand Oaks, CA: Sage Publications.

Delić, A., & Avdibegović, E. (2018). A user-centred approach to helping women survivors of war rape in Bosnia and Herzegovina. In A. Hamburger (Ed.), *Trauma, trust, and memory: Social trauma and reconciliation in psychoanalysis, psychotherapy and cultural memory* (pp. 69–78). London: Routledge.

Denzin, N. K., & Lincoln, Y. S. (2005). Introduction: The discipline and practice of qualitative research. In N. K. Denzin & Y. S. Lincoln (Eds.), *The sage handbook of qualitative research* (3rd ed., pp. 1–32). Thousand Oaks, CA: Sage Publications.

Frank, A. W. (1997). *The wounded storyteller: Body, illness, and ethics*. Chicago: University of Chicago Press.

Greenspan, H. (1998). *On listening to holocaust survivors: Recounting and life history*. Westport, CT: Preager.

Greenspan, H., Horowitz, S. R., Kovács, E., Lang, B., Laub, D., Waltzer, K., & Wieviorka, A. (2014). Engaging survivors: Assessing 'testimony' and 'trauma' as foundational concepts. *Dapim: Studies on the Holocaust, 28*(3), 190–226.

Habermas, T., & Bartoli, E. (2020). Development of autobiographical narrating: Possible implications for coping with social trauma. In A. Hamburger, C. Hancheva & V. Volkan (Eds.), *Social trauma. An Interdisciplinary Textbook* (pp. 201–207). New York: Springer.

Hamburger, A. (2017). Genocidal trauma: Individual and social consequences of assault on the mental and physical life of a group. In D. Laub & A. Hamburger (Eds.), *Psychoanalysis and holocaust testimony: Unwanted memories of social trauma* (pp. 66–91). London & New York: Routledge.

Hamburger, A. (2018). New thoughts on genocidal trauma. In A. Hamburger (Ed.), *Trauma, trust, and memory: Social trauma and reconciliation in psychoanalysis, psychotherapy and cultural memory* (pp. 13–22). London: Routledge.

Hamburger, A. (2020a). Social trauma—A bridging concept. In A. Hamburger, C. Hancheva & V. Volkan (Eds.), *Social Trauma. An Interdisciplinary Textbook* (pp. 3–16). New York: Springer.

Hamburger, A. (2020b). Video testimonies. Videotestimony Research. In A. Hamburger, C. Hancheva & V. Volkan (Eds.), *Social Trauma. An Interdisciplinary Textbook* (pp. 343–354). New York: Springer.

Herman, J. (2015). *Trauma and recovery*. New York: Basic. (Original work published 1992).

Jaeger, J., Lindblom, K. M., Parker-Guilbert, K., & Zoellner, L. A. (2014). Trauma narratives: It's what you say, not how you say it. *Psychological trauma: theory, research, practice and policy, 6*(5), 473–481.

Keats, P., & Keats-Osborn, W. (2014). Qualitative evidence in trauma research: The case of the journal of traumatic stress. *Canadian Journal of Counseling and Psychotherapy, 48*, 38–56.

Langer, L. (1991). *Holocaust testimonies: The ruins of memory*. New Haven: Yale University Press.

Larkin, M., Watts, S., & Clifton, E. (2006). Giving voice and making sense in interpretative phenomenological analysis. *Qualitative Research in Psychology, 3*, 102–120.

Laub, D., & Hamburger, A. (Eds.). (2017). *Psychoanalysis and Holocaust Testimony: Unwanted Memories of Social Trauma*. London & New York: Routledge.

Laub, D. (1992). Bearing witness or the vicissitudes of listening. In D. Laub & S. Felman (Eds.), *Testimony: Crises of witnessing in literature, psychoanalysis and history* (pp. 57–74). New York: Routledge.

Leavy, P. (2014). Introduction. In P. Leavy (Ed.), *The Oxford handbook of qualitative research* (pp. 1–13). Oxford: Oxford University Press.

Mattar, S., & Vogel, E. B. (2014). The quality of the evidence: Qualitative research in trauma psychology. *Europe's Journal of Psychology, 10*, 363–375.

Newman, E., Walker, E. A., & Gefland, A. (1999). Assessing the ethical costs and benefits of trauma-focused research. *General Hospital Psychiatry, 21*, 1–10.

Parker, I. (2002). Qualitative research. In P. Banister, E. Burman, I. Parker, M. Taylor & C. Tindall (Eds.), *Qualitative methods in psychology: A research guide* (pp. 1–6). Open University Press. (Original work published 1994)

Smith, J. A. (1995). Semi-structured interviewing and qualitative analysis. In J. A. Smith, R. Harré, & L. van Langenhove (Eds.), *Rethinking methods in psychology* (pp. 9–26). London: Sage.

Traianou, A. (2014). The centrality of ethics in qualitative research. In P. Leavy (Ed.), *The Oxford handbook of qualitative research* (pp. 62–77). Oxford: Oxford University Press.

Vukčević, M., Momirović, J., & Purić, D. (2016). Adaptation of Harvard trauma questionnaire for working with refugees and asylum seekers in Serbia. *Psihologija, 49*(3), 277–299.

Willig, C. (2013). *Introducing qualitative research in psychology* (3rd ed.). McGraw-Hill: Open University Press.

Chapter 36
Videotestimony Research

Andreas Hamburger

36.1 Introduction: Background and Main Theoretical Concepts/Discussions

36.1.1 Testimony, History, and Veridicality

History is a condensed and identity building knowledge about the past, structuring it alongside the necessities of the present (see Rüsen, 2020; Assmann, 2020, both in this volume). However, it is a construction claiming veridicality. This is especially true for recollections of a traumatic past, where classifying the memory as a mere construction would deny its acknowledgment in the very same way the traumatic experience itself deprived the subdued victims of their own voice.

Video testimonies of survivors of a traumatic historical event evoke a somehow contrary reception: while historians hold reservations against the validity of a mere subjective recollection as a historical document or a proof for the reality of the said event, pointing at the distortions and reconstructive character of memory, psychoanalysts address the very process of construction and re-construction, taking the testimony as a document for personal experience. Psychoanalytic listening relates to the stories as they are reported, leaving it in the "uncertainty cloud" (Bion, 1963, p. 42), whether this story is historically "true" or subjective. This acknowledgment of "subjective truth," however, is not sufficient when it comes to trauma. In therapy with a traumatized person, we have to consider that one of the most haunting aspects of traumatization, be it abuse, rape, persecution, maltreatment, or more subtle forms of abasement and exclusion, is the lack of acknowledgment. Victims of sexual assault, for example, have a much better prognosis for recovery if their experience is acknowledged and they receive adequate understanding. Posttraumatic

A. Hamburger (✉)
International Psychoanalytic University Berlin, Berlin, Germany
e-mail: andreas.hamburger@ipu-berlin.de

© Springer Nature Switzerland AG 2021

A. Hamburger et al. (eds.), *Social Trauma – An Interdisciplinary Textbook*,
https://doi.org/10.1007/978-3-030-47817-9_36

psychopathology correlates highly with lack of support (Muldoon et al., 2019). The importance of acknowledgment is well known to every experienced clinician. Especially disturbing are the not so rare cases, where only traces of the past seem to be present. Psychoanalysts carefully explore these moments of not-knowing without leaping to conclusions.

36.1.2 Social Trauma, Uncertainty Cloud, and Acknowledgment

So, as psychoanalysts, with traumatized patients we have a double task. On one hand, we have to acknowledge the subjective truth of the patients' report without regarding it as pure phantasy (which would continue the disavowal they have experienced in the past), while on the other hand we have to acknowledge our own uncertainty too, since we do not know better than the patient herself what has happened. And if for the sake of relief from our sometimes hardly bearable countertransference feelings of helplessness and uncertainty, we launch into prematurely assuring the patient that we believe in the factual reality of what she herself remembers only vaguely or in a very fragmented way, we would again impose on her vulnerable mind an external certainty and decisiveness, repeating and perpetuating the "confusion of tongues between the adult and the child" (Ferenczi, 1988) in the transference. What we can do, however, in this situation, is to be aware of our own position in the unconscious relational field of transference.

36.1.3 The Video Dispositif

Quite opposed to the consulting room, sheltered by discretion and analytic reception, a videotaped interview or testimony is potentially open to the public. The interviewer is a representative of an anonymous number of recipients. This changes a lot, and we should have brief glance at the history of pictorial communication in psychology to understand the frame of our own enterprise if we work with video testimonies.

The pictorial presentation of clinical case reports has a long tradition even before psychoanalysis, the most famous example being the André Brouillet's (1887) painting of Charcot at the Salpêtrière demonstrating a hysterical patient: the patient, Blanche Wittman, showing her *Arc de Cercle* to the expectation of the doctor, at the same time imitates a picture that can be seen at the rear wall of the auditory, illustrating the typical pose. In a similar way, the video testimony as a *dispositif* is a breach to the analytic space, as Freud (1916) distinctly underlines:

> The talk of which psycho-analytic treatment consists brooks no listener; it cannot be demonstrated. A neurasthenic or hysterical patient can of course, like any other, be introduced

> to students in a psychiatric lecture. He will give an account of his complaints and symptoms, but of nothing else. The information required by analysis will be given by him only on condition of his having a special emotional attachment to the doctor; he would become silent as soon as he observed a single witness to whom he felt indifferent. (p. 17)

A video testimony comprises both the image and the "indifferent witness," who, according to Freud, would mutilize the witness on the spot.

Since the mid-twentieth century, film and video were used in ethnography, behavioral sciences, and sociology. However, the use of video in psychology was all but reflective, not to say naive: in contrast to ethnography and sociology, where the medium was reflected, psychology inadvertently displayed some dramaturgy: early psychology films served not only as a means of documentation but also as a means of public education at the same time. Specific features of the medium, such as recursive inspection, slow motion, and freezing offered an opportunity for detailed psychological research (Papousek, 2013; Tronick, 1989). The videographic tradition in sociology and ethnology is different. Here also, initially an objectivist approach prevailed, such as in Eibl-Eibesfeld's use of the angle lens for concealed ethnographic photographic documentation (Kaczmarek, 2008). This approach met with criticism relatively quickly, as it places the ethnologist in the position of a distant observer, even voyeur (Harms, 2006; Knoblauch, Schnettler, Raab, & Soeffner, 2006).

A prototype for the videographic staging in clinical-psychological fields of application is the orientation of the camera view toward the interviewee, as we also find it in the material of the Yale Videotestimony Study, which is oriented toward the traditional testimony video. Similar camera shots are also shown in the material of Spielberg's Shoah Foundation, which is carried out on a large scale, collected by a large number of interviewers.

36.2 Learning Outcome Related to Social Trauma

In psychotherapy, reported traumatic recollections, even if regarded as the "subjective truth," pose a challenge of reality acknowledgment. This challenge can be met by a position of acknowledging uncertainty regarding the veridicality of the account without distrusting the patient. In a video testimony research with survivors of social trauma, however, the interviewer/researcher cannot take a therapeutic stance for more than one reason: first, the video transcends the holding environment of the analytic space, by fixating its dreamlike flow to a reproducible document, which can be shared with third parties and even broadcasted. Second, as a historical event, the reported trauma is not just part of the micro- or mesosocial sphere of the survivor, but of a larger societal context that includes the researcher. Thus, the research itself is part of societal acknowledgment of the event and its historical interpretation. A video testimony is not just documented interview, but a potentially public display.

However, videographic documentation deprives the testimony of its open and unpredictable situation of witnessing in the presence of the other. But it fulfils the commandment of remembrance, which works against the disappearance of living memory and obliges it to be passed on. Thus, it creates a new immediacy in the process of reception. The immediacy that opens up here is not that of the witness—who is filmed—but of the video. The recipient is together with it, and in being together, he is also referred to himself (see also Goodman & Meyers, 2011).

36.3 Preferred Model of Explanation

The qualitative method of video testimony research described in this part has been established since 2007 in the context of the Yale Videotestimony Study (Laub & Hamburger, 2017). This project explored the testimonies of Holocaust survivors, who had been hospitalized as chronic psychotic patients in psychiatric institutions in Israel for decades, without awareness of their survivor history being a relevant factor in their psychopathology and treatment. In addition to the clinical-psychological questions of social long-term traumatization and retraumatization (Hamburger, 2017a), this study contributed to the question of preserving traumatic memories of the past.

36.3.1 Scenic Narrative Microanalysis (SNMA)

Scenic-Narrative Microanalysis (Hamburger, 2015a, 2015b) provides a formal analytic framework to analyze videotaped interactions, in the field of testimonial and therapeutic work and beyond. The method combines the psychoanalytic case discussion, naturalistic observation methods of qualitative infant research, and expert evaluation (Hamburger, 2017b, p. 228). At the same time, it attempts to meet the demands of qualitative validity and reliability criteria (Groeben, 2006; Miles & Huberman, 1994; Petry, 2016; Steinke, 2004; Winter, 2000a, 2000b). Its central feature is the evaluation of the transference-countertransference scene (Holmes, 2014) in identifiable emergent moments of the interaction ("Now Moments" or "Moments of Meeting"; Stern, 2004). Now Moments are experienced by both participants as being-together, when a habitual framework of the interaction is about to change, which draws both participants' attention to the present. The Boston Change Process Study Group (2010) has conceptualized the clinical process at the local or micro level (using video and audio recordings of psychoanalytic sessions), emphasizing change in nonsymbolic representations of intersubjective relational experiences (Lyons-Ruth, 1999). This process is structured by the aforementioned emergent moments, especially the "Moments of Meeting" where the implicit relational knowledge is rearranged; these moments of meeting are being mutually remembered by both interactants as experiences of a new and significant shift in relationship.

The procedure of SNMA builds on these observations. It consists of a manualized procedure of:

1. Transcription of the videographed material (psychotherapy session or else).
2. Independent examination by 4–6 trained raters with the task to identify and describe relationship-relevant moments in the session, using among other signals the introspective observation of their own emotional reaction to the text.
3. Selection of text sequences coded by the majority of raters as Now Moments or Moments of Meeting.
4. A moderated consensus session, audiotaped and partly transcribed, where the selected sequences are discussed and a psychoanalytic hypothesis of the nature of the occurring change in the transference-countertrasference relatedness of the interactants is formulated.
5. Interpretation of the interactional change in the session, using documented material from all steps of the process.

The method embraces the social-scientific reflections on videography, compatible with a relational-psychoanalytic position, where the unconscious is no longer understood as a part of the inner life of a single individual, but as an interactive process between patient/interviewee and listener or, respectively, between the testimony and its viewer. Systematic introspection on the part of the analyst/researcher leads to hypotheses as to the hidden "scene" of reenactment between the interactants, and in consequence to its interpretation in the shared research situation of the analytic space.

36.3.2 A Case Example

The study to be presented here is based on some of the Yale Fortunoff Archive Video Testimonies, a corpus of conservatively staged interviews (according to the psychological tradition of videography), where only the interviewee is portrayed by the camera, while the interviewer remains invisible.

The testimony of Shmuel B was taken at the Holocaust Survivor Home, Beer Yaakov, Israel, by Dori Laub; design and analysis have been meticulously described in Laub and Hamburger (2017).

The segment to be discussed here (min 22:07–27:22) is about Shmuel's report on deportation at the age of 14. The interviewee first denied any memories about atrocities in his native village, while the interviewer (led by his historical knowledge) insisted asking for details on persecuting Romanians. At a certain point, the witness, then, frankly stated, "I do not complain of them because the Jews made fun of them and then revenge came." This statement of guilt reversal (the Jews were the party responsible for their own extinction) provoked a strong emotional response in the rating group, from shock to blaming the interviewer for creating an interrogation-like atmosphere. Analyzing this group reaction, we understood that Shmuel's guilt reversal, well known among traumatized patients, might have triggered especially strong emotional responses on the part of the interviewer and the researchers, since both are in different ways part of the same societal context where the crime against humanity had taken place and still cannot be addressed unexcitedly. On the part of the raters' group, we noticed impulsive rage, as well as dizziness and paralysis; in the interviewer's case, we even observed an unconscious countertransference parapraxis in the minutes following this statement. From the reflection of these emotional reactions within the rater's group, it was inferred that the group was about to witness and partly repeat a reaction for and on behalf of the interviewer. He first gives in, assertively repeating Shmuel's words, and suddenly changes the topic—but in doing so, he starts to confuse places and dates already mentioned in the previous testimony. His question "And what did you see when you arrived in the new place? You are a 7-year-old child …" turned out as a paramnesia. In fact, the interviewer confuses his own age at the time of deportation from his home village not far from the interviewee's, with Shmuel's, who was already 14 years old when his family was deported. The rating group interpreted this as a partial fusion or merging of biographies, due to a counteridentification, with a temporary loss of reality control, which we understand as a communicative event. The interviewer is dragged into the fissures of the interviewee's mental life through the latter's fragmented narrative, thereafter forcing the interviewer himself to fill in the resulting gaps with entries from his own inner life. Under the specific condition of social trauma, the reparative function of the social environment is damaged, too, as it was the case in Shmuel B's life history.

The testimony exemplifies the specificity of genocidal trauma, where not only the injured memory of the survivor is at stake, but also in the emotional reactions of the witnesses: the interviewers and the researchers in the rating group.

The testimonial process itself, of which only a very brief example is presented here, had a healing aspect for the survivors (Strous et al., 2005), whose parental containment had been destroyed by the genocidal trauma of the Shoah, and was then symbolically restored through the reenactment in the process of the testimony. Reflecting upon the scars of social trauma in our own relatedness to the testimony—resulting in our proneness to denial, archaic fantasy, and repression—gives a voice to muted parts of our own mental lives as well. The survivors gave their testimonies not only to the "third ear" of the interviewers but also to the video camera, thus passing them on to us.

36.4 Practical Implications in the Field of Social Trauma

Working with video testimonies of survivors of social trauma requires an awareness of the social and cultural relevance of both giving and taking witness, as well as of documenting this personal process and writing it into the virtual archives (Pinchevski, 2017), a transformation that makes the testimonies part of the cultural memory in a different way. A video testimony serves to install a cultural narrative of the traumatic past; moreover, the testimonies become part of cultural imagery. Our decision to watch and listen to the witness is part of a societal negotiation about the past;

thus, scientific research inevitably is one stakeholder among others and can hardly claim objectivity. Media and other public discourse arenas often precede and evoke academic research. Saul Friedländer (2002) has noted that the increased interest of historiography in the Holocaust since the 1970s has followed the media staging of remembrance in the television series of the same name (quoted from Assmann, 2006, p. 262).

The increased appreciation of subjective testimonies as historically relevant data also calls into question the established distinction between verifiable historical facts and subjective memory (Friedländer, 1997). It is a new genre that also stands out from the traditional scheme of the autobiography. Assmann (2006) emphasizes that this newer generation of Holocaust video testimonies (cf. Kushner, 2006), unlike other video testimonies, does not aim for a narrative closure or a coherent autobiographical reference; they do not focus on the account of a person and his or her fate, but rather testify to the Holocaust itself from the perspective of the subject; they are a new genre in which history can be experienced by participating in its deliberately subjective recollection.

This concept of the video testimony on social trauma is in line with a performative turn in the humanities and overall culture. It is mirrored in a modern psychoanalytic paradigm change, replacing subsuming interpretation, which aimed to gain insight into unconscious, pathogenic conflicts, by "scenic understanding" (Lorenzer, 1970), which is based on the reflection of the analyst's unconscious participation in the interaction process. Assuming such a relational paradigm is indispensable for working with severely genocidally traumatized persons, since it lies at the very root of traumatization, as well as in its often decades-long perpetuation through denial as a social act (see Hamburger, 2017a, 2017b).

It was Dori Laub who put an emphasis on such a relational psychoanalytic concept of social trauma, when he pointed to the dimension of the transference and countertransference and the power of reenactment in interviews with survivors of social trauma. The same awareness for his own unconscious participation is necessary for the video testimony researcher, who is not present in the original interview, but works just with the archived material. In its videographic mise-en-scène, the testimony presents a message to the viewer, addressing a chain of further recipients beyond the interview situation, indeed beyond the lifetime of the witness. It creates an empty, unrepresented chair for the viewer, on which the observer is invited to take a seat.

Genocidal trauma can be understood as an interactive process: not as a lightning bolt that strikes once and leaves damage behind, but as an ongoing communicative scar (see Hamburger, 2017a). Cumulative retraumatization as a trauma-preserving condition occurs precisely when the recipients, the witnesses of the testimony, cannot bear the tension inherent in the situation and hastily leave the survivor alone – either by devaluating, diagnosing, and hospitalizing him or, conversely, by hastily attributing to his testimony a meaning, a message, a result, and a learning goal and thus dispense with its intolerability. When they get up hastily from the chair that the testimony had offered them.

36.5 Suggested Reading and Further Information

Goodman, N. R., & Meyers, M. B. (Eds.). (2011). *The power of witnessing: Reflections reverberations, and traces of the holocaust*. New York: Routledge.

Hamburger, A. (2015a). Refracted attunement, affective resonance: Scenic-narrative microanalysis of entangled presence in a holocaust survivor's testimony. *Contemporary Psychoanalysis*, *51*(2), 239–257.

Kushner, T. (2006). Holocaust testimony, ethics, and the problem of representation. *Poetics Today* 27(2), 275–295.

Laub, D., & Hamburger, A. (Eds.) (2017). *Psychoanalytic approaches to social trauma and testimony: Unwanted memory and holocaust survivors*. London: Routledge.

Shenker, N. (2015). *Reframing holocaust testimony*. Indiana University Press.

References

Assmann, A. (2006). History, memory, and the genre of testimony. *Poetics Today,* 2(2), 262–273.

Assmann, A. (2020). Cultural memory. In A. Hamburger, C. Hancheva & V. Volkan (Eds.), *Social Trauma. An Interdisciplinary Textbook.* (pp. 25–36). New York: Springer.

Bion, W. R. (1963). *Elements of psycho-analysis*. London: Heinemann.

Boston Change Process Study Group. (2010). *Change in psychotherapy: A unifying paradigm.* New York: W.W. Norton.

Ferenczi, S. (1988). Confusion of tongues between adults and the child. *Contemporary Psychoanalysis, 24,* 196–206. (Original work published 1949).

Freud, S. (1916). Introductory lectures on psycho-analysis. *The standard edition of the complete psychological works of Sigmund Freud, volume XV (1915–1916): Introductory lectures on psycho-analysis (parts I and II)* (pp. 1–240).

Friedländer, S. (1997). *Nazi Germany and the Jews* (The years of persecution, 1933–1939) (Vol. Vol. 1). New York: HarperCollins.

Friedländer, S. (2002). Im Angesicht der 'Endlösung': Die Entwicklung des öffentlichen Gedächtnisses und die Verantwortung des Historikers [Facing the 'final solution': The development of public memory and the responsibility of the historian]. In D. Borchmeyer & H. Kiesel (Eds.), *Das Judentum im Spiegel seiner kulturellen Umwelten. Symposium zu Ehren von Saul Friedländer* Judaism in the mirror of its cultural environments. Symposium in honour of Saul Friedländer] (pp. 207–23). Neckargemünd: Edition Mnemosyne.

Goodman, N. R., & Meyers, M. B. (Eds.). (2011). *The power of witnessing: Reflections reverberations, and traces of the holocaust.* New York: Routledge.

Groeben, N. (2006). Are there ways out of the self-inflicted irrelevance of the qualitative off-stream? *Forum: Qualitative Social Research, 7*(4), Art 34. Retrieved from http://nbn-resolving.de/urn:nbn:de:0114-fqs0604347

Hamburger, A. (2015a). Refracted attunement, affective resonance: Scenic-narrative microanalysis of entangled presence in a holocaust survivor's testimony. *Contemporary Psychoanalysis, 51*(2), 239–257.

Hamburger, A. (2015b). Roots in Jewish and Christian soil: A portrait of the holocaust researcher as an involved person. *Contemporary Psychoanalysis, Special Issue: The Evolution of Witnessing—Emergent Relational Trends in Holocaust Studies, 51*(2), 289–295.

Hamburger, A. (2017a). Genocidal trauma. Individual and social consequences of the assault on the mental and physical life of a group. In D. Laub & A. Hamburger (Eds.), *Psychoanalysis and holocaust testimony: Unwanted memories of social trauma* (pp. 66–91). London: Routledge.

Hamburger, A. (2017b). Scenic narrative microanalysis. Controlled psychoanalytic assessment of session videos or transcripts as a transparent qualitative research instrument. In D. Laub & A. Hamburger (Eds.), *Psychoanalysis and holocaust testimony: Unwanted memories of social trauma* (pp. 166–182). London: Routledge.

Harms, V. (2006). Produktion ethnographischer Filme im Stil von Paparazzi? Probleme der Ethik in der Visuellen Ethnologie [Production of ethnographic films in the style of Paparazzi? Problems of ethics in visual ethnology]. In A. Hornbacher (Ed.), *Ethik, Ethos, Ethnos. Aspekte und Probleme interkultureller Ethik* [Ethics, ethos, ethnos. Aspects and problems of intercultural ethics] (pp. 75–87). Bielefeld: Transcript.

Holmes, J. (2014). Countertransference in qualitative research: A critical appraisal. *Qualitative Research, 14*(2), 166–183.

Kaczmarek, J. (2008). Soziologischer film—Theoretische und praktische Aspekte [Sociological film—Theoretical and practical aspects]. *Forum Qualitative Sozialforschung/Forum: Qualitative Social Research, 9*(3), Art. 34. Retrieved from http://nbn-resolving.de/urn:nbn:de:0114-fqs0803343

Knoblauch, H., Schnettler, B., Raab, J., & Soeffner, H. G. (Eds.). (2006). *Video analysis: Methodology and methods: Qualitative audiovisual data analysis in sociology*. Frankfurt a.M.: Peter Lang.

Kushner, T. (2006). Holocaust testimony, ethics, and the problem of representation. *Poetics Today, 27*(2), 275–295.

Laub, D., & Hamburger, A. (Eds.). (2017). *Psychoanalytic approaches to social trauma and testimony: Unwanted memory and holocaust survivors*. London: Routledge.

Lorenzer, A. (1970). *Sprachzerstörung und Rekonstruktion: Vorarbeiten zu einer Metatheorie der Psychoanalyse [The destruction of language and reconstruction: Preliminary work on a metatheory of psychoanalysis]*. Frankfurt a.M. Main: Suhrkamp.

Lyons-Ruth, K. (1999). *The two-person unconscious. Psychoanalytic Inquiry, 19*(4), 576–617.

Miles, M. B., & Huberman, A. M. (1994). *Qualitative data analysis* (2nd ed.). Thousand Oaks, CA: Sage.

Muldoon, O. T., Haslam, S. A., Haslam, C., Cruwys, T., Kearns, M., & Jetten, J. (2019). The social psychology of responses to trauma: Social identity pathways associated with divergent traumatic responses. *European Review of Social Psychology, 30*(1), 311–348.

Papousek, M. (2013). Einsatz von video in der Eltern-Säuglings-Beratung und-Psychotherapie [Use of video in parent-infant counselling and psychotherapy]. *Praxis der Kinderpsychologie und Kinderpsychiatrie, 49*(8), 611–627.

Petry, X. (2016). Zur Geltung von Erkenntnissen in der Psychotherapieforschung [The validity of findings in psychotherapy research]. *Psychotherapie-Wissenschaft, 6*(1), 17–29.

Pinchevski, A. (2017). Counter-testimony, counter-archive. In D. Laub & A. Hamburger (Eds.), *Psychoanalytic approaches to social trauma and testimony: Unwanted memory and holocaust survivors* (pp. 242–254). London: Routledge.

Rüsen, J. (2020). The wounds of history—About the historical dealing with traumatic experiences. In A. Hamburger, C. Hancheva & V. Volkan (Eds.), *Social Trauma. An Interdisciplinary Textbook.* (pp. 43–54). New York: Springer.

Steinke, I. (2004). Quality criteria in qualitative research. In U. Flick, E. von Kardorff, & I. Steinke (Eds.), *A companion to qualitative research* (pp. 184–190). London: Sage.

Stern, D. (2004). *The present moment in psychotherapy and everyday life*. New York: Norton & Company.

Strous, R. D., Weiss, M., Felsen, I., Finkel, B., Melamed, Y., Bleich, A., & Laub, D. (2005). Video testimony of long-term hospitalized psychiatrically ill Holocaust survivors. *American Journal of Psychiatry, 162*(12), 2287–2294.

Tronick, E. Z. (1989). Emotions und emotional communication in infants. *American Psychologist, 44*, 112–126.

Winter, G. (2000a). A comparative discussion of the notion of 'validity' in qualitative and quantitative research. *The Qualitative Report, 4*(3/4), 2000. Retrieved from http://www.nova.edu/ssss/QR/QR4-3/winter.html

Winter, G. (2000b). A comparative discussion of the notion of 'validity' in qualitative and quantitative research. *The Qualitative Report, 4*(3), 1–14. Retrieved from https://nsuworks.nova.edu/tqr/vol4/iss3/4

Part VIII
Social Trauma and Education

Chapter 37
Education and Social Trauma

Dženana Husremović and Maida Koso-Drljević

37.1 Introduction

This chapter is structured so as to first introduce the reader with the position and purpose of education in the current global picture, with the special emphasis on the education policies in Europe. The second part of the chapter gives a brief overview of the main sociological perspectives on education, so the reader can gain a better insight in paradigms used by the government in order to create own education system. A discussion follows on the ways how nations or interest groups create education outcomes with the goal to install and further sustain collective identities and collective memories to protect large groups, their stereotypes, and internal interests.

Education is the main pillar of each society. It is a complex area in which participants not only gain knowledge and skills for future work but also internalize the values and cultural norms important for the society. So, there are many functions of education, and they are interconnected and contingent of one another. In short, one could say that the purpose of education is to support the development of the individual who will further develop the society and contribute to the respect of human rights and economic development. The European context of education is shaped in multiple layers. The European Union, through its institutions and branches, gives a framework used by countries in the process of development of national education strategies. The document entitled "Improving Competencies for the 21st Century" (European Commission, 2008) states:

D. Husremović (✉) · M. Koso-Drljević
Faculty of Philosophy, University of Sarajevo, Sarajevo, Bosnia and Herzegovina
e-mail: dzenana.husremovic@ff.unsa.ba; maida.koso@ff.unsa.ba

© Springer Nature Switzerland AG 2021

A. Hamburger et al. (eds.), *Social Trauma – An Interdisciplinary Textbook*,
https://doi.org/10.1007/978-3-030-47817-9_37

> Young people need a wider range of competences than ever before to flourish, in a globalized economy and in increasingly diverse societies. Many will work in jobs that do not yet exist. Many will need advanced linguistic, intercultural and entrepreneurial capacities. Technology will continue to change the world in ways we cannot imagine. Challenges such as climate change will require radical adaptation. In this increasingly complex world, creativity and the ability to continue to learn and to innovate will count as much as, if not more than, specific areas of knowledge liable to become obsolete. Lifelong learning should be the norm.

The European Commission notes that to advance well-being in the face of the twenty-first century challenges requires a new approach centered on providing citizens with adequate opportunities for self-fulfillment, access to education, employment, healthcare, and social protection in a context of solidarity, social cohesion, and sustainability (Gordon et al., 2009).

In order to create a common framework for education in Europe, the European Commission prepared a list of eight key competencies to be recognized by national education systems as common learning outcomes (European Commission, 2018). Some of them are basic life skills like literacy, numeracy, and scientific competencies. However, other competencies defined are equally important, and two most important for this book are social and civic competence and cultural competence.

What is the definition of competence? In the document *Key Competences for Lifelong Learning; a European Reference Framework* (European Commission, 2018), competence is described as a combination of skills, knowledge, aptitudes, and attitudes crucial for personal fulfillment, active citizenship, and inclusion and employability. As we can see, competence is not only knowledge or skill but also a deeply internalized value manifested as readiness to use knowledge and skills in different contexts and times. Social and civic competence includes the development of values and behaviors which enable individuals to effectively and constructively participate in a social relation within the diverse societies and equip them with the skills necessary for negotiation and a peaceful conflict resolution.

Major elements of knowledge within this competence include knowledge of the generally accepted norms and rules of conduct; understanding of concepts such as individual, group, society, and culture; understanding of European multiculturalism; understanding concepts such as democracy, citizen, and citizenship; and international declarations which ensure the universality of human rights. Emphasis within this competence is placed on the knowledge of emigration, immigration, and minorities in Europe and the world. In addition to knowledge, students are also expected to have social skills: constructive communication that involves tolerating the views and behaviors of others, expressing frustration and anger in a constructive manner, skills to separate private and professional spheres of conflict, and negotiation skills. Lastly, to round off all knowledge and skills to competency, young people should internalize attitudes and values that will allow them to show a genuine interest in and respect of others, willingness to overcome their own stereotypes and prejudices, to prefer collaboration and compromise over conflict, and a willingness to respond to injustice and discrimination.

The question we ask ourselves is: if we have agreed that this is important to us, then why do we have so much conflict and injustice, why do we continue to

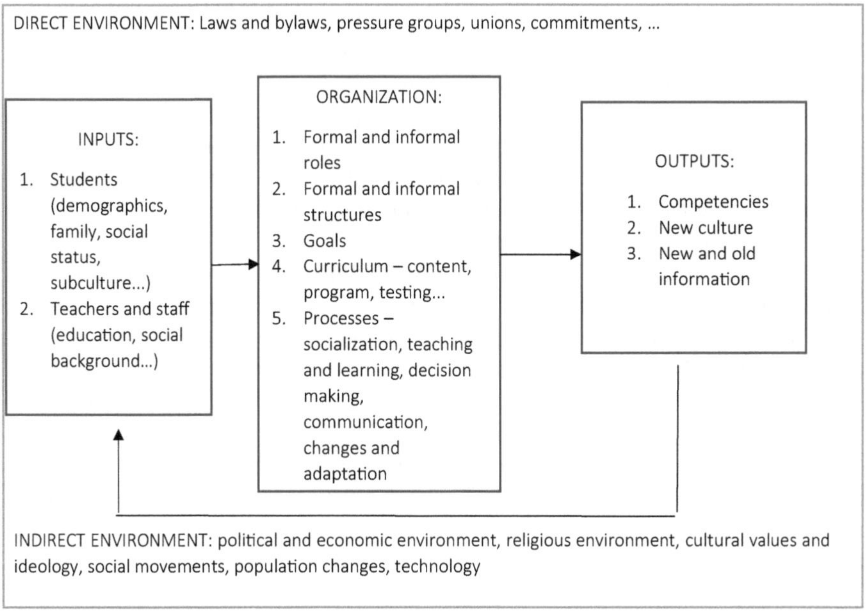

Fig. 37.1 Direct and indirect environments

discriminate against people, why do we not love migrants, and why are others always worse than us?

Answers to these questions urge us to understand the structures of educational systems and their interdependence with all elements of a community. To this end, we will use the Scheme of the Education System (adapted from Ballantine, 1989), which shows all the elements that influence the final educational outputs and outcomes (Fig. 37.1):

What we can see in this scheme is that the middle part—the educational organization and process—is immersed in a space where both direct and indirect factors act on it.

Different theoretical approaches explain factors that determine the educational system, its purpose and goals, and the changes that inevitably occur. These approaches generally differ in the degree of autonomy they attribute to the education system itself and, thus, to the emphasis on change factors.

37.1.1 Modernistic Approaches to Education

Liberal theoretical approaches are based on the humanistic philosophy of modernity. According to them, the main purpose of education is to promote the individual, as well as the well-being of the society. The most prominent theorist of the liberal approach to education was John Dewey (1859–1952). The liberal approach emphasizes that the educational system is highly autonomous and that changes should generally be attributed to internal factors, such as creativity and innovativeness of teachers and school staff. By treating teachers and other employees as key agents of change within the autonomous system, promoters of this approach believe that the teaching process should focus on important outcomes and have a constructive social impact. However, other social scientific approaches point out that the organization of education is dependent on economic, political, and cultural changes, that is, ideological changes in society.

Merritt and Coombs (1977) pointed out that all important decisions in education are related to events in politics and economics. This paradigm runs through several theoretical approaches. Thus, the functionalist point of view, most famously represented by Emile Durkheim and Talcott Parsons, assumes that the main purpose of education is to maintain consensus around social values, and that changes in education are generated outside of education, on political and social bases. Education is a subsystem of the society (together with the religious subsystem, the media, the police, and the judiciary) whose task is to enable the acceptance of social norms by all individuals through the process of socialization in order to integrate into the society.

In contrast to the functionalist approach, the Marxist or conflicting perspective on understanding education (with representatives Karl Marx and Louis Althusser) points out that education is a process that enables the ruling class to reproduce its dominance and other social classes. The educational system must reproduce the basic ideology of capitalism, that is, for young people to socialize in the idea of accepting capitalism as the best form and to accept the economic dominance of the ruling class (Kapo, 2012).

37.1.2 Postmodernist Approaches to Education

Postmodernist approaches are characterized by advocating that knowledge does not have a solid foundation, that is, that there is no ultimate truth, and, therefore, there can be no single best curriculum, method of learning and teaching, or unique educational outcomes. Pierre Bourdieu (1930–2002), as a forerunner of postmodernity, believes that the primary purpose of education is cultural reproduction, and that of the ruling class culture. A dominant culture is a type of capital that translates into wealth and power through education. Children who come from primary families belonging to the ruling class are already privileged at the outset because they understand the "code" implanted in them through primary socialization. On the other hand, children from the lower class are more easily eliminated from the education system due to a misunderstanding of the "code" of culture, and thus have less chance of advancing through society.

37.1.3 Nationalism, Collective Identities, and Education

Where, then, is nationalism in education? We could say that nationalism is the basis of building education. Modern education began to develop with the establishment of nation-states, and that entails pre-university, as well as higher education and scientific institutions. Modern institutions of education and science emerged as a result of the need of the nation-state to develop by producing its science and educating its citizens. Ernest Gellner (1925–1995) points out in his work *Nations and Nationalism* that a universal and standardized education is one of the main factors of modern society construction. The education system is the basis for the creation of a homogeneous cultural field and national integration. Gellner defines nationalism as "the endeavor to make culture and the political order the same, to supply a particular culture with one's own political vault, and only one such vault," (Gellner, 2006), and it is usually language that serves as the benchmark and boundary of a culture.

Nation is a term originated with the creation of modern nation-states, and it attaches to a specific territory (or national motherland), though there are also nations without a state (such as Kurds). Members of a nation share a common identity and very often shared kinship and origins. The nation defines the criteria by which it is judged whether one is a member of the nation or not. Members of one nation do not have to be like-minded, they can speak different languages and even live in other states, but if they are bound by elements defined by the nation as national, they will see themselves as belonging to one nation.

Nation-states are states where the state borders ideally or flatly coincide with the nation's borders. However, nation-states also include groups that do not belong to the dominant nation. They form ethnic groups who seek to achieve their equality or seek autonomy and separation from their home nation-state. Multiethnic states are countries where members of different ethnic groups live, but none dominates in number over the other. In today's world, once-national states are becoming increasingly multiethnic, owing to migration.

A socially defined category "ethnic group" includes a large group of people who identify themselves based on common elements such as common ancestors, cultural heritage, ideas and myths about their origins, language, religion, and other lifestyle elements.

Although this brief overview of the basic concepts of nation, ethnicity, nation-state may seem to have nothing to do with the topic itself, these issues are the basis of defining outcomes in education systems. The emergence of the state, the impact of migration, historical conquest and rule on the "state of the nation," the number and power of ethnic groups within the state, and their struggle for supremacy and domination, all left a mark on the collective memory, which is then sought to be reflected in the educational system. Individual education systems have the freedom and right to define what they see as important educational outcomes for their students and to define the content presented to children in education, and this opens the door for the impact of social trauma and collective memory on the learning outcomes themselves.

Therefore, the task of the education system is to maintain the collective memory of the group and to impute in the students a clear differentiation between us and them in order to maintain the elements of social trauma that, ultimately, lead to a potentially simple mobilization of forces in the event of any threat to group identity.

What are the main elements of this collective identity of large groups that are also affected by the education system? Vamık Volkan, in his books *Blind Trust* (2004), *Blood Lines* (1998), and *Killing in the Name of Identity* (2006), elaborates on these elements. According to Volkan (2004), the main type of large group is an ethnic group. He says:

> …I believe it is a privileged category of the large—group identity. … ethnicity reflects the feelings and thoughts that connect people with those who unconsciously and symbolically feel like their mothers or like other important caretakers of childhood. Thus ethnicity not only refers to a human sense of belonging at a basic emotional level, but also define "we-ness" by defining "other" who is not "like us." (p. 25)

Religion is one of the elements that historically tied people to large groups. However, the mere fact that people share a religion does not lead them to form the same ethnic group. For example, Bosniak Muslims from Bosnia and Herzegovina and Albanian Muslims share the same religion but do not belong to the same ethnic group. Second, an ethnic group can unite people of different religions. For example, people in France do not all share the same religion, but identify as French by their country, culture, tradition, and language.

However, religion is often an important determinant of defining collective identity. For example, in Bosnia and Herzegovina, the three main ethnic groups are Bosniaks, Croats, and Serbs. Although they share a common origin, what divides them is religion. Thus, in the last census in 2014, these three ethnic groups declared themselves as in the table below:

	Category (%)		Category (%)		Category (%)	
Group	Bosniaks	50.7	Serbs	30.75	Croats	15.43
Religion	Islam	50.11	Orthodox	30.78	Catholic	15.19
Mother tongue	Bosnian	52.86	Serbian	30.76	Croatian	14.60

Thus, these three ethnic groups are almost homogeneous in terms of religion and mother tongue. This is where we come to the second element of the formation of a collective identity, which is language. Language, as described in Volkan's book *Blind Trust*, is the way of establishing the sense of belonging because of its potential to incorporate the shared images of common history.

37.2 Learning Outcomes

The importance of the education system for each country and society is crucial. Children go to school to become employable, but even more so to be constructive citizens who contribute to the development of the society.

In light of this, it is important for readers too to reflect on their experience with educational systems and to consider what the system should look like. This would help societies overcome their social traumas, and that can be achieved by understanding the way in which the trauma interferes with the education system, especially with education policies, curriculum development, instructional design, and education process.

Students should develop the idea why it is important to insist on education which will be more open and just in all schools. This can be done by using several measures. Some of them are (1) redefining the standards for quality education in which the issue of diversity is highly valued; (2) using the teaching methodology that supports critical thinking, and (3) defining standards for textbooks that will help authors to offer the content for critical analysis and reflecting on universal values.

37.3 Preferred Model of Explanation: Examples from Educational Systems

The twenty-first century has brought many challenges to societies. Disintegration of the great multiethnic states (Union of Socialist Republics or USSR, Yugoslavia, etc.) and the awakening of national consciousness have raised the issue of ethnic identities as never before. Globalization and migration of all kinds should logically guide education systems toward new priorities in terms of education and upbringing of children for a life that respects diversity, solidarity, and equality for all citizens so that they can function in the future. However, we see that increasing the diversity of the societies did not lead to an increase in tolerance and acceptance of diversity, but rather opposite—increasing inequality and the incitement of racism and other *isms*. How much do educational systems contribute to this?

37.3.1 Segregation in Schools and Its Consequences

One of the most important studies that provided an overview of how key educational system variables sustain social trauma and differences was conducted by the Network of Educational Policy Centers (Golubeva, Powell, Kazimzade, & Nedelcu, 2009). This report provides a research finding about segregated schooling systems of minority groups and the consequences of such approaches. The following countries participated in the survey: Bosnia and Herzegovina, Estonia, Kazakhstan, Kosovo, Latvia, Romania, Slovakia, and Tajikistan. This was the first comparative study comparing the conditions of civic acculturation in separate ethnic majority and ethnic minority schools. Civic acculturation through the education system involves the process of transmitting and adopting attitudes and norms that are not included in the formal curriculum, but are part of the school environment (such as school climate and culture, rituals, celebrations, customs, and language norms).

Separate schools for ethnic groups are not uncommon in multiethnic communities. There are separate ethnic majority and ethnic minority schools in all countries that participated in this survey.

In the countries of Eastern and Central Europe, the Balkans, Central Asia, and the countries that emerged after the breakup of the USSR, there are not so many differences in socioeconomic status between individual ethnic groups. In these parts of the world, segregated education has come about due to the following:

- Historical circumstances (because they were part of larger multiethnic empires) or
- A peace agreement that led to a settlement of war conflicts, ensuring that children go to separate schools.

Although school selection is a voluntary process (parents choose the school, the state provides infrastructure), there are a number of visible and invisible barriers that prevent children from developing interculturalism, and, thus, the educational system contributes to the further extension of collective memories and identity which further segregates societies. The research started with the idea to evaluate the possibilities of desegregation of the school system according to the model of Amir, Shlomo, and Ben Ari (1984) in which four groups of variables are crucial for desegregation:

1. Structural variables—school status, funding, etc.
2. Model behavior variables—language, ethnic group status, and political power.
3. Variables related to goals and values—the perception of historical events, projections of the future, and perception of citizenship.
4. Affective variables—attitudes toward segregation/desegregation.

Thus, the main question here is to what extent do the elements that collectives seek to retain through future generations (and which are described through variables) lead to desegregation or further segregation?

37.3.2 The Influence of Structural Variables on the Segregation and Maintenance of Elements of Social Trauma

There are some specific situations in all countries that are part of this research.

37.3.2.1 Bosnia and Herzegovina

Bosnia and Herzegovina was a highly multiethnic society before the war. The war lasted from 1992 to 1995, resulting in significant human losses and displacement of the population. After the war, geographic territories became differently populated in terms of domination of one of the three ethnic groups—Serbs, Bosniaks, and Croats. In addition to the direct impact that the conflict had on educational infrastructure, postwar education policies became an instrument "to shape or strengthen divisions in society, intolerance and inequality, or to eliminate critical thinking citizenship opportunities" (Ramírez-Barat & Duthie, 2015).

Nationalist policies already started with the project of separate education and separate curriculum during the war, so today three curricula are used in Bosnia and Herzegovina: the curriculum in the Republika Srpska (Serbian as the mother tongue, and the national group of subjects (history, geography, and religious education) is taught from the Serb perspective); the curriculum in Bosnian (implemented in the Bosniak-majority schools, Bosnian as the mother tongue, and the national group of subjects is taught from the Bosniak perspective); and the curriculum in Croatian (Croatian as the mother tongue, and the national group of subjects is taught from the Croat perspective).

In addition, many parents who suffered during the war and developed posttraumatic symptoms refused to enroll their children at school for fear of being harmed for their ethnic identity. At first, members of the same ethnic group started initiating classes for children at homes, cafes, and restaurants, or to drive their children to schools in remote locations. In 2002, in order to address this difficult educational situation, the International Community adopted an Interim Agreement on the Special Needs and Rights of Returnee Children. One of the measures created under this Agreement is "two schools under one roof" (OSCE, 2018). These schools are mainly located in communities with mixed Croatian and Bosniak population. These schools are located in the same building, but everything else is physically separate: entrances, classrooms, toilets, and even hallways so that children do not meet.

37.3.2.2 Kosovo

Kosovo is also a multiethnic state dominated by Albanians (88%) and with a presence of Serbs (7%) and others (Bosniaks, Roma, Turks, etc.). Serbian children (in northern Kosovo) go to separate schools where Serbian teachers teach according to the curriculum of Serbia.

37.3.2.3 Estonia, Latvia, Slovakia, and Romania

In these four countries, there is a unified curriculum for all schools, but instruction is provided in the native language of the ethnic group. All schools have equal funding and do not suffer from structural discrimination. However, with the introduction of a new curriculum in 2000s in Latvia, which reduced the number of classes in Russian for Russian minority schools to 40%, widespread protests took place. A similar situation happened in Estonia.

37.3.2.4 Kazakhstan

Although there is a unique curriculum in Kazakhstan and, at first glance, it seems that there are no differences between minority and majority ethnic schools, there are very important structural elements that put minority students at a disadvantage. Primarily, there is the completion of the final graduation as a prerequisite for enrollment to higher education institutions. The education system caters to students from 23 different ethnicities. Ethnic Kazakhs comprise 73% of students, ethnic Russians 14%, and ethnic Uzbeks 4%. In 2012, the language of instruction in most schools was Kazakh (3819 schools), followed by Russian (1394), Uzbek (60), Uighur (14), and Tajik (2) (IAC, 2014). The high-school graduation exam is conducted exclusively in Kazakh and Russian, so children attending schools in Uzbek or Turkish must take this test in a language other than the language of instruction.

37.3.2.5 Tajikistan

In Tajikistan, 83% of the population are Tajik, while 12% are Uzbek. However, a still strong traditional family and negative attitudes toward gender equality have led Uzbek parents to choose to send their sons to Tajik schools (which provide higher quality education), while sending girls to Uzbek schools.

37.3.3 Language, Status, and Political Power: The Impact of Model Behavior

The second group of indicators dealt with issues of political participation and minority equality policy, and the findings of the study showed that there was a startling level of distrust and asymmetry in political power toward minorities. Students of majority ethnic groups considered it bad to have politicians from minority groups in the government, and this is especially emphasized in countries where the ethnic minority has been historically dominant in that country (such as in Romania and in Slovakia with this attitude toward the Hungarian minority, and in Estonia and Latvia toward the Russian minority). When students of majority ethnic groups were asked to comment on the presence of minority groups in history textbooks, their opinion was generally that they should not be specifically represented because they either contributed nothing or because it was not the history of their people but the history of the majority group. On the other hand, when students from minority ethnic groups were asked about their future careers and political participation, they expressed attitudes that showed that they felt inferior. Although everyone agrees that knowing the language of the majority gives an advantage in future life, students of minority groups feel that knowledge of their own language is very important.

37.3.4 *Perception of Citizenship*

The above-mentioned research has shown that over 80% of students support the paternalistic role of the state, and in view of the majority/minority ratio, this is even more emphasized among the majority.

37.3.5 *Attitudes toward Segregation/Desegregation*

This research has substantially shown that students agree that separate education is necessary and desirable, and this is especially pronounced among minority ethnic groups. The analysis showed that the most important factor for this opinion is how much school supports segregation. It is the school culture and climate that most influences individual support for segregated schooling.

The main findings of this study show that educational systems with separate education for ethnic groups are associated with the minority's notion of less political power, less protection from the state, and more ethnic prejudice against ethnic minorities, especially in the curriculum. Resistance to co-education in minority groups comes from their need to protect the group identity. On the other hand, the majority group students do not want the political participation of minority groups, nor do they think that they should be more represented in textbooks (especially history) but would be willing to go to school together. This apparent controversy comes from their belief that the state protects the majority and that their identity would not be compromised by co-education.

37.3.6 *School Books: Books Reflecting Society*

When we analyze the link between education and maintaining national identities, it is simply impossible to bypass the textbooks. These are the books where we can best see what one society considers important, what it wants future generations to internalize and how. Textbooks reflect the entire curriculum—the goals of education, content, and their interpretations. Antić (2013) outlines four approaches to defining textbooks. The first approach is encyclopedic, where the most important function of definitions is to provide representative content for students. The second approach defines the textbook through a pedagogical function, which itself can be different. Choppin (according to Antić, 2013) emphasizes four pedagogical functions: curriculum function—a source of data for curriculum-defined content; instrumental function—indicates learning and teaching methods and offers activities and structured learning; ideological function—represents a framework of value system and a desirable way of thinking; and documentary function—contains documents, records, and graphics that encourage understanding and critical thinking. The third approach in defining textbooks emphasizes the political, cultural, and ideological dimension. Since different interest groups are involved in the creation of textbooks, they are often the scene of different, and sometimes conflicting, interests of politics, professions, publishing, as well as society. Educational sociologists (such as Purves, Bowles & Gintis, Bourdieu, Apple, Craford, according to Antić, 2013) mentioned in the first part of this chapter believe that textbooks cannot be separated from politics and that they are an integral part of the process of maintaining social inequalities based on the cultural, ideological, and political power of dominant groups, and that their content seeks to strengthen the common historical memory. Finally, the fourth approach defines textbooks as agents of socialization and, in this sense, they are subject to value judgment and cultural and folk-psychological transformations, which are often not explicit, thus making the textbook a link between the formal curriculum and the actual curriculum realized with the students. No matter what approach is used to define textbooks; they will be an important educational tool that explicitly and implicitly frames the world of students.

The first way of research is to analyze the content of textbooks, which are quite common especially for history and social science textbooks. These analyses pay most attention to the selection of materials and presentation methods in order to establish the connection between real social and political processes. Other research focuses on how textbooks are used or the textbook development process, but content analyses are most common. In order to illustrate the link between the content of the textbook and the maintenance of social trauma, here we will mention the recent analyses from Bosnia and Herzegovina.

In 2017, the Open Society Fund of Bosnia and Herzegovina supported a comprehensive analysis of the content of so-called textbooks for group of national subjects (Soldo et al., 2017). This group of subjects includes mother tongue, history, geography, and religious studies. This content analysis was the second vawe after 10 years when the first analysis was conducted (Husremović, Powell, Šišić, & Dolić, 2007), when the main finding was that textbooks encouraged additional segregation and stereotypical views of their own ethnicity and other ethnicities. In those 10 years, BiH underwent educational reform that should have focused on learning outcomes and competencies needed for personal fulfillment, active citizenship, and social inclusion. Schools were supposed to foster creativity, problem solving, knowledge application, and self-education. With this new orientation, the education authorities in BiH opted for a "society of knowledge, humanity and values," recognized the importance of education in integration into the European Union, and committed themselves to adopt the world's economic and civilizational heritage. An extensive process of developing new curricula and textbooks was followed for all grades of the new 9-year school, which involved huge human, financial, and institutional resources.

The main objectives of the content analysis were to evaluate the results of the reform of thc textbook policy and the extent to which the textbooks, by their content, support social cohesion, tolerance and interculturalism, respect for human rights and fundamental freedoms, and the development of critical thinking. Questions the researchers wanted to answer were the following: (1) Are the values positioned as educational outcomes in the curriculum and textbooks of the national group of subjects? (2) Are universal values affirmed in textbooks? (3) Does the content of textbooks encourage the development of critical thinking? The main conclusions of this analysis were that textbooks, as a major tool in teaching, continue to rely fundamentally on the ethnocentric approach and conservative thinking. Thus, textbooks continue to promote the idea that the perspective of one's own group is the one and the best. A dominant national perspective is presented, in which primacy is given to the collective in relation to the individual, in which self-victimization is emphasized, wars are glorified, and violence is justified. A state or homeland is presented as a territory owned by an ethnic group that survives owing to defenses, victims, spilled blood, and its history is a series of events that prove its longevity, survival, and sovereignty.

The conclusions are usually limited to one perspective (the ethnic group that uses the textbook), which creates a sense of genuine truth for the student and universal values are not considered. This kind of thinking is at the root of stereotypes and prejudices, because it prevents questioning and flexibility in the attitude toward others, but also toward one's own group. Given that BiH is in Europe, textbooks also promote a Eurocentric worldview, with Europe as the center of the world, and topics such as colonization, poverty, and migration are rarely problematized. Somehow, the new textbooks seem to have returned to the past in the sense of abandoning humanistic ideas and ideals while favoring tradition, obedience, and maintaining our standing by embracing customs and the ideas of traditional faith and culture. Respecting traditions and customs (which are presented as a value) is particularly encouraged, as well as refraining from actions that could violate the established social norms. Obedience to authority is presented as a desirable virtue, and freedom of choice and personal responsibility are not something particularly desirable.

Thus, in order to maintain the primacy of collective identities, education authorities must ensure the transfer of elements of social trauma to young generations, with textbooks being an indispensable tool.

37.4 Practical Implications in the Field of Social Trauma

As seen in previous examples, education is the most important tool for the development of the society. Whether we talk about healing or perpetuating the problems, education is always involved.

Children do not learn how to compare events from different perspectives which helps develop prejudices. They do not internalize the fact that universal values cannot be particularized to one group, and they receive the messages that differences and pluralism are all right if Others are like Us and if Others are willing to assimilate completely within the majority group. So, is it realistic then to expect from them, when they become older, to truly appreciate the richness of differences?

This fact has become more prominent in the last decade with an increasing number of people moving from their home countries as part of forced or voluntarily migration. As stated in the report from European Social Survey (Heath & Richards, 2016), immigration is one of the most prominent political issues in Europe. Labor migration and continuous pressure to accommodate refugees and asylum seekers from war zones around the world makes the issue of migration management one of the top priorities for many societies. While many countries declare that they are welcoming and ready to help, we see a lot of tensions between groups of domicile people and migrants.

In order to prepare societies for future societal changes, social scientists must work with education stakeholders at all levels. Social scientists should be involved in curriculum development to secure that learning outcomes and contents are aimed at desegregation, development of critical thinking, and positioning the development of universal values such as justice, piece, and solidarity as the ultimate goals. Teachers themselves have to be the main models for what they teach. Therefore, their potential should be cherished not only for teaching but also for development of new, constructive, and open education policies.

37.5 Suggested Reading

Husremović, D., Powell, S., Šišić, A., & Dolić, A. (Eds.). (2007). *Obrazovanje u Bosni i Hercegovini: čemu učimo djecu?* Sarajevo: Fond otvoreno društvo Bosna i Hercegovina.

Soldo, A., Trbić, D., Husremović, D., Veličković, N., & Ibrahimović, N. (Eds.). (2017). Čemu (ne)učimo djecu: Analiza sadržaja udžbenika nacionalne grupe predmeta u osnovnim školama [What we do(not) teach our children: An analysis of the content of textbooks for the National Group of subjects in primary schools]. Sarajevo: Mas Media Sarajevo, Fond otvoreno društvo BiH.

Volkan, V. D. (1998). *Bloodlines : From ethnic pride to ethnic terrorism.* Boulder, CO: Westview Press.

Volkan, V. D. (2006). *Killing in the name of identity: A study of bloody conflicts.* Charlottesville, VA: Pitchstone Publishing.

References

Amir, Y., Shlomo, S., & Ben Ari, R. (Eds.). (1984). *School desegregation: Cross-cultural perspectives*. London: Routledge.

Antić, S. (2013). *Udžbenik kao instrument za konstrukciju i ko-konstrukciju školskog znanja (Textbook as an instrument for constructing and co-constructing school knowledge)*. Doctoral thesis. University in Belgrade, Faculty of Philosophy.

Ballantine, J. H. (1989). *The sociology of education: A systematic approach*. Upper Saddle River, NJ: Prentice Hall.

European Commission. (2008). *Improving competences for the 21st century: An Agenda for European Cooperation on Schools*. Communication from the Commission to the European Parliament, The Council, The Economic and Social Committee and the Committee of the Regions, European Commission, Brussels. Retrieved July 3, 2008, from eur-lex.europa.eu

European Commission. (2018). *Proposal for a council recommendations on key competences for lifelong learning*. Commission Staff Working Document. Retrieved from https://eur-lex.europa.eu/

Gellner, E. (2006). *Nations and nationalism* (2nd ed.). London: Wiley-Blackwell.

Golubeva, M., Powell, S., Kazimzade, E., & Nedelcu, A. (2009). *Divided education, divided citizens? A comparative study of civil enculturation in separate schools*. Zagreb: Network of Education Policy Centers.

Gordon, J., Halasz, G., Krawczyk, M., Michel, A., Pepper, D., Putkiewicz, E., & Wisniewski, J. (2009). *Key competences in Europe: Opening doors for lifelong learners across the school curriculum and teacher education*. Warsaw: CASE—Center for Social and Economic Research.

Heath, A., & Richards, L. (2016). *Attitudes towards immigration and their antecedents: Topline results from round 7 of the European social survey*. European Social Survey European Research Infrastructure Consortium (ESS ERIC).

Husremović, D., Powell, S., Šišić, A., & Dolić, A. (Eds.). (2007). *Obrazovanje u Bosni i Hercegovini: čemu učimo djecu?* Sarajevo: Fond otvoreno društvo Bosna i Hercegovina.

Kapo, M. (2012). *Nacionalizam i obrazovanje: studija slučaja Bosne i Hercegovine*. Sarajevo: Fond otvoreno društvo BiH.

Kottak, C. P. (2004). *Window on humanity: A concise introduction to anthropology*. McGraw-Hill Companies.

Merritt, R. L., & Coombs, F. S. (1977). Politics and educational reform. *Comparative Education Review, 21*(2/3), 247–273. Retrieved from https://www.jstor.org/stable/1187660

OSCE. (2018). *Dvije škole pod jednim krovom: Najvidljiviji primjer diskriminacije u oblasti obrazovanja u Bosni i Hercegovini*. Sarajevo: Organization for Security and Co-operation in Europe, Mission in Bosnia and Hercegovina.

Ramírez-Barat, C., & Duthie, R. (2015). *Education and transitional justice: Opportunities and challenges for peacebuilding*. International Center for Transitional Justice.

Soldo, A., Trbić, D., Husremović, D., Veličković, N., & Ibrahimović, N. (Eds.). (2017). *Čemu (ne) učimo djecu: Analiza sadržaja udžbenika nacionalne grupe predmeta u osnovnim školama [What we do(not) teach our children: An analysis of the content of textbooks for the National Group of subjects in primary schools]*. Sarajevo: Mas Media Sarajevo, Fond otvoreno društvo BiH.

Volkan, V. D. (2004). *Blind trust: Large groups and their leaders in times of crisis and terror*. Charlottesville, VA: Pitchstone Publishing.

Chapter 38
Education of Migrants and Vulnerable Groups: Trauma or Protective Factor?

Tinde Kovač-Cerović

38.1 Introduction

Education of children and youth from vulnerable, excluded, and discriminated against groups has increasingly become a task which education systems are expected to fulfill. Discussing minority education in a forced migration context embodies interdisciplinary considerations and requires the embracing of a critical analysis of exclusionary practices of education systems, building on the seminal work of Freire (1970), Bourdieau (Bourdieu & Passeron, 1977) and others, a social–political analysis of forced migration and of the variety of practices by nation-states and other actors toward asylum seekers, including the presence of stereotypes and segregation policies. It also requires a deep understanding of social trauma and mental health as well as research in the area of psychosocial well-being, healing, and reconciliation. Although research in each of these pivotal areas is abundant, the connections between the important bodies of research are rarely made. Good models and successful examples indicate the benefit of interdisciplinary approaches.

Migration has many types, directions, motivations, and durations, including international or in-country, economic or education-related, forced migrations, temporary displacements. All embody trauma risks and incur at least some, but often, major changes in social context, entrenched communication fabric, lifestyle, and rituals, as well as status and prospects. Here, we will focus on the most dramatic and demanding situation of international forced migration.

International migration is measured at approximately 3% of the global population amounting to around 240 million persons in 2015 (UNESCO, 2018). In recent years, it is increasing at an even steeper rate (OECD, 2019), and is expected to rise further, while new forms of migration, for example, related to climate change are likely to emerge. In most OECD countries in 2015, at least one out of five

T. Kovač-Cerović (✉)
Faculty of Philosophy, Department of Psychology, University of Belgrade, Belgrade, Serbia
e-mail: tkovacs@f.bg.ac.rs

© Springer Nature Switzerland AG 2021

A. Hamburger et al. (eds.), *Social Trauma – An Interdisciplinary Textbook*,
https://doi.org/10.1007/978-3-030-47817-9_38

15-years-olds were immigrants or had an immigrant background (UNESCO, 2018). Given recent immigration trends, this percentage could already be higher. The reliability of statistical data on migrant children is usually weak, hence policy targeting can become cumbersome even when extraordinary migration is triggered by major political turbulences and armed conflicts, and emergency measures should be in place. These difficulties also affect education providers, education systems, and new education policies. For example, as a consequence of conflicts in the Middle East, in the European Union alone, ca. five million new migrants arrived between 2013 and 2018, peaking in 2015 and 2016 with 1.2 million new asylum seekers each year (Eurostat, 2019). This process was marked by shifting political circumstances (Agustin & Bak Jørgensen, 2018), human tragedy (European Commission, 2015; Pinson, Arnot, & Candappa, 2010), but also by an increasing capacity of education systems to include migrants (Dovigo, 2018; OECD, 2018).

Similarly, dramatic refugee flows, sometimes more sometimes less numerous, regrettably occurred many times over the past few decades, such as during the civil wars in the former Yugoslavia, particularly Bosnia; or after the breakup of the Soviet Union, between Kyrgistan, Uzbekistan, and Tajikistan, in the Caucasus; during the exodus in Sudan, or persecution of minorities in Myanmar, and many more. In all these instances, the political circumstances, demographics, geographies, histories, and outcomes were quite different, but all bore the markers of social trauma and all disrupted the education path of hundreds of thousands, or even millions of children and youth leaving them in an education vacuum.

38.2 Learning Outcomes

In this chapter, we focus on two major points as learning outcomes that highlight the circular connections between social trauma, migration, and education.

For refugee/migrant children and youth education can have a lifesaving function; it provides not only job prospects, but also a sense of life continuity and self-esteem, as well as social integration and peer relationships (INEE, 2010; Kia-Keating & Ellis, 2007). On the other hand, education systems in host countries are faced with the need to adjust and change in order to respond to the needs of children arriving from war-afflicted regions and different cultures, speaking distant and diverse languages. Very often they fail to do so, creating instead new barriers to integration that the refugee/migrant children/youth need to overcome or endure. This way education can become a new source of social trauma for entire populations. The reader will be thus enabled to recognize the main barriers to education integration of migrant children in diverse settings and to select informed, appropriate, and comprehensive education interventions facilitating successful integration of migrant children in school, thus lowering the risk of their secondary traumatization.

International research repeatedly found higher dropout rates of migrant students compared to natives (NESSE, 2008; OECD, 2015; UNESCO, 2018), and lower educational outcomes of students with a migration background (UNESCO, 2018). Many of these children experience war and loss and suffer from trauma (Arnot & Pinson, 2005), feelings of guilt (Richman, 1998), behavioral problems (Candappa, 2000) and other "normal reactions to abnormal situations" (Srna, Kondić, & Popović, 2000). On top of these, they have to adapt to a new environment, social context, language, and are frequently confronted with schools that are not fully welcoming toward newcomers.

Migrant children, similarly to children from other excluded and vulnerable groups—such as the Roma population in Europe—can face multiple, nested layers of barriers in education structured around access, attendance, attainment, and progression (UNICEF, 2014). Access barriers can substantially hinder the right to education by logistical problems such as a lack of placement capacity in the neighborhood school, distance to school, a lack of transportation, and/or a lack of safety on the road (Bartlett, 2015; UNHCR, 2015). Creating additional placement possibilities with enlarged classes can also result in negative reactions from the domicile population (Bartlett, 2015; Kovács-Cerović & Vulić, 2016). Segregated schooling is another type of complex barrier, often promoted as a culturally and linguistically sound option, enacted as a consequence of segregated housing, but, in reality, it presents a suboptimal schooling environment that does not provide possibilities for language acquisition through peer interaction (NESSE, 2008), nor for progression and employability. Attendance barriers most often derive from inadequate or missing welfare support for education, and a lack of support for nonacademic needs of the students from vulnerable groups as mundane as basic physiological needs (food, clothing, shelter), psychological needs (safety, belonging, esteem) (Slade & Griffith, 2013), or access to transportation and school equipment. Children living in extreme poverty, slums, and refugee camps can miss out on schooling entirely if some of the required support is not duly organized. Attendance can easily be hindered by adversarial peer relationships or nonconducive school ethos as well (Krachman, LaRocca, & Gabrieli, 2018). Barriers to education attainment include differences between home and host country curricula (NESSE, 2008; UNHCR, 2015). Teachers' pedagogical competencies and competencies for working in truly multicultural environments are crucial, teachers' expectations from refugee/migrant children might be low (OECD, 2016), which, in turn, creates self-fulfilling prophecies (Rosenthal & Jacobson, 1968) lowering the attainment of vulnerable children.

Schooling burdened by such barriers easily closes the circle of premigration, migration, and postmigration traumatic experiences (Kuttikat, 2012). Afflicted children face three sets of traumas: the trauma of the past—the hardships in their homeland forcing them to leave, the trauma of the present—suboptimal life and depraved schooling experiences, and the trauma of the future—lacking hope and plan (Srna et al., 2000).

38.3 The Main Lines of Effective Integration Policies of Migrant Children and Youth in Education

Building on the Convention on the Rights of the Child, and observance toward economic benefits of population-wide quality education; local and national integration policies are developed and implemented globally, corroborated by global integration compacts such as the Inclusive Education Movement or the Decade of Roma Inclusion or, more recently, the European Commission's Communication on the protection of children in migration.

Analysis of education policies in this rapidly growing body of innovation and inquiry is currently the main road to knowledge production, gradually complemented by qualitative participatory research, airing the views and voices of those involved in the changing education realm. Regrettably, however, the least represented as researchers or critical participants are the migrant/vulnerable communities themselves.

An increasing number of recent policy analyses target the education of migrant children. Their main conclusion, put bluntly, is that we know what works best and what should be done, but countries rarely do all that; most often, they do not do enough, and sometimes they barely do anything. A comprehensive policy analysis of previous migrations identified key policy lines for effective and respectful integration of migrants (OECD, 2015): language integration, early childhood education and care, parental engagement, limiting concentration of migrants in disadvantaged schools and in lower standard classes as well as building the capacity of schools and teachers. However, in facing new refugee influx countries rarely relied on this body of knowledge; rather, they intensified their entrenched mechanisms of dealing with migrants without undertaking critical and creative reflections (Kornhall, 2016). The recent Global Education Monitoring (GEM) report (UNESCO, 2018) developed a migrant integration policy index anchored on five policies—access to advice and guidance in the host country education system, support to learning the language of instruction, monitoring of immigrant students' successes and needs, providing education support through teaching assistance, homework, and guidance, and teacher education programs addressing migrant students' needs and teacher expectations. The study found striking between-country differences in the volume of integration policy implementation, spanning from countries at almost maximum level of the index (Scandinavian countries, US, Canada and Australia) to countries in which the index was very low (e.g., Bulgaria, Turkey, and Croatia).

A recent Eurydice report (European Commission/EACEA/Eurydice, 2019) provides additional evidence on how only a small number of EU Member States embrace policies combining language integration and cultural diversity with whole school support to social, emotional, and cognitive development of the migrant child, while the majority are focusing only on some of the needed aspects.

Building on these arguments, it appears that almost no education setting takes up the full scale of recommended policies, thus leaving dangerous loopholes which impede and block the full integration of migrant children in the host country education system, thus paving the way for their exclusion from the society and labor market.

Two qualitative studies using a participatory and empowering approach can provide additional insight on ways of integrating essential support for education of children from vulnerable groups and forced migration. Both derive evidence from Southeast Europe, particularly Serbia, as one of the countries on the "Balkan route of migration," transited by several hundred thousand migrants between 2014 and 2016. In integrating the migrant children, Serbian schools relied on memories of having received almost one million refugees from other former Yugoslav countries during the 1990s, on Roma integration experiences, and on inclusive education policies implemented from the early 2000s.

The first study is situated in the context of the Decade of Roma integration, and embraces the situated wisdom of Roma pedagogical assistants (RPAs) working in schools to facilitate the inclusion of Roma students into mainstream education (Daiute & Kovač-Cerović, 2017). One hundred seventy-four RPAs shared their experiences, concerns, and reflections about their role in the social integration process, and about the situations of Roma children in education through diverse storytelling genres. The values analysis (Daiute, 2014) of the more than 600 texts (approximately 6000 thought units) gathered highlighted the authentic voice of the main actors in education inclusion. Especially, outspoken were the RPAs describing the unprecedented collaborative roles they play connecting all actors needed for successful integration and the wide array of obstacles they (and the Roma children) confront on the road to becoming educated, from facing discrimination, humiliation and abuse to poverty, neglect and history of exclusion. Joint reflections of RPAs and the researchers on the results, embodying empowerment and respect, contributed also to the RPAs in Serbia becoming "unique critical and reflexive participants in the education reforms" (Kovač-Cerović, 2018, p. 131) and effectively counteracting the social trauma of exclusion and discrimination they grew up with.

The second study used in the context of recent migration a similar methodology, involving children and youth both from the migrant and from the native community in Serbia (Daiute et al., 2019; Kovács-Cerović, Grbić, & Vesić, 2018). Results reveal the surprising power of peer relationships between local and newly arrived refugee children, albeit with a huge linguistic and cultural distance. Narratives of local children are abundant with enacting cultural models of helping, interacting, sharing, and making friends with the newly arrived migrant students in a welcoming and socially nuanced way. The migrant students used this narrative opportunity to reflect on their experience and knowledge widely beyond the here and now, capturing hardships of their losses and journeys, and their orientation toward high hopes in an idealized future. The research found both groups sharing emotional reactions of surprise, joy, and occasional sadness, and reflections on cultures with mutual recognitions of similarities and differences, thus displaying the possibilities of humane integration in school.

38.4 Practical Implications for the Field of Social Trauma

The risk of re-traumatization of children from forced migration groups and any other vulnerable group when encountering education barriers is immense. This calls for heightened awareness of educators and education policymakers and for their thoughtful actions to avoid and prevent segregation and discrimination, nurture welcoming school climate and peer relationships with local peers, involve parents, teachers and cultural mediators from the country of origin of refugees in the life of schools, increase teachers' expectations from children from these groups, ensure language immersion and support in order to acquire the language of instruction, and provide all needed noneducational support—just to mention the most important.

On the other hand, health and social work professionals need also to be aware of the multiplied benefits that children from vulnerable groups can gain if the typical education barriers are alleviated and dismantled for them and engage shoulder to shoulder with educationalists to achieve this aim for each and every child.

38.5 Suggested Further Reading and Information

Kovács-Cerović, T., & Vulić, I. (2016). *Supporting education of refugee/migrant children and youth*. ESP Working Papers Series. New York: Open Society Foundations.

OECD (2019). *International migration outlook 2019*. Paris: OECD Publishing.

UNESCO. (2018). *Global education monitoring report, 2019: Migration, displacement and education: building bridges, not walls*. Paris: UNESCO.

References

Agustin, O. G., & Bak Jørgensen, M. (2018). *Solidarity and the 'refugee crisis' in Europe*. Cham: Palgrave Macmillan.

Arnot, M., & Pinson, H. (2005). *The education of asylum-seeker and refugee children: A study of LEA and school values, policies and practices*. Cambridge, UK: University of Cambridge, Faculty of Education.

Bartlett, L. (2015). *Access and quality of education for international migrant children*. Background paper prepared for the education for all global monitoring report. Paris: UNESCO.

Bourdieu, P., & Passeron, J. C. (1977). *Reproduction in education, society, and culture*. Beverly Hills, CA: Sage.

Candappa, M. (2000). Building a new life: The role of the school in supporting refugee children. *MCT, 19*(1), 28.

Daiute, C. (2014). *Narrative inquiry: A dynamic approach*. Thousand Oaks, CA: Sage.

Daiute, C., & Kovač-Cerović, T. (2017). *Minority teachers—Roma in Serbia—Narrate education reform*. Belgrade, Serbia: Institute of Psychology, Faculty of Philosophy at the University of Belgrade and the Association of Pedagogical Assistants.

Daiute, C., Kovács-Cerović, T., Mićić, K., Sullu, B., Popović, K. & Vračar, S. (2019). *Policy echoes and unique positions across narratives along the Balkan route*. Paper presented at ECER, 2–6 September, Hamburg, Germany

Dovigo, F. (Ed.). (2018). *Challenges and opportunities in education for refugees in Europe. From research to good practices*. Rotterdam: Brill | Sense.

European Commission, European Civil Protection and Humanitarian Aid Operations. (2015). *Refugee crisis: A human tragedy beyond the facts and figures. News and stories.* Retrieved January 20, 2019, from https://ec.europa.eu/echo/blog/refugee-crisis-human-tragedy-beyond-facts-and-figures_en

European Commission/EACEA/Eurydice. (2019). *Integrating students from migrant backgrounds into schools in Europe: National Policies and measures*. Eurydice report. Luxembourg: Publications Office of the European Union.

Eurostat (2019). People on the move - Statistics on mobility in Europe. Accessed from https://ec.europa.eu/eurostat/cache/digpub/eumove/index.html?lang=en

Freire, P. (1970). *Pedagogy of the oppressed*. New York: Herder and Herder.

INEE (Inter-Agency Network for Education in Emergencies, UNESCO). (2010). *Minimum standards for education: Preparedness, response, recovery*. New York: UNESCO. Retrieved from https://www.right-to-education.org/sites/right-to-education.org/files/resource-attachments/INEE_Minimum_Standards_2010.pdf

Kia-Keating, M., & Ellis, B. (2007). Belonging and connection to school in resettlement: Young refugees, school belonging, and psychosocial adjustment. *Clinical Child Psychology and Psychiatry, 12*(1), 29–43.

Kornhall, P. (2016). *Reception of newly arrived migrants and assessment of previous schooling.* Peer learning activity in Stockholm Sweden 6–7 April 2016. Sweden: Ecorys.

Kovač-Cerović, T. (2018). Education policies for Roma integration with messages from the Roma pedagogical assistants in Serbia. *NORRAG Special Issue, 1*, 131–134.

Kovács-Cerović, T., Grbić, S., & Vesić, D. (2018). How do schools integrate refugee students? First experiences from Serbia. In F. Dovigo (Ed.), *Challenges and opportunities in education for refugees in Europe. From research to good practices* (pp. 77–112). Rotterdam: Brill | Sense.

Kovács-Cerović, T. & Vulić, I. (2016). *Supporting education of refugee/migrant children and youth*. ESP Working Papers Series. New York: Open Society Foundations.

Krachman, S. B., LaRocca, R., & Gabrieli, C. (2018). Accounting for the whole child. *Educational Leadership, 75*(5), 28–34.

Kuttikat, M. (2012). Migration traumatic experiences and refugee distress: Implications for social work practice. *Clinical Social Work Journal, 40*(4), 429–437.

NESSE (Network of Experts in Social Sciences of Education and Training). (2008). *Education and migration. Strategies for integrating migrant children in European schools and societies. A synthesis of research findings for policy-makers*. Brussels: European Commission.

OECD. (2015). *Immigrant students at school: Easing the journey towards integration*. Paris: OECD Publishing.

OECD. (2016). *Low-performing students: Why they fall behind and how to help them succeed.* Paris: OECD Publishing.

OECD. (2018). *Working together for local integration of migrants and refugees*. Paris: OECD Publishing.

OECD. (2019). *International migration outlook 2019*. Paris: OECD Publishing.

Pinson, H., Arnot, M., & Candappa, M. (2010). *Education, asylum and the 'non-citizen' child.* Hampshire: Palgrave Macmillan.

Richman, N. (1998). *In the midst of the whirlwind: A manual for helping refugee children*. Stoke on Trent: Trentham Books Ltd.

Rosenthal, R., & Jacobson, L. F. (1968). Teacher expectations for the disadvantaged. *Scientific American, 218*(4), 19–23.

Slade, S., & Griffith, D. (2013). A whole child approach to student success [special issue]. *KEDI Journal of Educational Policy, 2013*, 21–35.

Srna, J., Kondić, K., & Popović, M. (2000). *Psihologija izbeglištva [psychology of the refugee status]*. Beograd: IP Zarko Albulj.

UNESCO. (2018). *Global education monitoring report, 2019: Migration, displacement and education: Building bridges, not walls*. Paris: UNESCO.

UNHCR. (2015). *Education: Issue brief 1–6*. Geneva: UNHCR.

UNICEF. (2014). *Policy impact analysis: Providing additional support to students from vulnerable groups in pre-university education*. Belgrade: UNICEF and SIPRU. Retrieved September 16, 2019, from https://www.unicef.org/serbia/en/reports/policy-impact-analysis

Chapter 39
University Level Education on Social Trauma

Carmen Scher and Lisa Malmheden

39.1 Introduction: Background and Main Theoretical Concepts

An inquiry into currently offered postgraduate programs and courses that may be compared with the didactic and theoretical aspects of the master course of "Social Trauma" (as will be described in the following sections), shows multifaceted approaches while targeting the topic. For instance, the University of Nottingham located in Nottinghamshire, United Kingdom, offers a graduate program in Trauma Studies within their department of social sciences and education (University of Nottingham, n.d.). Aimed at broadening their students' expertise concerning the nature of *psychological* trauma within both groups and individual sufferers, the didactic foundation of the program is based on approaches centralized around *experiential learning*. That is, via small group learning, workshops, and seminars, as well as lectures, all emphasizing active and vibrant in-depth self-reflection regarding the topic of psychological trauma. In terms of these didactic features, similarities with the Course Social Trauma (CST) are indeed present, with a difference being, that an interdisciplinary integration of clinical traumatology, intercultural aspects, and sociohistorical approaches are key features of the CST. Further, King's College London has offered the internationally acclaimed program of War and Psychiatry (M.Sc.) since 2005 (King's College London, n.d.). The program covers methodological, cultural, historical, medical, ethical, and empirical aspects concerning how members of armed forces, as well as civilians, respond to the psychological trauma mainly of war. Additionally, short- and long-term consequences of genocide, terrorism, and forced migration are addressed; and the compulsory module Civilians and Extreme Trauma target both artificial *and* natural disasters,

C. Scher (✉) · L. Malmheden
International Psychoanalytic University Berlin, Berlin, Germany
e-mail: carmen.scher@ipu-berlin.de; lisa.malmheden@ipu-berlin.de

© Springer Nature Switzerland AG 2021
A. Hamburger et al. (eds.), *Social Trauma – An Interdisciplinary Textbook*,
https://doi.org/10.1007/978-3-030-47817-9_39

encompassing cross-cultural psychological and societal traumatological consequences resulting thereof. Didactic formats comprise group work, case analyses, and student presentations within the frames of lectures, seminars, and tutorials. Sessions are described as interactive and aiming to stimulate, for instance, systematic and reflexive investigation, thus including experiential learning in their didactic approach. Moreover, acknowledging *employability* as a guideline in the design of their program, the possibility of acquiring relevant “transferable skills” is declared. Another postgraduate program of a somewhat similar character, albeit with a larger focus on practical experience, is provided at the University of Tel Aviv, Israel (University of Tel Aviv, n.d.). Their 1-year-long program in English, Crisis and Trauma Studies (M.A. in social work), consists of a curriculum concentrating on psychological and psychosocial consequences of both natural (e.g., natural disasters, epidemics) and artificial disasters (e.g., genocide, war, forced migration), while using didactic aspects with a profound focus on what they have named “hands-on experience.” That is, in addition to providing lectures centering around theoretical, societal, and clinical aspects of collectively and individually experienced psychological trauma, the students are directly familiarized with practical implications of delivering acute and long-term interventions and support within exposed individuals and populations. This is done via “one-day-a-week” internships at different organizations, proceeding throughout the duration of the studies. Further, ‘site visits” to various psychosocial crisis centers are frequently organized, where the students learn directly from the professionals working within the institutions, as well as—when applicable—the possibility of hearing personal stories and experiences from clients. Finally, an additional type of postgraduate program which is frequent in scope concern the Holocaust and Genocide studies. Usually, these programs are grounded within the realms of a historical approach; yet, often, cross-disciplinary vantage points via political science, cultural and social anthropology, psychology, peace and conflict studies, and sociology are included. One such example can be found at the Dutch University of Amsterdam, which offers a postgraduate program in Holocaust and Genocide Studies taught in English (University of Amsterdam, n.d.). Through conventional lectures and seminars, together with discussions, independent group work, and tutorials, different cases of genocide and mass violence are closely and “comparatively” studied through the lenses of the aforementioned interdisciplinary points of view. Further, the students are encouraged to take part in excursions—for instance, to the International Criminal Court—organized throughout the studies.

As will be shown throughout the remainder of this chapter, some didactic and theoretical aspects of the previously mentioned graduate programs are included in the fundaments of the CST. Additionally, the unique angle of approaching the concept of social trauma in the format of summer schools, while carrying emphases on reflective intercultural, social, and interdisciplinary approaches together with practical relevance, will be demonstrated.

39.2 Learning Outcome(s) Related to Social Trauma

Some of the desired learning outcomes associated with the Social Trauma elective course (CST) are aligned with the construct of *employability skills,* mainly in terms of future cooperation with postwar countries, and their students of psychology, sociology, cultural sciences, and similar study courses. During the last decade, *intercultural competence* has received increased attention regarding its key association with employability (e.g., Busch, 2009; Jones, 2013; Stier, 2006). In line with Holmes and O'Neill's (2012) study regarding the importance of direct intercultural peer-to-peer encounters, the assumption "…that [the] developing [of] intercultural competence encompasses processes of acknowledging reluctance and fear, foregrounding and questioning stereotypes, monitoring feelings and emotions, working through confusion, and grappling with complexity" (p. 707) is highly relevant within the context of studying social trauma. Recognizing possible challenges of cross-cultural encounters (see Turner, 2009), the *self-reflection groups*—guided by an experienced psychology professor—provide a forum for venting, exploring, and ideally resolving possible conflicts; ultimately, fostering an internalized understanding of one's own role regarding direct or indirect experiences of social trauma, as well as of those belonging to the "cultural other." Thus, by granting the students of the course an intimate space of *small reflection groups*, and by further tasking the students with entertaining a self-reflective *learning portfolio* throughout the course, reflective abilities in terms of one's own historical, cultural, and societal narratives, as well as those of "cultural others," are encouraged. The "learning portfolio" is an academically widely used (Zubizarreta, 2009) learning and/or assessment tool, requiring its writer to elaborate on both acquired knowledge, as well as reflective aspects on the subject area (i.e., Häcker, 2005; Klenowski, Askew, & Carnell, 2006; McMullan et al., 2003). Moreover, we aim at taking one step away from the more commonly accepted notion of *a* teacher informing *a* student, and move closer toward a "*student-peer-teacher*" triangularity; resulting in a continuous interchanging of knowledge regarding each other's cultural, historical and societal narratives, and experiences.

39.3 Preferred Model: The International Interdisciplinary Masters Course "Social Trauma" (CST)

In 2013, the Balkan Network was established within the framework of the *Stability Pact for South Eastern Europe* via the financial support of Deutsche Akademischer Ausstauschdienst (DAAD). Until 2016, the project went under the name of *Trauma, Trust and Memory* (TTM), and between 2017 and 2018, it was called *Migration—Trauma in Transition* (MTT). As of 2019, the project is entitled *Social Trauma in Changing Societies* (STICS) and several fruitful outcomes have grown out of the collaboration throughout the years. One of these developments is the Masters Course in Social Trauma (CST), which is offered annually at one of the ten Balkan network universities in Bosnia and Herzegovina, Serbia, Bulgaria, Greece, Turkey, and Germany. Mainly available within the frames of summer schools, taking place during a time span of circa 9 days, the course consists of six overarching modules. Namely, those of Ethics, Developmental Psychology of Social Trauma, Clinical Psychology of Social Trauma, Social Psychology and Cultural Theory of Trauma, Memory Studies, as well as Specific Methodology and Practice in Social Trauma Research (specifically described in Hancheva, Scher, & Hamburger, 2018). Apart from welcoming students of different nationalities and ethnicities to take part in the course, internationality is further granted by staff from all involved universities taking shifts in teaching courses and seminars. Moreover, the interdisciplinary nature of the concept of social trauma is implemented by regular invitations of external keynote lecturers, who provide first-hand knowledge from their fields of expertise.

Before the beginning of the summer schools, an initial introductory lecture on the Concept of Social Trauma is held at the home universities of the respective students. When arriving at the location of the course—which shifts from year to year—students are assigned to groups consisting of approximately 20 individuals each. The sorting of individual participants into smaller groups is based on creating a representative diversity corresponding to that of the whole group. These constellations will stay put throughout the duration of the course in order to amplify cross-cultural encounters and work against the tendency of preferring to work together with students stemming from the same nation as oneself (DeVita, 2005). The previously mentioned *group reflections* are managed by professors who, however, do not have the function of leading the discussions, but rather engage as aids of the discourse, should that be needed. One student who participated in the Summer School in 2019 wrote the following sentences in her learning portfolio about the reflection groups:

> As a student used to an academic environment set up by certain rules and regulations, a somewhat unfamiliar space emphasizing group reflection and personal open expression was offered. Quickly it became clear that the STICS Summer School would allow a learning experience exceeding the frames of your ordinary academic encounter. A period of nine days—at this very moment still ahead of me—would not only engage my curiosity on an intellectual level, but on a very personal one as well; ultimately enabling a complex intertwining of the two.

Though this quote demonstrates only one student's perceived experience, a tendency can generally be identified throughout the learning portfolios of the students with regard to the fundamental importance of the group reflections for the overall learning experience. A similar trend is found within the literature on didactic approaches of higher education, where reflection is heavily emphasized as of crucial significance in the process of acquiring knowledge (see, for instance, Harvey, Coulson, & McMaugh, 2016; Rodgers, 2002; Rogers, 2001). An additional aim is to enable an internalization of the consequences of oneself as a descendant of a war-torn country, as well as the ability to grasp and internalize the experiences and hardships of the "cultural other." This is manifested in concrete interactions—often commencing within aforementioned group reflections—between students belonging to different ethnical or national groups, with a historical and societal narrative badgered with hostility toward each other, which may be characterized by a historical "victim–perpetrator" relationship. By fostering understanding and reflection concerning why and how one might *be perceived by the "other"* in terms of one's historical, cultural, and societal narrative, as well as gaining insights into how and why one's own narratives in its turn have shaped the *perception of "the other,"* the students are equipped—metaphorically speaking—with a lens through which emotional participation and self-reflection pave the way for robust intra- and interpersonal introspection and development. A similar experiential approach is emphasized within the seminars, which include aspects of interactive discussions, reflective practice, and group work. For instance, within the module of Specific Methodology and Practice in Social Trauma Research, small group work may consist of jointly constructing a hypothetical research question and designing a research project relevant to social trauma research. Finally, the students are asked to either present the results to the rest of the group, or share these ideas within their individual learning portfolios. Some of the activities, however, commence within the whole of the large group, such as lectures, public panels, and *large* group reflections. Experiential learning heavily influences the large group gatherings as well: one example of this is demonstrated within the module of Developmental Aspects of Social Trauma, where the fishbowl discussion method (Priles, 1993) is used to create a lively and reflective discussion environment.

Moreover, students are recommended to take part in excursions to memorial sites, which are organized within each summer school. This didactic feature of fundamental importance may be exemplified by the visit to the Potočari Memorial near Srebrenica by Bosnian, Serbian, Bulgarian, and German students and lecturers in 2013 (cf. Deutscher Akademischer Austauschdienst (DAAD), 2013). Direct descendants of former victims, together with individuals belonging to families consisting of previous perpetrators, shared the experience of jointly visiting this emotionally charged location. Conclusively, this resulted in a collective confrontation of the consequences of *what once had been,* and created a situation characterized by a profound mourning and an eloquent silence, ultimately fostering personal reflective processes in regards to one's own relation to social trauma. Usually, the learning groups of the annual summer schools similarly consist of individuals of different nationalities and ethnic groups; some of whom have been fierce enemies and gone through war and genocide in the past. Since the start of the project in 2013, these excursions are continuously cited by participants as leading to valuable—personal and theoretical—learning experiences, which enable awareness of how they unconsciously still carry traces of a social trauma having taken place in the past, even before their own lifetime.

A further approach within the STICS project are the transnational, transcultural, and autonomous fellow trainings. With an exclusive emphasis on peer-to-peer learning, students enrolled at the network universities are encouraged to suggest and autonomously organize discussions on specific topics regarding social trauma, while inviting students from corresponding network universities to participate.

39.4 Practical Implications in the Field of Social Trauma

By offering a curriculum carefully designed to address interdisciplinary theoretical, clinical, and emotional aspects, the students are prepared for future work within the multifaceted realm of social trauma. Importantly, this is not only done via fostering a theoretical and reflective awareness concerning the individual student's own possible experiences of social trauma, but also in terms of *interpersonal* skills while interacting with affected individuals of other cultures. That is, how one's own affiliation with a certain group, carrying a particular historical, cultural, and/or societal traumatic narrative—be it as perpetrators or victims—may influence unconscious thoughts or behaviors while interacting with individuals of other collectives.

Out of the more than 700 students who attended the Social Trauma course during its 7 years, many have been inspired to either carry out research projects of their own, or have initiated careers directly related to social trauma. The multifaceted curriculum offered within these frames provides emotional-reflective and didactical focuses which equip its students with tools of immense importance, should they choose to pursue working with individuals or groups who suffered under social trauma. By offering the students the forum of enhancing their intercultural, introspective, intellectual, and interpersonal competencies with regard to social trauma, a robust basis characterized by emotional and theoretical understanding is established.

39.5 Suggested Reading

Antioch University Los Angeles. (n.d.). *MA in clinical psychology, psychological trauma studies specialization*. Retrieved December 13, 2019, from https://www.antioch.edu/los-angeles/degrees-programs/psychology-degree/clinical-psychology-masters-programs/psychological-trauma-studies/

Hamburger, A. (2018). After Babel—Teaching psychoanalysis on a former battlefield. *International Forum of Psychoanalysis*. 27(1), 1–9.

Hamburger, A. (Ed.). (2018). *Trauma, trust, and memory. Social trauma and reconciliation in psychoanalysis, psychotherapy, and cultural memory.* London: Routledge.

Hamburger, A., Hancheva, C., Ozcurumez, S., Scher, C., Stanković., & Tutnjević, S. (Eds.) (2019). *Forced migration and social trauma. Interdisciplinary perspectives from psychoanalysis, psychology, sociology and politics*. London: Routledge.

Lesley University. (n.d.). *Clinical mental health counseling: Trauma studies*. Retrieved December 13, 2019, https://lesley.edu/academics/graduate/clinical-mental-health-counseling-trauma-studies

Stockton University. (n.d.). *M.A. in holocaust & genocide studies*. Retrieved December 13, 2019, from https://stockton.edu/graduate/holocaust-genocide-studies.html

The Chicago School of Professional Psychology. (n.d.). *M.A. in counseling psychology*. Retrieved December 13, 2019, from https://www.thechicagoschool.edu/chicago/programs/ma-counseling-psychology-trauma-and-crisis-intervention-concentration/

University of Haifa. (n.d.). *Weiss-Livnat International Program in holocaust studies.* Retrieved December 13, 2019, https://uhaifa.org/academics/graduate-programs/holocaust-studies/holocaust-studies-program-description

Uppsala Universitet. (n.d.) *Master's Programme in holocaust and genocide studies.* Retrieved December 13, 2019, from https://www.uu.se/en/admissions/master/selma/program/?pKod=HFF2M

References

Busch, D. (2009). What kind of intercultural competence will contribute to students' future job employability? *Intercultural Education, 20*(5), 429–438.

Deutscher Akademischer Austauschdienst (DAAD). (2013). *Vom Stabilitätspakt zur EU-Annäherung. 15 Jahre Akademischer Neuaufbau Südosteuropa* (pp. 22–25).

DeVita, G. (2005). Fostering intercultural learning through multicultural group work. In J. Carrol & J. Ryan (Eds.), *Teaching international students: Improving learning for all* (pp. 75–83).

Häcker, T. (2005). *Portfolio als Instrument der Kompetenzdarstellung und Reflexiven Lernprozesssteuerung*. Retrieved from http://www.bwpat.de/ausgabe8/haecker_bwpat8.pdf

Hancheva, C., Scher, C., & Hamburger, A. (2018). International master's study course in social trauma. In A. Hamburger (Ed.), *Trauma, trust, and memory. Social trauma and reconciliation in psychoanalysis, psychotherapy, and cultural memory* (pp. 249–254). London: Routledge.

Harvey, M., Coulson, D., & McMaugh, A. (2016). Towards a theory of the ecology of reflection: Reflective practice for experiential learning in higher education. *Journal of University Teaching & Learning Practice, 13*(2), 2.

Holmes, P., & O'Neill, G. (2012). Developing and evaluating intercultural competence: Ethnographies of intercultural encounters. *International Journal of Intercultural Relations, 36*(5), 707–718.

Jones, E. (2013). Internationalization and employability: The role of intercultural experiences in the development of transferable skills. *Public Money and Management, 33*(2), 95–104.

King's College London. (n.d.). *War and psychiatry Msc.* Retrieved December 13, 2019, from https://www.kcl.ac.uk/study/postgraduate/taught-courses/war-and-psychiatry-msc

Klenowski, V., Askew, S., & Carnell, E. (2006). Portfolios for learning, assessment and professional development in higher education. *Assessment & Evaluation in Higher Education, 31*(3), 267–286.

McMullan, M., Endacott, R., Gray, M. A., Jasper, M., Miller, C. M., Scholes, J., & Webb, C. (2003). Portfolios and assessment of competence: A review of the literature. *Journal of Advanced Nursing, 41*(3), 283–294.

Priles, M. A. (1993). The fishbowl discussion: A strategy for large honors classes. *English Journal, 82*(6), 49–50.

Rodgers, C. (2002). Defining reflection: Another look at John Dewey and reflective thinking. *Teachers College Record, 104*(4), 842–866.

Rogers, R. R. (2001). Reflection in higher education: A concept analysis. *Innovative Higher Education, 26*(1), 37–57.

Stier, J. (2006). Internationalisation, intercultural communication and intercultural competence. *Journal of Intercultural Communication, 11*, 1–11.

Tel Aviv University. (n.d.). *The international program in crisis & trauma*. Retrieved December 13, 2019, from https://en-socialwork.tau.ac.il/international/

Turner, Y. (2009). “Knowing me, knowing you,” is there nothing we can do? Pedagogic challenges in using group work to create an intercultural learning space. *Journal of Studies in International Education, 13*(2), 240–255.

University of Amsterdam. (n.d.). *Holocaust and genocide studies (history).* Retrieved December 13, 2019, from https://gsh.uva.nl/content/masters/holocaust-and-genocide-studies-history/holocaust-and-genocide-studies.html

University of Nottingham. (n.d.). *Trauma studies MA*. Retrieved December 13, 2019, from https://www.nottingham.ac.uk/ugstudy/course/Trauma-Studies-MA

Zubizarreta, J. (2009). *The learning portfolio: Reflective practice for improving student learning*. New York: John Wiley & Sons.

Index

© Springer Nature Switzerland AG 2021

A. Hamburger et al. (eds.), *Social Trauma – An Interdisciplinary Textbook*,
https://doi.org/10.1007/978-3-030-47817-9

W

MIX
Papier aus verantwortungsvollen Quellen
Paper from responsible sources
FSC® C105338

If you have any concerns about our products,
you can contact us on
ProductSafety@springernature.com

In case Publisher is established outside the EU,
the EU authorized representative is:
Springer Nature Customer Service Center GmbH
Europaplatz 3, 69115 Heidelberg, Germany

Printed by Libri Plureos GmbH
in Hamburg, Germany